W9-CDI-263

Mastering the requirements process

ACM PRESS BOOKS

This book is published as part of ACM Press Books – a collaboration between the Association for Computing (ACM) and Pearson Education Limited. ACM is the oldest and largest educational and scientific society in the information technology field. Through its high-quality publications and services, ACM is a major force in advancing the skills and knowledge of IT professionals throughout the world. For further information about ACM, contact:

ACM Member Services
1515 Broadway, 17th Floor
New York, NY 10036-5701
Phone: 1-212-626-0500
Fax: 1-212-944-1318
Email: acmhelp@acm.org
URL: http://www.acm.org/

ACM European Service Center
108 Cowley Road
Oxford OX4 1JF
United Kingdom
Phone: +44-1865-382388
Fax: +44–1865-381388
Email: acm_europe@acm.org
URL: http://www.acm.org/

Selected ACM Titles

Requirements Engineering and Rapid Development   *Ian Graham*

Software Reuse   *Ivar Jacobson, Martin Griss, Patrik Jonsson*

Object-Oriented Software Engineering – A Use Case Driven Approach
Ivar Jacobson, Magnus Christerson, Patrik Jonsson, Gunnar Övergaard

The OPEN Process Specification   *Ian Graham, Brian Henderson-Sellers, Houman Younessi*

The OPEN Toolbox of Techniques   *Brian Henderson-Sellers, Anthony Simons, Houman Younessi*

Documenting a Complete Java Application using OPEN   *Don Firesmith, Scott Krutsch, Marshall Stowe, Greg Hendley*

Bringing Design to Software: Expanding Software Development to Include Design   *Terry Winograd, John Bennett, Laura de Young, Bradley Hartfield*

Software Requirements and Specifications: A Lexicon of Software Practice, Principles and Prejudices   *Michael Jackson*

Mastering the
requirements process

——————— *Suzanne and James Robertson*

ADDISON-WESLEY

London · Boston · Indianapolis · New York · Mexico City
Toronto · Sydney · Tokyo · Singapore · Hong Kong · Cape Town
New Delhi · Madrid · Paris · Amsterdam · Munich · Milan

PEARSON EDUCATION LIMITED

Head Office:
Edinburgh Gate
Harlow CM20 2JE
Tel: +44 (0)1279 623623
Fax: +44 (0)1279 431059

London Office:
128 Long Acre, London WC2E 9AN
Tel: +44 (0)20 7447 2000
Fax: +44 (0)20 7447 2170
Website: www.awprofessional.com

First published 1999

© 1999 by ACM Press, A Division of the Association for Computing Machinery, Inc., ACM

The rights of Suzanne Robertson and James Robertson to be identified as authors of this Work have been asserted by them in accordance with the Copyright, Designs and Patents Act 1988.

ISBN 0 201 36046 2

British Library Cataloguing-in-Publication Data
A CIP record for this book is available from the British Library

All rights reserved; no part of this publication may be reproduced, stored in a retrieval system, or transmitted in any form or by any means, electronic, mechanical, photocopying, recording or otherwise, without either the prior written permission of the publisher or a licence permitting restricted copying in the United Kingdom issued by the Copyright Licensing Agency Ltd., 90 Tottenham Court Road, London W1P 4LP. This book may not be lent, resold, hired out or otherwise disposed of by way of trade in any form of binding or cover other than that in which it is published, without prior consent of the Publishers.

Many of the designations used by manufacturers and sellers to distinguish their products are claimed as trademarks. Pearson Education Limited has made every attempt to supply trademark information about manufacturers and their products mentioned in this book. A list of the trademark designations and their owners appears on p. ix.

10   9   8

Typeset by Meridian
Printed and bound in Great Britain by Biddles Ltd, Guildford and King's Lynn

The Publishers' policy is to use paper manufactured from sustainable forests.

—————————— *For one generation*

Margaret and Nick

and another

Carlotta and Cameron

Contents

Trademark Notice
Adobe Photoshop is a registered trademark of Adobe Systems Incorporated.
Microsoft Excel and Microsoft Word are trademarks of Microsoft Coporation.
UNIX is a registered trademark, licensed through X/Open Company Ltd.
(collaboration of Novell, HP & SCO).

Acknowledgments

Writing a book is hard. Without the help and encouragement of others it would be close to impossible, at least for these authors. So we would like to take a few lines to tell you who helped and encouraged and made it possible.

Andy McDonald of Vaisala was generous with his time, and gave us considerable technical input. We hasten to add that the IceBreaker product in this book is only a distant relation to Vaisala's IceCast systems. The Vaisala User Group, of which E. M. Kennedy holds the chair, also provided valuable technical input.

Thanks are due to the technical reviewers who gave up their time to wade through some fairly incomprehensible stuff. Mike Russell, Susannah Finzi, Neil Maiden, Tim Lister and Bashar Nuseibeh all deserve honorable mentions.

For the convenience of the reader, throughout this book we have used 'he' to mean 'he or she'. We the authors (one male one female) find the use of 'he/she' disruptive and awkward.

We would like to acknowledge our fellow principals at the Atlantic Systems Guild – Tom DeMarco, Peter Hruschka, Tim Lister, Steve McMenamin and John Palmer – for their help, guidance and incredulous looks over the years.

The staff at Pearson Education contributed. Sally Mortimore, Alison Birtwell and Dylan Reisenberger were generous, skillful and used such persuasive language whenever we spoke about extending the deadline.

And finally the students at our seminars: their comments, their insistence on having things clearly explained, their insights, their feedback have all made some difference, no matter how indirect, to this book.

Thank you, everybody.

Foreword

It is almost ten years now since Don Gause and I published *Exploring Requirements: Quality before Design*. Our book is indeed an exploration, a survey of human processes that *can* be used in gathering complete, correct, and communicable requirements for a software system, or any other kind of product.

GAUSE, DONALD C. AND GERALD M. WEINBERG. *Exploring Requirements: Quality Before Design*. Dorset House, 1989.

The operative word in this description is 'can', for over this decade, the most frequent question my clients ask is 'How can I assemble these diverse processes into a comprehensive requirements process for our information systems?'

At long last, James and Suzanne Robertson, in this book, have provided an answer I can conscientiously give to my clients. *Mastering the Requirements Process* shows, step by step, template by template, example by example, one well-tested way to assemble a complete, comprehensive requirements process.

One watchword of their process is 'reasonableness'. In other words, every part of the process makes sense, even to people who are not very experienced with requirements work. When introducing this kind of structure to an organization, reasonableness translates into easier acceptance – an essential attribute when so many complicated processes are tried and rejected.

The process they describe is the *Volere* approach that they developed as an outcome of many years helping clients to improve their requirements. Aside from the Volere approach itself, James and Suzanne, in this book, contribute their superb teaching skills to the formidable task facing anyone who wishes to develop requirements and do them well.

The Robertsons' teaching skills are well-known to their seminar students as well as to fans of their *Complete Systems Analysis* books. *Mastering the Requirements Process* provides a much-requested front-end for their analysis books – or for anyone's analysis books, for that matter.

ROBERTSON, JAMES, AND SUZANNE. *Complete Systems Analysis 1 & 2*. Dorset House, 1994.

We can use all the good books on requirements we can get, and this is one of them!

Gerald M. Weinberg
http://www.geraldmweinberg.com
February 1999

What Are Requirements?

in which we consider why we are interested in *requirements*

Requirements are the things that you should discover before starting to build your product. Discovering the requirements during construction, or worse, when your client starts using your product, is so expensive and so inefficient, that we will assume that no right-thinking person would do it, and will not mention it again.

So let us begin. You are about to build a new product. What does it have to do? Control an aircraft? Predict profitability for your organization? Turn satellite data into graphic displays for broadcast? These might describe the purpose of your product, but what are the things that it has to do to achieve that purpose? These things are its functional requirements. And what qualities must the product have? Does it have to be fast? Or easy to use? Secure from hacking? Whatever qualities it must have are its non-functional requirements.

This book tells you how to find these requirements. Moreover, it tells you how to know whether you have found the correct requirements.

Any endeavor where the outcome is important, is best done by using some kind of orderly process. This book presents *Volere*, a process and a requirements specification template for gathering, confirming, and documenting the requirements for a product. Our examples anticipate that the product will contain a significant software component, either custom-built, or commercial off-the-shelf (COTS) software, or a maintenance project. However, the process explained by this book can be used for any kind of product. Currently it is being used, amongst other things, to gather the requirements for products as dissimilar as a submarine, a banking system, a telephone network and a wheel clamping system.

> *This book is for people who want to discover the requirements before constructing their products*

This book is about a requirements process – a process that begins before systems analysis does. Systems analysis builds models of a proposed system based on descriptions supplied by the assumed users. The requirements process uses interviews and other trawling techniques to determine not only what the product must do, but also how it must do it. In other words, the requirements are a complete description of the product, not just its functions and data. The requirements process is a thorough exploration of the intended product with the intention of discovering – in some cases inventing – the functionality and behavior of the product. The output of this requirements process is a specification that is used as input to systems analysis, and later to design of the product

It is fairly obvious that the requirements must be known before constructing the product. Most organizations that we consult with do some kind of systems analysis to find out what the product must do. That is, they build models of systems using DeMarco's data flow notation, or McMenamin and Palmer's event-response models. Some use variations on these two, and nowadays more and more organizations are using some form of object-oriented analysis, usually using unified modeling language (UML) notation. We have no argument with any of this. In fact, if you are not already doing systems analysis using some kind of modeling technique then we encourage you to start. Right now.

If you are already doing systems analysis, then read on. Requirements are not an extra burden, but something that will enhance your analytical life. To see how it works, look at the development lifecycle illustrated in Figure 1.1. The two initial activities, the Requirements Process and Systems Analysis, determine the business problem to be solved or opportunity to be addressed, and what the product will do to contribute to a solution.

There is a fair amount of overlap between the requirements and the analysis activities. During the course of this book you will see it. Analysis modeling is necessary for setting the scope of the work and so on. In fact, we make use of analysis models to describe the requirements process. We will also use analysis models to explain some of the concepts of requirements. We do not assume knowledge of analysis modeling, but neither do we provide a complete explanation of it. The commentary accompanying the models should be sufficient for you to understand them.

Once you have finished with our requirements process then systems analysis begins in earnest. The functionality that you have discovered during the requirements process is modeled to prove its correctness. That is, you demonstrate that the functionality and the data will work together correctly to provide the outcomes that the client expects. Most systems analysis disciplines provide models that help you to do this.

Once the functions and data are known to be correct, the task of the designer is to devise a way of making it happen in the technological world. Product Design translates the requirements into a plan to build some physical reality that will, in the real world, do what is required. Design determines what devices are to be used, what software components are necessary, and how they are to be constructed. It derives ways of making the required characteristics into real-world artifacts. But note that the design process needs requirements as input. Designing without requirements is no more than inventing without knowing if the invention is useful. It is important to the success of the product that design decisions are not taken before the relevant requirements are known.

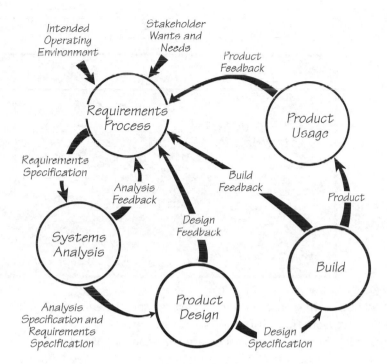

Intended
Operating
Environment

Stakeholder
Wants and
Needs

Product
Feedback

Requirements
Process

Product
Usage

Requirements
Specification

Analysis
Feedback

Build
Feedback

Product

Systems
Analysis

Design
Feedback

Build

Analysis
Specification and
Requirements
Specification

Product
Design

Design
Specification

Figure 1.1

The diagram illustrates the role of requirements in the development lifecycle. The Requirements Process studies the work to devise the best possible product to help with that work. As an outcome of this process, the Requirements Specification is a complete description of the functionality and the behavior of the product. Systems Analysis produces working models of the functions and data needed by the product as its specification. Product Design turns the abstract specifications from requirements and analysis into a design for the real world. Once built, the product is used and this inevitably provides more new requirements.

Once the product is built, it is used, and immediately begins to evolve. Users demand more and more functionality, and the product must grow to accommodate this. (Remember when Microsoft Word used to come on one floppy disk?) Evolution is not a process that we control or prescribe, but it is one that we must accept. Requirements for a product are not frozen the moment that it is built. They evolve over a period of time, and any requirements process must take this into account.

Requirements and Systems Analysis

Requirements Gathering and Systems Analysis have a degree of overlap – the requirements gatherer uses analysis models to help find the requirements, the systems analyst uses the requirements to help model the functionality and data.

In the beginning, the requirements activity is dominant. The only analysis models being built are context diagrams and perhaps exploratory data models. The requirements gatherers are busy discovering the business goals, the product, what it has to do, what qualities it must have, what constraints it must conform to and what interfaces it has to the outside world.

Figure 1.2

The overlap between Requirements Gathering and Systems Analysis varies as the development of the product progresses. Initially, there is very little analysis done, and the majority of the effort is taken up with gathering and verifying requirements. As development continues, the analytical activity grows to occupy a continually greater proportion of the effort, until all the requirements are known, and the remainder of the effort is directed to Systems Analysis.

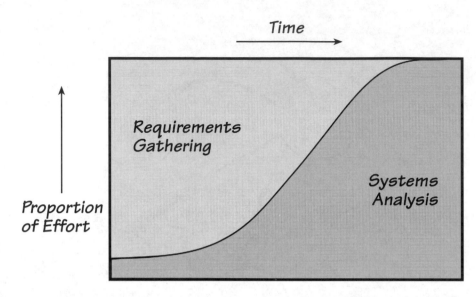

READING

ROBERTSON, JAMES AND SUZANNE. *Complete Systems Analysis: the Workbook, the Textbook, the Answers.* Dorset House, 1994.

JACOBSON, IVAR ET AL. *Object-Oriented Software Engineering – A Use Case Driven Approach.* Addison-Wesley, 1992.

As the knowledge of the product increases, and the business events and use cases evolve from fuzzy intentions to known quantities, the systems analyst can model them more precisely, and provide valuable feedback to the requirements process. Similarly, the growing knowledge of the requirements feeds the analytical process, enabling it (the analysis) in turn to become more productive.

The proportion of effort expended on systems analysis increases as time goes on, until finally the requirements are defined and systems analysis continues for a short time until the product is completely understood. This is illustrated in Figure 1.2.

The craft of systems analysis is well documented. There are several books that cover this area. Some are mentioned in the margin. The requirements activity is not so well documented. This book explains a process for producing the correct requirements. It will be expanded as we proceed through the book.

So Why Do I Need Requirements?

The requirements must be specified before attempting to construct the product. If you do not have the correct requirements, you cannot design or build the correct product, and consequently the product does not enable the users to do their work.

Sadly, this is not always the case. Steve McConnell reports that 60% of errors exist at design time. Jerry Weinberg confirms this with statistics that show that up to 60% of errors originate with the requirements and analysis activities. So although developers of products have the opportunity almost to eliminate the entire largest category of error, they choose, or worse their managers choose, to rush headlong into constructing the wrong product. And thus they pay many times the price for the product than they would have if the requirements and analysis had been done correctly in the first place. Keep in mind that poor quality is passed on. It is as simple as that.

The cost of good requirements gathering and systems analysis is minor compared to the cost of poor requirements. But you have bought this book. We shall not preach to the converted any longer. If you need more justification for installing a quality requirements process, do this: measure the cost to your organization of repair to sub-standard products, and opportunity lost by not having the correct products. If the cost of this wastage is insignificant, then stop reading this book. You already have your requirements process under control.

Otherwise, read on.

READING

McCONNELL, STEVE. *Code Complete*. Microsoft Press, 1993.

WEINBERG, JERRY. *Quality Software Management. Volume 4 Anticipating Change*. Dorset House, 1997.

So What is a Requirement?

A requirement is something that the product must do or a quality that the product must have. A requirement exists either because the type of product demands certain functions or qualities, or the client wants that requirement to be part of the delivered product.

Functional Requirements

Functional requirements are things the product must do – an action that the product must take if it is to provide useful functionality for its user. Functional requirements arise from the fundamental reason for the product's existence.

> *The product shall produce an amended de-icing schedule when a change to a truck status means that previously scheduled work cannot be carried out as planned.*

Functional requirements are things the product must do

This requirement is something that the product must do if it is to be useful within the context of the customer's business. In this case, the customers for the product are the counties and other authorities that have responsibility for dispatching trucks to spread de-icing material on freezing roads.

Non-functional Requirements

Non-functional requirements are properties, or qualities, that the product must have. In some cases the non-functional requirements are critical to the product's success:

Non-functional requirements are qualities the product must have

> The product shall determine 'friend or foe' in less than 0.25 seconds.

and sometimes they are requirements because they enhance the product:

> The product shall use company colors, standard company logos and standard company typefaces.

Non-functional requirements are usually attached to the product's functionality. That is, once we know what the product is to do, we can determine how it is to behave, what qualities it is to have, and how big or fast it should be.

Constraints

Constraints are global requirements. They apply to the entire product, and are preferably defined before beginning work on gathering the requirements. For example, the purpose of the product is a constraint – individual requirements must contribute to this purpose. The users of a product are a constraint, as they dictate the usability of the product:

Constraints are global issues that shape the requirements

> Passengers on board an aircraft will use the product.

There may also be constraints placed on the eventual design and construction of the product. For example:

> The product shall run on the company's existing UNIX machines.

The constraints are determined early in the requirements process, and thereafter used to gauge the correctness and appropriateness of the requirements as they are gathered.

The Template

All of the requirements and constraints, regardless of their type, are written in a requirements specification. This is a complete description of the product's capabilities. Specifications can take many forms. We (the authors) have arrived at a useful form of requirements specification, and documented it by using a template that can act as the basis for your own requirements specifications.

Volere is the Italian word for 'to wish' or 'to want'

The Volere Requirements Specification Template is a compartmentalized container for a requirements specification. It gives you a framework for writing a specification.

Requirements can be categorized into useful types. Each of the template's sections describes a type of requirement and its variations. The intention is that as you discover the requirements with your users, you add them to your specification, using the template as a guide to necessary content.

The complete Volere Requirements Specification Template is in Appendix B

The table of contents for the template categorizes the contents of a requirements specification as follows:

Product Constraints – *restrictions and limitations that apply to the project and the product*

1 The Purpose of the Product – *the reason for building the product and the business advantage if we do so*

2 The Client, Customer and other Stakeholders – *the people with an interest in the product*

3 Users of the Product – *the intended end-users, and how they affect the product's usability*

4 Requirements Constraints – *limitations on the project, and restrictions on the design of the product*

5 Naming Conventions and Definitions – *the vocabulary of the product*

6 Relevant Facts – *outside influences that make some difference to this product*

7 Assumptions – *that the developers are making*

Functional Requirements – *the functionality of the product*

8 The Scope of the Product – *defines the product boundaries, and its connections to adjacent systems*

9 Functional and Data Requirements – *things the product must do and the data manipulated by the functions*

Non-functional Requirements – *the product's qualities*

10 Look and Feel Requirements – *the intended appearance*

11 Usability Requirements – *based on the intended users*

12 Performance Requirements – *how fast, big, accurate, safe, reliable, etc.*

13 Operational Requirements – *the product's intended operating environment*

14 Maintainability and Portability Requirements – *how changeable the product must be*

15 Security Requirements – *the security, confidentiality and integrity of the product*

16 Cultural and Political Requirements – *human factors*

17 Legal Requirements – *conformance to applicable laws*

Project Issues – *these apply to the project that builds the product*

18   Open Issues – *as yet unresolved issues with a possible bearing on the success of the product*

19   Off-the-Shelf Solutions – *ready-made components that might be used instead of building something*

20   New Problems – *caused by the introduction of the new product*

21   Tasks – *things to be done to bring the product into production*

22   Cutover – *tasks to convert from existing systems*

23   Risks – *the risks that the project is most likely to face*

24   Costs – *early estimates of the cost or effort needed to build the product*

25.   User Documentation – *the plan for building the user instructions and documentation*

26   Waiting Room – *requirements that might be included in future releases of the product*

Browse through the template before going too much further in the book. You will find a lot about writing requirements, together with a lot of food for thought about the kinds of requirements to be gathered.

Throughout this book, we will refer to requirements by their type. By this we mean the types as shown in the above list of the template's contents.

The Shell

Individual requirements have a structure. There are a number of components for a requirement, each contributes something to your knowledge, and each is necessary to understand the whole requirement.

The components are all used, and all have a contribution to make. Although they may at first sight seem rather bureaucratic, we have found that their value repays the effort used to gather the information. The components will be described as we work our way though the process.

The shell is completed progressively. It is not practical to find all components of one requirement before moving on to the next. For this reason, we have the shell printed onto cards, and use the cards when we are interviewing users, quickly scribbling each requirement as we discover it, and completing the card as we learn more about the requirement. See Figure 1.3.

There are a number of automated tools on the market for recording, analyzing and tracing requirements

This low-tech approach gives us an initial flexibility, and does not hinder us as we work at the user's place of work to gather the requirements. We usually keep them grouped according to the use case they belong to (See Event/ Use Case # in the upper right of Figure 1.3) as that makes it easier to find individual cards in the deck. When we think that the requirements are well formed, we store them using an automated tool.

Requirement #: **Unique Id**   Requirement Type: **Template section**   Event/use case #: **Origin of the requirement**

Description: **A one-sentence statement of the intention of the requirement**

Rationale: **Why is this requirement considered important or necessary?**

Source: **Who raised this requirement?**

Fit Criteria: **A quantification of the requirement used to determine whether the solution meets the requirement.**

Customer Satisfaction: **Measures the desire to have the requirement implemented**   Customer Dissatisfaction: **Unhappiness if it is not implemented**

Dependencies: **Other requirements with a change effect**   Conflicts: **Requirements that contradict this one**

Supporting Materials: **Pointer to supporting information**

History: **Origin and changes to the requirement**

Copyright © Atlantic Systems Guild

Figure 1.3

The requirements shell. We use a 5" by 8" card, printed with the shell components, for our initial requirements gathering. Each of the components contributes to the understanding and testability of the requirement. Although a copyright notice appears on the card, we have no objections to any reader making use of it provided the source is acknowledged.

The Volere Requirements Process

The remainder of this book explains how you can successfully gather, verify and document requirements. Each chapter covers an activity of the process, or some aspect of requirements gathering that is needed to complete the activity.

As you work through the process, keep in mind that it is a guide for producing *deliverables*. In other words, what you do with the process is driven by relevant deliverables, not procedures.

Once you understand the process, it is not necessary to read the book in the presented order – although there may be some terminology that assumes knowledge from previous chapters. The following chapter gives an overview of the process, and a complete model of it can be found in Appendix A.

We are aware that your requirements needs are different from other readers', and that you will therefore be interested in exploring some aspects of the process before others. So once you know the basic outline of the process, please feel free to plunge in wherever you feel it will be most valuable.

We hope that you find our book useful.

2 The Requirements Process

 in which we find our way around the generic requirements gathering process

Whether you are building custom systems, building systems by assembling components, using commercial off-the-shelf software or making changes to existing software, you still need to explore, capture and communicate the requirements

See Appendix A for the complete Volere Requirements Process

We based this book on the Volere Requirements Process and its associated Specification Template. The process is a generic requirements gathering and specification process whose principles can be applied to both large and small systems. In addition you can apply the requirements principles no matter what your system development environment.

Whether you are building bespoke systems, building systems by assembling components, using commercial off-the-shelf packages or making changes to existing software, you still need to explore, capture and communicate the requirements. The Volere process is a guide for how to discover and write testable requirements. Each part of the process is described in detail in one of the chapters in this book.

The Volere Requirements Process Model in Appendix A contains a detailed model of all of the activities and the connections between them. Take a moment now to flip to Appendix A and make yourself aware of its contents. As you see, the model is very detailed. Rather than diving straight into all that detail and complexity, let's stand back and look at a simplified view of the overall process. Such a view is shown in Figure 2.1.

At various places throughout the book we will use this simplified version of the process model. For the most part the simplified version is faithful to the complete version in Appendix A. However, there are times when, for the sake of making an explanation simpler, or making it easier for you to see what we are talking about, we have made some minor changes and simplifications. Please be aware of this and be sure you use the detailed model for any of your important implementation decisions.

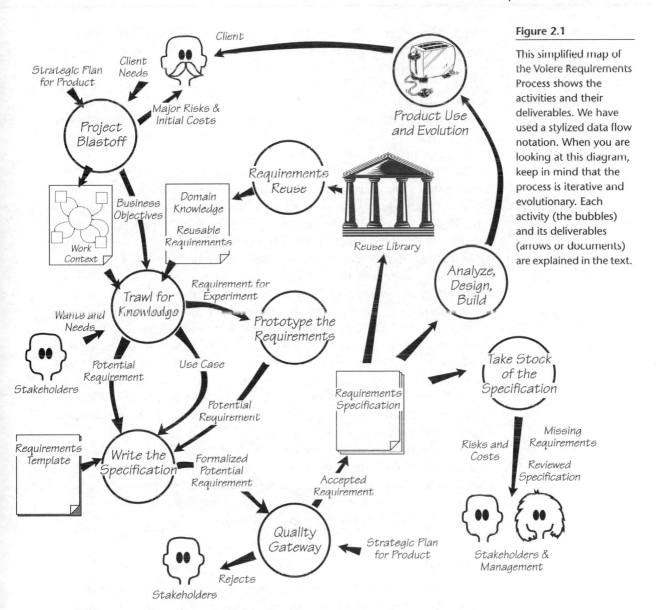

Figure 2.1

This simplified map of the Volere Requirements Process shows the activities and their deliverables. We have used a stylized data flow notation. When you are looking at this diagram, keep in mind that the process is iterative and evolutionary. Each activity (the bubbles) and its deliverables (arrows or documents) are explained in the text.

In Figure 2.1 you see all of the main activities in the Volere Requirements Process, and how they are linked by their deliverables. The deliverables are shown as moving from one activity to the next. This, to some extent, represents the concept that the output from one activity is input to the next. However, do not take this too literally, as it is usually necessary for activities to iterate and overlap before producing the final output.

For an example of this, look at the *Trawling, Writing* and *Quality Gateway* activities. *Trawling* discovers several requirements, they are made rigorous by writing them down in the prescribed manner, and then the *Quality Gateway* inspects them to determine if they are correct enough to be added to the Requirements Specification. Any rejects are sent back to the originator, who probably takes them back to the trawling activity for clarification and further explanation.

This iteration goes on until the specification is considered complete, and then it goes to the Stock Take activity. If this review uncovers serious faults, then part of the process is repeated.

Note that there is no end to the requirements process. When a product is delivered and your users start using it, then evolution kicks in. As people use the product, they discover new uses for it, and want it to be extended. This raises new requirements, that in turn go through the same requirements process. Just as the product evolves on its own, you may choose to make it evolve by building the early versions with a minimal amount of functionality, and augmenting it by a planned series of releases. The evolutionary nature of the requirements process is designed with this in mind.

Note also the people around the periphery of the process. These people supply information to the process, or receive information from it. These people are some of the *stakeholders* – the people who have a vested interest in the product. They participate in the requirements process, and as well have tasks that fall outside the scope of the process. For example, some of the stakeholders participate by being the users who give you the requirements in the trawling activity. Another stakeholder is your client who tells you the business objectives for the product, and pays for the development.

Some stakeholders play a role completely outside the process. In Figure 2.1 you can see that management stakeholders receive the risks and the costs from the process to enable them to assess the viability of the project.

As we discuss the process throughout this book, we will also discuss the different stakeholder roles and responsibilities.

The Process

The process is not just for new products that you are developing from the ground up. Most product development that is done today is aimed at enhancing an existing product, or making a major overhaul to an existing product, or suite of products. A lot of today's development involves commercial off-the-shelf products, or other types of componentware. Whatever your development method, the requirements for the final outcome are still necessary.

Let's look briefly at each of the activities. In subsequent chapters, they will be covered in more detail. The intention here is to give you a gentle introduction to the process, and how the parts of it fit together. If you want more detail for any of the activities, feel free to jump to the relevant chapter before completing this overview of the process.

Keep in mind as we go through the process that we are talking as if we are working with a brand new product, and are starting from scratch. This is not always the case with requirements projects. In Chapter 14, Whither Requirements?, we talk about projects that are already underway, and projects where the requirements are changing.

A Case Study

Let's look at a project that is using this process. We would like you to meet Karen. Karen works for Saltworks Systems and is the lead requirements analyst on the IceBreaker project. This project is to develop a product that predicts when ice will form on roads, and schedules trucks to treat the roads with de-icing material. The major reasons for having this product are so that the road authorities can be more accurate with their predictions, schedule the road treatment more precisely, and thus make the roads safer. They also anticipate that they will reduce the amount of de-icing materials used.

Now let's follow Karen as she works her way through the requirements process. Karen works closely with the project manager. In fact, some of the things that she is doing in this project overlap the responsibilities of a traditional project manager. This IceBreaker project is putting an emphasis on requirements, and so project issues and requirements tend to go together. Let's see how this works for Karen.

Project Blastoff

Imagine launching a rocket. $10 - 9 - 8 - 7 - 6 - 5 - 4 - 3 - 2 - 1$ – blastoff! If all it involved was the ability to count backwards from ten then even Tierra del Fuego would have its own space program. The truth of the matter is that before we get to the final ten seconds of a rocket launch, a lot of preparation has taken place. The rocket has been fueled, the courses plotted, in fact everything that needs to be done before the rocket gets off the ground. We can't really have '$10 - 9 - 8 - 7 - 6 - 5$ – hey, hold it! The astronauts aren't aboard.'

Back to reality. Karen calls a blastoff meeting to prepare the project, and ensure its feasibility before launching it.

She invites the principal stakeholders – the client, the main users, the lead developers, technical and business experts, and other people who are key to the success of the project. Saltworks Systems are developing the product for worldwide sale. However, Northumberland County Highways Department have agreed to be the first customer, and are helping with the requirements. Naturally, Karen has invited the key Northumberland people to the blastoff.

> " The likelihood of frost or ice forming is determined by the energy receipt and loss at the road surface. This energy flow is controlled by a number of environmental and meteorological factors (such as exposure, altitude, road construction, traffic, cloud cover, wind speed). These factors cause significant variation in Road Surface Temperature from time to time and from one location to another. Winter night-time road surface temperatures can vary by over 10 °C across a road network in a county. "
>
> *Source: Vaisala News 1997*

Northumberland is a county in the far north of England

This part of the process is shown in detailed model form in Project Blastoff (Diagram 1) in the Volere Process model in Appendix A

Refer to Chapter 3 for a detailed discussion of Project Blastoff

The blastoff is a joint application development (JAD) meeting where the principals lock themselves away and work together until they have achieved the blastoff's objectives – gathering enough facts to ensure that the project has a worthwhile objective, is possible to achieve, and has commitment from the stakeholders.

Karen leads the group in a brainstorm to identify all the stakeholders – the people who have an interest in the product, and thus have requirements for it. If she doesn't know who the stakeholders are, she won't be able to find all the requirements. The blastoff group identify the various people who have some interest in IceBreaker – the road engineers, the truck depot supervisor, and so on. As Ice-Breaker will be using weather forecasts, Karen adds weather people to the list of stakeholders, along with the road safety experts and ice treatment consultants. The group identifies other stakeholders as they study the context of the work.

Karen facilitates the group as they determine the scope of the work that she is to study. Note that at the moment, she is only concerned with the scope of the work. Later, her investigations will reveal the precise scope of the product that she is to build to help with this work. She draws a context model on a whiteboard as the group discusses the extent of the work, what it should include and what they consider to be outside the scope of the ice forecasting business. This is illustrated in Figure 2.2.

Figure 2.2

Karen builds a consensus among the stakeholders as to the context of the work that needs to be studied. The product that she eventually builds will be used to do part of this work.

The blastoff determines the product's purpose. Karen keeps the team working at this until they produce a statement that clearly says what they want the product to do. She also ensures that the group agrees that the product is worthwhile, and that the organization is capable of building and operating it.

While she has the group together, Karen produces a preliminary estimate of the costs involved from her model of the scope of the work. She also makes an early assessment of the risks that the project is likely to face. She discusses these with the stakeholders. Although they may be bad news, she knows that it is always better to get an idea of the downside of the project (risk and cost) before being swept away by the euphoria of the benefits that the new product will bring.

Finally, she gets the stakeholders to arrive at a consensus on whether the project is worthwhile and viable – the go/no go decision. Karen knows from bitter experience that it is better to cancel a project early than have it stagger on for months or years consuming valuable resources with no chance of success. So she works hard to have the group carefully consider whether or not the product is viable, and whether its benefits are greater than its costs.

The project blastoff deliverables are described in the Volere Requirements Specification Template. Refer especially to the first eight items. You can find the template in Appendix B

Trawling For Knowledge

Once the blastoff is completed, Karen starts trawling. She leads her team of requirements analysts into learning about the work that was identified by the blastoff. She starts with the work context model that the blastoff stakeholders produced when they identified the scope of the work. (You can see this in Figure 2.1.) She breaks the work into business events, and assigns requirements analysts to each of the events for further detailed study. The analysts use techniques such as apprenticing and use case workshops to discover the true nature of the work. These techniques are described in Chapter 5, Trawling for Requirements, and are favored as they involve the users closely in capturing the requirements. Once they understand the work, Karen and her team can decide the best product to help with this work. They then gather the requirements for the product. See Figure 2.3.

Refer to Chapter 4 for a detailed discussion of business events and use cases, and how to use them

Refer to Chapter 5 for details of the trawling activity

When they are trawling to discover the requirements, Karen and her team work mainly with the users as they describe the work that they do, and the work that they hope to do. The product they will build is intended to help with the work, so the team must understand that work. They must also understand the users' aspirations about what the work should or could be, and together with the users, invent the best product.

Karen assigns some of the team as apprentices to the users. They work closely with the users to understand the work. Meanwhile, other team members are gathering information by interviewing some of the stakeholders.

The relevant part of the Volere Process model (Appendix A) is Project Blastoff (Diagram 1)

Figure 2.3

The blastoff activity delivers the foundation for requirements trawling. The blastoff determines the scope of the work to be studied, and the business events that have an effect on that work. The stakeholders identified by the blastoff contribute requirements to the trawlers. The outputs of the trawling activity are the potential requirements – they still have to pass the quality checks.

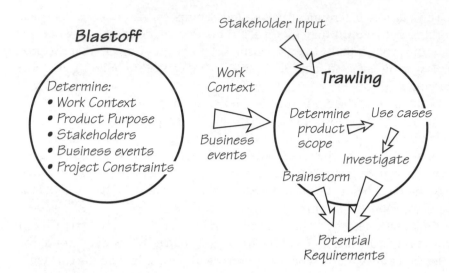

The client has said that the product might eventually be sold to other road authorities. Karen uses some of her resources to do a survey of these potential users and their needs.

Of course, the product that Karen intends to build for her client is not just an automation of the procedures that they do at the moment. To deliver a really useful product, Karen's team will have to invent a better way to do the work, and build a product that helps with this better way of working. The inventing part of the requirements process is done by the team when they hold brainstorms to generate ideas for particular aspects of the product. These techniques, and others, are elaborated in Chapters 4, Event-driven Use Cases, and 5, Trawling for Requirements.

Prototyping and Scenario Modeling

Sometimes requirements analysts get stuck. Sometimes there are requirements that are not properly formed, or the user can't explain them, or the requirements analysts can't understand them. Or the product is so groundbreaking that nobody really knows the requirements. Or they just need to work with something more concrete than a written requirement. This is when they use prototypes.

This part of the process is shown in detailed model form in Prototype the Requirements (Diagram 5) in the Volere Process model in Appendix A

A prototype, as we use the term in this book, is a quick and dirty version of a potential product – probably only part of the product. The intention of the prototype is to present the user with a simulation of the requirements. There are two approaches to building requirements prototypes: high fidelity (uses some kind of automated technology) and low fidelity (mainly uses pencil and paper or some other familiar means). Karen's team construct

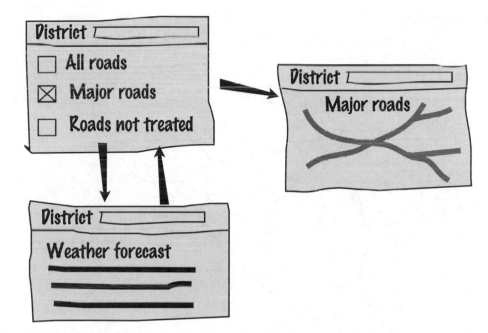

Figure 2.4

A low fidelity prototype built to provide a quick visual explanation of some of the requirements and to elicit some misunderstood or missing requirements.

some high fidelity prototypes built using one of the specialized software tools, and some low fidelity prototypes that they draw on whiteboards, paper, or anything they can lay their hands on, as in Figure 2.4. The team like using the low-fi prototypes as they can generate them quickly and the users enjoy the spontaneous nature and inventiveness of these prototypes.

They also build scenarios. Scenarios are stories constructed to show the steps that are needed to complete a particular piece of work. The users lead the effort here as they demonstrate to the analysts how the work is done and where there might be exceptions to the norm. When the analysts fully understand the work, they use the scenarios to generate the requirements for the product that will help with that part of the work. These techniques are elaborated upon in Chapter 11, Prototyping and Scenarios.

Refer to Chapter 11 for a detailed discussion of prototyping and scenario modeling

Whatever form of prototype they use, the output from this activity is a number of requirements. Of course, they have to write them down.

Writing Them Down

At this stage of the requirements process, Karen refers to all requirements as 'potential requirements'. The reason for this is that so far, the requirements have not passed the tests that get them through the Quality Gateway. But before they can be inspected by the gateway, they need to be written down in a consistent format.

This part of the process is shown in detailed process model form in Write the Requirements (Diagram 3) in the Volere Process model in Appendix A

Figure 2.5

Potential requirements are discovered by the Trawling and Prototyping activities. These potential requirements are brought into a consistent format by the Writing activity, before being inspected by the Quality Gateway. Only by passing through the gateway can they become part of the Requirements Specification.

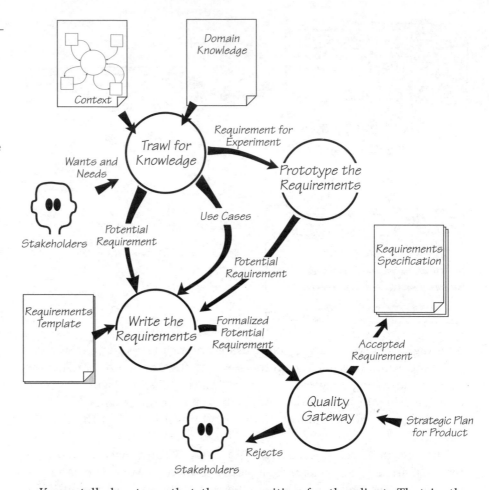

Chapter 9 describes the fit criteria in detail

Karen tells her team that they are writing for the client. That is, the requirements are the business requirements, and must be written using business language so that the client can understand them and verify their correctness. Of course, the requirements also need to be written so that the product designers can build precisely what the client wants. To meet this need, the analysts will add a fit criterion to each requirement. A fit criterion is a measurement of the requirement. Its purpose is to quantify the requirement so that the testers can determine precisely if an implementation meets, in other words fits, the requirement.

The analysts use two devices that make it easier to write a specification. The Requirements Specification Template is an outline of a requirements specification. The analysts use it as a guide for their specification documents. The second device is a Shell. Each requirement is made up of a number of components, and the shell is a convenient layout for ensuring that each requirement has all the correct constituents.

Of course, the writing activity is not really a separate activity. In reality it is integrated with the activities that surround it – Trawling, Prototyping and the Quality Gateway. However, for the purposes of understanding what is involved in writing correct requirements, we have chosen to look at it separately. Figure 2.5 illustrates all this.

Refer to Chapter 8 for a detailed discussion of Writing Requirements

Quality Gateway

The Quality Gateway (Figure 2.6) is the single point that every requirement must pass through before it can become a part of the specification. Karen has set up a gateway where one of her analysts and a senior user are the only people who are authorized to pass requirements through the gateway. Together they check every requirement for completeness, relevance, coherency, traceability, and several other qualities before they allow it to be added to the specification.

The customer has on several occasions said 'I am not going to have any requirements that I do not understand, nor will I have any that are not useful, or don't contribute to my work. I want to understand the contribution that they make, that's why I want to measure each one.'

The Quality Gateway is detailed in Diagram 4 of the Volere Process model in Appendix A

Figure 2.6

The Quality Gateway ensures a rigorous specification by testing each requirement for completeness, correctness, measurability, absence of ambiguity, and several other qualities before each requirement can be added to the specification.

Chapter 10 describes the Quality Gateway tests

The requirements analyst has a different, but complementary approach to testing requirements. He says 'I need to ensure that each requirement is completely unambiguous, and that I can measure it against the client's expectations. If I can't put a measurement to it, then I can never tell if we are building the product that the client really wants.' This measurement is the fit criterion, and the Gateway process ensures that a fit criterion is attached to each requirement.

Another reason that Karen has set up a Gateway is to prevent requirements leakage. This is where new requirements seem to find their way into the specification without anybody really knowing where they came from, or what value they add to the product. Karen knows that if the only way into the specification is through the Quality Gateway, then she is in control of the requirements, and not the other way round.

Reusing Requirements

Before starting on any new requirements project, Karen goes through the specifications that were written for previous projects, looking for potentially reusable material. Sometimes she finds dozens of requirements that she can reuse without altering them. More often she finds requirements that although they are not exactly what she wants, they are the basis for the requirements that she will write in her new project. See Figure 2.7.

Figure 2.7

Requirements for any product that you build will never be completely unique. Thus you can take advantage of previous projects by reusing their requirements.

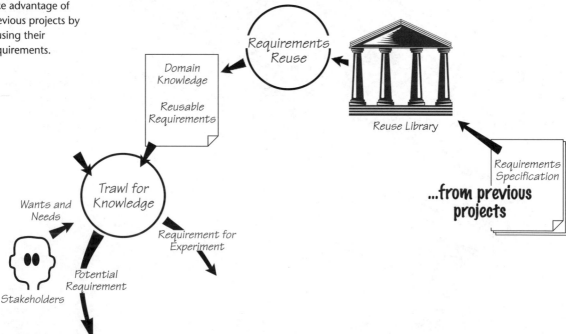

Karen knows that the specifications for products similar to the one that she is working on at the moment are rich sources for her to mine. She knows that the rules for road engineering do not change between products; that she does not have to rediscover them. She knows that the business of vehicle scheduling does not radically change every year, so her trawling process can take advantage of some requirements from previous projects.

The point about reusing requirements is that once a requirement has been successfully specified for a product, and the product itself is successful, then the requirement does not have to be reinvented.

See Chapter 12 for more on Reusing Requirements

In Chapter 12 we discuss some ways that you can take advantage of the knowledge that already exists in your organization, and how you can save yourself time by recycling requirements from previous projects.

Taking Stock of the Specification

The Quality Gateway exists to keep bad requirements out of the specification. However, it deals with one requirement at a time. When she thinks that the specification is complete, Karen runs a specification stocktake. This checks for missing requirements, that all the requirements are consistent with one another, and that there are no unresolved conflicts between the requirements.

This is the subject of Diagram 7 of the Volere Process model in Appendix A

In short, this is her check that the specification is really complete, and suitable for her to pass on to the next stage of development.

Karen uses this review as an opportunity to reassess the costs and risks of the product. Now that she has a complete specification, she knows a lot more about the product than she did at blastoff time. Once the requirements specification is complete, Karen and her team have a precise knowledge of the scope and functionality of the product, so they remeasure its size and from that assess the cost to construct it.

See Chapter 13 for more on Taking Stock of the Specification

They also know at this stage what kinds of requirements will cause the greatest risks. For example, the users may have asked for a kind of interface that their organization has not built before. Or they have to use untried technology to build the product. Do they have the people capable of building the product as specified? By reassessing the risks at this point, they give themselves a better chance to build their product successfully.

Post Mortem

Karen considers a post mortem to be so important to improving her process that she facilitates all her post mortems herself. She conducts her post mortems as a series of interviews with stakeholders and group sessions with the developers, and polls all the people involved in the process with the questions:

'What did we do right?'

'What did we do wrong?'

'If we had to do it again, what would you do differently?'

By asking these questions, and looking for honest answers, Karen gives herself the best chance of improving her process. Her idea is very simple: do more of what works and less of what doesn't.

Your post mortem can be very informal – a coffee time meeting with the project group or the project leader collecting email messages from the participants. Alternatively, if the stakes are higher, it can be formalized to the point where it is run by an outside facilitator who canvases the participants, both individually and as a group, and publishes a post mortem report.

The most notable feature of post mortems is that the companies that, as a matter of normal procedure, make post mortems a part of their process consistently report startling improvements in their processes. Post mortems are probably the cheapest investment you can make in your own process.

If we did the project again tomorrow, what would we do differently?

Tailoring Your Process

The itinerant peddler of quack potions, Doctor Dulcamara, sings the praises of his elixir, guaranteed to cure toothache, make you potent, eliminate wrinkles and give you smooth beautiful skin, destroy mice and bugs, and make the object of your affections fall in love with you. The rather fanciful libretto from Donizetti's opera *L'elisir d'amore* points out something that, although very obvious, is often disregarded. There is no such thing as the universal cure.

We really would like to be able to present you with a requirements process that has all the attributes of Doctor Dulcamara's elixir – a process that suits all projects for all applications in all organizations. But we know from experience that every project needs a different process for the simple reason that every project is different. However we have learnt that there are basic concepts of the requirements process that, once understood, can provide the basis for building your own process. Instead of looking for a magic potion we have distilled experience from a wide variety of projects to provide the basis for tailoring your own requirements process.

The process we have just taken you through is a generic process – it is not aimed a specific type of product, nor at a specific type of organization. The process contains the things that you have to do to produce a complete, accurate requirements specification. It contains descriptions of the deliverables that any requirements project must produce. In fact, we prefer you to think in terms of the deliverables, not so much the process that delivers them.

Think of the deliverables more than the process that delivers them

We have also observed that between organizations, there are huge cultural differences. The access to users is different, the stakeholders see their responsibilities differently, and so on. This means tailoring.

To tailor this process you need to understand each of the deliverables produced by the process – the rest of this book will discuss these in detail. Once you understand the content and purpose of each deliverable, ask how each one (provided it is relevant to you) would best be produced within your project environment using your resources. Ask:

● What is the deliverable called within your environment? Use the definitions of the terms used in the generic process model and identify the equivalent deliverable in your organization.

● What is the deliverable used for within your environment? If the deliverable does not have an agreed purpose within your environment then omit it from your process.

● Who produces the deliverable? Specify which parts of the deliverable are produced by whom. Also, when several people are involved you need to define the interfaces between them.

● When is the deliverable produced? Map your project phases to the generic process.

● Where is the deliverable produced? A generic deliverable is often the result of fragments that are produced in a number of geographical locations. Define the interfaces between the different locations and specify how they will work.

● Who needs to review the deliverable? Look for existing cultural checkpoints within your organization. Do you have recognized stages or phases in your projects when peers, users or managers review your specification?

The generic model describes deliverables and procedures for producing them. The tailoring task is determining how your project will produce them.

Summary

The process focusses on the deliverables that you need to produce in order to build a testable and traceable requirements specification. The deliverables provide early metrics for managing the project. You can tailor the procedures for gathering, eliciting, writing and testing requirements so that they suit your technical and cultural environment. The requirements template and the requirements shell are sample deliverables that you can tailor to your own environment using your own terminology. The generic process provides the key to understanding requirements concepts so that you can implement those concepts within the constraints of your project.

3 Project Blastoff

 in which we find out what we really know about the product, and start to measure early in the project

The Project Blastoff is a short burst of activity that puts together all the pieces that are necessary to get your project off to a flying start and to ensure that your project is viable and well founded.

The blastoff (see Figure 3.1) identifies the work that the product is to become a part of, and determines the precise purpose that the product is to fulfill. The other deliverables from the blastoff help to qualify the project, and are used as inputs to the remaining requirements gathering activities.

The blastoff deliverables lay the foundation for the project:

- Purpose of the project – a short, measurable statement of what the product must achieve for the business.

- The client – who is the product being built for?

- The customer – for commercial products, who is going to buy the product?

- The stakeholders – who are the people with a vested interest in the product?

- The users – who is going to operate the product? And what are their capabilities?

- Constraints – are there any design solutions that must be used? How much time and money is available for the solution?

- Names – what terminology is to be used in this project?

- Relevant facts and assumptions – what does everybody need to know?

- The scope of the work – just what are the boundaries of the product and the project?

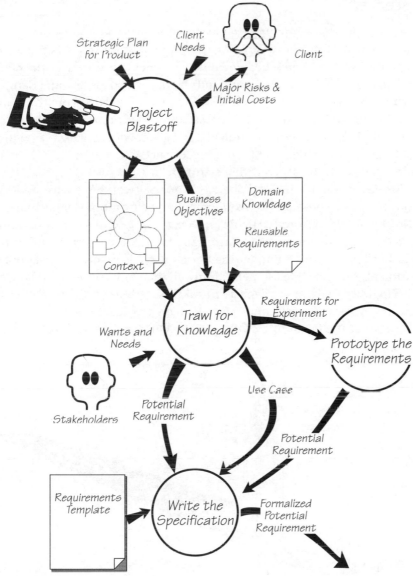

Figure 3.1

The blastoff activity is used to get the project off the ground and to ensure that the foundations for a successful project are in hand. A complete model of the blastoff process is to be found in Diagram 1 in the Volere Process model in Appendix A.

- The estimated cost – how much effort, or money, must be expended to bring the product to fruition?
- The risks – a short risk analysis to reveal the main risks faced by the project.

Taken together, these deliverables give you enough information to make the final deliverable from the blastoff:

- Go/no go decision – is the project viable, and does the cost of producing the product make it worthwhile?

IceBreaker

Road weather stations have been available for more than 20 years, and today there are more than 5000 installed in 25 countries around the world.

Source: Vaisala News 1997

IceBreaker is the case study that we have built to illustrate the requirements process. IceBreaker uses a variety of data to predict precisely when ice will form on roadways. It then schedules and dispatches trucks to treat the roads with de-icing material (a salt compound) before the roads become dangerous. The IceBreaker case study uses subject matter knowledge from the many ice forecasting and road de-icing systems, and other products produced by Vaisala (UK) Ltd, and Vaisala worldwide. We acknowledge Vaisala's permission to use their material, and their kind cooperation. See Figure 3.2 for an illustration of an IceBreaker weather station.

IceBreaker is Karen's project. She works for Saltworks Systems, and her responsibility is to produce the requirements specification. Her customer is the Northumberland County Highways Department, who will be providing information and requirements. Northumberland is a county in the north east of England, tucked up under the border with Scotland. The Highways Department is responsible for maintaining all the roads in that county. One of the Highway Department's most critical tasks is to keep the roads free of ice during winter when icy conditions are likely to cause accidents.

Let's start at the beginning of the project. Our first question is 'Why are we doing it?'

Figure 3.2

An IceBreaker weather station. This device transmits data about the weather and road surface conditions to the part of the product that predicts when roads will freeze. The product then dispatches trucks to treat the roads with de-icing material.

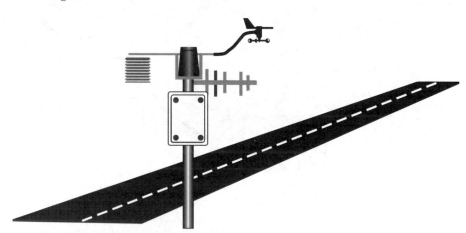

Product Purpose – What Do We Want This for Anyway?

The product purpose is the highest-level customer requirement

The product purpose describes the reason for building the product – what will this product do that will help our work?

The product purpose is the highest-level customer requirement. That is, it is the business need. All the other requirements that you gather must contribute in some way to the purpose. We are going to test all requirements against this statement of purpose. Thus it will pay you to spend a little time during the blastoff to reach a consensus on the purpose, and to write it clearly, unambiguously and in such a way that it can be measured.

Usually at the beginning of a project, the purpose of the product is vague, or is stated in terms that almost any solution could satisfy. How do you make it clearer? Start with a statement of the user problem or background to the project. (We make this problem statement the first part of all our specifications. See the template in Appendix B for a suggested format.) Those stakeholders who represent the user or business side of the organization, should confirm that you indeed understand the problem, and that your problem statement is a fair and accurate one.

The customer has given us this background:

Roads freeze in winter and icy conditions cause road accidents that kill people. We need to be able to predict when a road is likely to freeze so that our depot can schedule a de-icing truck in time to prevent the road from freezing. We expect a new system will provide more accurate predictions of icy conditions by using thermal maps of the district and the road temperatures from weather stations installed in the roads, in addition to the weather forecasts. This will lead to more timely de-icing treatment than at present which will reduce road accidents. We also want to eliminate indiscriminate treatment of roads which wastes de-icing compounds and causes environmental damage.

Once you, and your blastoff group, know and can articulate the problem, you can begin to formulate an appropriate solution. This solution is what the product will do to help with, or alleviate, the problem.

The problem appears to be road accidents due to ice on the roads, and the solution to the problem is to treat the roads to prevent the ice from forming (and presumably to melt the ice if it has already formed). Thus we can say that the purpose for this product is:

PUTTING THIS TO WORK

> Purpose: To accurately forecast road freezing times and dispatch de-icing trucks.

The purpose of the product should be not only to solve the problem, but also to provide a business advantage. Naturally, if there is an advantage, you must be able to measure it.

The business advantage is the reduction, ideally the elimination, of accidents due to ice. The County is particularly interested in reducing the accident rate. We have been told:

The new system will lead to more timely de-icing treatment than at present which will reduce road accidents.

Thus we can say that the business advantage of the product is:

The goal, or purpose of the product, not only solves the problem, but also provides a business advantage

> *Advantage: To reduce road accidents by forecasting icy road conditions.*

Is this *measurable*? Yes. The success of the product can be measured by the reduction in the number of accidents where ice is a contributing factor.

> *Measurement: Accidents attributed to ice shall be no more than 15% of the total number of accidents during winter.*

PAM – Purpose, Advantage, Measurement

We have stated a measurable goal, and monitoring the accidents for a winter or two is reasonable. As accident statistics and police reports are already collected, we should have no trouble establishing if our product is successful or not.

But is this a *reasonable* goal? Is the elimination of most of the accidents due to ice worth the cost and effort of building the product? And where did '15% of the total' come from anyway? The Northumberland County Highways Department representative at the blastoff assures us that this is a target figure set by the County. If it can be achieved, then the County Council will be happy, and they are prepared to spend money to achieve the target. Note that at this stage if there was no concrete goal, or if the effort (we will deal with estimating the effort shortly) was too great for the business advantage, then now is the time to call a halt.

Is it *feasible*? Can a 'timely de-icing treatment' lead to a reduction in accidents? And to as little as 15% of the total? One of the reasons for having the main stakeholders at the blastoff is to have questions like this answered. One of the stakeholders (see later in this chapter for how stakeholders are selected) is from the National Road Users Association. She assures us that their research shows that ice treatment is effective, and that the expected reductions are realistic.

Is it *achievable*? The stakeholders representing the product designers and builders, the technical experts from the hardware side, and the meteorologist, all assure the blastoff participants that the technology is available, or can be built, and that similar software problems have been solved previously by the team.

Note the aspects of the purpose or goal:

● Purpose – a statement of what the product is to do.

● Advantage – what business advantage does it provide?

● Measurement – how do you measure the advantage?

● Reasonable – is the product construction effort greater than the advantage?

● Feasible – can the product achieve the measure?

● Achievable – does the organization have (or can it acquire) the skills to build the product, and operate it once built?

Sometimes products have more than one purpose statement. Look at the customer's statement:

We also want to eliminate indiscriminate treatment of roads which wastes de-icing compounds and causes environmental damage.

This reveals another purpose for the product:

> *Purpose: To save money on winter road maintenance costs.*

The advantage stemming from this purpose is that the customer believes that accurate forecasts will reduce the cost of treatment as less de-icing material will be used. By preventing ice from forming on road surfaces, damage to roads will be reduced. (When ice forms in cracks in the surface, it expands as it freezes and forces the crack to expand. Eventually this results in significant holes in the road surface.)

The advantage is straightforward:

> *Advantage: Reduced de-icing and road maintenance costs.*

And the measurement of 'reduced costs' is usually expressed in monetary terms:

> *The cost of de-icing shall be reduced by 25% of the current cost of road treatment, and damage to roads from ice shall be reduced by 50%.*

Naturally we need to know the current costs so that we will know when they have been reduced by 25% and 50%. If there is supporting material available then cite it in your specification:

> *Supporting Materials: Thornes, J.E., 1992: Cost-Effective Snow and Ice Control for the Nineties. Third International Symposium on Snow and Ice Control Technology, Minneapolis. Minnesota, Vol. 1, Paper 24.*

The engineers also know that applying too much salt compounds to roads damages the environment. By having a more accurate treatment, less material will find its way to the environs of the roads, and less damage will result. This means that more accurate forecasts give us another advantage:

> *Advantage: To reduce damage to the environment by unnecessary application of de-icing compounds.*

The advantage can be measured by comparing the amount of de-icing material used by the product with that used at present.

> *Measurement: The amount of de-icing chemicals needed to de-ice the council's roads shall be reduced by 50%.*
> *Supporting Materials: Thornes, J.E., Salt of the Earth. Surveyor Magazine, 8 December 1994, pp. 16–18*

Note that the purpose statements result in an advantage and a measurement. It is a simple fact that if you cannot express an advantage for the purpose, or the advantage is not measurable, then it should not be part of your specification. For example, if the purpose of a product is something vague like:

> *Purpose: To improve the way that we do business.*

You cannot build the right product unless you know precisely what the product is intended to do, and how the product's success is to be measured

the advantage of this is unclear. Do we want the business to make more money, or do we want the business process to function more smoothly? Or something else? The discipline necessary to give the purpose an advantage and a measurement means that fuzzy or ill-defined purposes are far less likely to find their way into your specifications.

You cannot build the right product unless you know precisely what the product is intended to do, and how the product's success is to be measured.

Whether or not the using organization achieves the target set by the product purpose may depend on the way that it uses the product. Obviously if the product is not used as intended, then it may fail to meet the advantages for which it was built. Thus the statement of product purpose *assumes* that the product will be used as intended.

Keeping Track of the Purpose

Once you have established the purpose, you also need to keep the project aimed toward it. It is always possible that the product purpose gets forgotten as the requirements analysts and the users explore the work and the proposed product. As more and more requirements are discovered, and more and more exciting new features are proposed, there is a possibility that the product will be formed so that it no longer meets the original purpose, and thus the original advantages will not occur.

If the purpose is worthwhile enough to justify launching the project, then it is worthwhile enough for the final product.

The Quality Gateway runs each requirement through a series of tests. One of the tests ensures relevancy. The product purpose statement is used as the yardstick for relevancy – if the requirement does not contribute in some way to the purpose, it is not relevant.

Who's Paying for This? – The Client and the Customer

Developing a new product is expensive. Who pays for it? Let's assume that you work for an organization that is about to launch into the development of a new product. Let's further assume that the development effort will involve, in total, about 50 people from different parts of the organization. Now, who pays for their time? Whose budget is about to carry the cost of some, if not all, of the people and effort shortly to be expended?

Whoever it is, he or she is your client. On the simple basis that money talks, the client, by paying for the development, has the last say in what that product does, how it does it, and how elaborate or how sparse it must be.

There is also someone else to consider – the customer who buys your product. What is it that he or she wants from your product? Shouldn't that be your guide when you gather the requirements? In some cases the distinction between customer (buys the product) and client (pays for development) is blurred. Both have to be satisfied. During the blastoff you identify and describe both. Let's consider what we have to know about these people:

● Know your client, and your customer (if applicable);

● Know what they want;

● Understand the customer's problems;

● Understand the client's aspirations;

● Know what is acceptable and unacceptable to the client and the customer.

Let's look at both the client and the customer.

The Client

The client pays for the development of the product. He is probably present at the blastoff. (You should be a little worried if he is *not* there.) Consider the possibilities for your client.

The client might be your user management. If you are building a product for in-house consumption, then the cost of construction is most likely borne by the manager of the users who will be the ultimate operators of the product. Their department, or their work, is the beneficiary of the product, so it is reasonable that their manager pay for it.

The client pays for the development of the product

The client may be your marketing department. If you build products for sale to people outside your organization, then the marketing department may assume the role of client. In other words, it is the marketers that you have to satisfy.

Consider your own organization. What is its structure? Who pays for product development? Who reaps the benefit of the business advantage that the product brings? Who is it you have to satisfy with your product?

The client for the IceBreaker product is Mr Mack Andrews, the chief executive of Saltworks Systems. Mr Andrews has made the commitment to invest in building the product. We write this into our requirements specification:

> The client for the product is Mr Mack Andrews, the chief executive of Saltworks Systems.
> Eventually the client would like to sell the product to customers in other countries.
> The client has said that he is solely responsible for approving changes in the scope of the product.

There are several things to note here. We name the client. It is now clear to everyone on the project that Mack Andrews is taking responsibility for investing in the product. Note also the other information provided about the client. This is used as the project progresses, and may have a bearing on some of the requirements, particularly the usability and portability requirements.

The client is recorded in section 2 of the specification. See the Volere Template in Appendix B for an explanation of the sections and their contents.

The Customer

The customer buys the product. You have to understand your customers well enough to specify a product that they will buy, and find useful and pleasurable

The customer buys the product once it is developed. You may already know the names of your customers, or they may be hundreds or thousands of unknown people who might some day put down their money and walk out of the store with your product under their arm.

In either case, you have to understand them enough to specify a product that they will buy, and find useful and pleasurable.

In some cases, the customer and the end user of the product are the same person. These are products with a retail price aimed at domestic or small office users. In other cases, your customer will buy your product for use by others. For example, you may be developing a new intranet product. Your customer is the office (or similar) manager who buys multiple copies of your product and expects his office staff to use it.

In any case, you must know what it is that will appeal to the customer. What requirements will he pay for? What will he find useful? What window-dressing features are attractive, and what is downright trivial? To be able to answer these questions may make a huge difference to the success of your product.

For the IceBreaker product, the Northumberland County Highways Department have agreed to be the first customer.

> *The customer for the product is the Northumberland County Highways Department represented by director Jane Torville.*

As there is a single customer (at this stage) it would of course be advisable to invite that customer to participate as a stakeholder in the project. In this case the customer will be actively involved in selecting which requirements are useful, choosing between conflicting requirements, and making the requirements analysts aware of her problems and aspirations.

Saltworks Systems has further ambitions for the IceBreaker product. They suspect that a successful de-icing forecasting system could be sold to other county councils. If you are going to build the product with this aim in mind, then your requirements specification should include an additional customer. Statement:

> *Potential customers for the product include all the county councils in the United Kingdom. A summary of the requirements specification will be presented to the Highways Department managers of all the county councils for the purpose of discovering additional requirements.*

The customer should always be represented by a stakeholder who is active on the project. Where there are many customers, there is a need to have a customer representative. This can be the marketing department, a representative from a user group, a senior user from one or more of your key customers, or a combination of domain and usability experts from within your organization. Or some other person. The nature of your product, the structure of your organization, your customer base and probably several other factors will decide who is to be the customer representative on your team.

Users – Get to Know Them

Users are the people who will ultimately operate your product. For in-house products, they are usually the people who work for your client. For external products, the user and the customer may be the same person.

The original Vaisala de-icing prediction system was built for Cheshire County Council in 1986. The designers of the product were Thermal Mapping International and The Computer Department. The product is now installed by all counties in the United Kingdom and has more than 100 customers overseas.

The purpose of identifying the users is so that you can understand the work that they do

The purpose of identifying the users is so that you can understand the work that they do. After all, your product is intended to help with this work. You also have to know their characteristics so that you can write the correct usability requirements. You have to build a product that these people can and will use. The more you know about them the better the chance you have of building a suitable product.

Different users make different demands on your product. For example, if an airline pilot is to be a user then he would have very different usability requirements from, say, a member of the public. Similarly, if members of the public are to be users, then 'person without cash' and 'person with only one arm free' would raise their own usability requirements.

There are always too many potential users, and too many that might be forgotten or overlooked. We recommend that you build a checklist of the categories of people that might conceivably use your product. As a starting point, make a list of the roles that people might play in connection with your product:

- What are the jobs of the people who might use your product?
  – doctor, clerk, engineer
- What other roles might people have?
  – neighbor, child, student
- Where will people be when they are using your product?
  – traveler, mountain climber, in the bath
- What are the nationalities of the people who might use your product?
- Are there any organizations who might use your product?
  – central banking, passport office, supermarket chain

READING

Don Gause and Jerry Weinberg give a wonderful example of brainstorming lists of users in their book. Gause, Don and Gerald Weinberg. *Exploring Requirements: Quality Before Design.* Dorset House, 1989.

Add to this by brainstorming a list of potential users for each product that you build.

For each of the user categories that you have on your list identify the particular attributes that your product must cater for.

- People with disabilities – consider all disabilities;
- Non-readers – consider people who cannot read and people who do not speak the home language;
- People who need reading glasses – this is particularly near and dear to one of the authors;
- People who cannot resist changing things like fonts, styles, and so on;
- People who will probably be carrying large parcels or a baby;
- People with luggage;

- People who do not normally use a computer (yes, there are such people on Earth);
- People who might be angry, frustrated, or in a hurry.

For the users, write a section in your specification to describe, as fully as possible, all the known and potential users and their attributes. For their attributes, consider the user's:

- Subject matter experience;
- Technological experience;
- Intellectual abilities;
- Attitude to job;
- Attitude to technology;
- Education;
- Linguistic skills;
- Age – older people have different life experiences from young people, and may not adapt as quickly to completely new concepts;
- Gender – men and women may have different perceptions.

At this stage, any users you identify are *potential* users. That is, you do not yet precisely know the scope of the product – this is determined later in the process – so at this stage you are identifying the people who could possibly use the product. Remember that people other than the intended users might end up using your product. It is better to identify superfluous users than fail to find them all.

READING

For more on identification of user characteristics and user-centered design refer to: MAGUIRE, MARTIN. *User-Requirements Framework Handbook.* Husat Research Institute. April 1997. www.npl.co.uk/inuse

People other than the intended users might end up using your product. It is better to identify superfluous users than fail to find them all

Stakeholders and Consultants

Stakeholders are people who have an interest in the product – they will build it, they will manage it, they will use it, or they will in some way be affected by its use. Stakeholders are people who have some demands on the product, and hence must be consulted in the requirement gathering activity.

Consultants are people who, although the product may not affect them, know about some of the requirements for it. For example, you may choose to consult with usability experts before deciding the usability requirements for your product. The expert may never use your product, but nevertheless can assist you with its requirements. For the sake of convenience, we will treat consultants as a type of stakeholder.

The principal stakeholders are the users, client and customers. We have already looked at them, so now let's consider the other people who have an interest, in the product.

Every context is composed of individuals who do or do not decide to connect the fate of a project with the fate of the small or large ambitions they represent.

Source: Bruno Latour, *ARAMIS or the Love of Technology.*

The problem that we often face is that we do not know who all the stakeholders are, and thus we fail to consider them. This results in a string of change requests when the product starts being used, and has an adverse effect on people we had overlooked. When any new system is installed, somebody gains, and somebody loses power. This may be a subtle gain or loss, or it may be wholesale. People may find that the product brings them new capabilities, or people may not be able to do their jobs the way they used to do them. The moral of the story is clear – find everybody who will be affected by the product, and find their requirements.

Stakeholders should be listed in section 2 of the requirements specification. It is useful to list them, if for no other reason than to use as a checklist of people to be consulted. However, we know that you will find a record of the people involved in the project useful in other ways.

Let's consider who might be stakeholders by looking at candidate categories, and from them derive the kind of stakeholder and their participation.

Management

Consider any category of management. Does the board of directors have any interest in the product? Is it a strategic product? Do any managers other than those directly involved have a stake?

Project sponsor, sometimes called the executive sponsor. This is the person in the organization who takes ultimate management authority for completing the product.

Project manager/Project leader – the person or people who manage the day-to-day project effort.

Business Subject Matter

This constituency includes the people who are experts in the business. Domain analysts, business consultants, business analysts, people who have some specialized knowledge of the business subject, and thus can contribute to the requirements for the product.

Developers

The developers are the people who will be part of the building effort for the product. The product designers, programmers, testers, systems analysts, technical writers, database designers and anyone who is somehow involved in the construction. It is not necessary to have all these people at the blastoff, as some of them will be involved for only part of the construction.

When you do know the people involved, then record their names. Otherwise, use this section to list the skills and duties that you think will most likely be needed to build the product.

Inspectors

Consider safety inspectors, auditors, firefighters, technical inspectors, possibly government inspectors. It may well be necessary to build inspection capabilities into your product.

Market Forces

The marketing department of your organization probably represents this constituency. When building a product for commercial sales, the market is a potent source of requirements. For example, note how quickly new technology is built into personal computers. Any new product in this arena that does not include the latest technology is consigned to the also-ran category by the market place.

Legal

Consult your lawyers, or possibly the police, for legal requirements. Also include in this constituency any standards that are relevant to your product. You will have to determine who are the standard bearers, for they are stakeholders.

Opposition

People who do not want the product. Although they may not be the most cooperative of people, it would be as well to consult them. You may find that, if the requirements are different from the commonly perceived version, the opposition may turn into supporters.

Professional Bodies

Your industry may have professional bodies that expect certain codes of conduct, or certain standards to be maintained by any product built in the industry.

Public Opinion

Are there any user groups for your product? They will certainly be a major source of requirements. For any product intended for the public domain consider polling members of the public as to their opinion. They may have demands on your product that could make the difference between acceptance and rejection.

Government

Some products rub up against government agencies for reporting purposes, or they receive information from the government. Other products have requirements that necessitate consulting with the government. Although the government may not assign you a person full time to your project, you should nevertheless nominate the agency as a stakeholder.

Special Interest Groups

Consider handicapped interest groups, environmental bodies, foreign people, old people, gender-related interests, novices, or almost any other group that may come in contact with your product.

Technical Experts

The people in this constituency may not necessarily build a part of the product, but they will almost certainly consult on some part of it. For the stakeholders from this constituency consider the usability experts, the hardware people, the experts in the technologies that you might use, specialists in software products, or experts from any technical field that the product could use.

Cultural Interests

This constituency is more applicable to products that will be in the public domain. For example, is it possible in these politically correct times that your product could offend someone? Are there religious, ethnic, cultural, political or other human interests that can be affected by your product? Consider inviting a representative from these groups to be a consultant for the project.

Adjacent Systems

Adjacent systems are the systems that directly interface with the product. These are described fully in the section on setting the scope of the product later in this chapter, and this will be more meaningful after you have read that. However, for the moment consider that any system that has direct contact with your product also has an interest in the requirements of the product.

Carefully look at the adjacent systems for people with an interest in the product, or where the adjacent system is an automated one, consider that you may have to spend some time looking at its specifications to find if it does indeed have any special demands by interfacing with your product.

Involve the Stakeholders

There is a paradox here. The stakeholders are identified by the blastoff, but the blastoff is a meeting of the main stakeholders. It may be necessary to have a short session to identify the main stakeholders before the blastoff.

During the blastoff you normally hold a brainstorming session to identify all possible stakeholders. Use the section above as a checklist to guide you, and add other categories unique to your project.

Inform all your stakeholders that they are stakeholders, and that you will be consulting them about requirements for the product. It is polite to inform them of the amount of their time you require, and the type of participation that you have in mind. A little warning always helps them to think about any requirements they may have.

The greatest problem concerning stakeholders is the requirements that you miss if you do not find all the stakeholders, or if you do exclude stakeholders from the requirements gathering process.

The greatest problem concerning stakeholders is the requirements that you miss if you do not find all the stakeholders, or you do not include stakeholders in the requirements gathering process

Requirements Constraints

Requirements constraints are global requirements – they have an effect on all, or at least most, of the requirements that you gather. Constraints refer to any limitations on the way the product is produced.

Constraints cover such subjects as design constraints, constraints on the amount of time, or money, that may be spent on the project. In other words, these constraints are restrictions that are imposed on the requirements gathering activity.

The constraints are probably already known to your management, or your marketing people, or your project sponsor. The task at blastoff time is to elicit and record them. We have included a section in the requirements specification template for constraints. Have a quick look at the template after you have finished with this section of the blastoff.

Appendix B, the Volere Requirements Specification Template

Solution Constraints

Part of the constraints section of your specification should describe any mandated designs, or solutions to the problem.

For example, you may be told that the only acceptable solution is one that will run on a personal computer. In other words, your management, or some other party, has expectations about the eventual design, and no other design is allowable. While we deplore designing the solution before knowing all the requirements, it may be that for some overriding reason – marketing, cultural, managerial, political, expectations, financial – there is only one design solution that will be accepted. If this is the case, it should be part of your specification.

Any partner applications should also be brought to light and recorded at the blastoff. Partner applications are those other applications or systems with which your product must cooperate. For example, your product may have to interface with several existing products. Thus the interfaces to those products become constraints on your product. Mandated operating systems are included here.

Commercial off-the-shelf (COTS) applications are also included here. Either your product must interface to COTS applications, or make use of them in the eventual solution. There may be good reasons for mandating this, and then again, there may not. The blastoff is the ideal opportunity for you to reach a consensus with the stakeholders as to whether the decision to incorporate COTS software is indeed wise.

Project Constraints

Financial constraints do two things: they indicate how elaborate the product may be, and they give you a good idea if the product is really wanted

This section of the specification also contains information about the financial and time constraints on the project. These constraints are determined at blastoff time, and affect the requirements that you gather later. If you have a $100,000 budget, there is no point in collecting the requirements for a million-dollar product.

Time constraints can be imposed to enable the product to meet a window of opportunity, to coincide with coordinated releases of associated products, to meet the scheduled startup of a new business venture, or for many other scheduling reasons. If this type of constraint exists, then you and your team must be aware of it. Keep in mind that a time constraint is not the same thing as an estimate of the required time.

Financial constraints do two things: they indicate how elaborate the product may be, and they give you a good idea if the product is really wanted. The blastoff delivers a go/no go decision. The budget is input to that decision.

Naming your Babies

Names are important. During the blastoff you begin to collect and record the names that are used by the project. Each project or product has names that are particular to it. This is the terminology that you are trying to capture, along with an agreed meaning.

Record the names in section 5 of the specification. This is a glossary that serves as a reference point for the project. We are always amazed at how many misunderstandings are caused when there is no central glossary available, and how effective good names can be at communicating meaning. It is worth expending effort in this area to ensure smooth communication later on in the project.

For example, the IceBreaker project added this to their glossary during the blastoff.

> *Weather Station — a collection of hardware capable of collecting and transmitting road temperature, air temperature, humidity and precipitation readings. Weather stations are installed in eight locations in Northumberland.*

Weather stations are also used as ice detection systems on airport runways. Two examples are Birmingham, UK, and Hokkaido, Japan.

The advantage of starting to define terminology at blastoff time is that you make the words visible so that the stakeholders can discuss them and change them to reflect the consensus as to their meaning. Later your detailed systems analysis uses this glossary as the basis for building a complete data dictionary.

The advantage of starting to define terminology at blastoff time is that you make the words visible so that the stakeholders can discuss them and change them to reflect the consensus as to their meaning

Setting the Scope

Firstly, the scope that we are interested in at the beginning of the project is the scope of the work. By work, we mean the business activity that the user needs the product to support. The work can be a commercial activity, some scientific or technical work, or indeed anything at all, so long as it involves some processing and some data. The reason for being interested in the work is that if, and only if, we can understand the work, then we can build a product that can help with the work. After all, the intention is to deliver a product that fits seamlessly with the work it supports.

We set the scope by dividing one lot of work (the work we are about to study) from another (the work that surrounds our work). Keep in mind here that any piece of work you will ever come across is somehow connected to other works. When your organization produces an invoice (this is work), it sends it to another work, in this case your customers' payments systems.

The work of the IceBreaker product is to predict the time that a road will freeze. It is connected to sensing devices that send it data. The sensing devices do the work of determining the atmospheric conditions and road temperatures. The sensing device work in turn is connected to another piece of work, that of the weather. The weather is connected to the position of the earth as it orbits the sun, and that in turn is connected to the work of the galaxy. You can only say that there is no more connecting work when you reach the edge of the universe. Usually you can stop a little short of that.

To determine where one lot of work finishes and another starts, consider the responsibilities of the work (Figure 3.3). That is, what is my piece of work responsible for producing, and what is the adjacent piece of work responsible for accepting? What does my work need from an adjacent work in order to get started with its responsibility?

Figure 3.3

Work exists to produce things – data, documents, goods, or almost anything. The responsibility of the work ends when the product is completed and passed to another piece of work. Thus we can use the *output* of the work as a clear delimiter between the work areas.

Note that we are talking about the things that move from one work to another – tangible things like data, documents, phone calls or even hard physical goods.

The Product Purpose and Other Constraints

Setting the scope of the work means that you are deciding how much work you will study before determining the requirements for the product. When you are considering what is part of your work and what is part of another work, keep in mind the product's purpose. It constrains what is inside and what can be safely left outside your work. You must ensure that whatever is inside your scope is enough to meet the objectives set for the product.

Similarly, the budget available and the time allowed temper the scope.

Domains of Interest

A domain of interest is a subject matter area. In this case your work comes under that subject or subjects. For example, 'Insurance' is a domain, and any product built to process some aspect of insurance comes under the insurance domain. To look at it another way, there are things in the insurance domain that have to be part of any product within the insurance domain.

Let's consider the domains for IceBreaker. Our client has told us:

Roads freeze in winter and icy conditions cause road accidents that kill people. We need to be able to predict when a road is likely to freeze so that our depot can schedule a de-icing truck in time to prevent the road from freezing. We expect a new system will provide more accurate predictions of icy conditions by using thermal maps of the district and the road temperatures from weather stations installed in the roads in addition to the weather forecasts. This will lead to more timely de-icing treatment than at present which will reduce road accidents. We also want to eliminate indiscriminate treatment of roads which wastes de-icing compounds and causes environmental damage.

Look through this statement. Domains are subjects that you will need to know something about if you are to build a product. For example, the statement begins with the word 'roads'. *Roads* is likely to be a domain, as any product that predicts freezing roads will need to contain some knowledge of roads – where they are located, what they are made of, what are the conditions that make a road freeze.

'icy conditions ... We need to be able to predict when a road is likely to freeze'. This suggests a domain that covers the subject of temperature, and if the product is to make predictions, the behavior of temperature. This is the domain of *weather*.

'schedule a de-icing truck ...' suggests that *scheduling* is a domain, as the product needs to have a knowledge of how to schedule, or the aspects of scheduling that are common to any scheduling product.

The product also needs to have a knowledge of *trucks* – how fast they can travel, their capacity for de-icing material, and so on. This knowledge is needed for the product to make realistic schedules.

'We expect a new system will provide more accurate predictions of icy conditions by using thermal maps of the district and the road temperatures from weather stations installed in the roads in addition to the weather forecasts.' This sentence confirms the weather domain, and also introduces the domain of *thermal maps*. Thermal maps represent a geographical area as being made up of a series of isotherms – lines that join points of equal temperature. These are similar to the weather maps that are published in newspapers showing isobars – lines of equal air pressure. Given the temperatures at a few points in a district, a thermal map can be used to extrapolate temperatures for all parts of the district. As we need to know how temperatures throughout a district behave, we can say that thermal maps are a domain.

This gives us the following domains:

● Roads
● Weather
● Scheduling
● Trucks
● Thermal maps.

Now let's make use of this.

Setting the Work Context

PUTTING THIS TO WORK

The work context defines the work that you intend to study, and the other systems that surround your work. You can think of this as 'What is your work responsible for, and what is the responsibility of others?' We show this division of responsibility by building a context model that shows the work and its connections to surrounding works.

Let's start by looking at the adjacent systems, which are the works that surround our work. These can be derived from the purpose of the product, the background information, and the domains of interest.

For each of the domains, ask:

● Is there a physical entity that represents this domain? For example, the weather domain is represented physically by the weather stations and the weather forecasting bureau.

● Does this domain provide data, policy or both to the work? For example, if the work needs data about the domain, then it must be supplied by a data connection between an adjacent system and the work. If the domain supplies policy, then it is built into the work. For example, the scheduling domain is a set of rules, or guidelines about scheduling. This is policy that is part of the processing rules for the work.

● Where will I go to get information about this domain? Are there external, or unmentioned sources that I need to reference in order to study this domain? This does not affect the context of the work. If you consult with some source then it does not necessarily show up on the context model, but you should have listed it as one of the stakeholders or consultants.

For the domain of roads, the physical representative is the Road Engineering Department. They are the people who build and maintain the roads, so it is appropriate that they inform the ice predicting work about the roads. This means that there will be one or more data flows between an adjacent system called Road Engineering Department, and the work. This department will also be a source of information about roads.

For the weather domain, the physical representatives are the weather stations and the weather forecasting bureau. The weather stations transmit their temperature readings, so this will be a flow of data between the adjacent system and the work. Similarly, the weather bureau becomes an adjacent system, with corresponding flows of data to the work.

The client has told us that the Truck Depot is the adjacent system that will represent the domain of trucks. One of the main reasons for the work's existence is to schedule the trucks, so we would expect to see flows of this nature between the work and the depot.

First-cut Work Context

Using our knowledge of the work's responsibilities and the information from the domains given above, we can build a model showing the work in its context. The model is shown in Figure 3.4.

The work context shows where the responsibilities of the work, and that of the adjacent systems, start and end. The flows of data between these identify which work is done by the work, and what must be done by an adjacent system. For example, there is a flow shown in Figure 3.4 called *Truck Change*. This advises the work about changes to the de-icing trucks – new trucks added to the fleet, those taken out of service, modifications to trucks that would affect the way that they are scheduled. Why is this flow there? The answer is that the work needs to know about trucks because it allocates trucks to roads when it produces the de-icing schedule. But what if we

The work context shows where the responsibilities of the work, and that of the adjacent systems, start and end

Figure 3.4

The work context diagram identifies the boundary of the work that we intend to study. The diagram shows the work as a single, as yet uninvestigated entity, surrounded by the adjacent systems. The named arrows represent the data that flows between the work and the adjacent systems. The adjacent systems are the representatives of the domains. The Truck Depot represents trucks, the Weather Station and the Weather Forecasting Bureau represent the weather domain, Road Engineering the roads, and, inevitably, Thermal Mapping Supplier represents the domain of thermal maps. The remaining domain, scheduling, is represented by policy inside the work, and thus has no external connection.

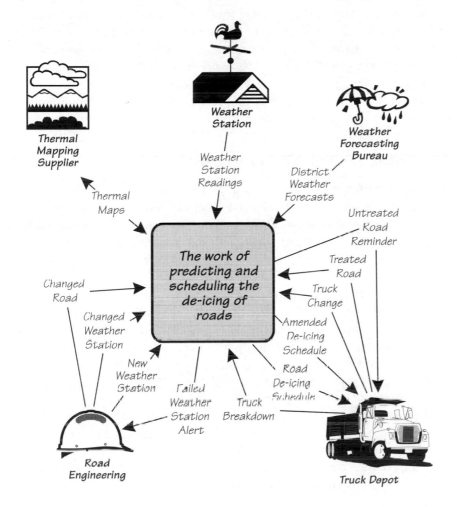

changed this responsibility? What if the depot became responsible for determining which truck was allocated to which road? The flow would be different. In fact, that flow would not appear on the context at all, as there would be no need of it.

The point is that the flows around the boundary of the work point clearly to its responsibilities. By defining these flows, we define the precise point at which one work ends and another starts.

There is a common problem setting the context – often we see contexts that are for the software product only. Remember that you are investigating some work, and the eventual product will become part of that work. To build the best possible product you need firstly to understand the work, and then decide how much of it you can automate or change.

Also consider the possibility that by enlarging the scope of the work you will find other possibilities for automation or improvement. Too often, before we understand the work we think of an automation boundary, and never rethink it. This means of course that the 'hard stuff', the work that we did not intend to automate, is not considered. But by casting our nets wider, we can very often find aspects of the work that would benefit from automation, and in the end turn out to be cheaper than we thought.

The moral of the story is firstly to understand the work. Then decide what product best supports that work.

The moral of the story is firstly to understand the work. Then decide what product best supports that work

READING
ROBERTSON, JAMES AND SUZANNE. *Complete Systems Analysis – the Workbook, the Textbook, the Answers.* Dorset Ho, New York, 1994

How Much is This Going to Cost?

At this stage there are so many measurable facets of the context that there is no real excuse for not measuring. The point of measuring is to understand the size of the work that has to be studied. Although we do not know at this stage the precise boundaries of the product, measuring the work will give you enough of an idea of the size of the task to make your decisions about whether or not to proceed with the project. (We discuss setting the precise scope of the product in Chapter 4, Event-driven Use Cases.)

The obvious measurables at this stage are the number of adjacent systems on the context model, and the number of inputs and outputs. While it is not the ultimate measure, counting the inputs and outputs will give you a far better idea of size than merely guessing. If your context has somewhere above 20 inputs and outputs, then it falls into the 'average cost per input/ output' range of estimating. Simply put, there is an average cost of an input/ output. This can be measured by going back to previous projects, counting the number of inputs and outputs on the context, and dividing this number into the cost of systems investigation.

More accurate costs can be gained by determining the number of business events that affect the work. We will discuss this fully in Chapter 4, but for the meantime if you will accept that the business events can be derived from the context model, then their number is a determining factor in the cost of the product. It is of course necessary to know the cost to your organization of analyzing the average business event. You can learn this from previous projects, or if necessary, run a benchmark. Multiply the cost per event by the number of events to give a reasonably accurate measure of the price you will have to pay for requirements gathering and systems analysis.

More accurate still is function point counting. At this stage you will need to have an idea of the data to be stored by the work, and this can usually be known in a short time if you have some experienced data modelers on your team. Function point counting measures the amount and the complexity of the data processed by the work, and adjusts these counts by weighting factors according to the type of work. Enough is known about function points that you can find figures for the average cost per function point of systems investigation.

The point is not so much which measuring system you decide to use at this stage, but that you measure. There is too much of a penalty for not measuring. If you do not make even the most basic of measurements, then any predictions you do make must be based on nothing more than guesswork. Guesswork and optimism usually lead to unrealistic project schedules, and these in turn force developers to cut corners and scrimp on quality. Inevitably, the project gets into trouble when the shortcuts turn out to cause *longer* delivery times (it always happens), and the users lose confidence in the integrity of the product and its developers. There is too much evidence of the downside of not measuring, and too much known about measuring, to have any excuse for not doing it.

The ultimate deliverable from the blastoff is a decision on whether to go ahead with the project. An accurate cost of construction is a key input to this decision.

We will talk more about function point counting in Chapter 13, Taking Stock of the Specification

READING
Function Point Counting Practices Manual. International Function Point Users Group, Westerville OH.

The ultimate deliverable from the blastoff is a decision on whether to go ahead with the project

Risky Business

We face risks every day. Just leaving your home to go to work involves some risk – your car won't start, the train will be late, you will be assigned to share an office with the boring person with body odour problems. But, we go to work each day as we know the risks, and consider the outcome worth the risk.

However, once we are at work, we might well plunge into situations where we have no idea of the risks involved, and thus no idea whether the outcome is worth braving the risks.

Pop quiz time – have you ever worked on a project where nothing went wrong? Okay, okay. Something always goes wrong. Now, did you ever try and figure out ahead of time what could go wrong, and do something to prevent it going wrong, or at least allow for the mishaps by budgeting for them? This in its simplest sense, is risk analysis.

The blastoff process includes a short risk analysis. The team assesses the risks that are most likely to happen, and the risks that would have the greatest impact if they become problems. For each risk, they assess the probability of it becoming a problem, and its cost or schedule impact. At the same time, they agree on early-warning signs – what happenings will signal that the risk is becoming a problem. In some cases where the risks are considered serious, a risk manager is assigned to monitor for the telltale signs that some risks are becoming problems.

Risk management is common-sense project management. You know that problems will occur, so why not be aware of them? The literature on risk management is growing. We like Capers Jones' *Assessment and Control of Software Risks*, as it gives some very valuable checklists. For example, Capers cites the following as the most serious risks – the ones that can do the most damage.

READING

JONES, CAPERS. *Assessment and Control of Software Risks.* Prentice-Hall, 1994.

BOEHM, BARRY. *Software Risk Management.* IEEE Computer Society Press, 1989.

1 Inaccurate metrics. The risk of not measuring correctly and how this can disrupt productivity.

2 Inadequate measurement. Tracking tends to miss major efforts. Unpaid overtime, management effort, user effort and so on are not counted correctly, or vastly underestimated if they are considered at all.

3 Excessive schedule pressure. This contributes to low quality, canceled projects, high attrition in software personnel. The problem usually starts with deadline by decree, instead of measuring.

4 Management malpractice. This is usually due to inadequate, or no, training of software managers.

5 Inaccurate cost estimating. This leads to massive errors in estimating, and thus the project is never on a sound footing.

6 Silver bullet syndrome. Naive belief that a single factor, often a new technology, will lead to huge productivity gains. See the weekly trade press for details.

7 Creeping user requirements. The average creep for projects is 30% of requirements arrive *after* the requirements process. Eighty per cent of MIS projects suffer from this.

8 Low quality. This means delays to releasing the product.

9 Low productivity. Often due to some of the problems listed above.

10 Canceled projects. Nah! Couldn't happen to us.

But perhaps the risks that are most relevant at this stage are the requirements-related risks. For example:

- The absence of a clear and measurable purpose for the product;
- Lack of client involvement;
- Lack of stakeholder involvement;
- Little or no agreement on requirements;
- Requirements creep;
- Gold plating;
- No measurements put on requirements (fit criteria and customer satisfaction/dissatisfaction);
- Rapidly changing requirements;
- Inadequate change control for the requirements;
- New or unknown business area with uncertain needs.

The most noticeable effect of doing risk analysis is that it makes the risks visible to all the stakeholders. By being aware of the risks, they can contribute to risk mitigation. Similarly, the project team make their management aware of the risks, and the impact if they become problems.

To Go or Not to Go

The deliverables that you produce during the blastoff provide the basis for assessing the viability of your project. When you take a good look at what these deliverables are telling you, you can decide whether or not it makes good business sense to press the button and launch the project.

Consider your deliverables:

- Is the product purpose clear?
- Is it measurable and viable?
- Is it possible to achieve the objectives of the project?
- Can you reach agreement on the context of the work?
- Does the high probability/impact of the risks make the project unfeasible?
- Is the cost reasonable for the product's benefit?
- Are the stakeholders willing to be involved?
- Do you have sufficient justification to invest in the project?
- Do you have enough reasons not to invest in the project?
- Is there any further investigation that you should do before pressing the button to start the project?

The point is to make an objective decision based on facts. For some reason it is always very difficult to stop a project once it is underway and has consumed some resources. Ed Yourdon refers to these as 'death march' projects – they stagger along for years when most of the people involved know that they were never viable enough to have been started in the first place. A little consideration at this stage can prevent poor projects from being started, and give good projects a flying start.

Blastoff Alternatives

You don't have to have a meeting, but you do need to know all the facts that the meeting would deliver

We have suggested here that the stakeholders get together for a couple of days and derive all the blastoff deliverables. We understand that in a lot of organizations this, despite its merit, is simply not possible. There are other ways.

While being together is important, it is the deliverables that really matter. Some organizations come up with these in other forms. For example, a lot of companies write a business plan, or some similar document, that covers a lot of the topics that we advocate. This is fine as long as you have an objective, quantifiable plan and it is circulated and agreed by the stakeholders.

Some organizations use feasibility studies as a way of getting their projects started. Of course the feasibility study must honestly look at the costs and risks as well as the benefits from the product. Provided the study delivers realistic numbers, then it will serve. We make the proviso that all the stakeholders have seen and commented on the accuracy of the feasibility study.

You don't have to have a meeting, but you do need to know all the facts that the meeting would deliver.

Summary

The Project Blastoff is about knowing. Knowing what you want the product to do for you, and what it will cost to build it. Knowing the scope of the work that is to be studied in order to gather the requirements for the product. Knowing who the people are that will be involved in the project, and having them know what is expected of them. Knowing the users, which in turn will lead you to knowing the usability requirements for the product.

The project blastoff is about knowing

Knowing the constraints on the project – how much money have you got to spend, how much or how little time have you got to deliver the product? Knowing the words to be used on the project. Knowing whether you can succeed.

The blastoff delivers knowledge. What is better, it delivers it at a time that it is most useful – at the beginning of the project when crucial decisions have to be made.

The blastoff deliverables will reappear later in this book. Some of them are used as input to the mainstream requirements activities. None of them is wasted.

Event-driven Use Cases

in which we discuss a fail-safe way of
partitioning the work into use cases, and along
the way discover the best product to build

The scope of the work that you have established is probably too large to be studied as a single unit. Just as you cut your food into small pieces before eating it, it is necessary to partition the work scope into manageable pieces before examining it to find the product's requirements.

The work is partitioned into use cases. Use cases are a unit of work that the user finds useful. This definition is a little vague and arbitrary, because each user may have different ideas as to what they find useful to have as a unit, and these ideas may be different from those of the developers.

So instead of making arbitrary choices as to what constitutes a use case, let us base our partitions on something tangible and recognizable. In this chapter we lay out a set of heuristics that guides you to defining what a use case is, and how to find the most appropriate use cases. Almost as a by-product of this, you will find the most useful product that you can build. See Figure 4.1.

Understanding the Work

Any area of work that we study today is likely to be too big to understand comfortably. When we say 'work', we do not mean just a computer system – either the current system or an anticipated one. Instead, we mean the system for doing business. We include the human tasks, the computers, the low-tech devices like telephones and photocopiers, in fact *anything* that is used to produce your client's goods or services. You are studying the work with a view to automating some of it with your product. Until you understand this work, and its desired outcomes, you cannot know precisely what product is the optimum one to build. That will be revealed by further study.

Figure 4.1

Breaking the system into smaller pieces is usually started during the Project Blastoff. At that stage you determined the business events that affect the work context. Business events are things that happen outside the scope of the work, and the work must make a response to them. During the trawling activity, we study the events and their responses, and from them determine the part of the response that will be done by the automated product. Prototyping is often done to help decide the best product scope. It is the part of the work done by the product that we refer to as a use case. Note that we arrive at the use cases by analyzing the responses to business events, hence the term 'event-driven use cases'.

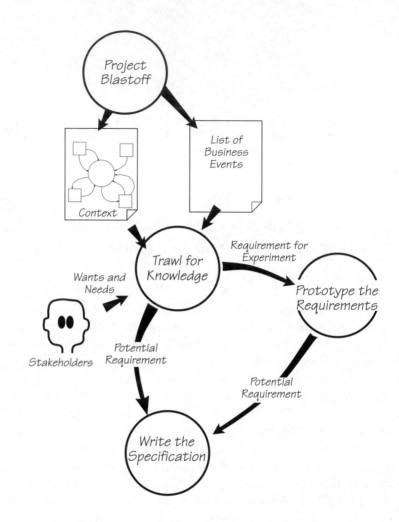

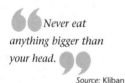 *Never eat anything bigger than your head.*

Source: Kliban

Because of the large scope of this work, not only will we as systems analysts and designers fail to understand the work if we try and digest it in its entirety, but our customers and users have no chance of explaining it to us. By finding smaller, more specialized parts of the work, we have a better chance of finding users who are experts in that part of the work.

We need to break our work into smaller pieces. For the purposes of requirements gathering and systems analysis, we are looking for pieces that:

● Are 'natural' partitions – they are an obvious part of the work;

● Have the least number of connections to other parts of the work;

● Have a clearly defined scope;

- Have rules for defining their scope;

- Have boundaries that can be observed and quantified;

- Can be named using names that are recognizable to the business experts – client, customer, users;

- Their existence can be readily determined;

- Are known to the users;

- We can locate one or more users who are experts for that part of the work.

Use Cases and Their Scope

The term 'use case' was first used by Ivar Jacobson to describe an amount of work to be done. He chose to break the system into smaller units, as he felt that object models were not scalable. So to conquer the complexity and largeness of modern systems, Jacobson said it was firstly necessary to partition them into convenient chunks, and that these chunks should be based on the user's view of the system. The wisdom of this is beyond questioning.

However, Jacobson leaves us with some loose ends. For example, his definition of a use case does not indicate precisely where a use case starts and ends. He also uses the term 'actor' to mean that user role, or perhaps another system, that is outside the scope of the system. The 'system' in this usage is presumed to be the automated system. Which leads to the question 'How can we know the automated system before we understand the work for which it is to be used?'

Think about this – if the responsibilities of the actor and the system are established at the beginning of the analysis process, and the requirements gathering focusses on the automated system, then how will we ever understand the work that the actor is doing, or the work that the automated product *could* be doing for the actor?

Without understanding the actor's true task – which will surely happen if we exclude him from the analysis study – we run the risk of missing opportunities for automation, or automating where a non-automation would be a better solution. We also could be guilty of building products that are not as useful as they might be, as well as running the risk of constructing interfaces that ultimately do not satisfy the user.

So let us instead firstly establish the scope of the work. This work scope must include the intended actor and the work that he is doing, as well as having knowledge of the systems that are adjacent to the work. Once we have established a satisfactory scope for the work, we will break it into smaller pieces. From these pieces we will determine the use cases.

READING

JACOBSON, IVAR ET AL. *Object-Oriented Software Engineering – A Use Case Driven Approach*. Addison-Wesley, 1992.

Think about this – if the responsibilities of the actor and the system are established at the beginning of the analysis process, and the requirements gathering focusses on the automated system, then how will we ever understand the work that the actor is doing, or the work that the automated product could be doing for the actor?

PUTTING THIS TO WORK

This is how we intend to proceed:

- Firstly, establish the scope of the work.
- Establish the adjacent systems that surround the work.
- Identify the connections between the work and the adjacent systems.
- From the connections, identify the business events that affect the work.
- Study the response to the event.
- Determine the best response that the organization can make for the event.
- Determine the product's role in the response.
- Determine the use case or cases for the product.
- Derive the requirements for each use case.

Each of these steps is straightforward. Each contributes to correctly understanding the work and specifying the best product for it.

The Work

READING

BEYER, HUGH AND KAREN HOLTZBLATT. *Contextual Design. Defining Customer-Centered Systems.* Morgan Kaufmann, 1998. Beyer and Holtzblatt have some wonderful insights into work, and how we should be looking at it. This book is highly recommended.

The work is the business activity of your client. Whatever this activity is – whether it is commercial, scientific, engineering, or any other form of activity – the automated product that you intend to build is a tool that will help with the work. The product will automate or streamline some of the existing processes, or it will change the work by adding new functionality. Either way, the product is simply a tool to help with the work. Thus it is imperative to understand that work.

To understand the work you must firstly know how it relates to the outside world. Consider this: work exists to provide services to the outside world. In order to provide those services the work must receive information and signals from the outside world, as well as send messages to it. To locate your work in the real world, you must be able to demonstrate how the work connects to the adjacent systems. Adjacent systems are the active parts of the world that surround your work. In other words, you are showing how your work relates to its business environment.

The most convenient and useful way to show the work's connections to the outside world is to use a context diagram. Figure 4.2 shows the context diagram for the work of predicting when roads are due to freeze, and dispatching trucks to treat them with de-icing material. The work is surrounded by adjacent systems that supply the data that is necessary for this work, or receive services and information from the work. The point of the diagram is to define the boundaries of the work so that you know precisely what you are studying.

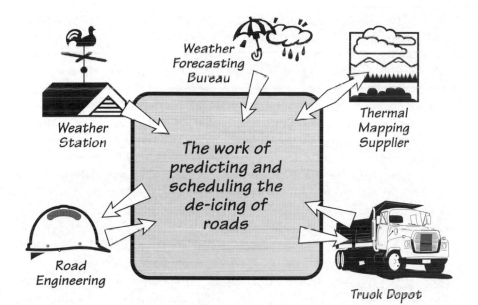

Figure 4.2

The context of the work. The central area of the diagram shows the scope of the work that you are about to study. The product that you eventually build will be part of this work. The outside world is represented by the adjacent systems – Weather Station, Truck Depot, and so on. The arrows represent flows of information between the adjacent systems and the work.

The work to be studied must include anything that can be affected by your product. For example, if you are building a product that is intended to automate part of some existing work, then the study context should include as much of the existing work – human activities, together with any existing computer systems – that could possibly influence the eventual product. For embedded systems, there may be no human activity in your work, but the work to be studied must include any devices that can be changed by the current development. Even if you are building some electro-mechanical device, such as an ATM (automated teller machine), and most of the human participation is outside the product boundary, you must still include in your work context the work that the human will be doing with the device.

The work to be studied must include anything that can be affected by your product

The Outside World

On the surface, the context diagram shows the work to be studied and its connections to the outside world. However, this diagram bears a lot closer examination, particularly in the area of the *adjacent systems* as they have an important effect on our work.

The adjacent systems are the parts of the world that have connections to our work. They are systems, in that they behave like any other system: they contain processes and consume and/or produce data. We are interested in them because they are often customers for the services provided by our work, or they supply services needed by our work. You can see this by looking at the connections established by the context diagram. It is through these connections that the adjacent systems have an important influence on the work.

RULE OF THUMB

The work context includes anything that you are permitted to change, and a few things that you are not

RULE OF THUMB

The further away from the anticipated automated system you look, the more useful and innovative your product is likely to be

To find the adjacent systems, you sometimes have to go outside your own organization. Go to the customers for your organization's products or services. Go to the outside systems that supply information or services to your work. Go to the other departments that have connections to the work. Use the guideline that the further away from the anticipated automated system you look, the more useful and innovative your product is likely to be.

You may sometimes find that your work is strongly connected to one or more computer systems. Or you are making an enhancement to an existing computer system. In this case the computer system(s), or the parts that you are not changing, are the adjacent systems. The interfaces between your work and the existing computer systems are critical. They are difficult to define, but you can never know the extent of your work, and eventually your product, if you do not define the interfaces clearly.

Do not be limited by what you think might be the limits of a computer system, but try and find the furthest practical extent of any influence on the work

Consider it this way: the adjacent systems are the reason that the work exists – they are customers for the services produced by the work.

The work produces these services either on demand, or at pre-arranged times. Whenever it is producing something, the work is responding to a business event.

Business Events

Businesses respond to events. It's that simple. Let's say that you bought this book in a bookshop. You found it on the shelf, thought it was useful and interesting, and approached the cash desk. At that moment, you started a business event – you wanted to buy the book. The sales assistant responded to this event by scanning the bar code, asking you for the cover price plus any applicable tax, perhaps asking the credit card company for authorization, ringing up the sale at the cash register, and putting the book in a bag before handing it to you. That, or something similar, is the bookshop's pre-planned response to that particular business event.

READING

McMENAMIN, STEVE AND JOHN PALMER. *Essential Systems Analysis*. Yourdon Press, 1984. McMenamin and Palmer were the first authors to use events as a way of partitioning systems. Their words on the essence of the system are also worth reading.

When you pay your credit card bill at the end of the month, it is another business event (seen from the point of view of the credit card company). The credit card company responds to this event by checking that your address has not changed and then recording the date and amount of your payment.

In both cases, you initiated a business event. The piece of work that you were dealing with – selling books or recording payments is work – has some pre-planned response to the event. Note what happened here: you do not own, nor do you control the bookshop or credit card company. But in both cases you make them do something. In other words, those businesses have a prescribed amount of work that is set up to be done whenever an outside body (the adjacent system) triggers a business event.

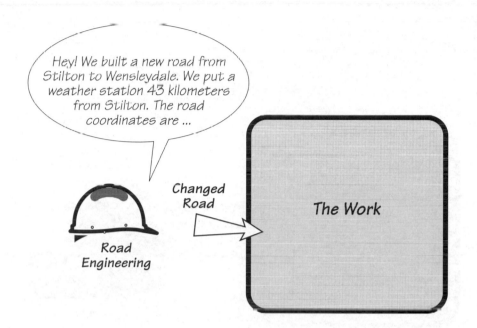

Figure 4.3

A business event has taken place outside the scope of the work. The work learns that it has happened by the arrival of an incoming flow of data. The work responds to this business event.

We will treat the response to each event as a unit of work to be studied. We can do this because the responses are fairly isolated from each other, and are therefore useful cases for study.

Note that business event responses are triggered by the arrival of a data flow – the book and your payment at the cash desk; your payment slip and check at the credit card company. Or to put it another way, a data flow arrives from an adjacent system. This means that the triggering of the event is outside the control of the work. The trigger is not prompted by the work. Once it happens, then the work initiates its response (see Figure 4.3). Before we look at the response, let's look at another kind of business event.

Once a business event happens, the work initiates its response

Triggered by the Passage of Time

Temporal business events are triggered by the passage of time – it becomes time for the work to do something. 'The passage of time' means that a pre-determined date or time has arrived. For example, your insurance company sends you a renewal notice shortly before the anniversary of your policy. You bank sends you a statement on the fifteenth day of every month (or on whatever day you have arranged to have it sent). 'The passage of time' may also mean that a certain amount of time has elapsed since another event happened. For example, a computer operating system may check the available memory 2.4 microseconds after the last time.

The usual response to a temporal business event is to produce some information and send it to an adjacent system. Consider the example in Figure 4.4.

Figure 4.4

The temporal business event happens when a pre-arranged time is reached. This is either periodic (for example, the end of the month, or 5 p.m. each day), or a fixed time interval (three hours since the last occurrence). The normal response is to send some information to an adjacent system.

Once the prescribed time for the event has arrived, the work's response is to do whatever is necessary to produce the output. This almost always involves the retrieval and manipulation of stored data. Once again, we will use the response to the temporal business event as our unit of study.

But first, we have to know what the events are in order to study them.

Finding the Business Events

PUTTING
THIS TO
WORK

We have seen how business events are things that happen to the work. So how do you discover what is happening to the work? The answer is fairly straightforward. If something happens to the work, then the work must receive notification of that happening. This means that there must be some sort of communication between the outside world (remember that events happen outside the scope of the work) and the work itself. In the case of time-triggered events, there is also a communication but this time it flows from the work to the outside. (There is little point in the work doing something if it fails to tell anyone or anything that it has done it.)

The place to look for communication between the work and the outside world is the work context diagram. This diagram, originally seen during the Blastoff, is reproduced in Figure 4.5.

Note the data flows that connect the adjacent systems to the work. Some of these you have already seen when we discussed business events. For example, the flow called Changed Road is the result of the event when the Road

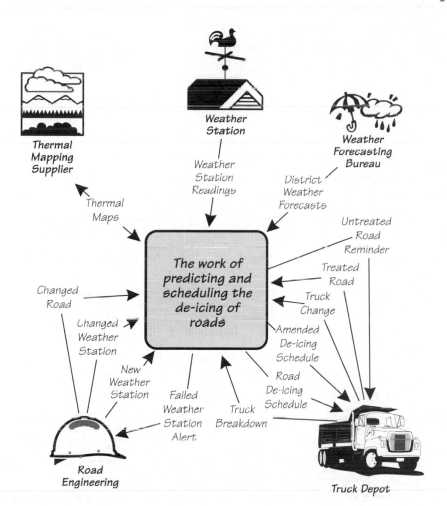

Figure 4.5

The work context diagram shows the connections between the work and the outside world. Each connection is generated by an event. By studying the connections, we can determine the events.

Engineering department makes changes to a road. They advise the work so that the scheduling work can update its own stored data about roads. The flow called Road De-icing Schedule is the result of a pre-arranged time being reached. The work produces a schedule of the roads to be treated and sends it to the Truck Depot.

Each of the flows that enters or leaves the work is the result of a business event. There is no other reason for an external communication to exist. If you look at each of the flows, you can determine the event that caused it. In some cases, there may be several flows attached to the same event. For example, when the Truck Depot advises a changed status for a truck (the input flow is Truck Breakdown), the work responds by making a new schedule – one of the trucks is out of service, and the other trucks have to be re-scheduled to compensate – and this flow is shown as Amended De-Icing Schedule.

Each of the flows that enters or leaves the work is the result of a business event

Look at the following list of events and their input and output flows. Compare it with the work context diagram shown in Figure 4.5, and reconcile the business events with the data that flows to and/or from the work.

Event name	Input and output
1 Weather Station transmits reading	Weather Station Readings (in)
2 Weather Bureau forecasts weather	District Weather Forecasts (in)
3 Road engineers advise changed roads	Changed Road (in)
4 Road Engineering installs new weather station	New Weather Station (in)
5 Road Engineering changes weather station	Changed Weather Station (in)
6 Time to test Weather Stations	Failed Weather Station Alert (out)
7 Truck Depot changes a truck	Truck Change (in) Amended De-icing Schedule (out)
8 Time to detect icy roads	Road De-icing Schedule (out)
9 Truck treats a road	Treated Road (in)
10 Truck Depot reports problem with truck	Truck Breakdown (in) Amended De-icing Schedule (out)
11 Time to monitor road de-icing	Untreated Road Reminder (out)

READING

ROBERTSON, JAMES AND SUZANNE. *Complete Systems Analysis: the Workbook, the Textbook, the Answers.* Dorset House, 1994.

Each of the flows on the context is attached to one, and only one, business event. When the flow leaves the work, then it is as a result of some event having happened, and the work having responded in some way, and sending some information to an adjacent system. Alternatively, when the flow enters the work, it is as the result of an event having happened. The adjacent system notifies the work of the event, and the work now has to do something in response to the event.

It is the work's *response* to the event that is interesting to the requirements analyst. Let's look at that.

The Work Responds to Events

The event response is the unit of work that we will study

For every business event, there is a pre-planned response to it – the work that happens whenever the business event happens. There is usually a collection of identifiable processes, an amount of data that is retrieved and/or stored, output generated, messages sent, or some combination of the above. In other words, some work is done.

You can isolate this work – it is fairly unconnected from other event responses. You can find one or more stakeholders who are expert in this part of the work, and they can describe the work precisely and in detail. They can describe both the normal cases where everything goes according to plan, and exceptional cases where almost nothing goes according to plan. You can observe the work. After all, business events are known to the stakeholders, and they can show you how the organization responds to any of them. For example, it would not be hard to find someone in your favorite bookshop who can take you through the process of selling a book. We will discuss techniques for doing this in the next chapter.

The response to a business event is continuous. That is, it includes everything that the work does until there is nothing left to do that can logically be done at that time – all the processes have been completed, all the data to be stored by the response has been stored, and all the adjacent systems have been notified.

This means that any event response is a group of processes surrounded by adjacent systems and data stores. In other words, the response is isolated from other processes within the work. Its only connection is through stored data. Consider the example in Figure 4.6. Once the triggering data flow enters the work, the response is a continuous series of processes. Processing continues until all the necessary work has been done to satisfy the business event, and any data associated with the event has been stored.

The product that you are going to build will contribute to the work done in response to the event. Your product will not change the real work, it just changes the way that it is done. But before you can design the optimum product, you must understand the work that it supports. Most importantly, you must understand your client's desired outcome of the work. So for the moment, forget the details and technicalities of the event response, and instead look outside the organization to see what kind of response is needed, or wanted, by the organization's customers and suppliers.

Let's start our look outside the organization by looking at the systems that are adjacent to the work that you are studying.

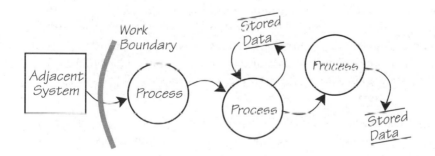

You can find one or more stakeholders who are expert in each event

Figure 4.6

The work's response to the business event is to continue processing until all the active tasks (the processes) have been done and all the data retrieved or stored. You can think of the response as a chain of processes and their associated stored data. Note that the processes are surrounded by a combination of data stores and adjacent systems.

The Role of Adjacent Systems

The adjacent systems are the systems that supply the work with information, or receive information and services from the work. An adjacent system might be an organization, an individual, a piece of technology or a combination of all three. The adjacent system is the customer for the business event. When you examine the response to an event, consider what the adjacent system would like from that event. Consider that the adjacent system may want to do more than passively supply information to, or receive a service from the system. Consider the type of service that your organization could provide if the adjacent system participates in the activities that make up the response.

An adjacent system might be an organization, an individual, a piece of technology or a combination of all three

Let's start with external business events. Consider adjacent systems and their role, or potential role, in the business events that they initiate.

- What are the technological capabilities of the adjacent system? Is it capable of interacting with the product? Is it human? Does it have some interactive technological capability?

- What is the desired outcome from the point of view of the adjacent system? What are it's aspirations at the time of triggering the event? Keep in mind that the intentions of the adjacent system may be disguised by the technological limitations of the products that are currently in use by the work.

- What is the desired outcome from the point of view of the work? What is it that the work wishes, or is capable, of providing? To do this satisfactorily, you will have to ignore the technology that the work used in the past, and current organizational limitations.

We are trying to discover the intentions of the adjacent system when it started the event. What outcome does it have in mind? Does the current work scope place restrictions, or some burden, on the adjacent system? If the adjacent system is a customer for the work, what can the work do to provide a better service when it responds to this event? Does the adjacent system want to participate in the event response? In other words, does it want to do some of the work, or have more control over the work by doing some of it itself? If you changed the current technology of the work, would the adjacent system want to change the way that it interacts with your work?

Get inside the brain of the adjacent system

Get inside the brain of the adjacent system. What does the adjacent system really want from the work, and what can your product provide?

There are some wonderful examples of businesses that got to the brain of their customers:

- American Airlines changed the way that travel agents booked flights by providing a terminal that links directly into their SABRE reservation system.

- First Direct is the fastest growing bank in the United Kingdom. They realized that people did not want to go to a branch of their bank, and so provided a complete banking service where all transactions are conducted over the telephone, the Internet or by mail.

- There has been a huge growth in businesses that act as a virtual store: customers order from catalogs for delivery the next, and sometimes the same, day.

- Internet commerce is growing at an amazing rate. People are finding it more convenient to buy things while sitting in front of a computer. Almost any commodity – food, underwear, books, securities, vacations, and of course software – can be bought from a web site.

- Some British supermarkets are now providing banking services for their customers at the checkout registers.

These businesses are successful. They have increased profitability by providing a better service – one that is more in tune with the aspirations of the adjacent systems that uses their services and products.

The product that you build is largely shaped by the adjacent system. Obviously we need to understand the adjacent systems, and their potential role in the work. So let us look more closely at the types of adjacent systems, their characteristics and capabilities.

The product that you build is largely shaped by the adjacent system

Active Adjacent Systems

Active adjacent systems behave dynamically. They can interact with or participate in the work. Active adjacent systems are usually humans. They initiate events, and when they do, have some objective in mind. They can work with the product by exchanging data and other signals, until their objective is satisfied. An example of an active adjacent system, a bank customer interacting with the bank, is shown in Figure 4.7.

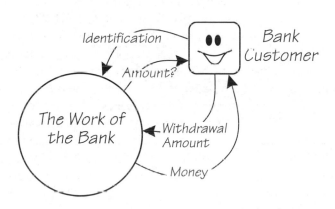

Figure 4.7

An example of an active adjacent system interacting with a bank. The bank customer initiates a business event, and then supplies information, or does whatever is needed until she achieves her desired outcome. In this case the event is a customer withdrawing money from her account. The precise nature of the flows between the work and the adjacent system are dependent on the technology being used by the bank.

In this example, we see that the active adjacent system interacts with the work. This interaction can be face to face, or it can be by telephone; the adjacent system can interact with a machine, or the interaction can take place over the Internet. But for the moment, let's ignore the technology being used. Instead, let's look a little more closely at the nature of the active adjacent system:

RULE OF
THUMB

Active adjacent systems
are usually humans.
They initiate events with
an objective in mind

- You (the requirements analyst/product designer) can predict its behavior within reason.
- You can expect it to respond to signals from your work. As long as there is some perceived benefit to the adjacent system, it will obey (more or less) instructions from the work. For example, if an adjacent system is using an ATM, then it is likely to comply when the ATM asks for the customer's PIN (personal identification number).
- The adjacent system will respond in a suitably short time. It is reasonable to say that the adjacent system will act promptly so as not to delay the transaction any more than necessary.

What can we make of that? Firstly, as the active adjacent system can interface directly with your work, you should consider it as *part of the work*, not just an inert outside body. Of course you must understand the desires and motivations of the active adjacent system. This will be a rich area of product innovation if you do.

For an example, let's consider a bank customer using an ATM. Don't think of the ATM as being an automated product, but the boundary of the work. The customer is currently outside the work. Let's imagine that this bank customer – the adjacent system – is a lady out of her office for lunch. She approaches your ATM. Now, what does she really want when she goes to the ATM? Just cash? A statement? If that is all you are prepared to give her, then you may be sadly short of the mark.

Consider whether you can change the scope of your work to provide a better service to the adjacent system, and if by allowing the adjacent system to participate in the work, it will receive a greater benefit from your work

Get inside the brain of the adjacent system. *Why* does she want the cash? Is she intending to pay her electricity bill on the way back to her office? If so, why not offer her the opportunity to pay it at your ATM? Does she want the cash to buy something? Why not extend the ATM card to act as a debit card in retail outlets so she doesn't have to bother going to the ATM in the first place? Does she just want to look at her account balance? Why not give her the facility to do so at home via the Internet or telephone?

While we are looking into the brain of this lady, what else does she want? Does she want the bank to identify each cash withdrawal so that her monthly statement tells her which members of her family made each of the withdrawals? Does she want a limit on withdrawals made by her children? Does she want to go to an ATM at all? Would she rather do most of this at home? Or at the supermarket?

Figure 4.8

Business events are initiated by the truck depots. As they wish to be more closely involved with the product, we make the supervisors active adjacent systems. This will probably result in part of the automated product being located in the truck depots so that the supervisors can have direct interaction.

Note that we are ignoring the technology being used by our existing businesses. While this may seem cavalier, it is only by ignoring current technology and its limitations that we are able to see the opportunities for providing products that are closer to the innermost needs and wants of our customers.

Let's look at this using IceBreaker as an example. At the moment, the ice forecasting work communicates with the truck depots by telephone. But let's get inside the brain of the adjacent system, which in this case is represented by the supervisors who run the depots. When we interview the supervisors we find that they wish to manipulate the IceBreaker product. They feel that if they – not the central clerk as at present – have control of it, they can make better decisions about scheduling within their areas. They feel that it will also keep them closer in touch with the de-icing effort, and that they can get a faster response if they have to reschedule when a truck unexpectedly goes out of service. See Figure 4.8.

By looking closely at the adjacent system, in this case an active one, we learn more about its aspirations and needs. We consider the adjacent system's technological capabilities and intentions as to the outcome of the business event. In this case we found that the adjacent system (the truck depot supervisor) wanted to avoid waiting on the telephone, wanted to play a more active part in the event and wanted an immediate response to scheduling requests.

The result of getting into the brain of the adjacent system is a product that extends outside its traditional work boundary to have a point of presence in the truck depots. In other words a better, more usable product.

The result of getting into the brain of the adjacent system is usually a product that extends outside its traditional work boundary

Autonomous Adjacent Systems

An autonomous adjacent system is some external body, such as another company, a government department, a customer who is not directly interacting with your work. The autonomous adjacent system acts independently of the work being studied, but has connections to it. Autonomous adjacent systems communicate through one-way data flows.

RULE OF THUMB

An autonomous adjacent system sends and/or receives a single-stream data flow. It does not interact with the work

For example, when your credit card company sends you a monthly statement, you (the credit card account holder) act as an autonomous adjacent system. You have no interaction with the credit card company, you are acting as a sink for the information that they send to you. You make no immediate response to the statement: you wait until *you* decide to pay the bill. In other words, you are acting willfully as seen from the viewpoint of the credit card company.

Similarly, when you do pay your credit card bill, you are again an autonomous adjacent system from the point of view of the work of the credit card company. You send your check by post, and have no expectations about participating in the response that the work makes upon the arrival of your check. Another example of an autonomous adjacent system is a weather station sending a reading to the ice prediction work. This is shown in Figure 4.9. The weather stations are programmed to transmit readings of the air and road-surface temperatures periodically. When the weather station does transmit, it is a business event. The response of the work is to record the readings. The transmission is one way. No signal is sent back to the weather station, nor does it interact with the work. Thus the weather station acts autonomously from the work.

Autonomous adjacent systems use a one-way communication, either because of their technology, or their preference. However, be careful to determine that this is really their choice, and not a result of your own business' technological decisions. If an autonomous system is your customer, then it may well prefer to be connected directly to your product – in other words become an active adjacent system – and not deal remotely.

Figure 4.9

When the weather stations transmit their readings, the readings arrive as a complete packet of data. The work accepts the readings and processes them according to a pre-planned policy. There is no advantage in the product interacting with the weather station, as there is no reason, and indeed it is not possible, for the weather station and the proposed product to have some kind of conversation. Thus we can set the boundary of the product at the boundary of the work.

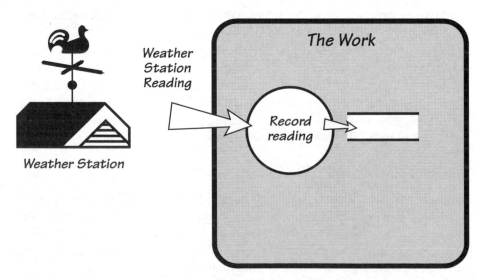

Keep in mind when considering the nature of adjacent systems that the same physical entity can be different types at different times. For example, when you send a check to pay a bill, you are autonomous, but when you go to that business and make an inquiry, or interact with the same business on the Internet, you become an active adjacent system.

For business events involving autonomous adjacent systems, the scope of the response starts and/or ends with the adjacent system. The product boundary is pushed as near as possible to the adjacent system, but may not be pushed into the autonomous adjacent system. While the developers of the product cannot change an interface with an autonomous adjacent system without negotiation, it may be the autonomous system would welcome the change. Thus we need to understand the content, format, delivery medium and frequency of the incoming and outgoing data flows, and most importantly, the motivations and desires of the adjacent system.

Let's look at another example of a business event involving an autonomous adjacent system. This is shown in Figure 4.10. The weather forecasting bureau sends the weather forecasts for the district by fax. If we look at the bureau we see that they cannot, or will not, send the data to the work any other way. Thus their method of transmitting their data makes them an autonomous system. The faxes are not a suitable medium for the product to utilize, so we must employ clerks to act as interpreters of the faxes and enter the weather data into the IceBreaker product. Thus the best boundary for our product is to interface with the clerks rather than directly with the autonomous weather forecasting bureau. We use the term actor – in this case the clerks – to define to whom or what we have chosen to have a direct interface with the product.

The main effect that an autonomous adjacent system has on the work is that it does not involve itself in the response to the business events that it triggers. Similarly, when it is the receiver of the output of a business event, such as a report or invoice, then it is a passive receiver of the output, and makes no attempt to respond immediately.

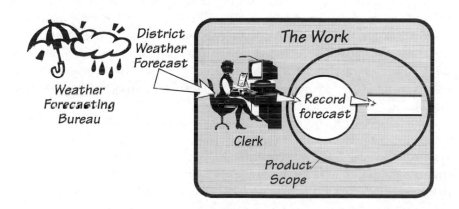

Figure 4.10

The adjacent system is autonomous, and is using a transmittal medium such that it is not practical for the product to receive it directly. An active adjacent system has been substituted to interact with the product.

Thus there appears to be little opportunity to involve autonomous adjacent systems in the work. However, before you decide that there is no opportunity, be certain that the adjacent system actually chooses to be autonomous, and is not forced to be so by your work's technology. For example, our bank forces us to fill in forms whenever we need a new service from them. That makes us autonomous, and the business event starts when the completed form reaches the bank. We would much prefer to initiate the event with some direct interaction – telephone, the Internet or face-to-face meeting – and then give the information they need. That way, the bank could make use of the information they already hold about us, and not ask us to fill in yet again our name, address, account number, and so on.

From the point of view of requirements gathering, it is necessary to understand the autonomous adjacent system to the point that you understand precisely the interface between it and the work, and that the interface is what is desired. Thereafter, you must understand the response that the work makes to the business event involving the autonomous adjacent system.

Cooperative Adjacent Systems

RULE OF THUMB

Cooperative adjacent systems are computerized

Cooperative adjacent systems can be relied on to behave predictably when called upon. In other words, they cooperate with our product to bring about some desired outcome. This is almost always done by means of a simple request–response dialog. A cooperative adjacent system might be another product that contains a database used by our work, an operating system, or any other system that provides a documented, predictable and immediate service to our work. We can access the cooperative adjacent system, store data in it, or request some service from it. At all times, the behavior of the cooperative adjacent system is predictable and consistent.

An example of a cooperative adjacent system: The Thermal Mapping Suppliers provide data that is used by the de-icing prediction work. In particular, this data is used by the event that schedules the trucks to treat the roads. The thermal mapper has the data on a database, and allows it to be accessed by the IceBreaker product. As the data is fairly volatile, it is considered good sense to access the data when it is needed, rather than IceBreaker maintaining its own version of the data. To put it simply, the product will have on-demand access to the thermal mapping database.

An example of a cooperative adjacent system is shown in Figure 4.11. When the ice prediction work asks for data from the database, the adjacent system responds with the requested data in an agreed timely manner. Thus the cooperative adjacent system receives a single input, the request for thermal conditions for a district, and has a single output in response. The

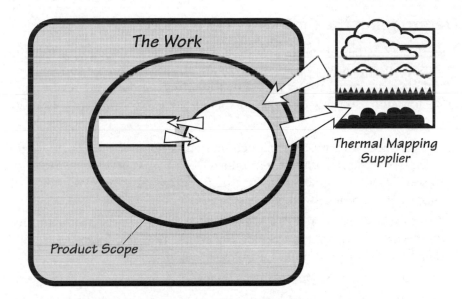

Figure 4.11

The system maintaining the thermal map database is an adjacent system – it is not owned by the de-icing business, and is the responsibility of another party. However, the de-icing system may access the data, and when it does, expects to get it quickly.

response is quick enough that the requesting product is prepared to wait for it.

This immediate interaction means that you can consider the cooperative adjacent system to be *part of the response to the business event*, or from the point of view of the product, part of the use case. The processing of the use case does not stop when it reaches the adjacent system – even though the adjacent system is not part of the product – but continues until the desired outcome of the event has been reached. We generally include it in our models of the event response, as illustrated in Figure 4.12.

It is unlikely that you will need, or want, to change the interfaces with the cooperative system. As cooperative systems are black boxes, their services are stable, and there is rarely much to be gained from trying to change them. The reason for wanting to change is if the product you decide upon needs a different service.

Figure 4.12

The processing for an event response does not stop when it involves a cooperative adjacent system. Even though the adjacent system is outside the scope of the work, due to its ability to respond immediately, it can be considered as a part of the work. The ↔ symbol indicates that this is a special type of adjacent system. That is, the data flow 'passes through' the adjacent system. This kind of adjacent system does not initiate events, nor does it act as an external sink for data flows.

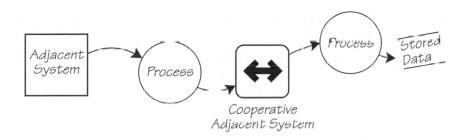

Determining the Best Product to Build

PUTTING THIS TO WORK

The product is the part of the work that you choose to build – this usually means the part that you choose to automate. In today's highly competitive world, there are great prizes for building the correct product, and severe penalties for failing to do so. So what factors are involved in determining the best product to build?

● The product's purpose. This was determined earlier in the project blastoff. It tells you what the product is intended to do – what problem it attempts to solve – and has a measurement (the fit criteria) that tells you how the success of the product will be measured.

● The work context model that shows you the scope of the work, and its connections to the outside world. The connections are indicated by the data that flows to and from the adjacent systems.

● The adjacent systems. Some of them are customers for the product's services.

● The stakeholders that you identified earlier have an effect on the product's boundary. Are the developer stakeholders capable of building a certain product? Can the users operate it? How much is the client willing to pay? There is no formula for making use of the stakeholders' capabilities and capacities, but it pays to keep them firmly in mind when making the decisions that are about to come.

● The influences from outside bodies. For example, there are professional bodies that have an influence on standards of behavior, or codes of conduct, for different industries. These may have some bearing on the product that you intend to build. Also consider the law applicable to the industry or the activity. Are you prohibited from building a certain type of product, or does the law encourage certain product behavior? Does public opinion matter? What effect will it have on your product?

● The market position that your organization holds. What kinds of product will enhance its position, and what kinds of product will harm the market's perception of your organization?

It is only by firstly understanding the work, and then automating part of it, that we achieve a seamless fit between our product and the work

Establishing the Product's Scope

Any product that you build is to become part of your client's work – part of the means of responding to a business event. As we have discussed, it is natural and necessary to study this work. Once you have achieved an intimate understanding of the work, you then decide how much of the work is to be done by your product.

It is wrong to start with a product, and then force-fit it into the work. Nor can you start with a preconception of what the product should be without

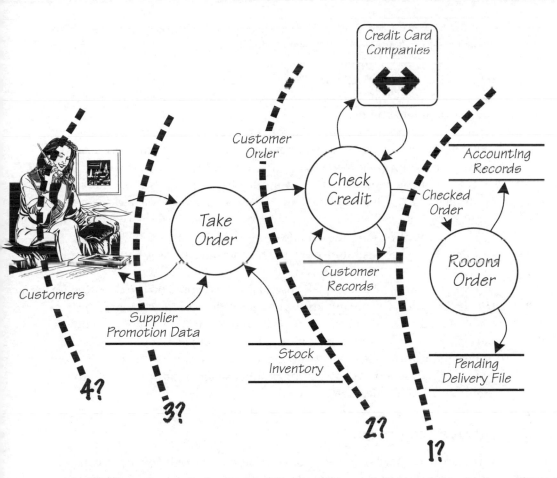

understanding the work that it is to become a part of. It is only by firstly understanding the work, and then automating part of it, that we achieve a seamless fit between our product and the work. So let us look at an example of how we determine how much of the work is to become the product.

Consider the situation depicted in Figure 4.13. This is a fairly typical response to a business event. In this case, a customer is ordering some groceries over the telephone with the intention of having them delivered to her home. Now, what is the best place to put the product boundary? Or thinking of it another way, what will make the most useful product?

What about the product that would result from boundary number 1? An operator would enter the checked order and the product would record the order once it has been authorized by the credit card company. This is not a very useful product, as it leaves the operator most of the work to do.

Then how about boundary number 2? The user would take the order over the telephone and enter it into the product, which would then do the credit card check and record the order. Not bad, but perhaps we could do better.

Figure 4.13

Once you understand the complete response to the business event, it is possible to establish the best scope of the product. The heavy dotted lines represent alternative product boundaries.

Getting the right product scope is crucial to getting the right requirements

Boundary number 3 means that the order taking is automated. This means that customers would make a telephone call to a product capable of voice recognition. Provided there are no questions or any serious responses needed, the customers get the advantage of calling 24 hours a day. Alternatively, customers could log on to the grocery company's web site and enter their own orders on-line.

But wait. That solution might be convenient for the grocery company, but what about the customer? What does she really want? What service should the grocery company provide to her to keep her loyalty?

To answer the question, let's look at the beginning of the business event. Or more usefully, what happened *before* the company became aware that the event had happened? It is reasonable to say that the customer went around the house counting groceries and determining what she needed to order. So from the customer's point of view, the business event started some 30 minutes ago.

From her point of view, a really useful product would do the counting for her. If the grocery company knew the quantities of grocery items the customer already had, and knew her consumption rates, then it would not be necessary for the customer to call at all. The company could call the customer and inform her of what she needed, and arrange a suitable delivery time. In other words, we extend the product scope out until it gets into the brain of the adjacent system.

> *We extend the product scope out until it gets into the brain of the adjacent system*

Innovative Products

If you are to compete in today's commercial market, or if you are to compete with the other agencies offering to build software or any other product for in-house consumption, then innovation is your greatest ally. Forget software development productivity: buying off-the-shelf software beats that hands down. Climbing up the CMM (capability maturity model) ladder won't do you a bit of good if you cannot build innovative products that thrill your client and your customers.

Part of your job as a requirements analyst is to invent a better way to do the work. Let's consider invention.

Firstly, you cannot invent a better way of doing work by merely automating yesterday's methods. Or by re-automating yesterday's automation. It is only by rethinking the organization's response to its business events that you will come up with products able to compete with your competitors.

Examine the business events that affect the work, particularly those that are initiated by active adjacent systems, or autonomous adjacent systems that could become active if given the chance.

> 66 *Our job is to give the client, on time and on cost, not what he wants, but what he never dreamed he wanted; and when he gets it, he recognizes it as something he wanted all the time.* 99
>
> Source: Dewys Lasdon, designer.

Consider the very beginning of the business event. Not the beginning where an operator sits down at a computer and enters some data, but the real beginning. What is it that the adjacent system is doing when she triggers the event? Can you extend your product scope to include that activity? For an example of this, let's look at the check-in procedure for passengers flying in Virgin Atlantic's Upper Class. Upper Class passengers are given a limousine ride to the airport (a welcome piece of innovation for a start). Instead of the limo driver dumping the passenger at the terminal, and letting them lug their bags to the check-in desk, Virgin have installed a drive-through check-in at some airports. Passengers check in while they are still in the car. In other words, Virgin considers that the business event is triggered when the passenger reaches the airport, *not* when she reaches the check-in desk. Think about your business events. Do they really begin at the boundary of your work, or do they start well before they reach your organization?

Consider the **real** *beginning of the business event*

Consider also that the consumer is about to become king. Consumers today are much better informed than they have ever been, and have access to information that previously was denied them. Consumers can cruise the Internet to find the best available prices, and make comparisons between almost all commodities and services. Geography no longer matters. Consumers can order goods from anywhere in the world, for home delivery in one or two days. Customer loyalty, that escape route for traditional companies, is rapidly disappearing to be replaced by customer demand for better service and convenience. If you are about to build some automated product, and it does not provide better service and greater convenience to your organization's customers, then perhaps you are wasting your time. Today, there are few other reasons for building automated products.

Consider giving your customer control of his transactions. People want to do some of the work themselves. Supermarkets are introducing – to much acclaim – self-scanning of their groceries rather than queuing for the checkout. People are shopping at home, ordering customized products that they have specified themselves using interactive web sites. People buy shares over the Internet without advice or intervention from a broker or trader. Innovative solutions are more and more exposing their organizations by giving the customer more and more access to previously guarded activities.

READING

PETERS, TOM. *The Circle of Innovation*. Alfred A. Knopf, 1997.

When you determine the best product to build, you must firstly understand the work that it is to support. You determine which part of the work should be automated. However, this process is not simply marking off some existing functionality and automating that. Rather the process is more along the lines of inventing a better way to do the work. Better in this sense means providing some benefit to your organization's customers.

The eventual product is determined by a blend of a number of factors. There are others, but we always consider at least:

- Customers' needs and wishes,
- Degree of participation desired by the adjacent systems,
- Stakeholder concerns and aspirations,
- Product purpose,
- Customer service,
- Client expectations,
- Project constraints,
- Cost/time to implement,
- Benefit to organization,
- Required speed of response/volumes,
- Security,
- Operational cost,
- Ability to build,
- Ability to use,
- Competitors' products,
- Established practice,
- Legacy systems,
- Available/desired technology.

The part played by the adjacent system is dependent on its capabilities and willingness to participate. Thus for each adjacent system we must study its:

- Ability to respond in a timely manner;
- Willingness to respond;
- Technological compatibility with the work – participation can only be achieved if there is an effective communication link that does not require slow translations;
- Policy with regard to responding;
- Proximity to the work – this affects the medium of communication, and perhaps the time taken;
- Ownership – adjacent systems that have a different ownership may be less inclined to participate;
- Interests – is it in the interests of the adjacent system to participate, or are its own interests better served by not participating?

There is no formula for applying these factors. Each project has different priorities. It is up to you and your stakeholders to consider the factors, examine alternative product boundaries and determine which mix of factors yields the optimal product.

Does Technology Matter?

Technology is important to our study only when it is outside our work. That is, the technology used by the adjacent systems matters, as it affects the way that they communicate with our work. However, for the purpose of requirements gathering, the *technology inside the work is disregarded*.

In the above examples, if the thermal map supplier used a technology that prevented it from responding in real time when the de-icing work asked for data, then it would be classed as a autonomous adjacent system. In this case the technology of the adjacent system affects the way that our own work behaves. Similarly, an active adjacent system can only play a part in the work if it is technologically capable, and personally willing. The truck depot supervisor was both, and thus was an active adjacent system, and played a part in the response to the events that he triggered.

So much for the technology of the adjacent systems. The technology *inside* the work is irrelevant for gathering the requirements. If we are going to gather accurate requirements, we must disregard any technology that currently exists, and suppress any thought we may have about future technology. Keep in mind that 'technology' here means humans, paper and low-tech devices. Imagine for the moment that *no* technology exists inside your work.

The reason is simple. Any work that you look at contains technology – machines, computers, people, paper and so on – and procedures. Often the procedures have been set up with a particular technology in mind. If the technology changes, then the procedure is no longer relevant. The implication of this is that any requirement you gather must not be a technological requirement, but must be a requirement for the work itself. All too often we have observed that technology was hiding the real requirements.

This means looking past any current implementation, and indeed looking past any implementation that you might envision for the future. As good or as bad as those technologies may be, they have the same effect: they prevent us from seeing the real requirements. If we are going to see the real work, then we have to see it without its technological trappings. In other words, what is the underlying policy, or the *essence*, of the work that you are studying?

The essential requirements are those that would be there regardless of the technology used to implement them

Once you have gathered the essential requirements, then it is time to select the appropriate technology for the product.

To see this essence clearly, for it is not always apparent, it is easier to look at smaller pieces of the system. These small pieces give you a clearer view of the work: one that isolates the work to do with a single subject – the response to one business event.

Event-driven Use Cases

PUTTING
THIS TO
WORK

For each business event, consider the response that the work makes. Consider if this response is what the adjacent system desires, or needs. In other words, consider if the organization is making the correct response to the adjacent system.

Determine the scope of the product for each business event response. When you are doing this, consider if the adjacent system is capable of making a different contribution to the work than it currently does. Do not assume at the beginning of the project what the responsibilities of both the product and the adjacent system will be, but derive them from an understanding of what will make a useful product.

The part of the response that is done by the product is a use case. But note how we got to this point – the use case is a part of the work, and we found it by examining the work and how the work responds to outside demands. The involvement of the adjacent systems determines, or largely determines, the role that the product should play in the work's response.

An event-driven use case is that part of the response to a business event that is done by the automated product

Thus the use cases are derived from the business events that are the driving force of the work.

Sometimes, for technical reasons, you might choose to implement a business event with a number of use cases. There may be reasons why you wish to subdivide the work inside the computer into smaller pieces. There will also be the opportunity to reuse use cases that have been developed for other parts of the product, or other products.

Use cases can be linked together using 'uses' and 'extends' links. These constructs are similar, and they mean that one use case can make use of the functionality of another.

The selection of use cases is somewhat driven by technical considerations, but if the product is to be recognizable and usable by its intended users, then the use cases must be based on the original business events.

Part of selecting the use cases is selecting the actors who will interact with the product.

Actors

Actors are the people or systems that interact with the automated product. In some cases, as we have shown above, the actors are adjacent systems that are outside the organization that owns the product. In other cases, we appoint actors from inside the organization, as the adjacent systems cannot, or will not, act as we need them to.

Figure 4.14 shows the use cases that were selected for the IceBreaker product, and the actors that operate each of the use cases.

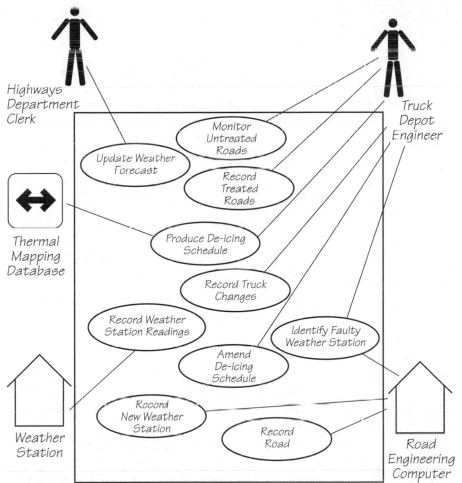

Figure 4.14

The use case diagram for the IceBreaker product. This shows the event-driven cases, the actors involved in each, and the product's boundary. An active actor is represented as a stick figure. Autonomous actors are shown as houses, and the cooperative one as a rounded square with arrows.

The significance of the use cases for the requirements analyst is that the requirements are written for each use case. After all, the use cases represent the components of the product that is to be built, so it is appropriate that you describe the use cases in terms of requirements. Note that the requirements are written for the actor. In other words, each requirement says what the product has to do to allow the actor to complete his work satisfactorily.

Summary

By employing the idea of the business events, we can carve out a rational piece of the work for further modeling and study. By understanding the effect that each of the adjacent systems has on the work, we understand the limits of the product's scope. We arrive at the scope by modeling the

Figure 4.15

This shows the flow of processes that we perform to find the appropriate use cases. The response to each business event is examined and an appropriate product scope determined. The use cases are the part of the response that is to be done by the product. The requirements are written for each use case.

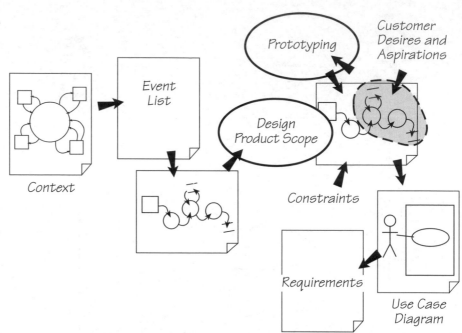

behavior of the work, not by presupposing that there will be a user and a computer, or being bound by the existing technology.

By using business events to partition the work, we have a guide for finding all the pieces of the work that are bound together for the same business reason. Figure 4.15 illustrates this.

Event-driven use cases are the parts of the business event response (activities and data) that are carried out by the product. Actors are selected to interact with the use cases, based largely on their aspirations about that part of the work. The use case becomes the anchor for the requirements. That is, each use case is studied and its requirements determined. By breaking the product into these small, convenient units, we can understand the real work that the product is expected to do. It is only by understanding the real work that we can build products that are truly relevant and useful.

Trawling for Requirements

in which we go fishing for requirements and
discuss some useful techniques

The term 'trawling' comes from our partner Steve McMenamin (a source of many useful and descriptive images). We use it because it evokes the nature of what we are doing here: running a net through the organization to catch every possible requirement. The trawling analogy is appropriate because the trawlers catch more fish than they really want – the skipper fishing for cod may not be interested in the herring caught up in his nets. He can always throw them back. However, with a little experience, the captain will know where to fish so that he gets the fish he wants, and not the ones that he doesn't. See Figure 5.1.

Any inappropriate requirements that get caught up in your net will be filtered out by the Quality Gateway. So if you do find a few extraneous requirements from your trawling, don't be too concerned. The Quality Gateway will reduce the requirements to the most appropriate ones. At this stage you should be concentrating on finding all the requirements and not missing any. In practice, this may mean gathering a few too many, which is always better than gathering a few too few.

Responsibility

Trawling is instigated by the requirements analyst. However, he does not do it alone. The requirements analyst, the users and other stakeholders collaborate to gather the requirements. Let us explain their roles.

We build products to help us do work. For our purposes it doesn't matter whether the work is processing insurance claims, analyzing blood samples, designing automotive parts, predicting when ice will form on roads, keeping

The requirements analyst and the users collaborate to gather the requirements

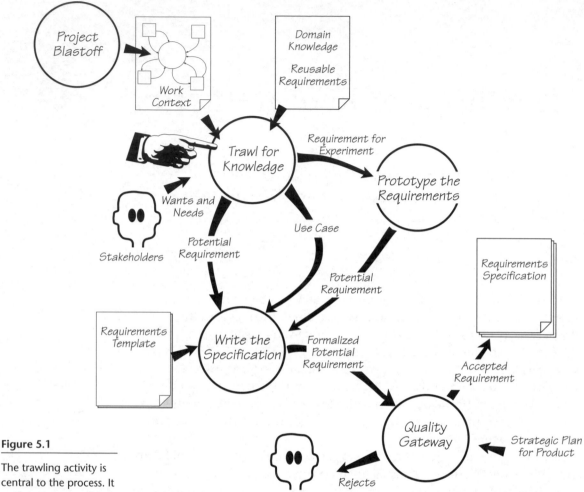

Figure 5.1

The trawling activity is central to the process. It uses the outputs of the Project Blastoff as its starting point for collecting the requirements from the users and other stakeholders. Prototyping runs as a parallel activity. Note that the requirements gathered at this stage are *potential* requirements. They still have to pass the quality checks of the Quality Gateway.

track of a things to do list, controlling a telephone network, or one of many other human activities. There are things to do, data to store, and for one reason or another, you have been asked to build a product that helps with this work.

To state the obvious, you are gathering requirements for a product that will help with some aspect of somebody's work.

Users, Customer and Client

The stakeholders who play the roles of users, customer and client are the source of knowledge about the work. They are the people who know what the work is, as well as having a vision of what the work should be. Therefore the users, customer and client have the responsibility to provide the requirements analyst with their knowledge of the work. Further, the people who play these roles have the responsibility to discuss and determine the feasibility of the requirements analyst's ideas for the work and the product.

The Requirements Analyst

The analyst is a translator. He has to understand what the user is saying about the work, and translate this into a specification for a product. But there is more to it. The requirements analyst has to inject something new into the process: his vision of what the product might be. In other words, the requirements are not simply the passive interpretation of an existing piece of work, but contain inventions that will make the work easier, better, more interesting and more pleasant. Thus the requirements analyst must:

● Observe and learn the work, and understand it from the point of view of the user. As you work with your users, you observe their work and question them about what they are doing, and why they are doing it. Each piece of information you hear is treated at several levels simultaneously.

● Interpret the work. A user's description of some work must be treated as factual. After all, the user is the expert on that part of the work. The analyst must filter the description to strip away any of the current technology or way of doing things in order to see the essence of the work, not its incarnation. (We will talk more about this later in this chapter.)

● Invent better ways to do the work. Once he sees the essence, or the real work, he interprets what the product must do to satisfy that part of the work. At the same time, he is inventing a product that will improve the work by providing the best help with it.

● Record the results in the form of a requirements specification, and analysis models. It almost goes without saying that the analyst must ensure that he and the user have the same understanding of the product, and that the user agrees that this is the product he wants.

Not so easy as it first appears.

There are techniques to help with the task of trawling for requirements. Like all techniques, none of them works all of the time, so your task is to select the technique that best fits the situation. As we go through the techniques, try to connect each of them to your own situation, and consider where and when each would be most advantageous.

Consider your users. They will be very conscious of some requirements and will bring them up early. There are others that we call the 'unconscious'

*Conscious
requirements are
those requirements
that are uppermost
in the users' minds,
this is often
symptomatic of
something that
the users want
to improve.*
Unconscious
*requirements are
those that the users
do not mention
because the users
know so much
about them that
they are assuming
everyone else will
have the same
knowledge.*
Undreamed of
*requirements are
the things that the
users will ask for
when they realize
that they are
possible*

requirements – the things that are so ingrained into the users' work that they have forgotten they exist. The techniques that capture the conscious requirements may not necessarily work for the unconscious ones. Then there are the 'undreamed of' requirements – those functions and features that the users and customer are unaware they could have. Undreamed of requirements are there because the users do not realize that they are possible. This may be because of a lack of technological sophistication, or they may have never seen their work in the way that you will show it to them. Whatever the reason, part of your responsibility is to bring these requirements to the surface.

All the requirements must be uncovered and captured during the trawling activity. Remember that requirements are requirements whenever you find them. Just because you do not find them at the requirements stage, does not mean they will never be found. It just means that they will be found during maintenance and product usage when it is far more expensive to build them into the product.

Trawling

The trawling activity is multi-faceted. The requirements analyst has to understand the work that the user currently does, and determine the work that the user, customer or the client, desires to be done in the future. The future work depends somewhat on the desires or aspirations of the adjacent systems.

The trawling activity uses some of the outputs from the blastoff activity. The blastoff has determined the context of the work, the purpose of the product and the constraints that apply to any solution. These guide the analyst as the work is studied and the requirements are gathered. The blastoff has also determined the stakeholders involved in the project, and the potential users. Naturally, the requirements analyst needs to know who to interview and who to study to get an understanding of the work.

The business events play a major part in trawling. As a rule of thumb, the requirements are gathered one business event at a time. The analyst studies the work that is currently done in response to the event or the work that would be done in response to a new event, and as an outcome of his interviews with the users, stakeholders and client, determines what the desired response is to be. That is, how must the current response be altered to take advantage of new technology or new opportunities to provide a better service or reduce costs, and how will the proposed product assist in this new response. Figure 5.2 illustrates this.

Thus the trawling activity is both a study of the work, and an invention of a better way to do that work.

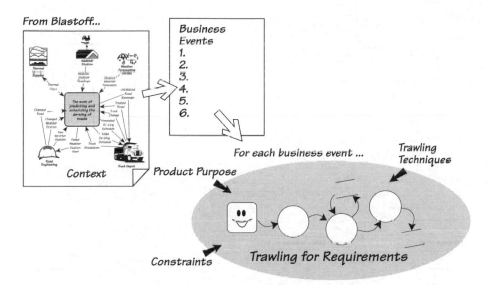

From Blastoff...

Business Events
1.
2.
3.
4.
5.
6.

Context

Product Purpose

For each business event ...

Trawling Techniques

Constraints

Trawling for Requirements

Figure 5.2

Business events are determined from the flows from the adjacent systems on the context. The response to each business event is studied so that the analyst understands what the desired response is to be, and what contribution the product is to make to that response.

The trawling techniques that we describe in this chapter are aimed at:

● Studying the work that is currently done in response to a business event;

● Learning the desires and aspirations of the adjacent systems involved in the business event;

● Determining the best response that the organization can make to the business event;

● Determining the way that the product will contribute to the desired response;

● Determining and describing the requirements for the product.

Enough. Let's look at the trawling techniques.

The Role of the Current Situation

The first part of requirements trawling is observing the work. We suggest that when you are doing this you are not just a passive onlooker, but actively understand the work. The most effective way of doing this is by building a model.

You use models to help you understand the work – you can't build a model without understanding the subject of your model, but the modeling activity makes you ask all the right questions. When the model is finished, it means that you have understood the subject. You use models to record the work, and to demonstrate your understanding of it. Most importantly, since the model is a common language between you and your user, both of you can agree that you have the identical understanding of the work.

The current system for doing the work contains many functions that contribute to the business. Naturally these functions must be included in any future product

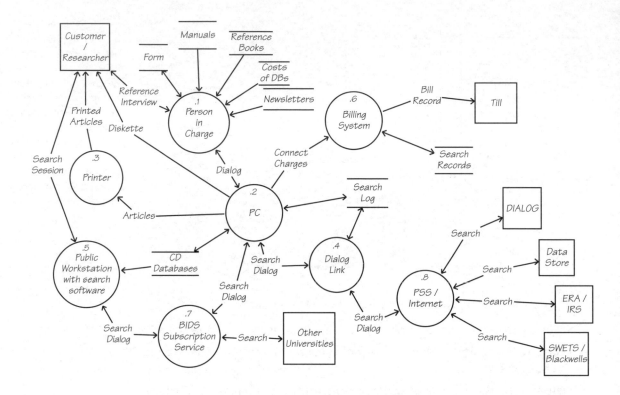

Figure 5.3

City University researchers' process for interrogating commercial databases. This model was built by the authors working with the user of the process. As the user described the work, the authors modeled and demonstrated their understanding. The model took about 15 minutes to complete.

When you model the current work, keep in mind that you are not attempting to specify a new product, but merely to establish the work that the users currently do. Most likely the users describe their work in a way that includes the mechanisms and technology they use to get the work done. These mechanisms are not requirements for the new system – you must look beyond them to see the underlying policy of the users' system. We call this the essence, and will discuss it fully a little later in the chapter.

Despite any bad reputation the current system for doing the work may have, it is not worthless. It will contain a lot of functions that are making a positive contribution to the business. Naturally these functions must be included in any future system. You may implement them differently with new technology, but their underlying business policy will remain almost unchanged. The objective of building a model of the current work is to find the parts to keep, and to understand the system that you are about to change.

Keep in mind that any modeling of the current system is as brief as possible, and is done as quickly as possible. Figure 5.3 shows a model of an existing system, built by the authors in conjunction with staff at City University, London.

You must restrict the amount of detail that you show in your models of the current system. There is little point in having a detailed model of the system that you are about to replace. There should be enough detail to give you an understanding of the work, and no more. The detail shown in Figure 5.3 is about right. That is, it shows the major parts of the current situation. It allows the user to verify that it is a correct representation of the work that he does, and gives the requirements analyst places to make further inquiries.

However, the aspect of the model that should not be restricted is the area of the business covered by the model. Here it is almost a case of 'the more the merrier'. Your models should cover all the work that is possibly relevant to your product, those parts of the business that could contribute to the new product, and those parts where operational problems have been experienced in the past. The other areas worth covering are those where the business is not well understood.

The point of having a large scope for your models is that if your new product is to be useful – that is, it makes the work easier, faster, better – then you are doing more than specifying an automated product. You are really in the

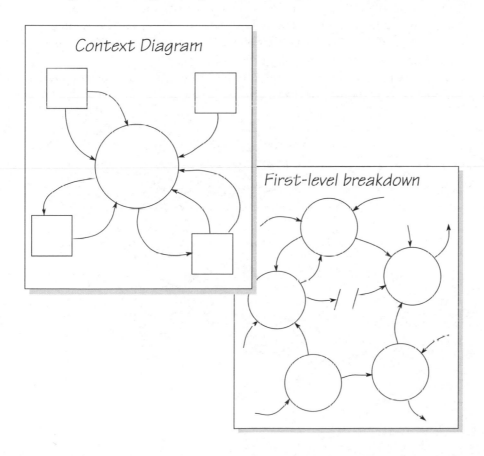

Figure 5.4

The first-level breakdown shows the processes contained with the context. The breakdown is used to confirm the context, and to partition the scope into areas of study.

business of reengineering the work. Thus the greater the scope of your study, the better your understanding, and the better the chance of finding areas that will benefit from improvement.

The current model confirms the context. During the project blastoff, you and the stakeholders built a context model to show the scope of the work. The model you build here confirms that all the appropriate parts of the work are included in the context (Figure 5.4). If at this stage you discover areas that would benefit from your attention, or parts of the work that need to be understood, or anything at all that should be included, then now is the time to adjust the context. This will of course have to be negotiated with the stakeholders, but far better to do it now than later.

An obvious benefit to be had from building current system models is finding out where to ask questions (Figure 5.5). As the model develops, it becomes more and more obvious what you don't know, and (sometimes) what the users don't know. This helps you to see where to concentrate your efforts.

It is of course impossible to change something without knowing what that something is. A study of the current system shows you how to fit something new into, or change, whatever currently exists. It also reveals the corporate and systems culture. The culture is not a requirement as such, but your new product has a far better chance of succeeding if you understand the cultural environment in which it will operate.

Thus the review of the current system is to ensure that you understand the situation before introducing any improvements.

Figure 5.5

Knowing where to ask questions is as useful as knowing the answers. If your model has flows going nowhere, processes without inputs, read-only or write-only datastores, or other incurred symbology, it usually indicates where you need to interrogate your users.

Apprenticing

Apprenticing is a wonderful way to observe the real work. Apprenticing is based on the idea of masters and apprentices. In this case, the requirements analyst is the apprentice, and the user is the master craftsman. The apprentice sits with the master to learn the job by observation, asking questions and doing some of the work under the master's supervision.

It is unlikely that many users can explain what they do in enough detail for the developer to completely understand the work, and thus capture all the requirements. For example, if you are away from your work, you tend to describe it in abstract terms, and describe generalized cases. An abstraction is useful in one sense, but it does not hold enough detail for it to work every time.

You cannot expect users to have enough presentation and teaching skills to present their work effectively to others. However, almost anybody is good at explaining what they are doing while they are doing it. If the user is doing his job in his normal workplace, he can provide a running commentary and provide details that may otherwise be lost. It is probably *only* while working that the user is able to describe his task precisely, tell you why he is doing things, and what exceptions can occur. You will see this the first time a user shows you his work-around for special cases.

To get the user to describe the work, you must not take him away from his work. Rather, the apprentice sits alongside the user, and receives a running commentary on the work as it happens. Each action is explained, and if not clear, the apprentice asks questions – 'Why did you do that?' 'What does this mean?' 'How often does this happen?' 'What happens if this piece of information is not here?' – and thus eventually sees all the cases, and the actions the user takes for each.

Apprenticeship can be combined with current system modeling. As the work is observed and explained, the analyst can sketch models of each of the tasks, and how they are connected by flows of data. Refer back to Figure 5.3 for an example of the type of model that is appropriate for an apprentice to build. As the models are built, the analyst feeds them back to the user for confirmation and to raise questions about any areas of uncertainty (see Figure 5.6).

The requirements analyst can use his term of apprenticeship to try out requirements and design ideas. As the work suggests them, the analyst can ask the user if an idea is feasible, if it would improve the work, and generate in the user's mind the notion that the analyst is more than an observer. That he (the analyst) is there to help improve the work.

We mentioned earlier that the requirements analyst is an interpreter as well as an observer. While observing the current work, the analyst must

READING

BEYER, HUGH AND KAREN HOLTZBLATT. *Contextual Design. Defining Customer-Centered Systems.* Morgan Kaufmann, 1998.

> *Nobody can talk better about what they do and why they do it than they can while in the middle of doing it.*
>
> Source: Beyer and Holtzblatt

 **PUTTING THIS TO WORK**

Figure 5.6

The requirements analyst learns the work while sitting at the user's desk. Sometimes models of the work are built while learning it.

abstract away from what he sees. He must overcome the user's close connection to the physical incarnation of the work. In other words, the procedures, the artifacts, the technology and so on that are currently used must be seen as a product of a previous designer. Someone, some time ago, decided that was the best way to do the work. However, times have changed. There may now be better ways – ways that take advantage of up-to-date technology, that use streamlined processes, that simplify the work or automate some or all of it.

So while the apprentice is learning the work by seeing the same tasks performed many times, he is also looking past how the user does the work to see the underlying essence of the work. We will come back to essence a little later.

Observe Structures and Patterns

This is where the analyst both observes and interprets. By seeing the users at work over a period of time, the analyst can determine an abstract structure, or a pattern to the work.

The structure is a framework for the user to do his task for the normal cases, and also allows improvisation for the exceptions. The structure is most likely invisible to the user – people usually do not make the necessary abstraction and think in terms of work structure.

The analyst is also looking for the skills that people use, and how they see themselves when they do the work. What conceptualizations and metaphors do they use?

Having observed the structure, the analyst then looks for patterns. Does this structure match, or almost match, another structure? Is there a pattern to the work that also occurs elsewhere in the enterprise? The objective is to find similarities that can yield common requirements.

For example, one of our clients, the international section of a bank in London, had 20 different products. The products ranged over letters of credit, guaranteed foreign bank loans, guaranteed funds, and so on. The way the users handled each of these products at first looked to be different. However, a common pattern emerged as we studied the structure of the work – we were looking for similarities, not differences. We observed that each product was in fact a different way of guaranteeing that exporters got paid for their goods in foreign countries. The end result was that we found a common set of requirements, and were able to make a single core implementation, and then dress it differently for each of the products. In some cases, this different window dressing was little more than changing a few words and icons on screens.

We were looking for similarities, not differences

We suggest building abstract models of the work structure. Abstract in the sense that they do not specifically give technological names to things, or use terminology that distinctly belongs to one part of the organization. Nor should the models name any particular user, nor use terminology identified with a user. Thus the models are made remote from their source – they use categorizations rather than specifics. Instead of modeling the work the way a single user sees it, model the class of work, or as all users could see it.

PUTTING THIS TO WORK

The purpose of this kind of abstraction is to discover whether the same pattern exists in another part of the organization. It has been our experience that although the names and the artifacts may vary, the same work pattern will occur several times in one organization. We have used the recurrence of patterns firstly to understand the requirements more quickly, and then to re employ the implementation of one part of the work to suit another.

See Chapter 12 for more on patterns

Interview the Users

Interviewing the users is the traditional approach to requirements gathering. However, used on its own it may not be the most effective because it commonly expects the users to know and to be able to tell all their requirements.

We strongly suggest that interviews are not the sole method of gathering, instead use them in conjunction with other techniques.

The requirements analyst can draw up questionnaires in advance. While this gives some structure to the following interview, we have found very few users who are motivated enough to fill in a questionnaire prior to meeting the analyst. We suggest that you send the user, or whoever you are interviewing, an agenda of the topics that you wish to cover. This at least gives the user a chance to have material to hand, or to ask subject matter experts to be present.

The user should not be completely passive during the interview. We strongly urge you to build models – business event response, use case, scenario, and so on – while you are talking with the user during the interview. This gives you and your user immediate feedback, and means you can test the accuracy of what you are being told. We prefer that the user participate in the modeling efforts. You must accept that there will be notational differences: that does not matter, you can correct them later.

Feed back your understanding. Build models while you are interviewing the user

- Set the interview in context. This is necessary to avoid having your user talk about something that you do not wish to. It also allows him a chance, if he has not prepared for the meeting, to pull out gracefully. Use business events as an anchor. Users know about business events, and it makes for more directed conversations if you talk about their work one event at a time.

- Ask a question, listen to the answer, then feed back your understanding.

- Draw models and encourage the user to change them. We find that when the user is talking about a process, a data flow model is best for communication. We draw data models for information and mind maps to link different subjects.

- Use the user's terminology and artifacts, both conceptual and real. If the user does not use his own language, then he makes a technological translation into terms that he thinks the analyst will understand. This usually leads to the analyst missing nuances, and asking questions about terminology that inevitably lead to new discoveries. The artifacts are the things that the user uses in his daily work. They can be real things: papers, computers, meters, spreadsheets, machines, pieces of software and so on. Or conceptual things like status, contracts, schedules, orders and so on.

Thank the user for his time

- Keep sample artifacts and documents. They will inevitably cause you to raise questions when you examine them later.

- Thank the user for his time and tell him why it was valuable. After all, he has lots of other things to do. Talking to you is not the reason he is employed and he often views it as an interruption.

Getting to the Essence of the System

Part of interpreting the work is finding its essence. The essence of the system represents the fundamental reason that the system exists. For example, the fundamental reason for IceBreaker's existence, in other words its essence, is to accurately predict when roads are about to freeze. How it does this – the technology, the instruments, the computers and the people it uses – is its implementation.

It is important that you are able to separate the essence of the problem from its implementation. This is mainly to avoid recording requirements that exist because of the current technology. It is also to avoid accidentally reintroducing technology that may not be appropriate for the new product.

Try to imagine the essence separately from its implementation. Consider this: on the one hand you have technology – machines, people, and so on. Technology can be used to implement a solution to many problems. A computer doesn't know if you are running a spreadsheet or playing a game – it's just a piece of technology. On the other hand, you have the problem being solved. The problem is some piece of work, of business policy that can be stated without any attendant technology. It would exist regardless of any technological implementation. That is the essence.

It is important that you are able to separate the essence of the problem from its implementation

Of course, you can derive the essence from a technological implementation. For example, when you approach an automated teller machine, what is the essential piece of business that you wish to conduct? 'Withdraw money from your bank account' would be a logical answer. The things that you have to do like insert a plastic card, enter a PIN, and so on are to do with the technology that the bank chooses to use. The essence is that you access your account and withdraw money from it.

READING

McMENAMIN, STEVE AND JOHN PALMER. *Essential Systems Analysis*. Yourdon Press, 1984. The title refers to 'essence'.

Note how technology free that statement is – 'You access your account and withdraw money from it.' Consider it, and now consider how many other ways you could 'access your account and withdraw money from it'. There are lots of technological possibilities, but only one essence. And this is the point. The requirements you are looking for are the essential requirements. How they are implemented now, or will be in the future is not important to you at the moment.

This means that when you are trawling for requirements, you must look past the current implementation. You must also ignore the future technology too for that matter, however exciting it may be. Imagine the underlying concepts that are there because of the real work.

READING

ROBERTSON, JAMES AND SUZANNE. *Complete Systems Analysis: the Workbook, the Textbook, the Answers*. Dorset House, 1994.

For example, the current implementation of IceBreaker uses a computer to interpret the electronic signals from the weather stations and record the road surface temperature and moisture. The engineers use a PC to run their analyses of the freezing roads. But those devices are incidental to the essence

– they are just the means chosen to carry out the essence. Look past those devices and ask, 'What is this doing to help the work?' That underlying policy is the essence.

Why is this important?

If you write a requirement that contains a technological element, then that piece of technology becomes a requirement. For example, suppose that you have a requirement like this:

If a requirement contains the means of implementation then it is a solution, not a requirement

> *The product shall beep and put a flashing message on the screen if a weather station fails to transmit readings.*

What's wrong here? The problem is that the message is now consigned to a screen. Perhaps there are better ways, like telephoning the road engineers, sending an email message, launching a weather station diagnostic application, or one of many other possibilities. However, if you write the requirement like this:

> *The product shall issue an alert if a weather station fails to transmit readings.*

then it allows the designer to cast about and find the most appropriate solution. Consider this requirement for a ticket-selling product for a metro train:

> *The traveler shall touch the destination on a map.*

The analyst wanted to use a touch-sensitive map of the metro network, and have the travelers touch the station that they wanted to travel to. The product would compute the appropriate fare, and as a bonus show an illuminated pathway of the fastest route to the destination. This is no doubt a clever implementation. However, it is not the essence of the problem. While it may be a good way to implement the requirement, it is not the only one and there may well be better ones. If the requirement is expressed in its essential form, it looks like this:

> *The product shall accept the destination from the traveler.*

and the designer can now use other methods (within the constraints of the project) of getting the destination into the product. In this case it turned out that touching a map was not such a good idea, as studies showed that the majority of travelers did not know the rail network well enough to be able to locate their destination quickly enough.

The point is that we should not prejudge the implementation, no matter how well we think we understand the problem, nor how appealing the technology might be.

Business Event Workshops

For each business event there is a response made by the work. The business event workshop is a human activity where the responsible user describes or reenacts the work that is done in response to that event. The requirements engineer records all the actions, and from these derives the requirements for the product that will best help with the work.

But let's start at the beginning.

A business event is some happening that the work must respond to. One type of business event happens outside the work – it is instigated by the adjacent system. When we looked at event-driven use cases in Chapter 4, we showed how the work responds to this happening. We also discussed how the product does part of, and sometimes all of, the work of responding.

Chapter 4, Event-driven Use Cases

Each business event has an 'owner' – somebody, sometimes several people, who are the organization's experts on that part of the business. The intention of the workshop is to transfer knowledge of the business event from its owner to the requirements analyst. They lock themselves away in a JAD (joint application development) style workshop, together with any other interested parties, and construct scenarios to show the actions necessary to make the correct response to the business event. This is illustrated in Figure 5.7.

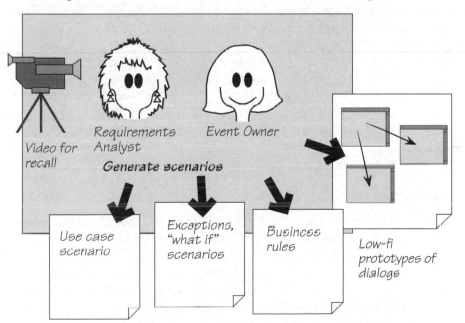

Figure 5.7

The business event workshop walks through the response to a business event. The user's needs for that work are determined, together with the contribution to be made by the automated product.

The deliverables from the business event workshop are:

- Purpose of the business event – the desired outcomes for the business;
- Scenarios of the work done to respond to the business event;
- 'What if' scenarios about the things that can go wrong when the event happens.
- The business rules that apply to that part of the work;
- The part of the work to be done by the product;
- The likely users of any product built for this business event;
- Prototypes for some of the steps – these are optional and must not be too detailed;

Purpose

The purpose of the business event is to focus on the outcome the organization hopes to achieve whenever the event occurs. Think of this in terms of *outcomes* and not *outputs*. For example, let's say that the business event is that a customer wants to rent a car. The desired outcome is that the customer drives away in the car of his choice, the rate selected is equitable, the details are recorded, and the transaction is completed with the minimum inconvenience to the customer at minimal cost. The outputs of the same business event are the rental document and some recorded data.

The purpose of the business event is to focus on the outcome the organization hopes to achieve

Note that an outcome is a business objective, not a way of achieving something. Outcomes are usually expressed from a higher-level view, such as the view of the organization or the organization's customer. Think of it this way: what are you trying to achieve, and why is that important? This should give your business event a solid reason for existing. It should not include technological statements, and should certainly not be tied to the existing technology or business methods.

You should be able to write the purpose of the business event in one sentence – if this business event happens, what state of affairs do you want to exist when the work has finished responding?

Scenarios

Scenarios are a series of actions that the business does to respond to the business event. In other words, what steps does the user go through to complete the required amount of work?

Steps are fairly high level, as the intention is not to capture every detail of what happens, but to have a broad-brush picture of the work. We suggest that you limit yourself to around half a dozen or so steps.

The first part of the workshop generates the scenarios. This involves the input from the users and other interested stakeholders. The use case is played through in order to extract from the user the essential things that have to happen. The result is a list of the steps that the product and the user must take. Later you turn these into functional requirements.

This last activity is discussed in Chapter 6, Functional Requirements

The 'what if' scenarios seek to find all the exceptions. Their name comes from the question 'what if [whatever] goes wrong?' The intention of this kind of scenario is to reveal all the exceptions, and from these derive the requirements needed to cater for the exceptional happenings.

'What if?' scenarios are covered more fully in Chapter 11, Prototyping and Scenarios

Business Rules

The business rules are management prescriptions that transcend and guide the day-to-day business decisions. Naturally any product that you build must conform to the business rules. The rules come to the surface as the user discusses the work for each business event. Later they will be used to guide the functional requirements, and to help to discover the meaning of stored data.

READING
WIEGERS, KARL. Use Cases – Listening to the Customer's Voice. *Software Development Magazine*, March 1997.

After the use case workshop, the requirements analysts derive and write the requirements. That is, for each of the use case steps, they ask the question 'What does the product have to do to complete this step?' At the same time, they will consider the non-functional requirements that are appropriate for this part of the work.

Deriving the non-functional requirements is covered in Chapter 7, Non-functional Requirements

Brainstorming

Invention is part of the requirements process. The product that the requirements analyst specifies should include new and better ideas for improving the work. Brainstorming is a method for generating new ideas.

Brainstorming takes advantage of the group effect. That is, you enclose a group of bright, willing people, and ask them to generate as many ideas as possible for the new product (Figure 5.8). They are told that all ideas are acceptable no matter how crazy they may seem, and that they must not slow the process down by criticizing or debating ideas. The objective is to be as imaginative as possible, and to generate as many ideas as possible.

Figure 5.8

A brainstorm is a gathering of interested people whose task is to generate new ideas for the product.

The best and most usable of the ideas will, with the client's consent, become requirements for the product.

There are some simple rules for brainstorming:

- Participants in the brainstorm should come from as wide a range of disciplines, with as broad a range of experience as possible. This mixture of backgrounds brings many more creative ideas to the session.

- For the moment suspend judgment, evaluation and criticism. Simply record requirements as they are generated. The practice of not stopping the flow is the fastest way to develop a creative and energized atmosphere for the brainstorm group.

- Produce lots of ideas. Come up with as many ideas as possible. Quantity will in time produce quality.

- Try to come up with as many ideas as you can that are unconventional, unique, crazy, wild, and so on. The wilder the idea, the more creative it probably is, and is often likely to turn into a really useful requirement.

- Piggyback a new idea on an old one. That is, build one idea on top of another.

- Write every idea down, without censoring. 'Ideas disappear faster than water evaporates unless written down.' – Alex Osborne, the founder of brainstorming.

- If you get stuck, seed the session with a word pulled randomly from a dictionary, and ask participants to make word associations that have some bearing on the product. That is, generate ideas using the word as a springboard.

After the brainstorming session, the lead requirements analysts and the client evaluate the ideas. Some of them will be worthless, but they will have served their brainstorming purpose by inspiring other, more practical ideas. Keep the best of the ideas, and providing there is a reasonable chance of implementing them within the project constraints, turn them into requirements.

Some of the ideas may need to be merged with others. In other words, there may be two half-formed ideas that when put together make a fully formed idea. You may also find the inspiration to take some of the brainstormed ideas and turn them into practical requirements.

Some of the ideas might need further investigation. Bring other trawling techniques that we have described in this chapter into play to explore the ideas further.

Mind Maps: a Useful Tool

We use mind maps all the time. We use them for note taking, for planning, for summarizing, for exploring ideas. But let's start at the beginning.

A mind map is a drawing and text combination that attempts to represent information the way that your brain stores it. Our brains store information by making associations. We link each new piece of information to something, or some things, that we already know. The mind map imitates this storage mechanism by using lines to link words and pictures that represent the information. Figure 5.9 shows a mind map on the subject of mind maps.

Mind maps are useful devices for organizing your thoughts as you don't have to write a lot of text. The keywords and links between them are sufficient. Pictures help as they can replace a lot of words, and are more easily remembered than words.

The benefit of mind maps for requirements work is that generally you are being told many aspects of a product that your client would like to have. Many of these aspects are linked, and many are dependent on others. By drawing your interviews in mind map format, you are more likely to see the connections, as well as spot connections that the client has not made, but should be explained to you. Think of the mind map as a more versatile note-taking tool. Versatile, as you can replace all the text it takes to establish connections by drawing a line.

Figure 5.9

A mind map about mind maps. The central area shows the topic, and each of the main limbs shows one of the main concepts connected to this topic. See the 'Concepts' branch for a breakdown of the types of concepts that you might use. Each of the other branches is a concept related to mind maps. The 'Note taking' branch tells you that mind maps are faster at taking notes as you use only the key words. Study this mind map before moving on.

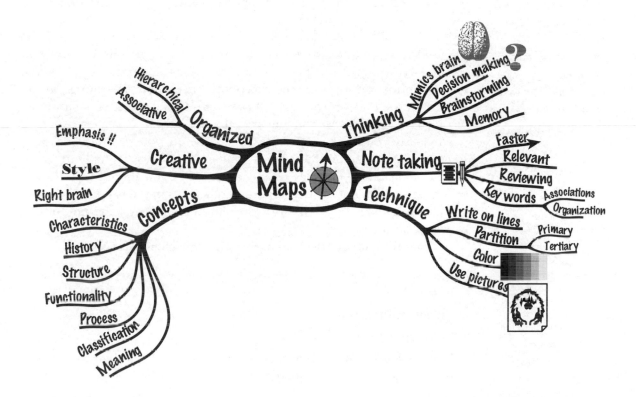

Although mind maps may at first seem a little daunting, be assured it is worth your while to read a little about them, and to experiment by drawing mind maps of conversations, meetings, planning sessions and most importantly, requirements interviews with clients.

Video: the Secret Weapon

Video can be used to co-develop systems. Users and requirements analysts participate in workshops and brainstorms – the proceedings are videotaped. Interviews and on-site observations are also taped. The tapes are used firstly to record, and then confirm, the proceedings. Additionally you can show videotapes to the developers who do not get the opportunity to meet face to face with the users.

Video can be used as an adjunct to interviewing and observing the users in their own workplace. Users have their own way of accomplishing tasks. They have their ways to categorize the information that they use, and ways to solve problems that they have found worked well for them in their own situation. Thus by using video to capture the users at work, you are capturing *their* ways of doing their jobs and their concerns, and not imposing your own expectations and preferences.

Video can also be used in a more structured way. Select a use case and ask the users to work through typical scenarios that they encounter with that activity. As they work, the users describe the special circumstances, the additional information they use, the exceptions, and so on. The shrugs, grimaces, gestures that are normally lost when taking notes are faithfully recorded for later playback and dissection.

Obviously you must ask their permission before you begin to videotape someone. Keep in mind that whoever you are taping will initially freeze in front of the camera, but they usually relax after a few minutes and forget that it is there. Do not ask any important questions in the first five minutes, as the answers may be given for the benefit of the camera, and not for the benefit of accuracy.

We suggest that you try video in the following circumstances:

- Videotape users and developers participating in use case workshops and brainstorms;
- Videotape interviews, on-site observations;
- Videotape the users at work;
- Videotape a business event. Ask the users to work through the typical response to an event, and to describe how they do their jobs.

READING

BUZAN, TONY. *The Mind Map Book*. BBC Books, 1995.

RUSSELL, PETER. *The Brain Book*. Routledge & Kegan Paul, 1979.

Video records help fill in the spaces between the paragraphs of more formal written documentation by retaining off-hand remarks, body language, facial expressions (like raised eyebrows), indications of stress in using the program, the ease of using the keyboard, and so on. Since it retains more information than language, which is simply an abstraction of the information on the tape, it retains the information more faithfully.

Source: DeGrace and Stahl

READING

FRANÇOISE BRUN-COTTAN AND PATRICIA WALL. Using Video to Re-present the User. *Communications of the ACM*, May 1995, vol.38, no.5

DEGRACE, PETER AND LESLIE HULET STAHL. *Wicked Problems, Righteous Solutions – a Catalogue of Modern Software Engineering Paradigms*. Yourdon Press, 1990.

Electronic Requirements

Today's technology provides access to unlimited potential requirements, especially useful when gathering requirements for commercial off-the-shelf software where the users are largely unknown. Using email and web searches you can gather clues for requirements. The problem with using this approach is that it is very easy to become swamped with requirements, many of which will be irrelevant. However, if you use this approach as a type of brainstorming technique – a first attempt to come up with some ideas – it can be very useful. Here are some ideas for putting it into practice.

- Use email to discuss requirements with a group of users. Useful when the users are geographically remote.

- Search the web for references to your domains of interest. This provides papers, contacts and directions for your search for requirements.

- Narrow the search by including the names of your business events and use cases. Searching the web often provides thousands of references. Your business events help you to be more specific about your reason for interest in the domain.

- Design a requirements survey and send it to potential users. If you don't know who the users are or there are too many for you to talk to, then design the survey and send it to representatives of potential users.

- Leave a requirements survey at your web site and ask visitors to give you feedback. Your visitors are interested in your product; ask them to give you feedback so that you can improve it.

- Offer a benefit. Make it worthwhile for someone to fill in your survey, for example, people are often interested in receiving results of the survey. Or make it into a competition where completing the survey makes them eligible for a prize.

Document Archeology

Document archeology is determining the underlying requirements by inspecting the documents and files used by the organization. It is not a complete technique, and should be used in conjunction with other techniques, and with caution. Document archeology is reverse engineering the documents used or produced by the current work. In other words, you are digging new requirements out of the material used by the old work. You are looking for requirements that are to become part of the new product. Obviously not all of the old work is to be carried forward. But where a current system exists, there will always be plenty of material that is grist for your requirements mill (see Figure 5.10).

Figure 5.10

Document archeology starts with you collecting samples of all documents, reports, forms, files, and so on. Gather anything that is used to record or send information, including regular telephone calls. User manuals are rich sources – they describe a way to do work.

Inspect the documents you have collected (for simplicity's sake, the term 'document' will mean anything you have collected) looking for nouns, or 'things'. These can be column headings, named boxes on forms, or simply the name of a piece of data on the document.

For each 'thing' ask:

● What is the purpose of this thing?

● Who uses it, why and what for?

● What are all the uses the system makes of this thing?

● What business events use or reference this thing?

● Can this thing have a value? For example, is it a number or a code or quantity?

● If so, to what collection of things does it belong? (Data modeling enthusiasts will immediately recognize the need to find the entity that owns the attribute.)

● What is that thing used for?

● Does the document contain a repeating group of things?

● If so, what is the collection of things called?

● Can I find a link between things?

● What process makes the connection between them?

● What are the rules attached to each thing? In other words, what piece of business policy covers the thing?

● What processes ensure that these rules are obeyed?

● Which documents give the users the most problems?

These questions will not in themselves reveal all the requirements for the product. They will, however, give you plenty of material and direction for further investigation.

You are looking for capabilities from the current work that are needed for the new product. This does not mean you have carte blanche to replicate the old system. After all, the reason that we are gathering requirements is to build a new product. However, an existing system will have some capabilities in common with its replacement.

But be warned. Because a document is output from a current computer or manual system, it does not mean that it is correct, nor does it mean that it is what is wanted by the client. It could well be that the client wants to get rid of that document as it serves no useful purpose, or could be replaced by something better.

We suggest that you use document archeology as part of your data modeling approach. Most of the above questions are commonly used in the discipline of data modeling. Of course, some of document archeology is used as a foundation for object-oriented development. The current documents, if used cautiously, reveal the classes, or categories of the data. They also reveal the attributes of data stored by the system, and sometimes suggest operations that should be performed on the data.

As a rule, we always keep artifacts – documents, printout, lists, manuals, screens, in fact anything that is printed or displayed – from our interviews because we find we often refer back to them. Make a habit of asking for a copy of any document or screen that is mentioned.

Snow Cards

The Volere Snow Card represents the low-tech approach to requirements gathering. A snow card in shown in Figure 5.11.

In our requirements seminar we place piles of pre-printed snow cards on the students' tables. The students use them to record requirements during the workshops. What surprises us is that although the snow card is a low-tech device, the students remove all the unused ones at the end of the seminar. Later we get emails telling us how much they like using snow cards for the early part of the requirements gathering process.

An architect, William Pena, coined the term 'snow card'. Pena's architectural firm used white cards to record requirements and issues relating to buildings they were designing – hence the term 'snow'. They taped cards containing unresolved issues to the conference room walls, and used this visual display to get a quick impression of the progress of the building.

We use cards when we are interviewing clients and users to record requirements as we hear them. Initially the requirement is not fully formed, so we

Figure 5.11

The Volere snow card. The card is printed with the shell components. It is designed to capture all aspects of a requirement, and is filled in as information becomes available.

Requirement #:	Requirement Type:	Event/use case #:

Description:

Rationale:

Source:
Fit Criterion:

Customer Satisfaction:	Customer Dissatisfaction:
Dependencies:	Conflicts:
Supporting Materials:	
History:	

Volere
Copyright © Atlantic Systems Guild

We were intrigued to see a snow card with an address and postage stamp on the back

Requirements tools are changing constantly. The Internet is the best resource for information on currently available tools and their capabilities

might simply capture the description and the source. As time progresses and the requirements become better understood, the components of the requirement are progressively completed on the card.

The advantage of loose cards is that they can be distributed among analysts. We have several clients who make use of cards in the early stages of requirements gathering. They find it convenient to pin them to walls, to hand them to analysts for further clarification, to mail them to users (we were intrigued to see a snow card with an address and postage stamp on the back) and generally be able to handle a requirement individually.

This low-tech approach is usable in the early stage of requirements gathering. However, you will find that an automated tool will begin to pay dividends as the work progresses and the number of requirements grows. The tool does not have to be elaborate – many of our clients find that a word processor is satisfactory. If you wish to invest in a dedicated requirements tool, then the market place is alive with vendors waiting to sell you an amazing amount of processing capacity. Look about, there is bound to be something that suits your requirements for recording requirements.

Finding the Best Work

So far you have seen a number of techniques that assist you to gather the requirements for the product you intend to build. So what is this product? We have said that the product is intended to help with the work. So let's start by looking at the work. But what work are we interested in? The current work? Your guess at what the future work might be? Are we looking for a technological solution, or a business solution?

The answer is all of these.

The unspoken task of requirements analysis is to determine what the work should be in the future, and how the product can best contribute to that work. Or to put it another way, the requirements analyst's task is to find the best work. The best work is the optimum way that the organization can respond to business events. Business events are usually requests from the outside world for the organization's services. The optimum way for the organization to respond is to provide the most valuable service (from the customer's point of view) at the cheapest cost in time or materials or effort (from the organization's point of view).

Once you know the priorities, then your task shifts to one of inventing the way that the organization will respond to the business event. This means designing the task of the users (if any) and designing how much of the response will be carried out by the product. It includes determining exactly what the product will do to contribute to the best work. Your requirements specification describes this contribution.

> *The unspoken task of requirements analysis is to determine what the work should be in the future*

Refer to Chapter 4, Event-driven Use Cases, for more on how to determine the best product boundary

Summary

Trawling is about gathering requirements. The techniques we have presented here are tools to help you to do something very difficult – to extract precise information from the brain of another human. And this is the crux of it – you have to do this work, there is no tool yet invented that can do it for you.

The tools that we have not covered are those that are attached to either side of your head. Listening is the most important technique in requirements gathering. If you can listen to what your client, your user, and your other stakeholders are saying, and understand what they mean, then the tools we have discussed in this chapter will be useful. On the other hand, if the requirements analyst does not listen, then the probability of specifying the product that the user wants is highly unlikely.

The trawling techniques are communication tools. They will help you to open a dialog with your users, and to provide the feedback that is so essential to good communication. Use them well and watch your requirements come to life.

> ❝ *You have two ears and one mouth. I suggest that you use them in that proportion.* ❞
>
> Source: G.K. Chesterton

6

Functional Requirements

 in which we look at those requirements that are there because of the product's fundamental reason for existence

The functional requirements specify what the product must do. They relate to the actions that the product must carry out in order to satisfy the fundamental reasons for its existence. For example, this is a functional requirement:

> *The product shall determine which road sections pass through areas that are predicted to freeze.*

It describes an action that the product must take if it is to carry out the work for which it is intended.

Chapter 5, Trawling, and Chapter 11, Prototyping and Scenarios

In the previous chapter, we described how to trawl for requirements. The trawling activity and the prototyping activity reveal the functional requirements. See Figure 6.1.

Functional Requirements

Functional requirements are:

- Specifications of the product's functionality;
- Actions the product must take – check, calculate, record, retrieve;
- Derived from the fundamental purpose of the product;
- Not a quality – for example, 'fast' is a quality, and therefore it is a non-functional requirement.

Think of the functional requirements as the business requirements. That is, if you speak with a user or one of the business people, they will describe the

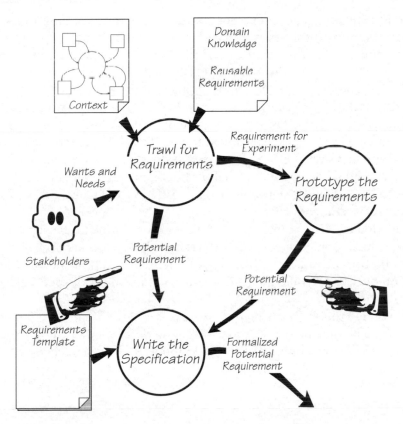

Figure 6.1

The functional requirements are discovered during the trawling and prototyping activities. At this stage they are not necessarily rigorous nor complete. The writing activity formalizes each requirement.

things that the product must do in order to complete some part of their work. Later, when you design solutions for the requirements there will be other technical requirements that you introduce because of the technology used by your solution. Technical requirements are sometimes lumped together with the business requirements and referred to as 'functional' requirements because they refer to functions of the design or the solution. However, it is more accurate and less confusing to separate technical solution requirements from functional business requirements. The functional requirements are a specification of the real work, or business, independent of the way that work will be carried out.

Keep in mind that the requirements specification will become a contract of the product to be built. Thus the functional requirements must fully describe the actions that the intended product can perform. So a requirement for the requirements is that the product's builder be able to use them to construct the product desired by your client.

Technical solution constraints, sometimes referred to as 'system' requirements, are specified either as requirements constraints (section 4 of the template) or as one of the types of non-functional requirement (sections 10–17 of the template)

How to Find Them

Keeping in mind that the functional requirements are things that the product has to do, then you can make use of any other artifact you have that describes the product's actions. For example, the context of the business has been broken into business events, and from these the product's use cases are determined. Each of the use cases is itself described by a scenario – a series of steps that complete the functional tasks of the use case.

Each of the steps in the scenario is a task that the actor describes. In other words, a task is something that the actor identifies as being part of the work of the use case. These tasks, or steps, are described in the actor's language, and thus are probably general and at too high a level to describe the details of the product's capabilities. However, the steps provide a vehicle – a thinking technique – for determining all of the functional requirements that are needed by each of the steps. Figure 6.2 illustrates this gradual breakdown of the use case's functionality.

Let's look at an example of a use case scenario. In the IceBreaker road de-icing system, one of the use cases is 'Produce Road De-icing Schedule'. The actor for this use case is the Truck Depot Engineer. He is the one that triggers the product to schedule the de-icing of the roads in his district. See Figure 6.3.

If you see this from the point of view of the actor, then the product has to carry out some tasks if it is to achieve the outcome desired by the engineer. We suggest that this scenario will produce the desired outcome:

Figure 6.2

Use the idea of use case steps as a way of discovering the functional requirements for a use case. Each of the steps is a task as seen by the actor. The functional requirements are what the product does to fulfill those tasks.

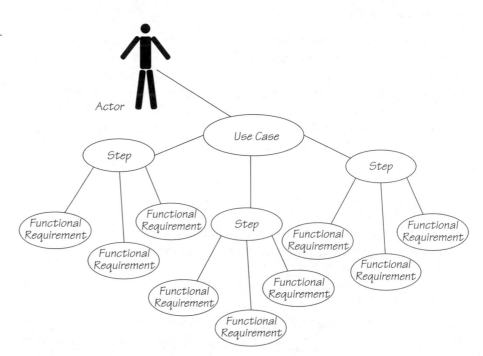

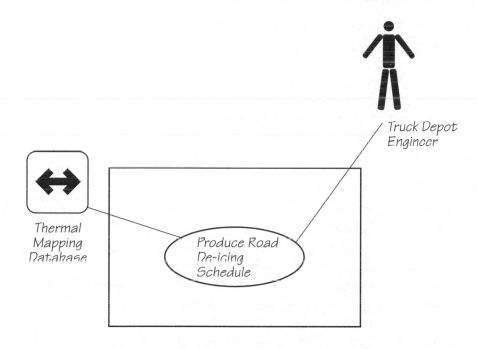

Figure 6.3

When the product produces the road de-icing schedule it has interfaces with two adjacent systems: the actor is the Truck Depot Engineer and the Thermal Mapping Database is a cooperative adjacent system.

- Product accepts a scheduling date and district identifier from the engineer.
- Product fetches the relevant thermal maps.
- Product uses the thermal maps, district temperature readings and weather forecasts to predict temperatures for each part of the district.
- Product determines which roads are likely to freeze and when they are likely to freeze.
- Product schedules available trucks from the depots responsible for the freezing roads.
- Product advises the engineer of the schedule.

The steps in this use case are enough, in general terms, to get the work done. They can be verified with the actor or the client for the product development. There are a limited number of steps in the scenario to avoid the possibility of getting lost in the details, and to keep it all in the user's language.

Once you and your user have agreed the steps, ask 'What does the product have to do in order to complete this step?' For example, the first use case step is:

- Product accepts a scheduling date and district identifier from the engineer.

RULE OF THUMB

Limit the number of use case steps to seven to help avoid getting lost in the details

The first functional requirement is fairly obvious:

> *The product shall accept a scheduling date.*

Now we ask whether there is anything special about the scheduling date and we discover that the scheduling is never done more than two days in advance. This gives us another functional requirement:

> *The product shall warn if the scheduling date is neither today nor within the next two days.*

Another requirement is:

> *The product shall accept a valid district identifier.*

We can discover another requirement if we inquire what is meant by 'valid'. The identifier might be valid in that it is one of the identifiers known by the product, but it must also be valid in that it is the identity of the district intended by the engineer. This leads us to another functional requirement:

> *The product shall confirm that the district selected is the one wanted by the engineer.*

Sometimes a use case step might lead to several requirements, and sometimes it can be represented by one requirement. However, the number of the requirements is not important. The objective is to discover all the requirements you need to build the product that your client is expecting, and that your user needs to do the work.

Let's consider another of the use case steps in our example:

> ● *Product determines which roads are likely to freeze and when they are likely to freeze.*

This one leads us to three more requirements:

> *The product shall determine where in the district it is predicted to freeze.*
> *The product shall determine which road sections pass through areas that are predicted to freeze.*
> *The product shall determine when the road sections will freeze.*

These three requirements are enough to satisfy the step from the use case scenario.

Level of Detail

Note the level of detail. These requirements are business requirements that can be verified by the business people. If you assemble all the requirements for a use case, then they should be enough to describe what the product does to complete the work of the use case. In other words, the user should be able to tell you whether there is enough functionality for the product to be useful, and whether the functionality is correct given the intended outcome of the work.

Later the product designers may add more requirements. These will be the technical requirements, things that are needed to make the technology work. For example, the product interfaces with the thermal map suppliers. This interface, together with any requirements that are needed for the product to work with the supplier's system, will have to be specified.

Note also that the requirements we have identified are not, as yet, measurable and thus testable. Later you will determine a fit criterion for each requirement. The fit criterion is a measurable way of stating the requirement, and is needed for the testers to determine whether the delivered product has indeed met the intention of the user. Fit criteria are harder to determine, and take time. Thus it is advisable for the time being to capture only the intention of the user and thus not interrupt the flow of requirements gathering.

If you are at all bothered by this seemingly casual approach to requirements, then please glance ahead to Chapters 8 Writing the Specification and 9 Fit Criteria and assure yourself that the requirements, in the end, are written so that they are complete, watertight and testable.

Refer to Chapter 8, Writing the Specification, and Chapter 9, Fit Criteria, for details on how to write all the individual components of each requirement, and how to make it testable

Of course, all the time that you are gathering requirements you are trying to spot ambiguity.

Watch out for Ambiguity

Whether your source of requirements is written documents or verbal statements from interviews, you should be on the lookout for ambiguity and the misunderstanding that comes from it. Ambiguity comes from several sources. Firstly, the English language is full of homonyms. The language contains an estimated 500,000 words. These words have been added to the language and used by many different people over a long period of time. This gradual growth has led to different usages and meanings of the same word. Consider the word 'file' used so commonly in information technology. As well as its meaning of an automated storage place for information, it also means a metal instrument for abrading or smoothing; a collection of documents; a row of people as in 'single file'; a slang term for an artful or shrewd person; as well as being a verb meaning to rub away or smooth; and more recently used by lawyers when they file suits. The last word also means the clothing the lawyer wears in court, as well as the set of playing cards such as hearts, diamonds, spades and clubs.

But we not only have to contend with homonyms. If the context is not clear then it may also cause ambiguity. For example, if we have a requirement such as:

The product shall show the weather for the next twenty-four hours.

The meaning here depends on the type of requirement, and what is near it in the specification. Does it mean that the product is to communicate the weather that is expected to happen in the forthcoming 24 hours, or must it communicate some unspecified weather and continue to do so until a day has elapsed?

The use case will, to some extent, reduce ambiguity. For example, if we consider the requirement:

The product shall show all roads predicted to freeze.

Does the 'all' refer to every road known to the product? Or just those being examined by the user? If the use case scenario tells us that the user/actor has previously identified a district, or section of the district, then we may safely say that 'all' refers to the geographical area selected. When it is written, the fit criterion for this requirement will clarify the meaning of 'all'. And we certainly should not waste our user's time by laboriously qualifying every word of the requirement. Anything has the potential to be ambiguous. The key is to identify when it is reasonable to take the risk of ambiguity, and continually minimize that risk by clarifying the context.

The meaning of a requirement is dependent on its context. We loved the example erected by the city traffic authority in New York some years ago when they introduced red zones. These were sections of streets where the authorities were particularly anxious that traffic was not impeded. The zones were designated by red-painted curbs, and adorned by signs that read:

No Parking
No Stopping
No Kidding

Although the last directive is ambiguous the traffic authority made a reasonable judgment in taking the ambiguity risk. They decided that no driver was foolish enough to think the authority intended that drivers should not make jokes in their cars. The authority made a reasonable assessment of how the majority of drivers would interpret the sign.

Similarly, when one of the engineers says, 'We want to have the trucks treat the roads before they freeze', it is fairly clear that he does not mean that the roads have to be treated before the trucks freeze. At least, the context in which it was said should indicate the meaning.

Record the meaning of each word used by the project in section 5 of the requirements specification. This gives you a start at eliminating ambiguity.

Next, eliminate all pronouns from your requirements and replace them with the subject or object to which the pronouns refer. (Note the difference if we had said 'they' instead of 'the pronouns' towards the end of the preceding sentence.)

Write each requirement. Read it aloud. If possible, have a colleague read it aloud. Confirm with your user that you both understand the same meaning for the requirement. This may seem obvious, but 'send the bill to the customer' may mean that it goes to the person who actually bought the goods, or it may mean that the bill is sent to the account holder. It is also unclear as to whether the bill is sent immediately after the purchase or at the end of the month. A short conversation with the user/client will clarify the real intentions.

Also, keep in mind that you are writing a description of the requirement. The real requirement is revealed when you write the fit criterion. Until then, a good description is sufficient.

FOOTNOTE: Is there no end to ambiguity? Mike Russell pointed out that the sign also was not intended to mean 'No birthing of goats'.

PUTTING THIS TO WORK

Summary

The functional requirements describe the product's actions. As such they should form a complete, and as far as possible unambiguous description of the product's functionality.

The functional requirements are derived from the product use cases. The easiest way of doing this is to write a scenario that breaks the use case into a series of steps. Examine each of the steps and derive its functional requirements.

When you have enough functional requirements to complete the work of the use case, it is time to move to the next use case. As you progress you will discover that a requirement that you defined for one use case will also apply to other use cases. Then you can 'reuse' the work you have done by cross-referencing each requirement to all relevant use cases. When all the use cases have been treated this way, then you have defined the requirements that specify the functionality of the product.

7 Non-functional Requirements

 in which we look at those requirements that your product must have in order to do what it must do

Non-functional requirements are the properties that your product must have. Think of these properties as the characteristics or qualities that make the product attractive, or usable, or fast, or reliable. For example, you may want your product to respond within a specified time, or make calculations within given accuracy limits. Similarly, you may want your product to have a particular appearance, or be used by non-readers, or adhere to laws applicable to your kind of business.

These properties are not required because they are fundamental activities of the product – activities such as computations, manipulating data, and so on – but are there because the client wants the fundamental activities to perform in a certain manner.

Let's look at an example. One of the fundamental activities of the Ice-Breaker product is to record the road temperatures and moisture levels when this data is transmitted by the weather stations. Recording data is a functional requirement. Now let us say that data has to be recorded within half a second, and that once recorded, nobody except a supervising engineer is allowed to alter it. These are performance and security requirements. They are not part of the fundamental reason for the product's existence, but are needed to make the product perform in the desired manner. These are the product's non-functional requirements.

Non-functional requirements do not alter the product's functionality. That is, the functional requirements remain the same no matter what properties you attach to them. The non-functional requirements add functionality to the product – it takes some amount of processing to make a product easy to use, or secure, or interactive. However, the reason that this function-

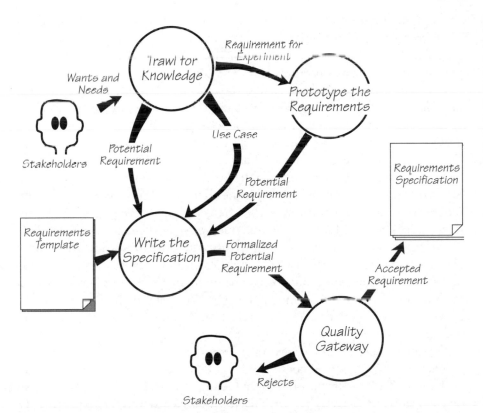

Figure 7.1

The non-functional requirements are discovered during trawling and prototyping. The writing activity formalizes the requirements. This chapter covers both of these activities.

ality is part of the product is to give it the desired characteristics. So you might think of the functional requirements as those that do the work, and the non-functional requirements as those that give character to the work.

Non-functional requirements make up a significant part of the specification (see Figure 7.1). They are important as the client and user may well judge the product on its non-functional properties. Provided the product meets its required amount of functionality, the non-functional properties – how usable, convenient, inviting and secure it is – may be the difference between an accepted, well-liked product, and an unused one.

The Non-functional Requirements

A use case describes an amount of work from the user's point of view. The functional requirements describe the actions with which the work is concerned. The non-functional requirements describe the experience that the user has while he does the work. In other words, the non-functional requirements are the characteristics of the work that are represented by the use case

A useful mental model is that functional requirements are characterized by verbs and non-functional requirements are characterized by adjectives

or the functional requirements. A useful mental model is that functional requirements are characterized by verbs and non-functional requirements are characterized by adjectives. Figure 7.2 illustrates how each piece of functionality has associated non-functional requirements.

Every product has a character that separates it from other products. You may have bought your hi-fi system because it has a different feel, or is easier to use than another. You may prefer the look and feel of one personal computer to another. You might have bought your electric toaster not because it makes the toast taste any different, but because you thought that the experience of using it would be better than the other toasters on display at the store. This experience, or look, or usability is the character of the product. The non-functional requirements describe the character, or the way that functions behave. So what non-functional requirements do you need for your product?

We have examined a large number of requirements specifications and extracted a list of the most useful properties for products to have. We came up with eight major non-functional requirement types, and within those, several sub-types or variations on the type. We have included these non-functional requirements in the template, and given each of the types an identifying number. The numbers that we are using in this chapter are the requirement types as they appear in the template.

There is nothing sacred about the type identifier, nor the categories that we have assigned to the non-functional requirements. Feel free to make your own categories. However, it does make it a lot easier to find the requirements if you have a classification system. If you know that there are different types of requirement, then you can use the types as a checklist, and ask questions about each of the different types of requirements.

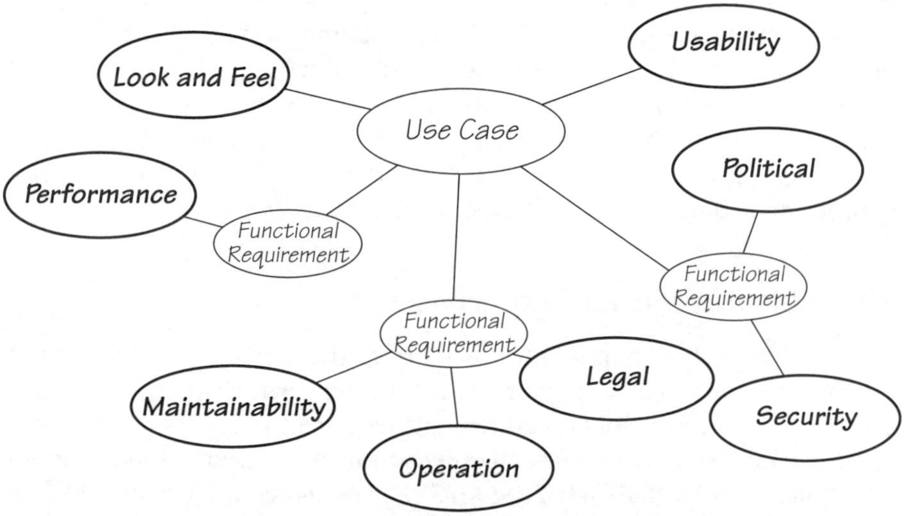

Appendix B, the Volere Requirements Specification Template

Figure 7.2

The non-functional requirements are properties that the functionality must have. The functionality can be represented either by a use case or a functional requirement – in this example, the use case has three functional requirements. The use case as a whole has to meet certain Usability and Look and Feel requirements. One of the functional requirements in this example has three associated non-functional requirements which specify that it must be maintainable to a desired standard, work correctly in a given operational environment and comply with given laws.

The non-functional requirement types that we use, and their type identifiers are:

10   Look and Feel Requirements – *the spirit of the product's appearance.*

11   Usability Requirements – *the product's ease of use, and any special usability considerations.*

12   Performance Requirements – *how fast, how safe, how many, how accurate the functionality must be.*

13   Operational Requirements – *the operating environment of the product, and what considerations must be made for this environment.*

14   Maintainability and Portability Requirements – *expected changes, and the time allowed to make them.*

15   Security Requirements – *the security and confidentiality of the product.*

16   Cultural and Political Requirements – *special requirements that come about because of the people involved in the product's development and operation.*

17   Legal Requirements – *what laws and standards apply to the product.*

Let's look at each of these in more detail. In some cases, the nature of the non-functional requirement will suggest to you how you might go about finding any requirements of that type that apply to your product. If nothing suggests itself, there will be a discussion later in the chapter on how you can go about eliciting all the non-functional requirements.

Keep in mind as you read though these requirement types that sometimes it is difficult to say exactly what type a requirement is. When this happens it is often an indication that you have several requirements posturing as one. Identification of the type is not the thing that really matters. What matters is that you identify all the requirements. The requirement type is a device to help you to find the requirements; you can think of it as a checklist. Later, when you add a fit criterion to the requirement, you make the requirement testable, and then the type becomes less important.

The requirement type is a device to help you to find the requirements; you can think of it as a checklist

Look and Feel Requirements – Type 10

The look and feel requirements describe the intended spirit of the product's appearance. Please note that the look and feel requirements are not the detailed design of an interface. While you might include some sketches of ideas, the intention is not to commit yourself to a design. The requirement is to specify the *intention* of the appearance.

For example, suppose you have a look and feel requirement like this:

> *Description: The product shall provide a graphic and colorful view of all the roads in a district.*

Note that this requirement does not commit the designer to displaying a map on a screen, but it does require that the designer provides some graphic view of roads, and that color should be used to enhance the information about the roads. Later, when we design the product, we consider whether a map on a screen, printed charts, holographic displays on clear panels, or any other alternatives will be the best way to implement this requirement.

Remember that this is only the *description* of the requirement. There is no way that a designer could know if an intended design for the product satisfies a requirement as loosely worded as this. For example, how much color should be used before the client considers it to be 'colorful'? How many pictures and symbols should be used before it is thought to be 'graphic'? We cannot tell without measurements for 'colorful' and 'graphic'.

The measurement of a requirement is its fit criterion. We will discuss fit criteria in depth in Chapter 9, but for the moment we ask you to accept that it is possible to measure such things as 'colorful' and 'graphic'. By adding this measurement, and agreeing it with the client, the designer and builder of the product can know precisely what it is they have to do to satisfy the client. In the same way, the fit criteria are the benchmarks that the product can be tested against.

For the moment, we will just write the descriptions of the non-functional requirements.

Consider the look and feel requirements that you might build into your next product. For example, among other appearances that might be appropriate for your product, you might want it to be:

● Highly readable,

● Apparently simple to use,

● Approachable, so that people do not hesitate to use it,

● Authoritative, so that users rely on it and trust it,

● Conforming to the client's other products,

● Colorful and attractive to children,

● Unobtrusive so that people are not aware of it,

● Innovative and appearing to be state of the art,

● Professional or executive looking,

● Exciting,

● Interactive.

Figure 7.3

The product's look and feel makes it attractive to the intended user.

Look and feel requirements are becoming more and more important as automated and software products move into consumer-oriented areas. Sophisticated products such as cameras, video cameras, personal organizers, and so on must appear to the intended customer to be relatively simple to operate, and yet carry a high degree of functionality.

Developers of products intended for the World Wide Web should place a great deal of emphasis on their look and feel. Your client has in mind the kind of experience he wants visitors to the site to have. Your task is to determine these requirements and to specify them with look and feel requirement descriptions like:

> The product shall be conservative.
> The product shall appear authoritative.
> The product shall be colorful.
> The product shall be attractive to a teenage audience.
> The product shall appear artistic.
> The product shall appear state of the art.
> The product shall have an expensive appearance.

You might be tempted to describe the required look and feel using a prototype. However, consider that the prototype does not express the requirement, but the result of the requirement. For example, suppose that your client asked for a product 'in the company colors'. While the prototype may be in the required colors, there is nothing about a prototype to tell the designer that the color is important. If he chooses to use different colors, or a different mix of colors, as well he might, then the requirement for 'company colors' will not be met. Thus it is important to write the requirement specifically, and not leave it to someone's interpretation of a prototype. The role of the prototype is to simulate possibilities to help you to discover and specify what the users' real requirements are.

If you know that your product is to be implemented using software, then some of your look and feel requirements can be described by citing the appropriate interface standards.

> *The product shall comply with the [Apple Platinum / Windows NT/ Motif / etc.] guidelines.*

And one requirement that you should consider is:

> *The product shall conform to the established look and feel of the organization's products.*

And we repeat, be careful not to design the interface – you do not yet know the complete requirements of the product. Designing is the task of the product's designers, once they know the requirements.

Usability Requirements – Type 11

Usability requirements describe the appropriate levels of usability, given the intended users of the product. Firstly, go to section 3 of your specification – the Users of the Product, and look at the descriptions of the users that you wrote and the classifications of their skill levels. What kind of people are they? What kind of product do they need to do their jobs? What kind of usability requirements will make a successful product for them? See Figure 7.4.

The usability of a product has an effect on productivity, error rates, and acceptance of the new product. Carefully consider what your client is trying to achieve with the product before writing the usability requirements.

For example, you might have a usability requirement:

> *The product shall be easy to use.*

This requirement may seem at first vague and idealistic, but remember that you will add a fit criterion that states how you will qualify 'easy to use' for your users. You could of course make the requirement more obvious by saying:

> *The product shall be easy to use by members of the public who may have only one hand free.*

Figure 7.4

Consider your intended
audience when writing
the usability
requirements.

or for a different user group:

> *The product shall be easy to use by graduate mechanical engineers.*

This captures the intention of your client, and for the moment, it is sufficient. However, a designer would be hard pressed to understand exactly what product to build, so later you will have to add a measurement such that the designer and the client have the identical understanding of 'easy to use'. We will discuss such measurements in Chapter 9 Fit Criteria. In the meantime, imagine how you would quantify the requirement that a product be 'easy to use'.

'Easy to use' and 'easy to learn' are slightly different. Easy to use products are designed to facilitate an ongoing efficiency. This may mean that there is some training to be done before using the product. For example, if you were specifying a product to be used in an office by office workers, you would be well advised to make it easy to use. Even if this means training people to use the product, the ongoing efficiency pays for this many times over.

Adobe Photoshop is a case in point. Photoshop is a complex product that offers an amazing wealth of utility for the manipulation of digital images. The

Photoshop learning curve is a steep one – there is lot to be learned and we would venture to say that it is not easy to learn. However, once learned, the features make manipulating images a straightforward, you might even say easy, task. Given the depth of functionality needed to do the task and the inherent complexity of the task, Adobe have made their product easy to use once you know how.

Easy to learn products are aimed at those tasks that are done infrequently, and thus may be forgotten between uses: for example, rarely used features of a software product, yearly reports and so on. Products that are used by the public – and thus no prior training is feasible – should also be easy to learn. For example, telephones in public places or dispensing machines.

You may describe your requirement as:

> *Description: The product shall be easy to learn.*

Or you may write:

> *Description: The product shall be able to be used by a member of the public without training.*

This may at first seem to fall into the 'Don't run with scissors' category of advice. However, it is a requirement – your client wants the product to be easy to learn. Later, when you add the fit criterion, you quantify 'easy to learn'. A suitable fit criterion might be:

> *Fit Criterion: 90% of a panel representative of the general public shall successfully purchase a ticket from the product on their first encounter.*

We had a client who wanted the product to be 'friendly'. We could think of no suitable measurement for 'friendly', so felt, naturally enough, that we could not write 'friendly' as a requirement. However, a little questioning revealed that the product he had in mind would appeal to the personnel consultants who were to use it. He knew that the consultants would be able to be more productive if they used the product, but he also knew that they would not use it, or would use it badly, if they didn't like it.

So now the requirements began to look like:

> *The personnel consultants shall like the product.*

We suggested to the client that we could evaluate whether or not we had met this requirement by measuring the number of consultants who, after an initial training period, preferred to work with the product rather than their old way. The client agreed with this – he told us that he would be satisfied if 75% of the consultants were using the product after a six-week familiarization period. He would use an anonymous survey to poll the consultants.

Thus we had our usability requirement:

> *Description: The product shall provide a preferred way of working for its users.*

and the fit criterion:

> *Fit Criterion: 75% of the consultants shall regularly use the product after a six-week familiarization period.*

Usability requirements can also cover:

● Rate of acceptance by the users;

● Productivity gained as a result of the product's introduction;

● Error rates (or reduction thereof);

● Being used by people who do not speak English (or the language of the country where the product is used);

● Accessibility to handicapped people;

and do not forget:

● Being used by people with no previous experience with computers.

The usability requirements are derived from a combination of what your client is trying to achieve with the usability of the product, and what the users expect. The characteristics of the users make a difference to their expectations. You as the requirements analyst have to discover these characteristics, and determine what levels of usability will make the product a pleasant and useful experience for them. Pay attention to usability, it often makes the difference between competing products.

Performance Requirements – Type 12

Performance requirements are written when there is a need for the product, among other things, to perform some tasks in a given amount of time, or for some tasks to be done to a specific level of accuracy.

The need for speed should be genuine. All too often we want things to be done quickly without there being a real reason for speed. If a task is to produce a monthly summary report, then there may be no need to do it quickly.

On the other hand, the success of the product may depend on speed.

> *The product shall identify an aircraft within 0.25 seconds.*

Capacity is a performance requirement. For example, the client for the IceBreaker product wanted to sell it to road authorities around the world. These authorities are responsible for varying sizes of geographical areas, and the client needed to ensure that the product could handle the largest area of any potential client. Initially we would have written the requirement as:

> *The product shall accommodate the largest geographical area of any road authority in the world.*

However, this is not a practical requirement to hand on to a designer, so eventually we refined it to:

> *The product shall have the capacity to manipulate 9000 roads, each having ten sections.*

When you are thinking about performance requirements, consider such aspects as:

- Speed to complete a task,
- Accuracy of the results,
- Safety to the operator,
- Volumes to be held by the product,
- Ranges of allowable values,
- Throughput such as the rate of transactions,
- Efficiency of resource usage,
- Reliability – usually expressed as mean time between failures,
- Availability – up time or time periods that users may access the product,
- Expandability of most of the above.

Performance requirements also cover the risk of damage to people or property. If your product is a lawn mower, then there is a genuine need for the product to avoid cutting off the user's toes. And Isaac Asimov included this in his laws of robotics:

> *A robot shall not injure a human being.*

Hardware is not the only thing to cause damage. You should consider whether your software product could cause damage, either directly or indirectly. The IceBreaker product schedules trucks to spread de-icing materials on roads. Environmental damage from this material can be serious, and thus the requirement states:

> The product shall schedule such that the minimum necessary amounts of de-icing material are spread on roads.

In some cases, you may want to specify a performance requirement for the *outcome* of a use case. This is not common, but it is worthwhile considering the effect that the product may have. We found this performance-related requirement:

> The product shall schedule such that the rescheduled de-icing truck is estimated to arrive at the breakdown location within 30 minutes of breakdown notification.

The performance requirements come mainly from the operating environment. Each environment has its own set of circumstances and conditions. The people, machines, devices, environmental conditions and so on, all place demands on the product. The way that your product responds to these conditions – how fast it has to be, how strong, how big, how often – are the appropriate performance requirements.

Operational Requirements – Type 13

Operational requirements describe the environment in which the product is to be used. In some cases this environment creates special circumstances that have an effect on the way the product must be constructed.

> The product shall be used in and around trucks, operating at freezing temperatures, at night. It is most likely to be raining or snowing. Salt and water are expected to come into contact with the product. Lighting will be poor. The user will be wearing gloves.

Consider the outcome if the above requirement had not been written.

Not all products have such an extreme environment – a lot of products are written for personal computers or workstations that are situated in offices with an uninterruptible power supply. But the seemingly simple environment may be more demanding than it first appears (see Figure 7.5).

Figure 7.5

Will the product work in
its intended operating
environment?

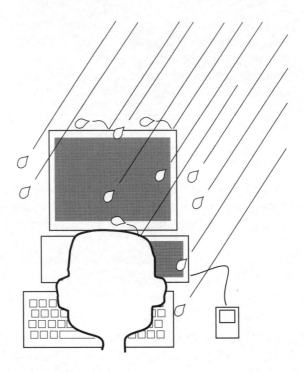

Chapter 4, Event-driven
Use Cases

Consider if the product has to collaborate with partner products, or access outside databases, or other systems that supply information. (These show up as actors on the product use case diagram.)

> *The product shall interface with the Thermal Mapping Database.*

You may have to describe the physical environment affecting the users when they use the product. This often means that there are special constraints on the way that the product is constructed. For example, if the product is to be used by people in wheelchairs, or people sitting in an aircraft seat, then you must specify it.

Operational requirements can cover:

● Operating environment,

● Condition of the users – are they in the dark, in a hurry, and so on,

● Partner or collaborating systems,

● Portable products.

Portable devices have their own special set of requirements. There is a need to specify if the product, or parts of it, is to be carried about. For example:

> *The product shall survive being dropped.*
> *The product shall be used in variable lighting conditions.*
> *The product shall conserve battery life.*

To find the operational requirements, look at the product boundary defined on the use case diagram and consider the needs of each of the adjacent systems, or actors. If necessary, interview the representative of each of them to find the requirements that result from the way that they go about their product-related work.

Maintainability Requirements – Type 14

Usually at requirements time you do not know the precise amount of maintenance that your product will undergo in its lifetime. Nor do you always know the type of maintenance that it will need. However, products are built where the types of maintenance can, to some extent, be foreseen. Consider if there are any expected changes to the:

● Organization

● Environment

● Laws that apply to the product

● Business rules

or other factors that may affect your product. If you know, or strongly suspect that the product will undergo relatively heavy maintenance due to expected changes, then you should specify the types of expected changes, and the amount of time allowed for those changes.

If the product is a software product, and you desire that it run on several different types of computer, then specify it.

> *The product shall be readily portable to the Linux operating system.*

Keep in mind that the requirements document is a contract to build. You are saying to the builder that you want to be able to port the product to another platform some time in the future, and that you will hold him accountable for the ability of the product to be adapted to a new machine. When you attach the fit criteria to this requirement you will specify the characteristics of the machine and the expected time or effort necessary to make the transition.

The IceBreaker product had this requirement:

> *The product shall be translated into various foreign languages. As yet, the languages are unknown.*

This requirement had a big effect on the product's designers. They designed the interface in such a way as to make it easy to add new languages. Naturally, they took into account the fact that different languages sometimes mean different cultures, and different ways of presenting data.

Security Requirements – Type 15

READING

PFLEEGER, SHARI LAWRENCE. A Framework for Security Requirements. *Computers and Security*, 1991, vol. 10, no. 6, pp.515–23.

Security is perhaps the most difficult of the requirement types, and potentially the one posing the greatest risk if it is not correct. When you are writing security requirements, consider the nature of security as it is applied to software, and allied products. Shari Lawrence Pfleeger in her 'Framework for Security Requirements' points out that security can be thought of as having three aspects:

- Confidentiality – data stored by the product is protected from unauthorized access and disclosure.
- Integrity – the product's data are the same as the source, or authority, of the data.
- Availability – the product's data and functionality are accessible to authorized users, and can be produced in a timely manner.

Confidentiality

The confidentiality aspect of security means that the data is not available to anyone except authorized users. You can achieve this by locking the product in a safe. But, if you want people to use it, then you have to provide a key to open the safe, and some way of controlling who or what is allowed to use the key. Locking our products away in safes is not all that practical, so we tend to use software 'locks' that have the same effect. That is, they prevent anybody except keyholders (the authorized users) access to the data.

When you write this kind of requirement, you are in fact specifying the allowable access – who is authorized, under what circumstances authorization is valid, what data and what functions are allowed to each authorized user.

> *The product shall ensure that the [name of] data (or function) can be accessed only by authorized users.*
> *The product shall distinguish between authorized and non-authorized users.*

The term 'authorized' may also need some explaining. For example, are all authorized users authorized all the time? Does access depend on time of day or location of the user at the time of access? Must a user collaborate with another authorized user to gain access? In other words, is the authorization conditional? If so, write these conditions as a requirement.

It may also be worth considering:

> *The product shall deliver data in a manner that prevents further, or second-hand use by unauthorized people.*

Availability

Availability means that authorized users are not prevented from accessing the data, and the security devices employed do not hinder or delay the users from getting what they want when they want it.

Availability also means that the data is, well, available. That is, it is not made unavailable by being archived off-site, or due to some malfunction. Thus you must consider requirements for prevention of the loss of data, and the recovery of lost data.

This begins to overlap with the Integrity topic, so let's jump straight to there.

Integrity

Integrity means that the data held by the product corresponds to the data as it was delivered to the product from an adjacent system (the authority for the data). Weather stations send data about temperature, precipitation and so on to the IceBreaker product. The weather station originates the data, and thus is the authority for the data. Any copies of this data, such as those held by IceBreaker, must be faithful to the weather station's version. The integrity requirement for the IceBreaker product is:

> *The product shall ensure that the weather data corresponds to the data transmitted by the weather station.*

This may at first seem obvious, but there are several other allied integrity requirements that you should consider:

- Integrity checks to prevent unintentional misuse by authorized users. This is, unfortunately, the most common form of data corruption.
- Audits to detect improper usage, either by authorized or non-authorized users.

● Proof of the integrity of the product after some abnormal happening, such as a power failure, an exceptional operating condition or unusual environmental conditions such as fire or flood.

You can also consider normal auditing as part of the security section of your specification. Most accounting products have a requirement to be audited. Not necessarily to prevent fraud or misuse, but to ensure that no mistakes were made, and that the results shown by the product are indeed correct. Audit requirements are often written to require that the product include an audit trail. The precise nature of your audit requirements must be negotiated with your own auditors. (This last paragraph is a subtle reminder to include the auditors as stakeholders in your project.)

... And No More

READING

CHUCK PFLEEGER. The fundamentals of information security. *IEEE Software,* January/February 1997

Consider the effect of adding '... and no more' to all of your requirements. This means that the product must do no more than the requirement specifies. For example, if the requirement is to find a name and address from a file, the product must not delete the name and address after finding it.

Consider this access requirement:

> *The product shall allow access to authorized users.*

the 'and no more' heuristic gives you a complementary requirement:

> *The product shall ensure that nobody but authorized users are able to gain access.*

For security reasons, you might consider adding an overriding requirement to your specification that says:

> *The product shall not do anything except that which has been specified as a requirement.*

Sometimes well-meaning product builders make the product perform faster or bigger, or add features that are not specified. While these properties may be beneficial to a part of the product, they may well have a detrimental effect on the product as a whole. We urge you to ensure that your development team does not build extra features of properties into your products without first negotiating their inclusion into the specification.

Security is important, and should be given a priority in relation to the value of misusing the product. For example, if your product is for a bank, or processes credit card or financial trading transactions, then the value of misuse (in financial terms) is very high. Similarly, if your product is intended for military use, then misuse may result in loss of life (perhaps even your own) or loss of a military advantage. Thus for financial, military or life-support products, security has a higher priority, and consumes more of the budget, than for many commercial systems.

You should consider calling in a security expert. Software developers are not usually trained in security, and the security of some functionality and data is so important, that the security requirements are best written by experts.

READING

PFLEEGER, CHARLES. *Security in Computing.* Prentice-Hall, 1997.

Cultural and Political Requirements – Type 16

Cultural and political requirements are special factors that would make the product unacceptable because of human customs, preferences or prejudices. These requirements can originate with almost any aspect of human behavior. The main reason for cultural requirements comes when we try and sell a product into a different country, particularly when their culture and language is very different from our own.

The first time we went to Italy, looking forward to experiencing the lively Italian atmosphere, we found an elegant, stainless steel coffee bar – the sort of place full of beautifully dressed people all talking at once. We went to the bar and ordered two cappuccini and two pastries. The barman gave us a lengthy explanation in Italian, shook his head and pointed to the cashier. Thus we discovered a cultural requirement. In Italian coffee bars it is normal firstly to go to the cashier and pay, then to go to the bar, to hand over your receipt and make your order (Figure 7.6). At the risk of being deprived of cappuccino we soon learnt to fit into the culture.

Figure 7.6

Sometimes cultural requirements are not immediately obvious.

If your reaction is 'Why on earth do they do it like that' then it is an indicator that you have discovered a cultural requirement

Discovering cultural requirements is difficult because they are often unexpected and at first glance sometimes appear to be irrational because they are outside your own culture. If your reaction is 'Why on earth do they do it like that' then it is an indicator that you have discovered a cultural requirement. Another technique you can use is to consider each requirement and ask yourself 'Is there anything about this requirement that is here purely because of my own culture?' We find that the best way to find cultural requirements is to have the help of someone from that culture.

If you are building a product for a number of different professions then it is likely that you will discover that they have different cultural requirements. For example, the advertising profession has a culture that is very aware of the latest design trends and this might spawn some special cultural requirements about using the most fashionable colors. On the other hand, these requirements might be irrelevant to the banking profession because their culture is different.

There are also requirements that come about for pure political reasons. These requirements are the ones for which it is usually impossible to write a coherent rationale. Why is this requirement important to the goals of this project – 'because I say so'. While we do not encourage this type of requirement, we accept that they exist and we are pragmatic enough to write them. Later activities, such as the Quality Gateway and estimating their cost, or simply making them visible might eliminate them.

Following are some items that you might consider cultural or political:

- Acceptable solutions – for example, should all components be made in [insert the name of a country you admire]?
- Unacceptable solutions – the product must include no products built by [insert name of a company that you dislike].
- Differentiating from existing products or work styles – the client may want any new product to look different from the existing products because he feels that it will have a beneficial effect on the workforce.
- Politics – a requirement with no justification other than 'I want it'.
- Religious observances.
- Political correctness – the product must not use terminology or icons that someone, somewhere on the planet might possibly take offense to.
- Spelling – Americans and British cannot understand why each other spells so strangely.

The more we build products for use in different walks of life, by different professions in different countries, the more we need to consider cultural requirements. Classifying a requirement as cultural or political requires a mixture of courage and creative thinking. Courage, because it often requires some probing personal questions to quantify these requirements. Creative, because it takes imagination to recognize something different from one's own culture. However, we find that if a requirement's reason for existence is not covered by one of the regular requirement types, then highlighting it as cultural/political is a good way to make sure you trap the requirement.

Legal Requirements – Type 17

The cost of litigation is one of the major risks for commercial software, and can be expensive for other kinds of software. You must make yourself aware of the laws that apply to your kind of product, and write requirements for the product to comply with these laws. Even if you are building software for use inside your own organization, be aware that there are laws applying to the workplace that may be relevant.

Start with your company's lawyers. They have far more experience with the law than you have. There are several things that you can do to facilitate compliance:

- Examine adjacent systems or actors. These are the entities that have contact with your product.

- Consider their legal requirements and rights. For example, are any of the disabled access laws applicable? Does the adjacent system have any rights to privacy of the data that you hold? Do you need proof of transaction? Or non-disclosure of the information your product has about the adjacent system?

- Are there any laws that are relevant to this product (or to the use case or the requirement)? For example, data protection, privacy laws, guarantees, consumer protection, consumer credit, right to information, and so on.

Adjacent systems and actors are defined in Chapters 3 and 4

A legal requirement is written like this:

> *The product shall comply with the [name of law].*

Once again, you will need help from your lawyers to know which law is applicable. The law itself may also make its own requirements. For example, automated products built for drug development use by the pharmaceutical industry must be self-documenting. The precise nature of this self-documentation varies. But it means that you (or somebody writing requirements for these applications) have to understand that these legal requirements exist and write them into your specification.

Similarly, some laws require products to display messages. This is a requirement for car batteries in some countries:

> *The product shall display the message 'Warning – do not drink the contents'.*

Similarly, you may be required to acknowledge copyright. If your product includes other products then it must acknowledge that by displaying the appropriate copyright notices.

Standards

Legal requirements are not limited to the law of the land. Some products must comply with standards. For example:

> *The product shall comply with our ISO 9000 Certification.*

Now that we have considered the content of the non-functional requirements, let's look at how we find them.

Finding the Non-functional Requirements

PUTTING THIS TO WORK

Like all requirements, the non-functional ones can come to light at any time. However, there are places that we can look that give us better opportunities to discover them.

Non-functional requirements may be uncovered by the functional requirements. For each functional requirement we can ask 'What properties or qualities must this piece of functionality have?' For example, let us suppose that there is a functional requirement:

> *The product must record changes to the road topography.*

Ask what non-functional requirements need be attached to it. The non-functional requirement types that we use are:

- Look and Feel
- Usability
- Performance
- Operational
- Maintainability
- Security
- Cultural and Political
- Legal.

Go down the list. Which ones are applicable? Some of the requirements that we came up with were these:

> The product shall have the appearance of a company product.
>
> The product shall be usable by road engineers.
>
> The product shall be able to calculate the changed road topography in less than 1.5 seconds.
>
> The product's functions that change the road topography shall only be accessible by users who are road engineers.
>
> The product shall keep an audit trail of all roads that are scheduled for treatment, and a record of their having been treated.

... and so on. It pays to keep the checklist of non-functional requirement types when interviewing your users, and at least for each use case, go through the list probing for examples of each type. Be aware that there is more to the non-functional requirements than a short checklist. Refer to the template for more explanation, and examples, of the non-functional requirements.

Non-functional requirements may apply to a use case in its entirety. For example, the usability of the use case called 'Schedule De-icing Truck' must be consistent for all of the functionality of the use case, and thus a single usability requirement applies to the use case. This makes sense, as there is only one type of user for the use case.

A suggested process for deriving the non-functional requirements is shown in Figure 7.7.

Prototypes can be used to drive out the non-functional requirements. Prototyping gives potential users the opportunity to try out the functions and thus the requirements gatherer can observe the way that the user thinks of the functionality. This leads to determining non-functional requirements such as usability, look and feel, security, and so on.

The client for the product may also have expectations that are relevant here. In many cases, the reason for building a new product is to provide a service to the users, or the customers of the business, and that service is dependent on one or more of the non-functional qualities. For example, providing portable, or highly usable, or secure functionality may be crucial to the development effort. Alternatively, your client may tell you that if you cannot provide an interactive and graphic display of the current trading position, then he does not want the product. Thus your client becomes the prime source of the critical non-functional requirements.

Once the functional requirements are met, it may be the non-functional qualities that make a potential customer buy your product. Consider the non-functional properties of products that you admire, or you have bought.

Figure 7.7

A process for finding non-functional requirements. For each functional requirement or use case, consider the factor in the first column. When you have an adequate knowledge of the factor, then question it about the requirement types in the second column.

For a use case or a functional requirement:

Who or what is/are...	*Do they or does it have these requirements?*
The users (3)	● *Look and feel (10)* ● *Usability – special considerations for this kind of user (11)* ● *Security (15)* ● *Cultural/political (16)*
The operating environment (4, 6, 7, 8)	● *Operational – particularly collaborating products (13)* ● *Performance – demands made by the environment (12)* ● *Maintenance – consider changes proposed for the environment (14)*
The client, customer (2)	● *Political/cultural (16)*
The adjacent systems (8)	● *Legal – special rights (17)* ● *Operational (13)* ● *Performance (12)*

(Numbers refer to sections in the template)

Then ask your client to what degree these are relevant to the product that you are specifying. Your client, or the marketing department, is the source of what will make customers buy the product. Make use of them.

Don't Write a Solution

Don't presuppose a design solution, or enforce a solution, by the way that you write your requirement. By the same token, don't adopt a current solution to a problem and write that as the requirement. For example, if you write

The product shall ask for a password when data is accessed.

then the product has a requirement to use passwords. This means that even if a better security device than passwords is available – and there are several better devices – then the product builder may not use it, and it prevents the designer from searching for an alternative, and possibly better, solution. By writing:

> *The product shall ensure that the [name of] data can be accessed only by authorized users.*

you allow the product designer the freedom to find the most effective solution.

The problem with writing a solution, instead of a requirement, is that technology is constantly changing. Almost all solutions lock in a technology, which may be out of date by the time that the product is built. By writing a requirement that does not include any technological component, you allow the designer not only to use the most appropriate, up-to-date technology, but also allow the product to change and adapt to new technologies as they develop.

Consider this usability requirement:

> *The product shall use a mouse.*

We can eliminate the technological component by saying:

> *The product shall use a pointing device.*

But the requirement can be improved by writing it as:

> *The product shall allow the user to directly manipulate all interface items.*

To follow the guideline of not writing solutions, examine your requirement. If it contains any item of technology, or any method, then rewrite it such that the technology or method is not mentioned. It may be necessary to do this several times before the desired level of technological independence is reached, but the effect on the design of the end product is worthwhile.

Summary

The non-functional requirements describe the qualitative behavior of the product – whether it need be fast, or safe, or attractive, and so on. These qualities come about because of the functions that the product is required to carry out. See Figure 7.8.

Figure 7.8

How many non-functional requirements does the user of a tap have?

At this stage you have written a description of the non-functional requirements. Some of them may seem a little vague, and some of them may seem to be well intentioned and little more. Please keep in mind that you have not finished the requirements, you have yet to write the fit criteria. When you do so you will write a measurement to quantify the meaning of each requirement.

Writing the Specification

in which we look at putting the requirements
into written form

Writing the specification refers to the task of putting together a complete description of the product to be built. It is appropriate to think of this activity as 'building' a specification – you assemble a specification during the requirements process rather than writing it all at once.

Writing the requirements is not really a separate activity, but is done partly during the trawling and prototyping activities when you discover the requirements, and partly during the quality gateway checks when you are ensuring that each requirement is complete. However, it makes sense in the context of this book to devote a chapter to discussing how a requirement is written. This is that chapter. See Figure 8.1.

Turning Potential Requirements into Written Requirements

When you are trawling or prototyping, the requirements you find will not always be fully formed. They are ideas or intentions for requirements. On the other hand, the requirements specification that you produce is the basis for the contract to build a product, and so it must contain clear, complete and testable instructions as to what has to be built. This is not exactly an easy task, but we have some aids to writing a successful specification – the template and the shell.

The template is a ready-made container for a specification, and the shell is the container for an individual requirement. Let's see how you can make use of them.

> *No matter how brilliantly ideas formed in his mind, or crystallized in his clockworks, his verbal descriptions failed to shine with the same light. His last published work, which outlines the whole history of his unsavory dealings with the Board of Longitude, brings his style of endless circumlocution to its peak. The first sentence runs on, virtually unpunctuated for twenty five pages.*
>
> Source: Dava Sobel, *Longitude*

Figure 8.1

The requirements are discovered by trawling and by prototyping. Before they are accepted into the requirements specification, they must be scrutinized by the Quality Gateway.
The role of the writing activity is to correctly and completely record each requirement.

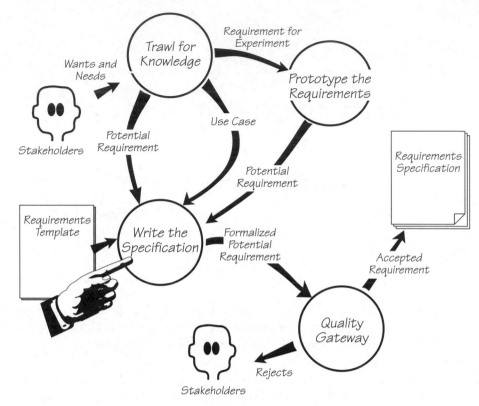

Bernard of Chartres used to say that we are like dwarfs on the shoulders of giants, so that we can see more than they, and things at a greater distance, not by virtue of any sharpness of sight on our part, or any physical distinction, but because we are carried high and raised up by their giant size.

Source: John of Salisbury

The Volere Template is found in Appendix B. This chapter will refer frequently to the template

The Volere Specification Template

Thousands of good requirements specifications have been written in the past. Your task of writing another one can be made easier if you make constructive use of some of the good specifications that have been written already.

The Volere Specification Template was made by 'standing on the shoulders of giants'. We (the authors) have borrowed useful components from specifications of successfully built products, and packaged the best of them into a reusable template that can form the foundation of your requirements specifications.

The Volere Template is a compartmentalized container for requirements. We examined requirements documents and categorized their requirements into types that prove useful for the purpose of recognition and elicitation. Each of the types is allocated to a section of the template. The template's table of contents lists these types:

Product Constraints

1 The Purpose of the Product
2 Client, Customer and other Stakeholders
3 Users of the Product
4 Requirements Constraints
5 Naming Conventions and Definitions
6 Relevant Facts
7 Assumptions

Functional Requirements

8 The Scope of the Product
9 Functional and Data Requirements

Non-functional Requirements

10 Look and Feel Requirements
11 Usability Requirements
12 Performance Requirements
13 Operational Requirements
14 Maintainability and Portability Requirements
15 Security Requirements
16 Cultural and Political Requirements
17 Legal Requirements

Project Issues

18 Open Issues
19 Off-the-Shelf Solutions
20 New Problems
21 Tasks
22 Cutover
23 Risks
24 Costs
25 User Documentation
26 Waiting Room

The template is set out in four main divisions. Firstly there are the *constraints*. Constraints are not exactly requirements, but they are issues that have a strong influence on the requirements and the outcome for the product. This part of the template covers such issues as the purpose of the product, the intended users of the product, and so on.

The next two divisions deal with the *requirements for the product*. Both the functional and non-functional requirements are described here. Each requirement is described to a level of detail so that the product's constructors know precisely what to build, and how you intend to test each capability of the delivered product.

The last division of the template deals with *project issues*. These are not requirements for the product, but are issues that must be faced if the product is to become a reality. This part of the template also contains a 'waiting room': a place to store requirements that are not intended for the initial release of the product.

The Product Constraints

Constraints are global requirements – they are factors that apply to the whole of the product. The product must be built within the stated constraints. Sometimes we know about the constraints, or they are mandated before the project gets underway. They are probably determined by management and are worth considering carefully – they drive the project and shape the product.

The constraints are written into the specification at blastoff time, although you may have some mechanism in place for determining them earlier. For the moment, put aside the way in which you find the constraints, and let us consider their content.

1   The Purpose of the Product

The initial section of the template deals with the fundamental reason that your client wants you to build a new product. That is, it describes the business problem that the client faces, and how the product will solve that problem.

The User Problem or Background to the Project Effort

This is a description of the work that the user is currently doing, and why it is not currently functioning as smoothly as desired. There must be some problems, otherwise you would not be being asked to develop a new product. The description may be quite brief,

> *Customers are unhappy with the length of time (10 days) it takes an order to reach them.*

or more fully describe the operational problem, usually giving the most weight to the most serious problems, and the problems that your intended product best addresses.

> Roads freeze in winter and icy conditions cause road accidents that kill people. We need to be able to predict when a road is likely to freeze so that our depot can schedule a de-icing truck in time to prevent the road from freezing. We expect a new product will provide more accurate predictions of icy conditions by using thermal maps of the district, road temperatures from weather stations installed in the roads and the weather forecasts. This will lead to more timely de-icing treatment than at present which will reduce road accidents. We also want to eliminate indiscriminate treatment of roads, which wastes de-icing compounds and causes environmental damage.

Give references to any material that supports your statement. Any problem that is serious enough to warrant new product development is serious enough to be well documented.

> Thornes, J.E., 1992: Cost-Effective Snow and Ice Control for the Nineties. Third International Symposium on Snow and Ice Control Technology, Minneapolis, Minnesota, Vol. 1, Paper 24.

It may be that there are no serious problems, but there is a business opportunity that your client wishes to exploit. In this case, describe that opportunity.

> We have a new range of products that will be the vehicle for expanding our customer base to include overseas customers. Our current customer billing system was designed 10 years ago to service a small volume of local customers. We want to build a new customer billing system to cope with the projected growth rate due to the new product ranges.

Alternatively, the project may be to explore or investigate possibilities. In this case the project deliverable, instead of a new product, would be a document proving that the requirements for a product can or cannot be satisfied.

> Our Northern and Southern branches have always operated as virtually separate companies. We suspect that we are duplicating a lot of work and not sharing useful experience. We want to investigate the effect of integrating the work of the Northern and Southern branch offices.

Goals of the Product

This part describes what we want the product to do, or how it will contribute to the overall goals of the work. Do not be too wordy in this section – a brief explanation of the product's goals is usually more valuable than a long, rambling treatise. Keep your words and sentences as short as possible. A short, sharp goal will be clearer to the stakeholders, and thus it is more likely that you can reach a consensus for the goal.

> *To reduce road accidents by accurately forecasting the de-icing of frozen roads.*

READING

THOMSETT, ROB. *Third Wave Project Management: A Handbook for Managing the Complex Information Management Systems of the 1990's.* Prentice-Hall/ Yourdon Press, 1993.

If a goal is worthwhile, then it must provide some advantage or benefit. Rob Thomsett, a prominent management consultant, says that there are only three benefits:

● Value in the market place

● Reduced cost of operations

● Increased value or service to customers.

Reducing road accidents can be counted as increasing a service to customers.

The advantage must be measurable. If it cannot be measured, then we suggest that it is not a worthwhile goal. In addition, if you cannot quantify the advantage then you can never tell if your product has achieved the advantage it was intended to produce.

For example, if your goal is:

> *To produce a distributed quality-focussed devolved groupware coordination and phased dynamic alliance monitoring solution.*

then we suggest that there is no advantage that we can see, and certainly nothing that can be measured. We would go so far as to suggest that you could never tell if the delivered product matched the goal. Instead of having a goal such as the above gibberish, we suggest that you look for a quantifiable benefit.

Later in this book we look at measuring requirements. Here we refer to the measurement as a *fit criterion*, and feel that it is so important that we have devoted a chapter to it.

Chapter 9, Fit Criteria

But let's go back to the clear goal:

> *To reduce road accidents by accurately forecasting the de-icing of frozen roads.*

The advantage of this goal is the reduction of road accidents. 'Reduction' is a measurable term, and coincides with the advantage that we set for the product. So by measuring the accident rate, we can tell if the product meets its goal. A suitable measurement for the above goal is:

> *Accidents attributed to ice shall be no more than 15% of the total number of accidents during winter.*

This measurement is easily testable – the data needed to verify that the product has achieved its goal is readily available. There may be other goals for this product, but be careful not to include every individual requirement in this section. A goal is an overriding requirement: it applies to the product as a whole. Thus

> *To save money on winter road maintenance costs.*

is a goal, whereas

> *The product shall record air temperature readings, humidity readings, precipitation readings and road temperature readings received from weather stations.*

is a functional requirement that contributes to the goal.

The goals are determined at blastoff time. You must ensure that the goals are reasonable, attainable, simply stated, worthwhile, and carry a measurement so that you can test the delivered product to ensure that it satisfies the goal. If the goal does not have these properties, then history demonstrates that it is unlikely the project will deliver anything useful.

The goal is used throughout the requirements gathering activity. Each of the requirements that you gather must contribute, even if indirectly, to the goal. Requirements that do not contribute are not relevant, and should be discarded.

2 The Client, Customer and Other Stakeholders in the Product

This section describes stakeholders – the people who have an interest in the product. It is worth your while to spend some time to accurately determine and describe these people, as the penalty for not knowing who they are can be very high.

Each of the stakeholders has demands on the product. That is, they are sources of requirements. If you do not discover all of them, then it is likely that you will not discover all of the requirements.

This section of the specification identifies the stakeholders. Wherever possible, give the name and contact details for the stakeholder.

The Client

The client is the person who pays for product development. For products developed for in-house consumption, the client may be the manager of the user department. For products intended for external sale, your client may be the marketing department, or product management.

The person with the budget is normally regarded as the client, and it is he that you have to satisfy with your product. Taking the time to understand who this is will help you to know what product you have to build. Name the client with an entry like this:

> *The client for the product is Mr Mack Andrews, the chief executive of Saltworks Systems.*

The Customer

The customer is the person who will buy your product. What kind of person is this? What attributes can you give to the customer, and what do you have to build to entice him to buy your product?

Describe the customer, and everything that you know about him.

> *The customer for the product is the Northumberland County Highways Department represented by director Jane Torville. Ms Torville has had many years of experience with de-icing roads, and will expect a state-of-the-art product.*

Other Stakeholders

The other stakeholders are people who have a vested interest in the product, or the development of the product. It is important to involve all the relevant stakeholders – failure to do so may mean either that you miss vital requirements, or that you end up with people actively working against your product.

Chapter 3, Project Blastoff

The stakeholders are identified at blastoff time. They are listed in this section of the requirements specification to formalize their involvement, and to give the requirements gatherers a knowledge of who are the relevant people to interview. Wherever possible, name the people who will be part of your project.

3   Users of the Product

Users are the people who will interact directly with your product. In this section, you identify all the people who might conceivably make use of the product. The users are determined when you identify the product boundary during trawling. In this part of the specification you describe them and their characteristics.

> The engineers located at the truck depot are the main user group. The engineers have a detailed knowledge of road types, road locations and road networks. They are all experienced in using personal computers for a wide variety of applications including word processing and computer aided design. All have a degree in engineering, and all of them speak English. Sonia Henning is the Road Engineering Supervisor.

> The Highways Department clerks are located at the Highways Department head office in Newcastle. Dick Button is the Clerical Supervisor. The clerks do not necessarily have any knowledge of the subject matter of roads and weather forecasts. Some of the clerks have used personal computers, however do not assume familiarity with technology. Most have GCSE O levels, they are aged between 18 and 60, and all can read and speak English.
>
> The clerks work for local government organizations. Refer to the employment rules for specification of the types of disabilities that must be catered for.

You can find a discussion of user characteristics in Chapter 3, Project Blastoff

The users determine the usability requirements. That is, you write usability requirements to suit the characteristics of the users.

Thus the better the description of the users that you write, the easier it is to determine the usability requirements. Make a point of including any unusual characteristics of the users – whether they might be angry, in a hurry, only able to use one arm, and so on. This is a section of specification where you, the requirements gatherer, specify your knowledge of the users. You take advantage of this work throughout the specification process to help you to define requirements that are relevant to these particular users.

4   Requirements Constraints

This section covers constraints on the way that the product must be designed, and constraints on the requirements. That is, they are conditions that restrict the requirements to specifying a product that falls within the constraint. Constraints are ordained – they are not raised by the product's demands, but by management policy.

Design constraints are those pre-existing design decisions that mandate how the final product must look, or technology that it must use or comply with. For example:

> *The product shall run on the existing network of personal computers.*

This constraint restricts any computerized solution to the existing technology. Thus the requirements may not specify a product that is so elaborate as to need a large mainframe to implement it.

Similarly, the client organization may have a standard that all new products are to use a specified programming language, or run on certain computers, or fit in with pre-existing products. While we discourage you from having any design at all in your requirements specification – design and requirements are not the same thing – there are always going to be mandates about the design that the client, or the organization, requires, and it would be unrealistic and unacceptable to ignore them. These constraints specifications also provide you with a way of identifying requirements that are not viable within the project constraints.

> *The product shall interface with the DM31 weather stations.*
> *The product shall interface with the Thermal Mapping Database.*
> *The product shall interface with the Road Engineering Computer System.*

Project constraints cover things like the budget, the time allowed to build the product, the deadlines, and so on. While these are by no means requirements, they do have the effect of constraining the requirements to those that can be built within budget. There is no point specifying a Mercedes Benz, if the time available, and the financial budget, only allow for a bicycle.

> *The budget for building the product is 1 million pounds sterling.*

There is another constraint on the product, which is the environment in which it must work. This is covered by section 13 of the template – Operational Requirements.

5   Naming Conventions and Definitions

Misunderstood words cause problems, and misunderstood names can cause hours of lost time, miscommunication between team members, and ultimately poor quality specifications. In section 5 of the requirements specification, start a dictionary to define the important terms to be used by the stakeholders. This will be enlarged and refined as the systems analysis proceeds, but for the moment, it should introduce the terms that the project will use, and the meaning of those terms to your project.

> *Weather Station – a weather station is capable of monitoring air temperature, humidity, precipitation and road temperature. Four road surface sensors can be attached to one weather station. Each sensor must be within 1 km of the weather station.*
>
> *Thermal Map – a region, or other geographical area is surveyed to determine the temperature differences at various parts of the area. The resulting thermal map means the temperature at any part of the area can be determined by knowing the temperature at a reference point.*

Firstly, check to see if there are any industry-standard dictionaries, or dictionaries that already exist in the organization. Naturally, a ready-made 14dictionary is going to save you time. Failing that, the names you use in the requirements specification should be the regular business names – the names that the users use in the everyday work. However, be prepared to suggest better names if the existing ones are misleading, or include references to obsolete technology.

Good names are easily distinguishable and self-documenting. They should invoke the right meaning, and thus save hours of explanation. Make the dictionary by writing each term and its definition. Include all abbreviations and acronyms that are used by your users.

The intention of this section is to be a reference for all the people that will work on the project. It is also used in the Quality Gateway to ensure that all terms used to write the requirements are those as defined in section 5. This section is the basis for the analysis data dictionary. As the analysis data dictionary evolves, many of the definitions from this section are expanded in the dictionary with their data composition.

6   Relevant Facts

Relevant facts are external factors that have an effect on the product but are not covered by other sections. They are not necessarily translated into requirements but may well be. Relevant facts alert the developers to conditions and factors that have a bearing on the requirements. For example, it may be that the IceBreaker product's specification would contain relevant facts:

> *Drivers cannot work more than three hours without a break.*

This means that the scheduling part of the product must not produce schedules that would require the driver to cover more than about 100 miles at a time.

> One ton of de-icing material will treat three miles of single-lane roadway.

Salt (NaCl) de-ices down to –6 °C. Calcium Chloride (CaCl) de-ices down to –15 °C.

Source: Vaisala

This fact must be taken into account when scheduling trucks to treat freezing roads. Note that it is not a requirement as such, but has a strong effect on the outcome of the product.

Relevant facts are usually discovered when you are trawling for requirements, and particularly when you are discussing the business rules with your users. The background information given by the relevant fact section is required reading for new people on the project.

7 Assumptions

The assumptions that are listed here are those being made by the project team. The intention is to alert management to factors that might have an effect on the product. The assumptions are usually about the intended operational environment of the product, but may be about anything that could, if the assumption does not come true, have a detrimental effect on the success of the product.

> Roads that have been treated will not need treating for at least two hours.
> Road treatment will stop at county boundaries.

By stating these assumptions, the analyst is saying to all the stakeholders 'Look at these. I am proceeding on the basis that these assumptions are true. The product that I specify assumes that they are true. If the product is *not* to stop road treatment at county boundaries, then please let me know right now.'

There may be other products that are being developed at the same time, and the delivery failure will affect your product. Similarly, you may be making assumptions about the performance, or capacity of some as yet untested product. If that product does not perform as you assume it will, then your product will be adversely affected.

> The Road Engineering's Apian system will be available for integration testing before November.
> Trucks will be capable of operating at up to 40 mph, and will have a material capacity of at least one-half ton, and no more than two tons.

Similarly, you may make assumptions about interfaces between the product under development and existing products. For example, the IceBreaker product is to interface with the weather stations. These stations are being developed by an outside organization. Obviously, if there are variations in the way that they transmit their information, then the IceBreaker product will not work as planned.

> The Bureau's forecasts will be transmitted according to their specification 1003-7 issued by their engineering department.

Also you may write assumptions about the availability and capability of bought-in components, the operational environment of the product, the capabilities of the development language, or anything else that will be used by the product.

8   The Scope of the Product

There are two scopes to be established. The earliest one is the scope of the work. This scope determines the boundaries of the work to be studied, and how it fits into the environment. Once you understand the work and the constraints, then you can establish the scope of the product. Keep in mind that the product has to fit seamlessly into the work, so it is appropriate to look firstly at the work.

You can use a context diagram to define the scope of the work. This diagram shows the work and its surrounding adjacent systems. Establishing the correct work context is crucial to the success of the product. It is worth investing all the care, and time, necessary to ensure that the context is sufficient for you to understand the parts of the customer's business that could potentially benefit from the product. When you understand the work then your objective is to identify the scope of the product that will achieve the business objectives within the constraints of the project.

The context, and how to establish it, is described fully elsewhere, and we urge you to look at Chapters 3 and 4 on Blastoff and Event-driven Use Cases.

Chapter 3, Project Blastoff. Chapter 4, Event-driven Use Cases

The requirements specification should include a context model showing the work and its environment. It should also include a diagram showing the scope of the product. We suggest a use case diagram for this; there is an example in Chapter 4.

The Shell

The first eight sections of the specification, covering the constraints and the context, use mainly free text. However, the functional and non-functional

Figure 8.2

The Volere Shell in its snow card form. Each 8" × 5" card is used to record a requirement. The requirements analyst completes each of the items when he discovers them, and thus builds a complete, rigorous requirement.

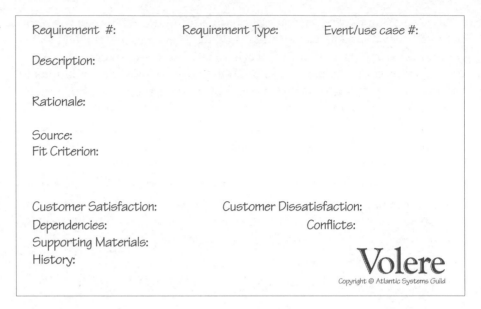

Requirement #:   Requirement Type: Event/use case #:

Description:

Rationale:

Source:
Fit Criterion:

Customer Satisfaction: Customer Dissatisfaction:
Dependencies: Conflicts:
Supporting Materials:
History:

Volere
Copyright © Atlantic Systems Guild

requirements must be written more formally and in a certain structure, and for this purpose we introduce the shell.

The shell is a container for an individual requirement. When you write your requirements, it is not sufficient to write natural language statements, as they lack the necessary rigor. We have found that there is a collection of components necessary to make a complete requirement, and have implemented these components in what we call a shell.

The shell can be implemented on cards, as shown in Figure 8.2, or can be automated. We find that cards are convenient when trawling for requirements, but at some stage we transfer the requirement to an automated tool. So now let us look at how the complete, formalized requirement is constructed.

As we treat each of the items that make up the requirement, consider how you will discover it, and how well it applies to your organization. For this activity, we will assume that you are using the Volere shell, or that you are using some mechanism to ensure that you capture all the relevant parts of each requirement.

Start by identifying the requirement. Each requirement has three pieces of identification: its number, its type, and the event(s) and/or use case(s) that spawned the requirement.

Requirement Number

Each requirement must be uniquely identified. The reason is straightforward – requirements must be traceable throughout the development of the product, so it is convenient and logical to give each requirement a unique number. We use 'number' meaning any unique identifier, although it can be any kind of identifier you wish. To keep this from being an onerous clerical task, we suggest you use a simple sequential number. It is not important how you uniquely identify the requirement as long as you identify it.

Requirement Type

The type comes from the Volere Template. The template's table of contents lists 26 sections, each of which contains a different type of requirement. Thus we use the template section number as the type – the purpose of the product is requirement type 1, functional requirements are type 9, look and feel are type 10, usability requirements are type 11, and so on.

Attaching the type to the requirement is useful in several ways:

● The requirements can be sorted into type. By comparing all requirements of one type, you more readily discover requirements that conflict with one another.

● It is easier to write an appropriate fit criterion when the type of requirement is established.

● By grouping all the known requirements of one type, it becomes more apparent if some of them are missing or duplicated.

Event/Use Case Number

The context of the work is broken into smaller pieces using the business events as the partitioning tool. For each business event you decide which part of the response to that event will be carried out by the product. It is this part of the response – the part being done by the product – that is referred to as a use case. When you identify each use case you identify the user or users who will interface with that part of the product. Each business event is given a number for convenient referencing. Similarly each use case is numbered. For traceability and change control purposes it is useful to keep track of all requirements that are generated by a business event. Each of your product use cases corresponds to a business event so you can use the same number to indicate the business event and the product use case. If, however, you choose to cluster your requirements into sub-use cases then you will need a separate numbering system for your use cases. Whatever your preference, you must tag each requirement so that you can identify which parts of the business it relates to (business events) and which parts of the product it relates to (use cases). Figure 8.3 illustrates how requirements are identified.

During later analysis, you will analyze each business event and use case separately. Thus it is convenient to be able to collect together all the require-

Figure 8.3

The requirement, type
and event or use case
identifiers.

Requirement #: **75**	Requirement Type: **9**	Event/use case #: **6**

ments for that part of the work. This will help you to find missing requirements, and to confirm the actions of a use case with its users.

Description

The description is the *intent* of the requirement. It is an English (or whatever natural language you use) statement in the user's words as to what is required. Do not be too concerned that it may contain ambiguities (but neither should you be sloppy with your language) as the Fit Criterion will eliminate any failings in the language. The objective when you first write the requirement is to capture the user's, or the client's, wishes. So for the moment a clear statement of the user's intentions suffices.

Rationale

The rationale is the reason behind the requirement's existence. It tells why the requirement is important, what contribution it makes to the product's purpose. Adding a rationale to a requirement helps you to clarify and understand it. Having this justification of the requirement helps you to assess its importance when you are testing for gold plating in the Quality Gateway activity.

Source

The source is the name of the person who raised the requirement in the first instance, or the person to whom it can be attributed. You should attach the source to your requirements so that you have a referral point if there are questions about the requirement, or if the requirement is rejected by the Quality Gateway. The person who raises the requirement must have the knowledge and authority that is appropriate for the type of requirement.

Fit Criteria

The fit criteria are quantified goals that the solution has to meet – they are acceptance criteria. While the description of the requirement is written in the language of the users, the fit criterion is written in a precise quantified manner so that solutions can be tested against the requirement.

The fit criteria set the standard to which the builder constructs the product. While they do not say how the implementation will be tested, they do provide the goals that the testers will use when they determine if each requirement has been met.

Fit criteria are so important that we have devoted an entire chapter to them.

Chapter 9, Fit Criteria

Customer Satisfaction and Customer Dissatisfaction

The *satisfaction* ranking is a measure of how happy the client will be if you successfully deliver an implementation of the requirement. The scale ranges from 1 to 5 where 1 means that the client is unconcerned about the outcome and 5 means that the client will be extremely happy if you successfully deliver a product that contains the requirement.

The *dissatisfaction* rating is also on a scale of 1 to 5. This time it measures the amount of *unhappiness* the client will feel if you do not successfully deliver this requirement. A 1 means that the client will be unconcerned if the product appears without this requirement, and the scale progresses through to 5 meaning that your client will be extremely angry if you do not successfully deliver this requirement.

For example, this is a fairly normal and unremarkable requirement:

> *The product shall record changes to the road network.*

Naturally your client is expecting the product to be able to record the road network so that it can tell the engineers which roads have to be treated. The client is unlikely to get excited over this requirement, so the satisfaction rating may be anything from 3 to 5. However, if the product cannot record changes to roads, you would expect the client to be rather angry, and thus would give a dissatisfaction rating of 5.

On the other hand, consider this requirement:

> *The product shall issue an alert if a weather station fails to transmit readings.*

This is a feature of the product that would be useful, and nice to have. Your client may give this a satisfaction rating of 5. However, the requirement is not crucial to the correct operation of the product – the engineers would eventually notice if readings failed to turn up from one of the weather stations. In this case the client may well rate the dissatisfaction at 2 or 3.

The satisfaction/dissatisfaction ratings are used to place a value against each of the requirements. The effect of asking your client to rate the satisfaction and the dissatisfaction is that he will consider the requirement more seriously. It also gives him an opportunity to let you know how he feels about each of the requirements. Later, these ratings will be weighed against the cost of the requirement.

The ratings are set either by your client, or a panel made up of the significant stakeholders. If the product is for sale to external customers, then these ratings should be done by a panel that represents the potential customers.

A complex case we have come across is one where portable telephones were being developed for sale in different countries. The marketing people had identified that the customers' priorities differed from country to country. Thus the value ratings had to be separately assessed for each target country.

Dependencies

Dependencies are other requirements that have an impact on this one. For example, there may be another requirement that will have to be changed if this one changes, or one whose data is linked very closely to the data that this one uses. Alternatively, there may be other requirements whose continued existence depends on the existence of this one.

Conflicts

Conflicts are other requirements that contradict this one, or make this one less feasible. For example, there may be a requirement that the product has to calculate the *shortest* route to the destination. There may be another that states the product is to calculate the *quickest* route to the destination. There could well be a conflict between these two if they are both considered to be the preferred route and if conditions dictated that the shortest was not always the quickest route.

Similarly, you may discover that a conflict between two or more requirements exists when you design the product and begin to look at solutions. It may be that the solution to one requirement means that the solution to the other is impossible, or severely restricted.

Conflicting requirements are a normal part of development. Don't be concerned that conflicts between requirements appear – as long as you are able to capture the fact that the conflict exists then you can work towards solving it.

Supporting Materials

Do not attempt to put everything in the specification. There will always be other material that is important to the requirements, and it may be simply referenced by this item.

> Supporting Materials: Thornes, J.E., 1992: Cost-Effective Snow and Ice Control for the Nineties. Third International Symposium on Snow and Ice Control Technology, Minneapolis. Minnesota, Vol. 1, Paper 24.

We suggest that you restrict entries under this heading to those references that have a direct bearing on the requirement.

History

This is the place to record the date that the requirement was first raised, dates of changes, date of deletion, date of passing through the Quality Gateway, and so on. Add the names of people responsible for these actions if you think it will help later.

Writing the Specification

The Requirements Template and the Requirement Shell are convenient devices to use when writing a specification. The template is a guide to the topics to be covered by the specification, and the shell is a guide to what to write for each requirement.

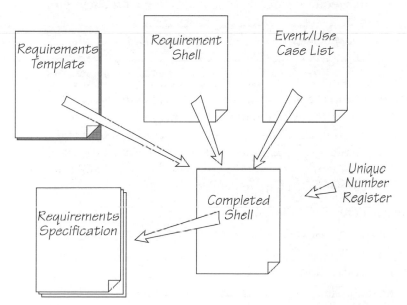

Figure 8.4

The specification is not so much written as gradually assembled. The template provides a guide to the types of requirements, and how to describe each one. The components for each functional and non-functional requirement are compiled using the shell as a guide. The Requirements Specification is an assembly of completed shells.

You will also need the Event List as functional and non-functional requirements are tagged to the business event, or use case, that spawned the requirement. As all requirements have a unique identification, you will also need some way of registering requirement numbers, or some other way of guaranteeing that each requirement carries a unique number. Figure 8.4 illustrates this further.

Now let us consider the remaining requirement types from the template, and discuss the appropriate entries for each of the sections.

9 Functional Requirements

Functional requirements are the things that the product must do. That is, the functional requirements describe functions or actions that are to be part of the product. You might think of the functional requirements as the fundamental activities of the product. For example, a functional requirement may be something like:

> *The product shall record the new weather stations.*

This states an action that if carried out, contributes to the goal of the product. If the goal is to predict when the roads will freeze, then it is necessary to collect data from weather stations, and thus it is necessary to know the existence and location of the weather stations. When new ones are added to the network, then the product must be able to record their details. Similarly, this requirement also contributes to the product's purpose:

> *The product shall issue an alert if a weather station fails to transmit readings.*

This requirement is necessary if the product is to know about failures of the stations, and the possibility of the product having incomplete data. Thus the collection of the functional requirements in the requirements specification describes the functionality of the product that you intend to build.

However, the example functional requirements shown above are not complete. And you may think that they are too casual and possibly ambiguous. To complete each requirement, you must:

● Give it an identification number.

● Designate the use case or business event that this piece of functionality is derived from.

● Write a description.

● If the rationale is not self-evident, then include it.

Figure 8.5

A complete functional
requirement using the
Volere shell.

Requirement #: **75**   Requirement Type: **9**   Event/use case #: **6**

Description: **The product shall issue an alert if a weather station fails to transmit readings.**

Rationale: **Failure to transmit readings might indicate that the weather station is faulty and needs maintenance, and that the data used to predict freezing roads may be incomplete.**

Source: **Road Engineers**

Fit Criterion: **For each weather station the product shall communicate to the user when the recorded number of each type of reading per hour is not within the manufacturer's specified range of the expected number of readings per hour.**

Customer Satisfaction: **3**   Customer Dissatisfaction: **5**

Dependencies: **None**   Conflicts: **None**

Supporting Materials: **Specification of Rosa Weather Station**

History: **Raised by GBS, 28 July 99**

Volere

Copyright © Atlantic Systems Guild

- Designate the source.
- Add a fit criterion.
- Describe any conflicts if they are known.
- Include any supporting materials that will be useful.

The complete functional requirement is illustrated in Figure 8.5. Let's look more closely at the description.

Description

Describe an action that the product must take. In other words, what the product must do. For example,

> The product shall record air temperature readings, humidity readings, precipitation readings and road temperature readings received from weather stations.

Note the level of detail. The requirement is written in plain English, provided it is not obviously ambiguous or open-ended. The description must be understandable and verifiable by your users and client. It is not yet complete – each of the requirements is given a fit criterion that tightens the definition by making it quantifiable and testable.

Usually the requirement can be stated in one sentence. If you find yourself taking more than one to describe it then you may in fact be describing

*It is good practice
to write each
requirement as a
single sentence*

several requirements. If the word 'and' appears, or you use two verbs in the sentence, then it might be that you are describing two requirements. It is good practice to write each requirement as a single sentence. It will cause you fewer problems when you come to write the fit criterion.

The functional requirements are usually derived from the steps of the use case. For example, the use case step:

> ● *Product determines which roads are likely to freeze and when they are likely to freeze.*

yielded these requirements:

> *The product shall determine areas of the same temperature from the map's isotherms.*
> *The product shall determine which road sections pass through areas that are predicted to freeze.*
> *The product shall determine when the road sections will freeze from the time interval of the map.*

Again, note the level of detail. It should be enough for your client (or the user or the domain experts) to verify that the product will work correctly.

Non-functional Requirements

Non-functional requirements are the properties that the product must have. In this section you describe the spirit of its appearance, how easy it must be to use, how secure it must be, what laws apply to the product, and anything else that must be built into the product, but is not a part of its fundamental functionality.

See Chapter 9, Fit Criteria, for details on how to quantify non-functional requirements

Non-functional requirements are written like other requirements, that is, they have all the usual components – they are identified, they have a type, a description, a fit criterion, and so on. Thus you write them just as you would a functional requirement (see Figure 8.6). The difference is that they are usually more difficult to quantify.

Project Issues

Project issues are not requirements. Rather they are project concerns that are brought to light by the requirements activity. It is appropriate to include these in the requirements specification because they help to understand the requirements.

Figure 8.6

A non-functional requirement.

Requirement #: **110** Requirement Type: **11** Event/use case #: **6,7,8,9,10**

Description: **The product shall be easy for the road engineers to use.**

Rationale: **It should not be necessary for the engineers to attend training classes in order to be able to use the product.**

Source: **Sonia Henning, Road Engineering Supervisor.**

Fit Criterion: **A road engineer shall be able to use the product to successfully carry out the cited use cases within 1 hour of first encountering the product.**

Customer Satisfaction: **3**   Customer Dissatisfaction: **5**

Dependencies: **None**   Conflicts: **None**

Supporting Materials:

History: **Raised by A.G. 25 Aug 99.**

Volere

Copyright © Atlantic Systems Guild

18 Open Issues

This section of the specification is for issues that have arisen from the requirements activity, but as yet have not been resolved. Usually the fact that you are probing around the user's business means that some questions come to the surface, and they cannot for the moment be answered. Similarly, as you are gathering the requirements for a future product, it may well be that the user is unsure of how something should be in the future.

> The feasibility study to determine whether to use the Regional Weather Center's on-line database is not yet complete. This affects the handling of weather data.

Changes happen all the time. Some of these changes are certain to affect your product. The Open Issues section may also contain notes on changes that are proposed, but whose final outcome is not yet established.

> Planned changes to working hours for drivers may affect the way that trucks are scheduled, and the length of routes that drivers are permitted to travel. The changes are still in the proposal stage, details will be available by the end of the year.

19 Off-the-Shelf Solutions

This section looks at available solutions, and gives a summary of their applicability to the requirements. This is not intended to be a full feasibility study of the alternatives, but should tell your client that you have considered some alternatives, and how closely they match the requirements for the product.

Note the intention of this section. It does not say that there are some wonderful solutions just waiting to be taken down from the shelf, and never mind if it doesn't fit the requirements all that well. Instead this section points to solutions that *may* be applicable, and are worth further study.

If there are no suitable products, then this section alerts the client that he may be faced with the cost of building something.

We suggest that the section has three headings:

- Is there a ready-made product, or commercial off-the-shelf software that could be bought?
- Can ready-made components be used for this product?
- Is there something that we could copy?

READING

MAIDEN, N.A.M., C. NCUBE AND A. MOORE. *Acquiring Requirements for Commercial Off-The-Shelf Page Selection: Some Lessons Learned.* City University, 1998.

For each of these, set out the alternatives that you feel are suitable, or give reasons why there is no suitable off-the-shelf solution. If your findings are preliminary, then alert the client to this. It is also useful to add approximate costs, availability, time to implement, and other factors that may have a bearing on the decision.

The point of this section is to consider alternative ways that the product can be implemented, not to try and force-fit the requirements into a marginal product.

20 New Problems

An all-too-common problem from a project perspective is preparing the change but not preparing for the change.

Source: Mike Russell

Changes to the existing order often bring with them adverse effects. This section gives you the opportunity to examine and highlight any problems that the installation of the new product will bring.

For example, there may be changes to the way that work is done, changes to interfaces with existing products, changes to jobs that people currently do.

While it is not necessary to describe every facet of every change, you should use this section as an opportunity to alert your client to problems that he might possibly face.

21 Tasks

What steps have to be taken to deliver the product? The intention of this section is to highlight the effort required to build the product, or steps needed to buy a solution, the amount of effort to modify and install a ready-made solution, and so on.

Whatever route you plan to follow to get the new product installed in the user's business area should be known, and described, at the requirements stage.

Although your organization may have a standard approach to constructing or buying products, there are usually variations caused by the requirements of the product. What you write here is used by management to assess the feasibility of the product, given the effort and cost required to produce it.

22 Cutover

When you install a new product, there are always things that have to be done before it can work successfully. For example, there are usually existing data files that have to be converted. There is often new data that has to be collected, procedures that have to be converted, and many other things that need to be done to ensure the successful transition to the new product.

Often there are periods where the organization will run the old and the new products in parallel until the new one has proven that it is functioning correctly.

This section of the specification is the place for you to identify the tasks necessary for the period of transition to the new product. This section is input to the project planning process.

23 Risks

All projects involve risk. By this we mean the risk that something will go wrong. Risk is not necessarily a bad thing, as no progress is made without taking some risk. However, there is a difference between unmanaged risk – say shooting dice at a craps table – and managed risk where the probabilities are well understood, and contingencies planned. Risk is only a bad thing if the risks are ignored and they become problems. Risk management is assessing which risks are most likely to apply to the project, deciding a course of action if they become problems, and monitoring projects to give early warnings of risks becoming problems.

READING
JONES, CAPERS. *Assessment and Control of Software Risks*. Prentice-Hall, 1994.

This section of the specification contains a list of the most likely and the most serious risks for your project. Against each risk include the probability of that risk becoming a problem, and any contingency plans.

It is also useful input to project management if you include the impact on the schedule, or the cost, if the risk does become a problem.

As an alternative, you may prefer to identify the single largest risk – the showstopper. If this risk becomes a problem, then the project will fail. The effect of identifying a single risk is that it concentrates attention on the single most critical area. Project efforts are then concentrated on not letting this risk become a problem.

This section of the book is not intended to be a thorough treatise on risk management. Nor is this section of the requirements specification meant to be a substitute for proper risk management. The intention here is to assign risks to requirements. To show clearly that requirements are not free – there is a cost, that can be expressed as an amount of money or time, and as a risk. Later, you can use this information if you need to make choices about which requirements should be given priority.

READING

BOEHM, BARRY. *Software Risk Management.* IEEE Computer Society Press, 1989.

CHARETTE, ROBERT. *Software Engineering Risk Analysis and Management.* McGraw-Hill, 1989.

24   Costs

The other cost of requirements is the amount of money or effort that you have to spend building them into a product. Once the requirements specification is complete, you can use one of the estimating methods to assess the cost, and express this as a monetary amount, or time to build.

There is no best method to use when estimating. The important issue is that your estimate is based on metrics that are directly related to the requirements. If you have specified the requirements in the way that we have described you have the following metrics:

- Number of business events
- Number of product use cases
- Number of requirements
- Number of requirements constraints
- Estimated number of function points.

You can use these metrics as the basis for estimating the time, effort and cost of building the product. Firstly you need to determine what each of these metrics means within the environment in which you are building the product. For example, do you know how long it takes you to do all the work necessary to implement a product use case? If you do not, then you can take one of the use cases and do a benchmark.

READING

Function Point Counting Practices Manual. International Function Point Users Group, Westerville OH.

If you have specified the requirements in detail then you can estimate the number of function points contained in the product. We favor function point counting – not because it is an inherently superior method, but because it is so commonly accepted, and so much is known about it, that it is possible to make easy comparisons with other products, and other installations' productivity.

It is important that your client knows at this stage what the product is likely to cost. You usually express this as a total cost to complete the product, but you may also find it advantageous to be able to point out the cost of individual requirements.

Whatever you do, do not leave the costs in the lap of hysterical optimism. Make sure that this section includes realistic numbers and coherent estimates and questions based on those numbers.

25 User Documentation

This section is a specification of the user documentation that will be produced as part of the product building effort. This is not the documentation itself, but a description of what must be produced.

> *The documentation shall include a user manual and on-line help.*

The reason for including this is to set your client's expectations, and to give your usability people, and your users, the chance to assess whether the proposed documentation will be sufficient.

26 Waiting Room

The waiting room is for requirements that cannot, for one reason or another, be part of the initial release of the product. If you are competent at gathering requirements, your users will often be inspired to think of more requirements than you can fit within the constraints of the project. While you may not want to include all the requirements in the initial version of the product, neither do you want to lose them.

When you decide to put a requirement into the waiting room it will not necessarily be written in detail. It might simply be one sentence summarizing an idea that someone has had. Just write enough so that the idea is trapped well enough for you to be able to assess it later.

The waiting room is a place to store requirements until you have the chance to use them. This has a calming effect on everyone because it shows that their ideas are being taken seriously. Your users and client know that the requirements are not forgotten, merely parked until they can be incorporated in the product.

Summary

Writing the specification is not a separate activity, but one that is done in conjunction with other parts of the process. Requirements analysts write requirements, or parts of requirements, whenever they find them. Not all requirements are completed at the same time.

However, this is not a random activity. Business events, use cases, the template and the shell make it possible to measure the degree of completion, and more importantly the areas in need of completion, at any time.

Writing a good requirements specification is important. A well-written requirements specification pays for itself many times over – the construction is more precise, the maintenance costs less, and the product reflects what the customer needs and wants.

Fit Criteria

in which we discuss how to make requirements
measurable and thereby testable

'Fit' means that a solution completely satisfies the requirement. That is, the solution does exactly what the requirement says it must do, no more and no less. However, before you can know whether or not a solution fits, you must firstly attach a quantification to the requirement. Once you have quantified the requirement, it then makes sense to measure your implementation. If the result of this measurement precisely matches that of the requirement, then you can be sure that your implementation fits your requirement. Without quantifying the requirement, it is impossible to know if the implementation matches the requirement. The quantification of the requirement is its fit criterion.

The fit criterion may quantify the behavior, the performance, or some other quality of the requirement. Fit criteria apply to both functional and non-functional requirements (Figure 9.1).

So far in this book you have seen how to write a requirement, but the part you have seen is the *description* of the requirement. This is the user's *intention* for the requirement. But to know precisely what is intended, you must quantify it in some way. Once the requirement has been expressed using numbers, there is very little room for misunderstanding.

Why Does Fit Need a Criterion?

If there is a requirement for the product to carry out some function, or for it to have some property, then the testing activity must demonstrate that the product does indeed perform that function, or that it possesses the desired property. To make such tests, the requirement must have a benchmark such

> *Using fit criteria recognizes the fact that you cannot design a solution to the requirement unless you have a way of knowing whether the solution meets the requirement*

> ❝ *I often say that when you can measure what you are speaking about, and express it in numbers, you know something about it; but when you cannot measure it, when you cannot express it in numbers, your knowledge is of a meagre and unsatisfactory kind.* ❞
>
> Source: Lord Kelvin

Figure 9.1

You can write fit criteria as soon as you discover the requirement, either in trawling or prototyping. However, you will find that you pay most attention to them when you are carrying out the Quality Gateway activity.

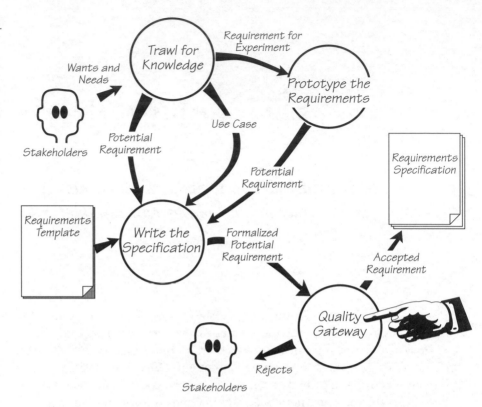

> *The idea is for each requirement to have a quality measure that makes it possible to divide all solutions to the requirement into two classes: those for which we agree that they fit the requirement and those for which we agree that they do not fit the requirement.*
>
> Source: Christopher Alexander, *Notes On The Synthesis Of Form*

that the testers can compare the delivered product with the original requirement. The benchmark is the fit criterion – some quantification of the product that demonstrates the standard that the product has to reach.

We should also consider the builders of the product. It stands to reason that once they know the performance criterion that the product has to meet, they will build to that standard. If they are told that their product has to be used underwater, and that the acceptance criterion is that the product must operate for up to 24 hours at a depth of 15 meters, then they are unlikely to build a product out of cardboard (Figure 9.2).

The problem of testing a requirement against an agreed measurement, is defining an appropriate measurement for the requirement. For example, if your client asks you for a product that is 'nice', then you must find some way of measuring the nicety of it. This measurement must of course, be agreed with your client, as it is his opinion on 'nice' that really matters. What we need is a way to quantify 'nice' so that the product's builders know whether or not they are heading in the right direction.

So let us find some measurements for 'nice'. Let's say that you interrogate the client and he tells you that to him, a 'nice product is one that is liked by the staff members who will use it'. A little more probing reveals that 'liked

Figure 9.2

If they know the performance criteria that the product must meet before it is accepted, the builders will, in all probability, build a product that will pass the test.

by the staff members' means that they take to it instinctively, and don't hesitate before using it.

This gives us something to measure. You can measure the amount of hesitation before using the product, the time elapsed before complete adoption of it, or you can survey the staff for user satisfaction after a period of time of using the product. Of course you have to agree with your client that your proposed measurement will in fact measure the quality that he seeks. Once it is agreed, then you have a fit criterion for a 'nice product'.

The point here is that anything can be measured, once you have found a suitable scale to measure it.

Scale of Measurement

The scale of measurement is the unit that you use to test conformance of the product. For example, if the requirement is for a certain speed of operation, then the scale is time – microseconds, minutes, and so on – to complete a given action or set of tasks. For a usability requirement, you can measure the time needed to learn a product, or the time taken before achieving an agreed level of competence, or perhaps even the error rate of the work done using the product.

There are scales of measurement for all sorts of qualities. Color can be measured by specifying its component colors as a percentage of cyan, magenta, yellow and black. Loudness and softness of sound is measured by decibels. An amount of light is measured by lumens. Typefaces can be measured by type names and point sizes. In fact there is a scale of measurement for almost everything. So far, the only thing that your authors have not been able to put a scale of measurement to is love.

To find an appropriate scale of measurement, start by analyzing the description and rationale that you have already established for the requirement.

> *Description: The product shall accept only British currency.*
> *Rationale: To prevent fraudulent use, and protect revenue.*

This requirement is about money, and ensuring that the product receives the correct amount of money. That is, it is not defrauded by accepting foreign currency. Thus a scale of measurement that suggests itself is a comparison of the amount of money that has been received with the amount that should have been received. This gives a fit criterion like this:

> *Fit Criterion: Actual valid sterling currency received by the product shall be equal to value of revenue recorded.*

Some fit criteria may, at first, be unattainable because of business, or real-life, constraints. Or your client may not be willing to spend whatever is required to meet the criterion. So you must adjust the fit criterion to allow for the product's operating environment, intended usage and client's budget. Think of these adjustments as *business tolerances*.

READING

FENTON, NORMAN AND SHARI LAWRENCE PFLEEGER. *Software Metrics: A Rigorous and Practical Approach.* International Thomson Computer Press, 1997.

> *Fit Criterion: Actual valid sterling currency received by the product shall be at least 99% of the value of revenue recorded.*

The 99% must not be arbitrary, it must be derived with the consent of the client and must be based on specified supporting material.

Let us consider the types of requirement, and how you can apply a fit criterion to each of them.

Fit Criteria for Functional Requirements

A functional requirement is something that the product must do: an action it must take. Thus the fit criterion specifies how you will know that the product has successfully done it. For functional requirements, there are no scales of measurement: the action is either completed or not. Completion depends on satisfying an authority — either the source of the data or the adjacent system that initiated the action — that the action has resulted in the correct manipulation of the data. The fit criterion for a functional requirement is supported by definitions of all of the terms mentioned in the fit criteria.

Functional requirements can be for different kinds of action. For example, if the action is to record something, then the fit criterion is that the recorded data complies with the data as known to the authority. For example:

PUTTING
THIS TO
WORK

> Description: The product shall record the weather station readings.
> Fit criterion: The recorded weather station readings shall match the readings sent by the weather station.

The authority in this case is the weather station: it initiated the action, and it is the source of the data. Thus you can say that the requirement is for the product to faithfully store the data (allow for the product to make necessary manipulations to the data) as sent from the weather station. If this is done correctly, then the product's data will conform to that transmitted by the station. Note that the fit criterion does not indicate how this is to be tested: it is simply a statement that the tester uses to ensure compliance.

If the functional requirement is to make some calculation, then the fit criterion says that the result of the calculation must be consistent with the authority's view of the data.

For example, if the requirement is that 'the product shall record ...', then the fit criterion reads 'the retrieved data will agree with ...' and cite the authority for the data. Usually this is the original source of the data. Where the requirement is 'the product shall check ...' then the fit criterion is 'the checked data conforms with ...' and again cite the authority for the data. 'The product shall calculate ...' results in a fit criterion 'the result conforms to ...' and this time give the algorithm (or source of the algorithm) for the result.

For the fit criteria to be complete the specification must contain a definition of the terms used in the fit criteria. If we are using the term Weather Station Readings then that term must be defined, otherwise the fit criterion ceases to be precise because it can be interpreted in more than one way.

The general rule for functional requirements is that the fit criterion ensures that the function has been successfully carried out.

For the fit criteria to be complete the specification must contain a definition of the terms used in the fit criteria

Section 5 of the specification template contains a definition of the terms used in the requirements specification. Refer to the Volere Template in Appendix B

Non-functional Fit Criteria

A non-functional requirement is a quality that the product must have, such as usability, look and feel, performance, and so on. The fit criterion quantifies that quality.

If you can't measure a requirement, then it is not really a requirement

Some of the non-functional requirements may at first seem difficult to quantify. However, you can place numbers against all of them. If you cannot quantify and measure a requirement, then it is likely that the requirement is not really a requirement. It might be several requirements, or it might be a requirement that has not been properly thought through. Alternatively, it might not be a requirement at all and should be deleted from the specification.

Let us look at some examples:

> *Description: The product shall be user friendly.*

This at first seems vague, ambiguous, and not at all lending itself to numbers. However, you can find a way to measure it. Start with the client: can he tell you more precisely what he means by 'user-friendly'? For example, does he mean easy to learn, or easy to use, or attractive and inviting, or some other meaning of 'user-friendly'?

PUTTING THIS TO WORK

Suppose that he clarifies his intention by saying 'I want my users to be quick to learn how to use the product'. This suggests a scale of measurement – the time taken to master given tasks. You can measure this by having a set of standard tasks and measuring the learning time needed before being able to do them successfully. Alternatively you can specify an amount of training time allowed before being able to use the product to a certain standard. Another measurement of how successful a user is at knowing the product could be the number of calls to a help desk or references to on-line help.

A suggested fit criterion for the 'user-friendly' requirement is:

> *Fit Criterion: New users shall be able to add, change and delete roads within 30 minutes of their first attempt at using the product.*

Earlier in this chapter you saw an example of a requirement that specified a nice product, and the client said that 'nice' meant the staff liked it. This gives you something to measure. If the staff like the product, then presumably they will use it. You could, for example, measure the rate at which they start using it, or how much they use it, or how soon word gets around that the product is good and users encourage each other to use it. All these are measurable and all quantify the client's desire that the staff like the product and use it (see Figure 9.3).

Figure 9.3

You could measure your users' liking for the product by surveying their work practices before and after introducing the product, or by measuring how long it would take them to start using it once it was available, or surveying them after a period of use to find their liking for the product.

> *Fit Criterion: Within three months of introducing the product, 60% of the users shall be using it to carry out the agreed work. From those users, the product shall receive a 75% or more approval rating.*

Note how determining the fit criterion clarifies the requirement. By searching for a measurement scale, the requirement is transformed from a vague and somewhat ambiguous intention to a fully formed, measurable requirement. Also note that it is usually not possible to get the complete, measurable requirement in the first instance. It is highly unlikely that your users will express themselves in such precise terms. Do not slow down the requirements gathering processes to make the requirement measurable, rather get the intention and go back to it and make it measurable later.

Product Failure?

The fit criterion can also be determined by asking your client 'What would be considered a failure to meet this requirement?' Let us suppose that the requirement is:

> *Description: The product must produce the road de-icing schedule in an acceptable time.*

Clearly the scale of measurement is time. Your client can tell you how much time he thinks would constitute a failure. For example, if the engineer has to wait for more than 15 seconds (or whatever) for the schedule, then the client will consider the product unacceptable. Thus the fit criterion, with suitable business tolerances applied, becomes:

> *Fit Criterion: The road de-icing schedule shall be available to the engineer within 15 seconds for 90% of the times that it is produced. The remaining times it will be available within 20 seconds.*

Sometimes, when you help the client to think about the requirement, you can define an agreed measure of acceptance. In other words, you make the requirement clear by making it measurable.

There will be times, however, when you discover that there is no agreement on a quality measure, and hence there can be no fit criterion. In these circumstances, it is possible that the original requirement is actually several requirements – each requirement has its own measurement – or the requirement is so vague, and its intention so unrealistic, that it is never possible to know whether it has been satisfied. For example: 'I want a product that my grandmother would have liked had she been alive today'.

Subjective Tests

Keep in mind that some requirements will have to be tested with subjective tests. For example, if the requirement is that a product to be used in the public domain is 'not offensive to any group', then the fit criterion must be along the lines of:

> *Fit Criterion: The product shall not be offensive to 85% of a test panel representing the makeup of the people likely to come in contact with the product. No more than 10% of the interest groups represented in the panel shall feel offended.*

The business tolerance here allows for the fact that you cannot count on 100% of humans passing any test. In this case the business tolerances shield the product from extreme minority views, while at the same time allow 'offensive' to be measured.

It is likely that a prototype, and not the delivered product itself, will be used for this kind of testing. Although the fit criteria are a measure of the product's performance, it is usually more cost effective to test prototypes built specifically for testing purposes.

Numbers used in fit criteria are not arbitrary. Let's say that there is a fit criterion 'to reduce the time to perform [some task] by 25% of the current time'. This means that the current time must be known and documented, not just guessed at. The reason for the target of a 25% reduction must be well understood, and agreed by the client. Ideally, the reasoning behind wanting 25%, and not 20% or 30%, is backed by empirical data taken from a study of the business.

Look and Feel Requirements

Look and feel requirements are about the spirit of the product's appearance, and the users' perception of the product.

For example, products in public areas may be required to be 'in company colors'. Colors are measurable – their RGB (red, green, blue) or CMYK (cyan, magenta, yellow, black) mixes specified, or a Pantone or other color scale number given – and the percentage of surface area colored can be measured.

Products that will have some software component may use conformance with cited interface guidelines as the fit criterion for look and feel. Usually these guidelines (Apple, Windows, Motif, and so on) are well documented, and it is fairly straightforward to find people qualified to certify that the product complies with the chosen guidelines.

For products that are required to be readable, there are several readability scoring systems. For example, the Flesch Reading Ease Score assigns a number according to several factors in the text. The highest score is 100, and a suggested score is in the 60–70 range. The Flesch–Kincaid Grade Level Score rates text against the US grade school levels of comprehension. For example, a score of 8.0 means that an eighth grader can understand it. Suggested scores for a standard document are in the 7.0 to 8.0 range.

Usability Requirements

Usability requirements are related to the intended users of the product. The product is usually required to be easy to use, easy to learn, able to be used by certain types of users, and so on. To write the fit criterion for these, you must find a measurement scale that quantifies the objective of the requirement.

Let's look at some examples.

> *Description: The product shall be intuitive and self-explanatory.*

To measure 'intuitive' you must consider the users to whom 'intuitive' applies. In this case you are told that the users will be road engineers, they will have an engineering degree, and have meteorological experience. When you know this, 'intuitive' takes on a different meaning.

> *Fit criterion: A road engineer shall be able to produce a correct de-icing forecast within ten minutes of encountering the product for the first time.*

Sometimes when the client says 'intuitive', he really means 'easy to learn'. In this case, you must ask how much time can be spent in training, and the resulting fit criterion might look like:

> Fit Criterion: Nine out of ten road engineers shall be able to successfully complete [list of selected tasks] after one day's training.

Fit criteria for usability requirements might also quantify the time allowed for given tasks, the error rates allowed (quantifying ease of use), the satisfaction rating awarded by the users, ratings given by usability laboratories, and so on. The important thing is to look for the real meaning of the requirement, and then confirm that meaning by having your client agree that the fit criterion is the correct measurement of that meaning.

The important thing is to look for the real meaning of the requirement, and then confirm that meaning by having your client agree that the fit criterion is the correct measurement of that meaning

Performance Requirements

Performance requirements are about the speed, accuracy, capacity, availability, reliability, and so on of the product. Most of the time, the nature of the performance requirements will suggest a measurement scale. Let us look at some examples:

The requirement is:

> Description: The response shall be fast enough to avoid interrupting the user's flow of thought.

The word 'fast' suggests that you measure time. A suggested fit criterion is:

> Fit Criterion: The response time shall be no more than 1.5 seconds for 95% of responses, and no more than 4 seconds for the remainder.

Similarly, fit criterion for an availability requirement might be:

> Fit Criterion: In the first three months of operation, the product shall be available for 98% of the time between 8 a.m. and 8 p.m.

As most performance requirements are themselves quantified, it should be fairly straightforward to write appropriate fit criteria. Naturally, if the requirement is given to you in correctly quantified terms, then the fit criterion and the requirement are the same.

Operational Requirements

These specify the environment in which the product will operate. In some cases the product has to be used in adverse or unusual conditions. Remember our example from the IceBreaker product:

> Description: The product shall be used in and around trucks, operating at freezing temperatures, at night. It is most likely to be raining or snowing. Salt and water are expected to come into contact with the product. Lighting will be poor. The operator will be wearing gloves.

The fit criterion is a quantification of ease of use, or the success of use, in the required environment. For the above, somewhat unusual, operational requirements, the fit criterion should quantify the ability of the operator to achieve specified tasks, and the ability of the product to withstand the conditions. For example:

> Fit Criterion: the operator shall successfully complete [list of tasks] within [time allowed] in a simulation of a 25-year storm (this is an accepted quantification of meteorological conditions) and the product shall function correctly after 24 hours exposure.

Operational conditions may also specify that the product must coexist with partner, or collaborating systems. The fit criterion in this case will cite the specification of the partner system:

> Fit Criterion: the interfaces to the DM31 Weather Station shall comply with the specifications issued by Saltworks Systems.

This is testable, at least by engineers from Saltworks, and points the product's builders toward a known and accepted standard.

Maintainability Requirements

These specify the expectation about the maintenance of the product. Usually the fit criteria for these requirements quantify the amount of time allowed to make certain changes. This is not to say that all maintenance changes can be anticipated, but where changes are expected, then it is possible to quantify the time allowed to adopt those changes.

> Fit Criterion: New users shall be added to the system with no more than five minutes disruption to existing users.

If the product is to be a software product, and there is a requirement to port it to another computer, then this is specified in the maintainability section. The fit criterion quantifies the amount of time, or effort, to make the port satisfactorily.

Security Requirements

Security requirements cover many aspects of the product, and the security of its operation. The most obvious security requirement is who, and under what circumstances, is allowed access to what parts of the product. The fit criterion could be something like:

> *Description: Only engineers using category A logons shall be able to alter the weather station data.*
> *Fit Criterion: Of 1000 alterations of the weather station data, none shall be from logons other than category A engineer logons.*

File integrity is part of security. The most common damage to computer files is done by authorized users accidentally corrupting the data. Thus there must be at least one requirement referring to file integrity. Its fit criterion would be something like this:

> *Fit Criterion: The product's data about static entities (weather stations, roads, etc.) shall conform to that held by all outside authorities.*

This fit criterion is saying that the product's data must agree with the authority for that data. As most data are transmitted to the product from the outside (changes to roads, new sensors, and so on), then the transmitter must be the authority. Thus if the product's data conform to the authority's, they are correct.

Cultural and Political Requirements

These requirements, by their nature, are subjective and difficult to quantify. The fit criterion is usually based on who will certify that the product is acceptable. The following examples of fit criteria should reveal their originating requirements:

> *Fit Criterion: The Shatnez Laboratory in Brooklyn shall certify that the product complies with the shatnez rules (We are indebted to Ethel Wittenberg for information on the Jewish prohibition on wearing a garment made of a mixture of linen and wool).*

> *Fit Criterion: Stan Hood of the auditing department shall approve the interface before it goes into production.*

> *Fit Criterion: The marketing department shall certify that all components are American made.*

Cultural requirements come about because different countries and different people have different customs, experiences and outlooks. When you are specifying fit criteria for cultural requirements, remember that words used in some countries are unknown in others that speak the same language. Make sure that you are not making assumptions about how the fit criteria will be interpreted by defining your terms in section 5 of your specification.

Legal Requirements

Legal requirements specify the conformance with laws. There is a fit criterion that will apply to most legal requirements: that your client wins a court case brought on by somebody using the product. However, fit criteria must be able to be tested in a cost-effective manner, and court cases are far too expensive to be indulged in lightly. Thus the majority of fit criteria will be along the lines of:

> *Fit Criterion: The legal department/company lawyers shall certify that the product complies with the [applicable laws].*

Legal requirements are also written to ensure that the product complies with cited standards. Most standards are written by organizations that either have people who certify compliance – 'standards lawyers' – or issue guidelines as to how you can certify compliance for yourself. In either case, fit criteria can be written to specify how compliance with the standard is to be verified.

Use Cases and Fit Criteria

A use case is a cluster of requirements. Each requirement, both functional and non-functional, has its own fit criterion. If we can measure each of the requirements, then we can measure the collection. Thus we can apply a fit criterion to the use case.

To be precise, the fit criterion for a use case is really made up of all the fit criteria belonging to all the requirements that make up that use case. If you want the solution to completely fit the use case then each of the related requirements' fit criteria must be satisfied. However, we find that it helps communication and understanding to also have a fit criterion for the use case.

> Use Case 8:
> Produce de-icing schedule
> Fit Criterion: The de-icing schedule shall include all roads that will freeze within the time interval specified by the engineer.

Note that this fit criterion is measuring the outcome of the use case. That is, it is quantifying your client's desired result of this use case. It describes the purpose of the use case, and your designer can use it as the standard that applies to the implementation.

The use case fit criterion is a summary of all the included requirements

The use case fit criterion is a summary of the intentions of all the related requirements. It does not replace the individual requirements' fit criteria, but it does help you to communicate more accurately about the intentions and the outcomes of the use case.

We suggest that you make use of fit criteria for use cases very early in your requirements gathering. During the blastoff (or whenever you break the work into business events) it is worthwhile eliciting from your users and client, success criteria for each of them. In other words, you are asking 'When this event happens, what do you want the outcome to be? How can I quantify that outcome?' This applies a fit criterion to a business event. As your business events evolve into use cases, the same, or very similar, fit criterion can be applied at the use case level. You will find, as we have, that an early fit criterion eliminates a lot of misunderstandings about what each event is intended to accomplish.

As you capture individual requirements, and their fit criteria, keep in mind that each of them has to contribute in some way to the purpose of the product. If you have a fit criterion attached to each use case, the gap between the requirement and the whole product is lessened. It is easier to look at the use case fit criterion to ensure that all the requirements you are capturing contribute to the use case as a whole.

Similarly when you are running a use case workshop, or testing the requirements for a use case, it helps communication with other stakeholders if you have a clearly defined, that is to say quantified, goal for that use case. That goal is the use case fit criterion.

Fit Criteria for Constraints

Product Purpose

We have already discussed writing the fit criterion for the product's purpose. We didn't call it a fit criterion back in Chapter 3, but that is what it is. We called it a measurement. Let's look quickly at it again. The product's purpose is a statement of what the product is intended to do or what problem it is intended to solve. If you are going to the trouble and expense of developing this product, then it makes a lot of sense to have an objective benchmark that you can measure the delivered product against.

This measurement of the purpose is exactly the same as a fit criterion for an individual requirement. The only difference being that the fit criterion measures a single requirement, whereas the purpose's measurement measures the whole product.

Refer to Chapter 3, Project Blastoff, for information on writing a measurable product purpose

Solution Constraints

The other constraints in this division of the specification do not need fit criteria, except for type 4 – Requirements Constraints. This type of requirement places restrictions on the way that the problem must be solved. In other words, it places mandates on the design solutions. For example:

> Description: The software part of the product must run with the Linux system.

This requirement comes about from a desire by management to continue, or to start to use the Linux operating system. It may (or it may not) have a sound technological basis, but that is beside the point. You are being told that any solution you deliver has to comply with this constraint.

We can test compliance – you either comply with the requirement or you don't – as long as whatever it is that you have to comply with is itself measurable. That means that you can test whether you have complied with a law, but you can't test if you have complied with a constraint that 'you shall be happy'. In the case of the Linux constraint, you could write:

> Fit Criterion: The software part of the product shall comply with the specification of S.U.S.E. Linux release 5.2.

Summary

The fit criterion is not a test. It is not the design for a test. It is, however, an unambiguous goal that the product has to meet. It is used as input to building a test where the tester will ensure that each of the product's requirements complies with its fit criterion.

Quantifying the requirement gives you a better opportunity to interact with your client and your users. By quantifying it you are confirming that you have indeed understood the requirement correctly, and that both of you have an identical understanding of it. You will also find that quantifying it ensures that the requirement is both wanted and necessary.

Adding a fit criterion to a requirement implies that the testers will become involved in writing the requirements. Testers should be involved early in the development cycle – we cannot stress this enough. Testers can help you to specify the fit criteria. This is not to say that the testers should write the fit criteria. It is perhaps not advisable for people to test something they have written themselves. However, testers are the best source of knowledge about whether or not something can be tested, and whether the fit criterion contains the appropriate quantification. In other words, the testers are consultants for the fit criteria.

The fit criterion is the requirement

The description that you write is the user's way of stating the requirement. However, if your user is like most of us, then he speaks using everyday language. Everyday language is, unfortunately, often ambiguous and sometimes not precise enough. Thus you need an adjunct to the requirement – a fit criterion that is stated in unambiguous and precise terms, and most importantly, uses numbers or measurement to convey its meaning.

Fit criteria are usually derived some time after the requirement description is first written down. You derive the fit criterion by closely examining the requirement, and determining what quantification best expresses the user's intention for the requirement. You might find that this close examination results in changes to the requirement. This is quite normal. The act of quantifying often shows us that the requirement was not properly understood in the first instance. However, with patience and persistence, and the wise use of numbers, you can ensure that each of your requirements is testable and real.

Quality Gateway

 in which we prevent unworthy requirements
from entering the specification

The Quality Gateway is each requirement's formal point of entry into the requirements specification. Why do we need a Gateway? Consider the life that a requirement leads before it arrives at the Quality Gateway: the requirement could have come from anywhere. You have used a variety of trawling techniques to discover the requirements. Each one was captured – regardless of its completeness or coherency – whenever and however it appeared. You caught requirements when they came out of people's mouths, when you observed them, when you read them. Your concern is to capture all the requirements and not to miss anything. The resulting potential requirements are in a variety of forms (interview notes, sample documents, videos, scenario models, rough sketches in your notebook ...) and states of completion, which makes them difficult to review. At this stage we call these *potential* requirements.

The writing process applies the template and the shell to the potential requirements and puts them into a consistent form. Now we can call them *formalized* potential requirements.

When the formalized potential requirement arrives at the Quality Gateway it should be complete enough to undergo the tests to determine whether it should be accepted into the specification or excluded. If it is excluded, then it is returned to its source for clarification, revision or discarding. See Figure 10.1.

It is worth emphasizing that you can, in fact you should, apply some or all of the Quality Gateway tests to a requirement at any stage of your requirements gathering. The way that you implement the Quality Gateway (who will do what, when they will do it and how many times they will do it)

Figure 10.1

The Quality Gateway is the activity where each requirement is examined to determine if it is suitable for inclusion in the specification. The point of the Quality Gateway is that the *only* way for a requirement to get into the specification is to pass through the Gateway successfully. For a detailed process model of the Quality Gateway, refer to Diagram 4 and its supporting material in Appendix A (Volere Requirements Process Model).

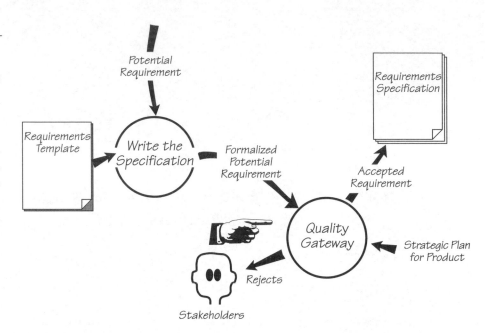

depends on how you decide to tailor the process to suit your project. We will talk more about ideas for tailoring later on. First we will concentrate on the tests that we apply to an individual requirement.

You will find that the Quality Gateway checks and tests are useful for most of the requirements specification. However, you will find that it is most applicable to:

● Purpose of the Product (type 1 in the specification template);

● Requirements Constraints (type 4 in the template. These are global restrictions on the requirements and the way that the product must be delivered);

● Functional Requirements (type 9);

● Non-functional Requirements (types 10–17 – requirements for the properties or qualities that the product must have).

Using the Gateway

The intention is to prevent incorrect requirements from being carried forward to the design and implementation where they will be more difficult and expensive to find and correct

As soon as you have a single requirement in your net you can start testing. The aim is to trap requirements-related defects as early as they can be identified. The intention is to prevent incorrect requirements from being carried forward to the design and implementation where they will be more difficult and expensive to find and correct.

To pass through the Quality Gateway and be included in the requirements specification, a requirement must pass a number of tests. These tests

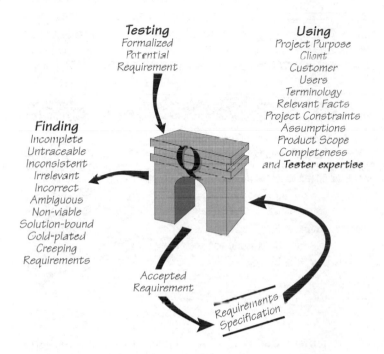

Figure 10.2

The Quality Gateway tests each requirement against the global constraints (sections 1–7 on the template) and the product scope defined by the use case boundaries (section 8). Accepted requirements are added to the specification.

ensure that the requirements are complete and accurate, and do not cause problems by being unsuitable for the design and implementation stages later in the project. This is illustrated in Figure 10.2.

We will discuss each of the requirements tests in a stand-alone manner. Once you are familiar with the tests, you can decide when, in your requirements process, it is appropriate to apply each of them.

Completeness

In Chapter 8, Writing the Specification, we discussed using the requirements shell as a way of making it easy to gather all the components necessary to make a complete requirement. That chapter contains a discussion of each component on the requirements shell.

The requirements shell is a container for an individual requirement. The shell identifies the component parts of a requirement. You can use the shell to help you test whether a requirement is complete. See Figure 10.3.

Chapter 8, Writing the Specification

The Requirements Shell is packaged as part of the Template in Appendix B

Are there any Missing Components?

The first test for completeness is to compare the requirement with the components that appear on the shell. While it is not always necessary to have every component for every requirement, if some components are missing then there should be a good reason for their absence.

Figure 10.3

An example of a
complete requirement
using the Volere shell.
There are no known
dependencies or
conflicts, and the
requirements analyst has
correctly marked the
requirement as having
none. This requirement
should pass the
completeness tests.

Requirement #: **75**   Requirement Type: **9**   Event/use case #: **6**

Description: **The product shall issue an alert if a weather station fails to transmit readings.**

Rationale: **Failure to transmit readings might indicate that the weather station is faulty and needs maintenance, and that the data used to predict freezing roads may be incomplete.**

Source: **Road Engineers**

Fit Criterion: **For each weather station the product shall communicate to the user when the recorded number of each type of reading per hour is not within the manufacturer's specified range of the expected number of readings per hour.**

Customer Satisfaction: **3**   Customer Dissatisfaction: **5**

Dependencies: **None**   Conflicts: **None**

Supporting Materials: **Specification of Rosa Weather Station**

History: **Raised by GBS, 28 July 99**

Volere
Copyright © Atlantic Systems Guild

The components of the shell come from successful requirements projects. They are items that we have, over the years, found to be valuable and to contribute to the clarity and reasoning of a requirement. They are measurements, or explanations, or pointers to other information or requirements that will be used at several stages of the project. Thus it is advisable to include as many as are appropriate for the requirement.

There are, however, times when they are not all necessary. For example, sometimes the *Description* makes it obvious why the requirement is important. In that case there would be no point in writing the *Rationale*. Sometimes the *Description* can be dropped, as there is a clear and readable *Fit Criterion*. Sometimes there are no *Supporting Materials*.

Naturally if one of the components is missing then it should be because it is not necessary rather than because it is too difficult or has been overlooked. If the component is missing because you are still investigating it, perhaps waiting for an answer from somebody, then write that on the requirement to forestall unnecessary questions:

Supporting Material: 10/10/99 waiting for county engineer to supply details of supporting material.

The completeness test says that each requirement shall have all relevant components, or you should record the reason why they have not been, or cannot be, completed.

Meaningful to All Stakeholders?

Once you are satisfied that the requirement has all the relevant components, you need to make sure that each component adds to the meaning and common understanding of the requirement.

This means that the requirement is written as clearly as possible. Conciseness, while admired, must not be adopted to such an extent that information that may add to the understanding has been omitted.

Test each component of the requirement and, from the point of view of each stakeholder, ask 'Is it possible to misunderstand this?' For instance in Figure 10.3 we see:

> Supporting Material
> Specification of Rosa Weather Station

so we ask 'Is it possible to confuse this?' 'Is there more than one specification of the Rosa Weather Station?' 'Is there any doubt about where to find this specification?' The answer to these questions helps us to be more precise about exactly what we mean and the resultant entry reads:

> Supporting Material
> Specification of Rosa Weather Station published Jan 22, 1998

RULE OF THUMB

From the point of view of each stakeholder ask 'Is it possible to misunderstand this?'

READING

For more on stakeholders' viewpoints refer to: SOMMERVILLE, IAN AND PETE SAWYER. *Requirements Engineering*. JOHN WILEY, 1998.

Testing Traceability

Remember the old story of the First World War general who needed to get a message back to headquarters. He gave the message to his next in command: 'Send reinforcements, we're going to advance'. The message was passed between runners and shouted to other messengers until at last it reached headquarters, except now the message was 'Send three and fourpence, we're going to a dance'. This is the sort of thing that happens when there are many intermediate transitions between the origin of a message and its final delivery. This is very much the same as a requirement going through the many stages before it is finally delivered as a working product. Each stage is a transformation, with the possibility that the requirement is misunderstood, applied wrongly, or somehow scrambled in the translation by one of the many people involved in the development of the product.

Thus it is vital that you are able to connect the original requirement with the part of the delivered product that implements that requirement. In other words, there is a connection from the beginning of the development process to the end of it – you can ensure that the requirement that is specified is actually the requirement that is implemented. Figure 10.4 illustrates this.

Figure 10.4

This model shows the connections between the elements of the requirements specification. We need to know these connections if we are to establish complete traceability. For example, the Product Boundary is delineated by a number of use cases (the * in UML notation means many) and each use case is a cluster of many requirements. A requirement can be subject to a number of Requirement Constraints, just as a Requirement Constraint may apply to many Requirements (the * to * association). The Work Context is made up of a number of Business Events, each of which can be implemented in the product as one or more Use Cases. (This is discussed in Chapter 4, Event-driven Use Cases.) To maintain traceability we need to have a system of knowing which requirements belong to which use cases, which business events are implemented with which use cases, and so on.

Is the requirement uniquely identifiable?

Is the requirement cross-referenced to business events, use cases, dependent requirements, conflicting requirements?

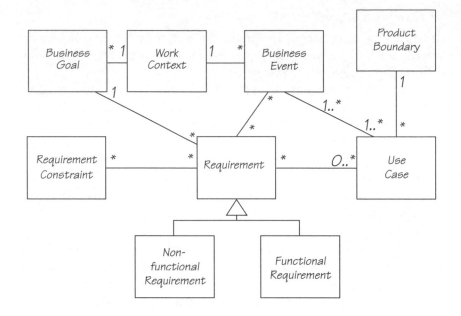

To make sure each of your requirements is traceable it must have:

- A unique identifier;
- An indicator of the type of requirement or constraint (these are listed in the template);
- References to all of the business events and use cases that contain this requirement;
- References to dependent requirements that might use the same subject matter, or have some change effect on this one;
- References to other requirements that are in conflict;
- Consistent use of terminology.

If the requirements are traceable, then when changes happen, it is far easier to find the parts of the product that are affected by the change and to assess the impact of the change on the rest of the product. Keep in mind that the requirements can change at any stage during the product's life. Keeping your requirements traceable means that you can design the most effective way to make the change.

Consistent Terminology

When a poet writes a poem he intends that it should trigger off rich and diverse visions for anyone who reads it. The requirements analyst has the opposite intention – he would like each requirement to be understood in the same way by every person who reads it. If the requirements specification is more like poetry, then it is open to any interpretation that seems reasonable to the reader. The danger of subjective appraisal of the requirement means that the product might be built to satisfy the wrong interpretation of the requirement.

To specify a requirement so that it is understood in only one way, we need to do two things. Firstly, define the terms we are using and the meaning of those terms within the specification. Section 5 of the requirements specification template is called Naming Conventions and Definitions. This section is a repository for the terms that are used for this project. The terms are given a definition that is agreed by the stakeholders. This section acts as a reference point for the words used to write the requirements.

Does the specification contain a definition of the meaning of every essential subject matter term within the specification?

The second act of consistency is to test that every requirement uses terms in a manner consistent with their specified meaning. It's not enough to define the terminology. We have to be sure that each term is being used correctly. For example, in a requirements specification that we assessed, we found the term 'viewer' in many parts of the specification. Our audit identified six different meanings for the term, depending on the context of its use. This kind of requirements defect always causes problems during design and/or implementation. If you are lucky, a developer will realize that there is inconsistency, but will have to reinvestigate the requirement. This almost always causes a ripple effect that extends to other parts of the product. If you are not lucky, the designer will choose the meaning that makes most sense to him and implement that one. Any stakeholder who does not agree with that meaning will then consider that the system does not meet the requirement.

One last word about inconsistency, you should expect it and you should look for it as part of the process of specifying requirements. When you discover inconsistencies they identify a need for further investigation and perhaps negotiation.

Is every reference to a defined term consistent with its definition?

Relevant to Purpose?

When you are trawling for requirements you are certain to come across some perfectly charming, well-stated, complete requirements that are irrelevant to the purpose of your product. This happens on most projects – users become enthusiastic and start adding everything they can think of, developers add requirements because they want to make the product all encompassing. However, this kind of irrelevancy quickly leads to requirements creep, with the probable result that the project runs significantly over time and over budget, and then doesn't deliver the product that the project set out to build in the first place.

Chapter 3, Project Blastoff, discusses how to define the purpose of the product

Does this requirement contribute to the purpose of the product?

In the chapter on project blastoff we discussed how to identify the purpose of the project and to write it down as quantifiable product goals. These goals are the arbiter of relevancy throughout the project.

To test a requirement for relevancy, compare its intention with the product goals. The test is fairly simple: does this requirement contribute to the purpose of the product? Does this requirement add something to the product that will, directly or indirectly, make the product meet its purpose?

As an example, imagine that you are working on the IceBreaker project and you come across the requirement:

> The product shall maintain a lookup table of the times of sunrise and sunset throughout the year.

At first this appears to be relevant. The product has to predict the formation of ice on roads, and ice usually forms at night – this requirement appears to contribute to the product goal:

> Product Goal:
> To accurately predict when ice will form on road surfaces and to efficiently schedule the appropriate de-icing treatment.

However if we dig a little deeper we discover that it is the temperature of the road surface that determines whether ice will form, and that road temperature is monitored and transmitted by weather stations. In other words, whether it is night or day does not override the actual temperature. Ice is perfectly capable of forming during the daylight hours, and so there is no reason for the product to have any knowledge of day or night.

Note that requirements can contribute *indirectly* to the product. There will be times when the requirement is for the product to do something that has no immediate connection to the purpose, however, without it, the product could not achieve its purpose. Also consider that a lot of the non-functional requirements contribute indirectly to the product's goals.

Irrelevant requirements should be returned to their source with a short explanation. Be prepared to invest a little time in this, as an 'irrelevant' requirement may mean that a stakeholder has misunderstood the purpose, or that a new business area is opening. In other words, you have to make a judgment whether the requirement is truly irrelevant, or the original scope has become incorrect because of business changes.

Let's consider the scope as it also determines relevancy. The scope of the product is determined during the blastoff. This should result in section 8 of the specification containing a work context diagram that shows the flows of

See section 8 of the template in Appendix B, Volere Template, for a sample context model. Also refer to Chapter 3, Project Blastoff, for information on how to set the context information between the work and the adjacent systems. You can use these flows as a test for relevancy.

For example, suppose that you are given a potential requirement like this. Does it fit within the scope we have defined for IceBreaker?

> *The product shall record the overtime worked by the truck drivers.*

Look at the product boundaries. A product context model (usually recorded in section 8 of the specification) shows the boundaries of the product. It shows the boundaries by the flows of information that enter or leave the product. Compare the above requirement with the boundary flows. Do any of the flows have anything to do with recording truck drivers' working time? Are there flows that indicate the product is dealing with working hours? Is there anything on the context model that indicates overtime hours should be stored within the product?

In this case there is nothing that makes the overtime requirement relevant. If it were to be included, then it would not connect to anything else in the product, and would be redundant functionality.

When considering relevancy, pay particular attention to the following sections of your specification:

Is every requirement relevant within the stated boundaries of this product?

- Users (section 3 of the specification template). Who are you building the product for, and is it a product suitable for these users?
- Requirements Constraints (section 4). Is the product relevant within the constraints? And have all the constraints been observed by the requirements?
- Relevant Facts (section 6). Are there any external factors that have not been taken into account by the requirements?
- Assumptions (section 7). The requirements should be consistent with any assumptions you are making about the project.

Testing Fit Criteria

Requirements can be ambiguous. In fact, any English language (or any other language) statement can be ambiguous. Natural language can also be subjectively understood. This is obviously not the way that we should write requirements, so as well as the natural language description of the requirement, we write a fit criterion. The fit criterion is a quantification of the requirement. In other words, as far as possible, the fit criterion uses numbers (numbers have no ambiguity) instead of words to express the requirement.

See Chapter 9 for a full explanation of how to write fit criteria

The fit criterion is a measurement of the requirement

The fit criterion is a *measurement* of the requirement that enables the testers to determine, without recourse to subjective judgments, whether the delivered solution meets, or fits, the requirement.

It is essential that each requirement has a fit criterion. The first question to ask is 'Does the requirement have a correctly defined fit criterion?' Any requirements that do not have one must be considered to be incomplete, as there is still a large degree of uncertainty about the requirement. It is this simple – if you cannot measure it, you don't understand it. Reject any requirements that do not have a valid fit criterion.

The next test for the fit criterion is whether it can be used as input to designing acceptance tests. You may need help from the testing people to do this. The fit criterion is not the test, but should indicate what kinds of tests need to be done to ensure that the delivered solution complies with the original requirement. At this stage you should also consider whether the tests could be cost effective.

Does each requirement have a fit criterion that can be used to test whether a solution meets the requirement?

The fit criterion must also meet the purpose of the product. We have discussed how the requirement must conform to the product purpose, so it obviously makes sense that the measurement of the requirement conforms to this purpose.

While the fit criterion uses numbers to express the requirement, the numbers themselves must not be subjective, but must be based on evidence. For example, suppose that you have a requirement that the product be easy to learn. This is a reasonable requirement, but it is subjective. We add a fit criterion that says given tasks must be able to be learned within 30 minutes of encountering the product. The question is 'Where did the 30 minutes come from?' Is it simply the whim of a stakeholder? Or is it based on evidence that anything longer than 30 minutes means the users will become discouraged and give up? It is of course useful if the requirement writer has included a reference to the evidence in the *Supporting Materials* component of the requirement.

The fit criterion uses a scale of measurement. For example, if the requirement is that something be fast, then the scale of measurement for the fit criterion is time. Check that the scale of measurement is appropriate for the requirement, and that acceptance tests run using that scale will in fact show the product fits the requirement.

The fit criterion measurement may include some business tolerances. For example, if the fit criterion specifies that a number of people have to perform certain tasks within certain time limits, then the business tolerance allows a small percentage of the test panel to fail. This tolerance exists because you cannot expect 100% of humans to be able to do everything. Similarly, products that handle material or deal with imperfect outside world artifacts might be allowed a certain margin of error, or business tolerance. Consider whether the business tolerance is based on appropriate evidence.

Viable Within Constraints?

Viable requirements are those that are workable within the project. That is, they comply with the constraints set down for the product. Constraints cover such things as the amount of time available to build the product, the anticipated workplace environment, the users of the product, constraints on the design of the product, and so on.

Each requirement must be tested for viability within the constraints. This means considering each of the constraints, and asking if the requirement contradicts it in any way.

For example, the users of the product are a constraint. Whatever product you are specifying must be consistent with those users. It must be easy for the user to operate it, but sophisticated enough to provide the needed functionality. As an example, this requirement for the IceBreaker product is not viable:

> Truck drivers shall receive the weather forecasts, and schedule their own de-icing.

Truck drivers do not have the necessary information at hand to predict the time that a road will freeze. Similarly, coordinating a number of trucks treating roads in a county is a matter for centralized control.

You might also consider whether the organization is mature enough to cope with a requirement.

Do you have the technological skills to build the requirement? It is easy to write a requirement, but it is sometimes a different, more difficult thing to construct a working solution for it. At this stage of the development, you should not pretend to have development capabilities greater than exist. This test is a matter of assessing – unfortunately there can be no measurement here – whether the requirement is beyond the technical capabilities of the construction team. You can, however, consider this question from the point of view of the experience of the team and the time and budget constraints placed on the project.

Do you have the time and the money to build the requirement? This test means estimating the time or money needed for the requirement, and assessing that as a share of the total budget. (The budgets should be listed as a constraint in section 4 of the requirements specification.) If the cost of constructing a requirement does exceed its budget, then the customer value attached to the requirement is a good indicator of how to proceed: high value requirements are negotiated, low value requirements are candidates for discarding.

Product constraints are described in sections 1–7 of the Volere Template in Appendix B

Do you have the technological skills to build the requirement?

Do you have the time and the money to build the requirement?

Is the requirement acceptable to all stakeholders?

Is the requirement acceptable to all stakeholders? This is simple self-defense. If a requirement is unpopular with some of the stakeholders, then history tells us that it is futile to include it in the product. Stakeholders have been known to sabotage the development of products because they disagreed with part or all of the product. Users have been known to ignore and not use products because not all of the functionality was as they thought it should be.

Are there any other constraints that make the requirement non-viable? Do any of the partner applications or the expected work environment contradict the requirement? Are there solution constraints – that is constraints on the way that a solution must be designed – that make the requirement difficult or impossible to achieve?

Requirement or Solution?

The more abstract the requirement, the less likely it is to be a solution

The description of a requirement is often stated in terms of a solution. We all unconsciously talk about requirements in terms of how we think they should be solved. We talk of solutions rather than requirements because of our personal experience of the world. This results in a statement that focusses on one possible solution – not necessarily the most appropriate one – and hides the real requirement.

Examine the requirement. Does it contain any element of technology? Or is it written in a way that describes a type of procedure?

The more abstract the statement, the less likely it is to be a solution. For example, if you write:

> *The product shall be easy to use.*

then it is a requirement. However, if you write:

> *The product shall have a graphical user interface.*

it is a solution. Note the use of technology 'graphical user interface' in the requirement.

Sometimes we unconsciously state solutions. For example, this is a solution:

> *The product shall have a clock on the menu bar.*

Both 'clock' and 'menu bar' are parts of a solution. We suggest that the real requirement is

> *The product shall make the user aware of the current time.*

When you write the requirement in an abstract manner, other solutions are possible. There are ways other than a clock to make people aware of the time. There are ways other than graphical user interfaces to make products easy to use.

Note that there will be requirements or constraints that sound like solutions. For example, if your product is shrink-wrapped software, and your client does not think that any interface except a graphical one would sell, then having a graphical interface becomes a requirement. However, this is more likely to be written in the Requirements Constraints part of the specification in section 4.

Examine your requirements. Examine any that are solutions and ask is that what the client really wants. Could you rewrite them as requirements without the technological content?

Also, ask 'Why?' For example, suppose that you have this requirement in your Quality Gateway:

> *Users shall use passwords to access the system.*

Why is this a requirement? 'Because we don't want unauthorized people to access confidential information.' Now you are discovering the real requirement:

> *The product shall provide access to confidential information only to authorized users.*

There are lots of ways to assure confidential access to information, passwords is just one of them.

Of course, from time to time people will come up with great ideas for solutions. Keep them in a special file labeled potential solutions, or add them to section 19 Off-the-Shelf Solutions of the requirements specification. You should always trap great ideas when you think of them. However, do not be tempted to distort the product's requirements to fit the great solution idea. It may be great, but it may also be the solution to another problem.

For more on writing requirements not solutions look at Chapter 6, Functional Requirements, and Chapter 7, Non-functional Requirements

Customer Value

The customer satisfaction/dissatisfaction ratings attached to a requirement indicate the value that the customer places on a requirement. The

The customer satisfaction/ dissatisfaction ratings indicate the value that the customer places on a requirement

See Chapter 13, Taking Stock of the Specification, for a discussion of how to use the customer value ratings to prioritize requirements

READING
For a good summary of QFD see MACAULAY, LINDA A. *Requirements Engineering.* Springer, 1996.

READING
For more on customer satisfaction and dissatisfaction ratings refer to: PARDEE, WILLIAM J. *To Satisfy and Delight Your Customer.* New York, 1996.

satisfaction rating is a measure of how happy the customer will be if you successfully deliver an implementation of the requirement, and the *dissatisfaction* rating measures the amount of *unhappiness* the customer will feel if you do not successfully deliver this requirement. See Chapter 8, the section on Customer Satisfaction and Customer Dissatisfaction.

We have found that this two-step approach helps people to think more objectively about a requirement rather than mechanically giving it a number on a scale from one to ten.

You may care to substitute Quality Function Deployment (QFD) for this exercise. QFD was developed by the Japanese car industry to ensure that all requirements are expressed 'in the voice of the Customer'. QFD includes a matrix for identifying the Customer Importance Rating. The difference between the Customer Importance Rating and Customer Value is that, rather than having one importance rating, Customer Value has two ways of rating each requirement.

The test to apply here is that the requirement carries an appropriate rating of the value that the customer places on the requirement.

Your customer, or a panel made up of the significant stakeholders, sets the ratings with your help. Later, these ratings will be weighed against the cost of the requirement and, if necessary, will be used to help make choices between requirements. Although this may seem to be something of an arduous exercise, knowing precisely how much value to attach to a requirement is very worthwhile. If you have a large number of requirements that have a satisfaction/dissatisfaction rating of 5/5, then it indicates that the values have not been thoughtfully rated. As this is the best opportunity your customer has of letting you know what is important and what is not, we suggest that you reject the ratings and ask that they be done again. Make sure that your customer understands that your reason for doing this is to understand what is most important to his business; then if you need to make tradeoffs you will choose the ones that are most relevant. Another reason for attaching customer values to the requirement is to determine what is, and what is not, gold plating.

Gold Plating

The term 'gold plating' comes from gold plated bathroom taps. Some people like to have gold plated taps. The water does not come out of the gold plated tap any better than it does from a chrome plated one. The difference is that the gold plated tap costs more. This term has been taken up by the software industry to mean features and requirements that contribute more to the cost of a product than they do to the functionality or usefulness.

Let's look at an example. Suppose there is a requirement for the IceBreaker product to play a piece of classical music at the beginning of each day. Knowing what we know about the IceBreaker product leads us to suspect that this is a gold plated requirement. It does not appear to contribute to the overall goals of the product. But maybe the truck depot supervisor thinks that the product would be more pleasing to the users if it plays music to them.

Does it matter if this requirement is not included?

This is gold plating. It is there because it might be 'nice to have'. Nobody would mind if the requirement were not included in the product. So the first test of gold plating is 'Does it matter if the requirement is not included?' If nobody can truly justify its inclusion, then it may be considered gold plating.

The second, and perhaps more reliable test, is to look at the customer values attached to the requirement. A low dissatisfaction rating indicates a requirement that is probably gold plating. After all, if the customer has said that it does not matter if this requirement is not included, then he is signaling a requirement whose contribution to the product is not vital.

A low dissatisfaction rating indicates a requirement that is probably gold plating

We hasten to add that we do not advocate excluding all gold plated requirements from your product. It is often a good idea to add that little something extra, that extra little bit of chocolate. Sometimes a little gold plating makes a big difference to the acceptance of the product. Sometimes we take great delight in unnecessary but delightful features – the screen saver, the sounds attached to alerts, changing screen colors and wallpaper, pictorial and customizable icons. The list of gold plated items that delight us goes on and on.

The point is that you should know if a requirement is gold plating and if you include it, it should be a conscious choice. If you discover that you cannot implement all of the requirements within the project constraints, then gold plated requirements are candidates for exclusion.

Requirements Creep

Requirements creep refers to requirements that enter the specification after the requirements process is supposed to be finished. Naturally, the requirements process is *never* finished (the product keeps on evolving) however there is a stage of the project when you decide that you are going to go ahead and build the product. The requirements that happen after this stage are the ones considered to be requirements creep.

Requirements creep has gained itself a bad name, usually because of the disruption to the schedules, and the bloated costs of product delivery. Without wanting to defend requirements creep, we do think it prudent to look at some of the causes of creep, and discuss how we can approach this problem.

Firstly, most creep comes about because the requirements were never gathered properly in the first place. If the requirements are incomplete, then as the product develops, more and more omissions must of necessity be discovered. The users, aware that product delivery is now imminent, ask for more and more 'new' functions. But are they really new? We suggest that they are requirements that in reality, were part of the product all along. They were just not, until now, part of the requirements specification.

Similarly, if the users and the clients are not given the opportunity to participate fully in the requirements process, then there is no doubt that the specification will be incomplete. Almost certainly the requirements will creep as delivery approaches and the users begin asking for functionality that they know they need.

We have also observed creep that came about because the original budget (for political reasons) was set unrealistically low. When the incredibly noticeable creep set in, it was not so much a matter of the requirements creeping, but the product bringing itself to its correct functionality.

Requirements also change. Quite often they change for the very good reason that the business has changed, or new technological advances have made change desirable. These kinds of changes are often seen as requirements creep. However, if changes that cause the new requirements happen after the official 'end' of the requirements process – and they could not have been anticipated – then this type of requirements creep could not have been avoided.

Whatever the reason, good or bad, you must be able to identify the reason for the creep. Moreover, you must be able to respond appropriately.

A little earlier in this chapter we spoke about the relevancy of requirements, and how the requirement must be relevant to the product purpose, and within the scope of the work. If requirements are creeping outside the scope, or are not relevant to the product purpose, then we suggest that you have serious cause for concern. Is the scope correct? Are the goals for the product correct and realistic? There is no way that we can diagnose your problem in this book, but we suggest that you look long and hard at the root cause of your requirements creep.

The best way of minimizing requirements creep is a good requirements process, with the active and enthusiastic participation of the stakeholders. That and having reasonably sized projects. Anything less and you must expect some creep to happen to your requirements. When it does, identify the cause, and use that to fine-tune your requirements process.

We have not spoken about the effect of requirements creep on your budget. Let's look at that along with another problem, requirements leakage.

Requirements Leakage

Requirements leakage refers to those requirements that somehow 'leak' into the specification. Another way to think about requirements leakage is unrecognized and uncontrolled requirement creep. Nobody knows where they came from, nor who is responsible for them. Nobody wants to own them. And yet, leaking requirements have an effect on the budget. If they are to be accommodated, then the project plan has to be adjusted.

Consider this: Capers Jones says that for the average project, about 35% of the requirements appear after the requirements process is deemed to have ended. That is, about a third of all the requirements have crept or leaked into the specification.

The effect of this is shown in Figure 10.5. The graph shows the cost of delivering functionality. You should have a graph like this to make everyone realize that functionality is not free. Look at what happens if we increase the size of the product by 35%. The effort needed goes up by a little more than that. And yet, this is the part of the product that somebody expected to get for free. When the requirements grow beyond what was originally anticipated, then the budget must grow proportionally. But how often do you hear 'Just one more little thing. It won't affect the budget'? It does affect the budget. Each requirement has a cost attached. So what to do about it?

The Quality Gateway must ensure that all requirements carry a source. This gives you the starting point that the originator of any requirement is known. Next the Quality Gateway must ensure that each requirement carries valid customer satisfaction/dissatisfaction ratings. These tell you what

READING

JONES, CAPERS. *Software Quality – Analysis and Guidelines for Success.* International Thomson, 1997.

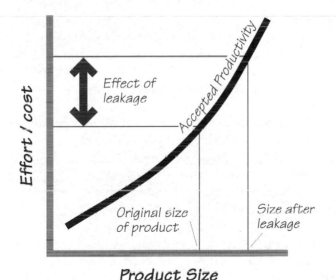

Figure 10.5

If you know the rate of productivity at your organization, then it is fairly simple to convert the size of the product into an amount of effort or a cost. However, if the size of the product increases, then the amount of effort needed naturally increases. It is this increase, due to uncontrolled requirements creep or leakage, that causes many projects to get into deep water.

value your client/customer places on the requirement. If it is high, then creeping requirements might be tolerated (with an adjustment to the budget). The Rationale attached to the requirement must also make sense. We have often found that leaking requirements do not make sense, or are outside the scope. If you are armed with the measurements that we advocate attaching to requirements, then you can confront the source of the requirement and justifiably reject the rogue requirement.

To stay in control means that you have to at all times be aware of how much functionality you are delivering. This implies that you measure the functionality of the product. Capers Jones advocates basing the development on a contracted number of function points at an anticipated cost per function point. Thus for a 1000 function point product to be delivered at $1000 per FP (about the US average) the cost would be $1,000,000. If the functionality to be delivered crept by 25%, that's 250 FP, and another $250,000 on the bill. While this does allow requirements to creep, it ensures that the creep is recognized, budgeted for and paid for.

As a footnote to this, we are now observing that some government departments are starting to contract out their software at a rate per function point. The size of the product can be anything that the government wants it to be, but the cost per function point of delivery remains the same. This idea may work for you.

Implementing the Quality Gateway

We have described the Quality Gateway as a process for testing requirements. Now you have to decide how you will do it in the context of your own organization.

The first decision is about who is to implement the Quality Gateway. Is it one person; if so who? Should it be a small group? If so, will it be testers, or quality people? Does the group include the project leader? Is the client represented? The answers to these questions are as varied as the organizations that have implemented Quality Gateways.

There is, as an important part of your organization, a culture. This culture is every bit as strong as the culture that you find if you go to different countries, or talk to people with different ethnic backgrounds, or observe groups of people who are outside your normal way of life.

Culture is an ingrained part of organizational life. And so you must respect this culture when you implement a Quality Gateway

Culture is an ingrained part of organizational life. And so you must respect this culture when you implement new procedures.

Does your culture allow for a group of people to sit in judgment on another person's work? Is the originator of a requirement expected (by the group) to be part of the inspecting process? Or does the originator expect to be part of the process?

The existing organizational culture will answer some of your questions about how you implement your Quality Gateway.

Formality is another question that we are often asked about. How formal does this need to be? Should we issue inspection reports? Should we hold pre-arranged Quality Gateway inspection meetings? And so on.

Most of the time we advise clients to keep their Quality Gateway procedures as informal as will allow the satisfactory checking of their requirements. Some organizations deal with complex, technical subject matter, and their Gateway is of necessity formal and rigorous. Some clients deal with more accessible subject matter, where all the participants in the requirements gathering process are well versed in the business, and their Gateways are so informal that they happen almost without anybody noticing.

The use of automated tools sometimes helps to reduce the amount of human intervention in the Quality Gateway process. Some requirements gathering tools can do the preliminary mechanical checking – ensuring that all the components are present, and so on.

Existing procedures may also play a part in your Quality Gateway. If people already have the job of inspecting work, then they are likely to be involved in your Gateway. If there are existing inspection procedures in place, then they should be adapted for requirements rather than try and implement a whole new process.

One large project we worked on implemented the Quality Gateway as a four-stage process. Firstly, each individual developer has a checklist and uses it to informally review and improve requirements throughout the development process.

The next stage is a peer review when another member of the team formally reviews each written requirement. We found it very effective for the peer reviewer to be someone from the test team. Rather than try and review the entire specification, these reviews are concerned with all the requirements that are related to a particular use case. The results of the review are recorded on the requirement as part of the requirement's history.

The third stage is a team review that includes customers and users. Problem requirements that have not passed the Gateway tests are presented by one person, and are discussed and possibly resolved, by the others.

The final stage is a management review that is most concerned with looking at a summary of the Quality Gateway successes and failures. The results of this are used to manage and fine tune the requirements project.

See Chapters 2, The Requirements Process, and 14, Whither Requirements?, for more on tailoring your process

Summary

The Quality Gateway applies a number of tests to formalized potential requirements. The Gateway tests individual requirements for:

- Completeness
- Traceability
- Consistency
- Relevancy
- Correctness
- Ambiguity
- Viability
- Being solution-bound
- Gold plating
- Creep.

Requirements are tested against the global constraints of the product. The primary objective of the Quality Gateway is to prevent bad requirements from becoming part of the specification. To this end, you must implement your Quality Gateway so that *all* requirements must pass through it before they can become part of the specification.

Prototyping and Scenarios

in which we use simulation techniques to help find requirements

Sometimes, when you are using a product, be it a hairdryer, a personal organizer, or a word processor, you often discover additional requirements:

'I wish that this hairdryer had completely variable speeds, rather than just two.'

'I would like the organizer to dial the phone for me.'

'I want the word processor to spell in several languages at once for when I am writing to foreign countries.'

Requirements often do not emerge until somebody is actually using the product. By then it is too late – the product exists. The objective of requirements gathering is to find the requirements before the product is built.

However, the requirements gathering activity is difficult. You are asking your client and users to *imagine* what they need their future product to do. Of course this is limited by people's imagination.

The idea of using a prototype is to give people something real. Or at least something that has the appearance of reality. The prototype makes the product real enough that potential users can think of requirements that might otherwise be missed. Our colleague, Steve McMenamin, refers to prototypes as 'requirements bait': when users see something useful, they immediately think of several other requirements. In other words, the prototype acts as an inspiration for further requirements. This way we capture the 'little extras' that might otherwise have waited until the product was in use before they were found.

The purpose of a prototype is to simulate aspects of the product and to make it real enough to help users think of requirements that might otherwise be missed

Prototypes can reduce creeping requirements by somewhere between 10% and 25%.

Source: Capers Jones

Prototypes are also used to play out the *consequences* of requirements. You know those strange requirements that always have a single advocate – the very person who swears he would be lost without it. Who knows if his requirement is a great idea that will make the product better, or merely a complex way of doing something that doesn't need to be done? The prototype does. When you build a prototype of hard-to-fathom requirements, you make them visible. This gives everyone the opportunity to understand them, discuss them, and then decide on their merits, or otherwise.

Figure 11.1 indicates that not all requirements are the subject of a prototype. Prototyping is potentially more expensive than other requirements gathering methods, and as such is reserved for situations where:

Figure 11.1

During trawling activity, some requirements are not clear, or you feel there is a need to experiment with the requirements. The prototyping activity builds simulations of a possible product, and tests these with the users. The intention is to give the users the opportunity to work with something real, and thus to have a better idea of what is needed to do their work. The requirements discovered by this process are treated the same way as requirements discovered by trawling techniques.

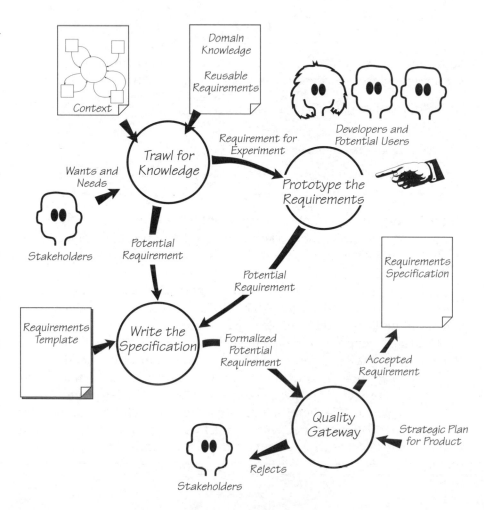

- The product has not existed before, and it is difficult to visualize.
- The users for the product have no experience with the kind of product, nor the proposed technology.
- The users have been doing their work for some time and are stuck in the way that they do it.
- The users are having trouble articulating their requirements.
- The requirements analysts are having trouble understanding what is required.
- The feasibility of a requirement is in doubt.

The prototypes that we are talking about here are 'throw away' prototypes – they are not intended to evolve into the finished product. They might, but that is incidental to the requirements gathering. Requirements prototypes are solely to help elicit requirements. They are there to get feedback from the users and to generate new requirements.

A prototype is a simulation. It attempts to appear as if it is a product that the users could use to do their work. But not the work that they have been doing in the past, rather the work that you envisage they might do in the future, given the help of the product that you are demonstrating. In other words, you are showing your users a prototype of a product, and asking them if they could do their job using that product. If the answer is yes, then capture the requirements demonstrated by that version of the prototype. If no, then change the prototype and try again.

Build a prototype that relates to the physical anchors in the user's world

The users who decide if your prototype is a reasonable demonstration of the proposed product are in a difficult situation. They bring with them to the prototyping exercise some work-related baggage. They have been doing their job for some time (you probably wouldn't be asking them to test your prototypes if they hadn't) and their perception of their work may be very different from yours. This requires tact on your part to understand what aspects of reality are uppermost in the minds of the people that you are dealing with. What are the metaphors they use for their work, and how do they envision themselves while they are doing their work? On top of this, you are asking them to tell you how they feel about doing different work, the work that you are proposing for the future. This could mean jettisoning artifacts and ways of working that they feel quite comfortable with. To turn away from the experience that they have gained, and to accept a new, and as yet untried, way of doing their work. No easy task.

The lesson that we learn from this is that we must always try and use prototyping techniques that conform, in some way, to the artifacts and experiences that are most familiar to the users. This means adjusting your prototyping approach for each situation.

Let us look at some of the possibilities that are available for prototypes and after that we can talk about how they could be employed. Let's start with the simplest and cheapest of them – the low fidelity prototype.

Low Fidelity Prototypes

To look at structure, the first prototypes are always paper.

Source: Hugh Beyer and Karen Holtzblatt

Low fidelity prototypes help the users to concentrate on the subject matter by using familiar media. Such things as pencil and paper, whiteboards, flip-charts, Post-it notes, index cards, cardboard boxes can be employed to build effective low fidelity prototypes. In fact anything that is part of the users' everyday life and does not involve an additional investment to purchase or learn.

The low fidelity prototype is not meant to look all that much like the finished product. This can be good and bad. The good part is that nobody is going to confuse it with an actual product. It is obviously built with a minimal investment in time, and most importantly gives no indication that it is anything but a prototype that is *meant to be changed*. The low fidelity prototype encourages people to iterate rather than expecting to get the answer with the first attempt.

Prototyping is more convenient, and ultimately more accurate, if based on a use case. The use case, covered fully in Chapter 4, is an amount of work that is almost certain to take place in a single, continuous time frame. It also has known outcomes, and if you have read this book carefully, you know it has a fit criterion that measures the success or not of outcomes of the use case. This gives us a self-contained amount of work as the subject of our prototype.

Let's see how this works with a use case.

Chapter 9, Fit Criteria

The use case called 'Monitor Untreated Roads' is suitable for our purposes here. The use case diagram is shown in Figure 11.2. This use case covers the situation where the engineer is checking to see that all the roads that are scheduled to be treated with de-icing material have been covered by one of the trucks. Thus we have to find all the requirements for this part of the product.

The reason that you are building this low fidelity prototype is to discover requirements that are part of the existing system and must be carried into the new, along with requirements that nobody has yet thought of. Let us suppose that the engineers are currently working with a system that supplies them with a list of roads, and we will use that as our starting point.

We can quickly sketch a low fidelity prototype of the current situation, and then begin to explore how we could improve it. The low-fi prototype does not get in the way. Its job is to quickly focus on what the product will do rather than on the mechanics of any particular implementation medium.

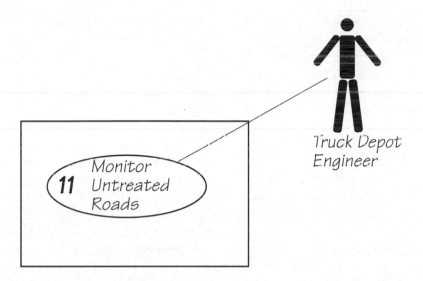

Figure 11.2

The truck depot engineers have the responsibility of ensuring that all roads in danger of freezing are treated with de-icing material. Use case number 11 – Monitor Untreated Roads – identifies a collection of requirements that the product must satisfy.

You can demonstrate each suggestion for improvement with another sketch. Once your users understand that you are attempting to simulate a possible solution to their problem, and that their input is not only welcome but necessary, they will almost certainly help you out and start suggesting their own improvements. Experience has taught us that once you get bright people started by making the problem visible, they tend to be very creative and imaginative – sometimes the problem shifts to one of keeping pace with their imagination.

PUTTING THIS TO WORK

Get started by sketching what the user might see when using the product for this use case. Ask the users what they would like the product to tell them and write a list of the things they mention like:

- Roads scheduled for de-icing,
- Roads that have been de-iced,
- Relative positions of roads.

Now ask the users how they would like the information to be given to them. Tell them there are no limitations. You are not designing the product, but are trying to capture all the things that it might possibly do to help them do their work. Sketch rough pictures to elicit ideas from the users. If they are having trouble getting started then inject some ideas of your own. Ask them to imagine that they are doing the job of monitoring untreated roads. Are there any other pieces of information that they need to do the job? Would they have to look for information somewhere else? Is all the information in the current version of the prototype necessary to do the job of monitoring untreated roads?

Let's say, that as the prototyping proceeds, and the engineers get to see your sketches, you hear the following:

'That's great. Now wouldn't it be good if we could see the major roads that have not been treated for three hours? But only the major roads – the secondary ones don't matter. Our current system can't distinguish between major and secondary roads.'

How long does it take you to add that to your sketch? About ten seconds? How long would it have taken to modify the installed product if the engineers had asked for this after delivery? Enough said.

By working with the engineers you generate a prototype that is generally quite different from what they have at the moment. That is the point of it – to change the work, and to discover new and better ways of doing the work. By encouraging the engineers to tell you more and more about the job, you find requirements that otherwise would not come to light. See Figure 11.3.

The low-fi prototype is not a work of art, rather it is an ideas generating device

When you draw a low-fi prototype (see Figure 11.4 for example), you demonstrate your ideas to the user, and encourage him to change them. Remember that a significant part of the requirements process is inventing a better way to do the work. The prototype is a vehicle for you and the user, and any other interested parties, to experiment with and to see how the proposed product would contribute to the new work.

Low fidelity prototypes give the best value if you use them early in the development cycle. The users can give you more feedback earlier when they are less fixed on the design, or appearance, of the product, and are more interested in the overall structure and broad-brush functionality. At this stage, the user's ideas for the product should be fluid, and quick and easy experimentation is going to yield the best product.

Figure 11.3

By drawing this low-fi prototype on a flipchart or whiteboard, with the help of the truck depot engineers, you identify their requirements. They want the product to highlight the major roads, within a district, that have not been treated, and are in a dangerous condition.

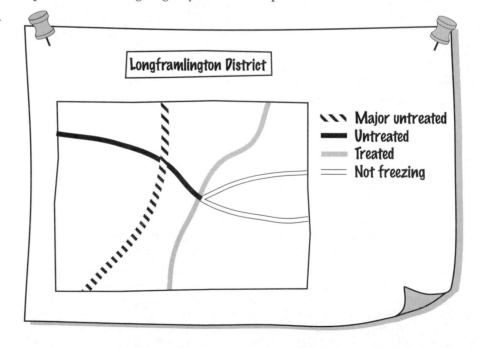

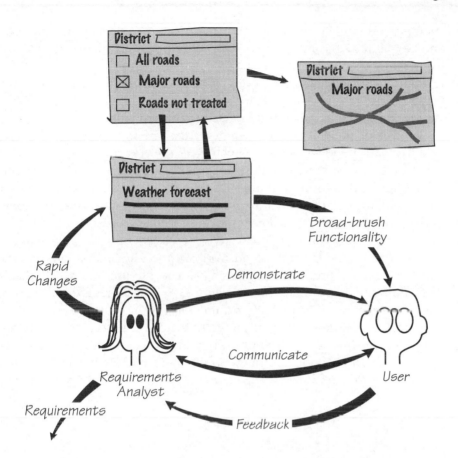

Figure 11.4

The informality of the low-fi prototype makes it an ideal medium for developers and users to communicate and iterate new ideas.

High Fidelity Prototypes

High fidelity prototypes are built using software tools. The hi-fi prototype is meant to look like the finished product. That is, whatever the use case does, the prototype will do. The intention is to give the user a chance to 'use' something that could conceivably be the final product.

Thus, the prototype behaves as the user would expect the final product to behave. It gives the user the chance to explore the prototype, hopefully with a view to suggesting improvements and new requirements. But herein lies the problem – if the prototype looks like the product, then will the user concentrate on the appearance, and possibly forego making functional improvements? This is, after all, the point of prototyping.

But putting aside the slight risk of users misunderstanding their role in the prototyping activity, the hi-fi prototype has a lot to offer. It is interactive and so encourages the user to explore. The icons and data displayed on the screen are representative of the data and icons used to do the work. The user should feel at home with the prototype – he can open windows, update data, and be told if he has made an error. In other words, this looks just like his real work.

The requirements analyst creates lifelike work situations, and asks the user to operate the prototype as if he was doing real work. By careful observation, the analyst will find some valuable requirements.

The first of these is missing requirements. The hi-fi prototype is more detailed than the low-fi version, which gives the user more opportunity to explore all the possibilities for the use case. For example, the error paths and the deviations that form the normal case can be looked at. 'What happens if I am using this and I find that there are no more trucks available, and some of the trucks have been scheduled to treat secondary roads?'

The hi-fi prototype is very effective for discovering usability requirements. As the user attempts to do work with it, the analyst can observe which parts of the prototype are pleasing and easy to use, and which usability features should be improved (see Figure 11.5). The user is also able to provide a lot of input to the usability requirements.

As well as the feedback you are getting from the users, consider the designer's contribution. It is most likely that any good designer has something to say, and ideas to contribute to the prototype. Designers, being the people they are, are usually happier working with real and visual objects,

Figure 11.5

The high fidelity prototype is a faithful demonstration version of the proposed product. The user 'uses' it in simulated work situations. This is an ideal opportunity to demonstrate the product to the client or customer. By using the prototype, the user changes the requirements so that the prototype conforms to his view of what the work should be. High fidelity prototypes have the advantage that it is easy to compare them to competitors' products.

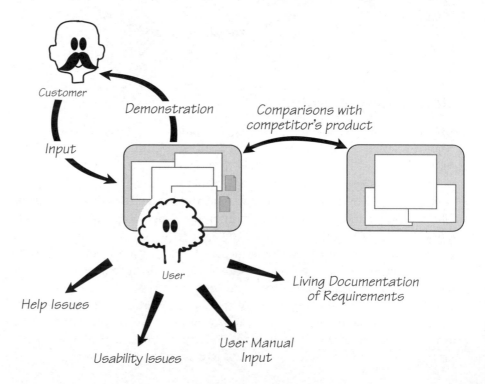

rather than abstract concepts. This makes the prototype a natural artifact for a designer to try out, and to improve. By showing your prototypes to your designers, you are almost certainly going to benefit from their new and better ideas.

Consider the value of a high fidelity prototype when you are developing a product for the mass market. The prototype in this case is a vehicle for soliciting feedback from customer representative groups. These are the people to whom you will be selling the product. Their feedback has to be a valid source of requirements. At the same time, the hi-fi prototype can be very useful for making realistic comparisons with competing products. Your potential customers will tell you their preferences and whether your product falls short of what they are willing to buy.

Scenario Models

Scenario modeling is a technique that has long been used in the world of the theatre, opera and films. A scenario model contains a number of scenes or episodes that tell a detailed story of a specific situation. The model is used for planning how the story will develop as each episode reaches its outcome.

Scenarios are used to illustrate a situation

This idea has been borrowed by requirements analysts as an aid to discovering requirements. Think of scenario modeling as a type of prototyping technique. Scenarios are used to illustrate a situation, and to bring the product to life.

The techniques that we use to build scenario models are a mixture of text and pictorial techniques aimed at exploring a story line and discovering exceptions. We suggest that you use business events or product use cases as the starting point for building scenario models. Let's look at one such event.

In the IceBreaker system, business event number 10 is 'Truck Depot Reports Problem with Truck'. The situation that surrounds this use case is that a truck has broken down, or encountered some other problem. The truck has already been scheduled to treat some roads, and its removal from the fleet leaves a gap in the schedule. Using the normal trawling techniques, you would have found the requirements related to the normal business response to the event – the depot finds out about the truck breakdown and reschedules all the roads that the truck was assigned to treat. Now let's use scenario modeling to discover any missing requirements by exploring the exceptions that can happen with this use case.

Text-based Scenario Models

We can simply use text for this kind of prototype. The advantage of using text is that it is familiar to everybody, and with a little help you can usually get the users to build some of their own scenarios.

There may be several scenarios for one use case. That is, each scenario explores what happens if there are different outcomes from processing actions. The scenario is broken into a number of episodes – each episode covers enough of the story to reach some outcome. For example, consider the following scenario that is exploring what happens if the depot tries to reschedule the work of a broken-down truck and there is no replacement available.

The scenario description and background set the scene for the scenario. Then as each episode is played out, consider the actions that the product takes, and the results, or outcomes, of those actions.

Business Event # 10 Truck Depot Reports Problem With Truck

Scenario: No truck is available to replace the broken-down one.

Background: Bill wants to schedule a truck within one hour.

Episode 1:

  Action: Bill (local engineer) asks the scheduling system for a truck

  Outcome: Scheduling system does not have a truck

Episode 2:

  Action: Bill telephones Erik (County coordinator)

  Action: Erik looks at his worksheet

  Outcome: No truck available

  Outcome: Erik declares emergency

Episode 3:

  Action: Bill telephones other Counties

  Action: Erik telephones other Counties

  Outcome: Another County loans a truck

Evaluation: Need to communicate with other Counties?

What happens if none of the other Counties has an available truck?

This scenario was built with the cooperation of the users. By writing down this and other scenarios, we discovered new requirements. In this case, we found that there was a need to communicate with other counties. This requirement had not been mentioned previously because people (unconsciously) assumed that the product would not be able to help with this. Once we understood the requirement it was possible for the product to automatically send an alert to other counties' depot controllers and thus get a more immediate response during an emergency.

We suggest you use this skeleton when you are building your own text-based scenario models:

> *Requirement # or Business Event # There may be several scenarios for a requirement or a business event*
> *Scenario: Description of what the scenario illustrates*
> *Background: Sets the situation for the scenario*
> *Each episode has a number of actions, and one or more outcomes. Include names of people if available to bring the story to life*
> *Episode 1:*
>   *Action:*
>   *Outcome:*
> *Episode 2:*
>   *Action:*
>   *Action:*
>   *Outcome:*
>   *Outcome:*
> . . . .
>   . . . .
> *Evaluation: What are the unanswered questions?*
> *What are the new requirements?*

Storyboards

Another technique for building a scenario model is to borrow the storyboarding technique from the film and cartoon industries. When a cartoonist is planning a cartoon he sketches a number of linked pictures. These pictures identify the story line and guide the cartoonist in how many detailed pictures he needs to draw.

When you build a storyboard scenario, you capture the same components as in the text-based scenario model – episodes, actions and outcomes. Instead of writing a description of each episode, roughly sketch a picture of the people involved. Stick figures are perfectly adequate, with cartoon bubbles to indicate the dialog. Sometimes one picture is enough to illustrate all the actions and outcomes in an episode; for more complex episodes you need a sequence of pictures.

Storyboards are less formal than text-based scenarios, and also a lot more fun. We find that they are a good starting point when you are trying to explore a business situation involving interactions between real people. Somehow, people identify with the cartoon figures (no matter how badly drawn) and give you a lot of input on what can happen during the course of the business event or use case.

Object Life History

Another type of scenario model that helps to discover missing requirements is an object or entity life history model. The idea is to take a key business object – one whose subject matter is the concern of a number of use cases – and use a state transition diagram to model all the things that might happen to that object during its lifetime. When you have completed the life history of the object, consider whether there are sufficient requirements to cover all the things that happen to the object.

In Figure 11.6 we see a state model for 'Road', one of the key business objects in the IceBreaker system. Each rectangle on the model identifies a different state of existence for this object. A state is a steady condition. For example, the Road object is normally in the condition of being safe to be used. It continues in that steady condition until something happens to change the state. In this case, the safe state is interrupted by a prediction being made that, due to ice, the road is about to become unsafe.

Once that happens, then the road is in a different state. It will remain in that state until something else happens to change it. The diagram indicates that either the road can be treated, in which case it moves back to being safe, or enough ice forms to make the road truly dangerous, in which case it is closed to traffic. Treating it or waiting for the ice to melt is the way to make this road safe to use again.

The story is told not so much by the states, but by the transitions between states

What's the point of this model? Like all scenario models, the object life history is concerned with telling a story. In this case it is the story of a road and the things that might happen to it (here, we are concerned only with the things that fall into the scope of the work that we are studying).

When the A1(M) road was predicted unsafe for use last January we could not treat it before it became unsafe for use and we had to close the road.

You can see this part of the story reflected in the state model in Figure 11.6.

However, the story is told not so much by the states, but by the transitions between states. These are the business events that affect the work. So far in this book we have been using events as a way of finding requirements, and this kind of prototype is using that same approach.

We had the requirements for all the events shown in the object life history model ... except one. When we built the first version of this model it said that a closed road would become safe for use when it is treated. When we showed the model to a user, he pointed out that the road would also become safe when the ice melts. In other words, there was a transition out of the Road closed state that we hadn't thought of.

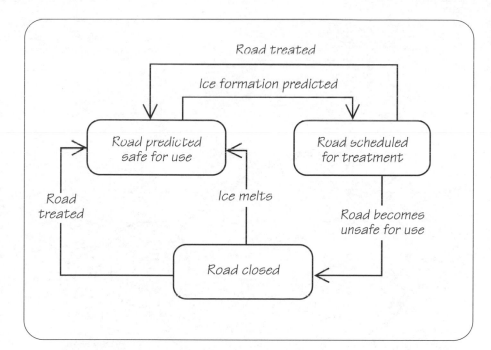

Figure 11.6

This state model for the business object Road identifies the states in which a road can exist and the events that cause a transition from one state to another.

The result of this is a new requirement – monitoring the condition of closed roads to see whether they have become safe without treatment. This of course means that there is a new event, which will have to be added to the context. Once done, the rest of the response to the event has to be explored, modeled and the requirements written.

Scenario modeling is fun, it has a playful, story telling aspect that encourages people to relax and be creative and imaginative. The act of building the model stimulates questions and uncovers other requirements.

Northumberland is very close to Scotland, and single malt whisky is popular. A good single malt is drunk without ice. We think this is a perfectly acceptable excuse for not realizing that ice eventually melts.

The Prototyping Loop

We have talked about a variety of different techniques that you can use for prototyping. There is a strategy for using any of them. Figure 11.7 shows this strategy as being made up of the prototyping activities of design and build, test and analyze. Let's look at these activities.

PUTTING THIS TO WORK

Design and Build

Design is the activity of deciding what it is that you are trying to model with your prototype, and what are you trying to achieve. The subject of the prototype may be a single requirement, or it may (more likely) be a use case. For the rest of this section, we will assume that you are prototyping a use case.

Figure 11.7

Prototyping begins with a requirement for experiment. In this case the requirement might be a single requirement, or more likely, a use case. The user tests the prototype, and the results are analyzed. Note the output of the Analyze process – requirements. The requirements that were learned through the test are recorded, and any needed modifications are used to redesign and rebuild. The process continues until the Analyze process ceases to reveal further requirements.

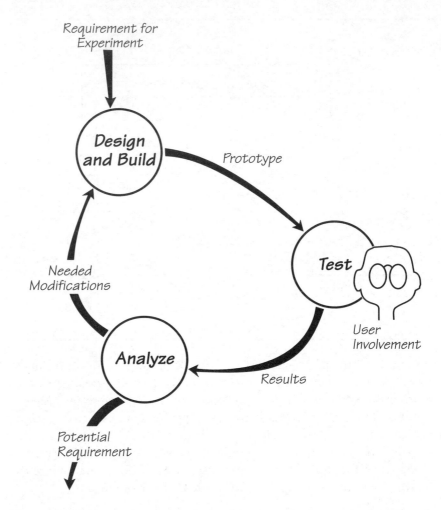

Now, what is the use case meant to achieve, and what are its functional outcomes? Once you have decided the functional outcome of the prototype, then that part of its design becomes clearer.

The other question is harder: what are you trying to achieve with this prototype? Are you looking for the functional requirements or non-functional ones such as usability? Are you exploring a use case which is largely unknown, or building a prototype to confirm the requirements for a fairly well understood piece of work? For any of these questions, consider how you will know when you have achieved your purpose. To put it another way, how will you measure the success of the prototype?

Also consider:

● Identifying the operational environment in which the product will eventually be used to do work. For example, this could be an office, a factory, a school, a laboratory, a family household or a public building. (You might already have defined this in section 13 Operational Requirements, of your requirements specification);

● Identifying whose input (people and roles) you need to get the results that you are aiming for. (You might already have defined this in your requirements specification – section 3 Users of the Product);

● Decide how you will make clear to each person why you need their input and what advantage they will get from being involved in the prototyping effort;

● Plan how you will run each prototyping session – will you work with the users or will you leave the prototype with them and return when they have had a chance to assess it?

Knowing the answers to these questions means that you slant the design of the prototype towards that objective.

Designing is mapping the world of the user into the prototype. What artifacts does the user want to see represented in the prototype? What are the user's metaphors for this use case, and how does he see the product's contribution to the work that he is doing?

Designing is mapping the world of the user into the prototype

We have already discussed building prototypes so we will not linger on that part of the process. Suffice it to say that given today's hi-fi prototyping tools, and the variety of low-fi methods, the actual construction of the prototype is a simple affair. Much of the time you can build your prototype in the company of the user.

Testing in the User Environment

Testing involves having the user use the prototype as a simulation of his work. In other words, your user is trying to work, and you are objectively recording his feedback.

The exact way that you run the tests depends on the kind of prototype you are using, and your objectives in using prototypes in the first place. Users can be left alone for some time to experiment with high fidelity prototypes, and later you meet up to discuss the results. Low-fi prototypes usually have to be demonstrated to the users, and the testing is therefore more casual and you get the feedback interactively.

Include your usability experts in your prototyping cycle

We strongly urge you to include your usability people in this kind of testing. It has been our experience that usability people are not invited to become involved until the product is very nearly in production. It is assumed that there will be only a few fine-tuning corrections to the usability aspects to complete the product. However, by this time it is far too late. Usability must be built into the product from the beginning, not bolted on at the last moment. We have included usability (section 11 in the template) for a very good reason – usability is a requirement. That is, it is an integral part of the product and not an optional accessory that can be sprayed on like a last-minute paint job.

The objective of prototyping is to get feedback. Let's look at how we analyze the feedback.

Analyzing the Results

Your aim in analyzing the results of the prototype is to identify potential requirements, and to determine whether it is worth modifying the prototype and running more tests in the user environment

There are two things you are analyzing for. One is potential requirements uncovered by the user, and the other is to determine whether it is worth modifying the prototype and running more tests.

Note in Figure 11.7 how one of the outputs of the analysis activity is a flow of requirements. When you look at the results of the prototype test, you are looking for requirements. Either the test confirms the requirements that you thought were correct when you built the prototype, or they are new requirements that the users have discovered by using the prototype.

It is important that you capture these requirements. The prototype alone may not be sufficient when it comes to understanding the requirements. The prototype is not the same thing as the requirements specification, instead it is a *simulation* of the specification. You still have to extract the real requirements, otherwise you are left with prototyping code that may not tell you what the underlying requirements are. Thus it is open to interpretation.

When you use prototypes, we urge you always to record the requirements, just as if you were not using prototypes. We have seen too many misunderstood requirements that resulted from designers making their own interpretation of the prototype to learn what they were to build.

Sometimes your prototyping results indicate that it would be worth modifying your prototype and testing it further. For example, the road engineers told us that they would like the product to identify roads in danger of closing, then they could make rescheduling decisions based on the seriousness of the closure.

A prototype is not the same thing as the requirements specification, instead it is a simulation of the specification. You still need to extract the real requirements

The seriousness factor was something new and its inclusion had an effect on a number of other requirements. We decided that a good way of learning more about the potential new requirements would be to modify the prototype and ask the engineers to test it again and provide more feedback.

Review the results of your prototyping. Are you still discovering new requirements? And how many of them? The number of requirements that you discover from your analysis is significant. Consider whether you have found enough requirements such that it is worthwhile to continue modifying and testing that prototype. Or were there too many? If you have a truly large number of requirements, does it indicate that you may not know enough about the work situation, and other methods would be more appropriate to learn how the work should be done?

Is your prototyping effort still contributing to your stated reason for building the prototype? If the answer is yes then you might decide to put more effort into modifying and testing the prototype. If your measurements indicate that you are learning less then you might decide that the prototype has served its purpose.

You could go around the prototyping loop several times, each time getting a different result. Consider your objectives and results each time. There is not much joy in being involved in an endless prototyping loop.

When you build a requirements prototype think of it as a technique for helping you to learn about the requirements so that the eventual product is based on real, well-defined user needs.

Summary

Requirements prototypes are simulation models designed to help learn more about the users' requirements. The aim of the prototype is to make it possible for people to imagine what it might be like to use the real product to do work and to stimulate them into remembering requirements they have forgotten, or thinking of ideas that might not otherwise occur to them until they are using the real product.

Low fidelity prototypes are a quick way of simulating a product using familiar technology like pencil, paper, whiteboard. Low-fi prototypes help to focus on what the product does rather than how it will appear. They help to discover missing functionality and to test the scope of the product.

High fidelity prototypes use prototyping tools and give a strong appearance of reality. They are particularly effective for discovering usability requirements.

Scenario models are a technique for bringing abstract subject matter to life by telling a story about a particular instance. These models are a powerful way of helping people to focus on details and discover exceptions that would otherwise be missed.

12 Reusing Requirements

in which we look for requirements that have already been written and explore ways to reuse them

To make a pot of tea: Warm the teapot with boiling water. Into the warmed pot put 1 teaspoon of tea per person plus one for the pot. Pour boiling water into the pot. Leave the tea to brew for 3–5 minutes depending on the strength of the type of tea you are using

In our everyday lives we all consciously, or more commonly unconsciously, reuse knowledge. If we are experienced drivers then we do not consciously think about how to drive. We can make a cup of tea without rediscovering how many spoons of tealeaves we should use. We write a letter without looking up where to put the recipient's address, and how to start and end the letter. In all these and many more daily situations, we are reusing knowledge. It is knowledge that we have gained by studying and practicing, what we have already discovered for ourselves, or more often what others have already defined. It does not occur to us to start all over and reinvent how to make a pot of tea. Instead we reuse the knowledge that already exists and enhance it to suit our particular situation.

When specifying the requirements for a product we are about to build, we can save a lot of effort if we start by asking 'Have these requirements or any similar to them, already been specified?'

What is Reusing Requirements?

Although they might have many of their own special features, the products that we build are not completely unique. Someone, somewhere has already built a product that contains some of the requirements that are germane to the work that you are doing. When you take advantage of work that has already been done, your efficiency as a requirements gatherer increases significantly. We strongly suggest that early in your requirements projects, you look for reusable requirements that have already been written, and incorporate these 'free' requirements into your own project. See Figure 12.1.

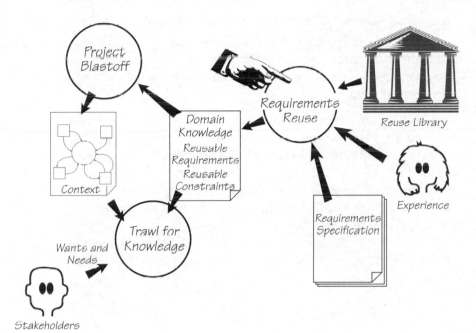

Figure 12.1

Reusing requirements entails making use of requirements that have been written for other projects. They can come from a number of sources – a reuse library of specifications, other requirements specifications that are similar or in the same domain, or informally from other people's experience.

But these requirements are not exactly free – you have to do something for them. Successful reuse starts with having an organizational culture that consciously encourages reuse rather than reinvention. If you have this attitude then you are in a position to include requirements reuse in your requirements process.

Naturally if you are going to determine whether you have any relevant reusable requirements, you need to know something about the work that you are investigating. When you run a project blastoff, pay particular attention to the first eight sections of the requirements specification:

Successful reuse starts with having an organizational culture that consciously encourages reuse rather than reinvention

Refer to Chapter 3 for more on how to run a project blastoff

1 The Purpose of the Product – are there other projects in the organization that are compatible, or that cover substantially the same domains or work areas?

2 Client, Customer and other Stakeholders – can you reuse a list of stakeholders to advantage?

3 Users of the Product – do other products involve the same users, and thus have similar usability requirements?

4 Requirements Constraints – have your constraints already been specified for another project?

5 System Terminology – you can almost certainly make use of someone else's glossary, and not have to invent all of your own.

6 Relevant Facts – pay attention to relevant facts from recent projects, they may well apply to yours.

7 Assumptions – do other projects' assumptions apply?

8 The Scope of the Product – your project has a very good chance of being an adjacent system to other projects that are underway in your organization. Make use of the interfaces that have been established by other work context models.

When you are looking for potentially reusable requirements, don't be too quick to say that your project is different from everything that has gone before it. Yes, the subject matter will be different, but if you look past the names, how much of the underlying functionality is substantially the same? How many requirements specifications have already been written that contain material that you can use unaltered, or at least adapted, in your own specification? See Figure 12.2.

We have found that significant amounts of specifications can be assembled from existing components rather than be invented from the ground up.

Figure 12.2

At project blastoff time the subject matter of the context, together with its adjacent systems and boundary data flows, should indicate the potential for reusing requirements from previous projects.

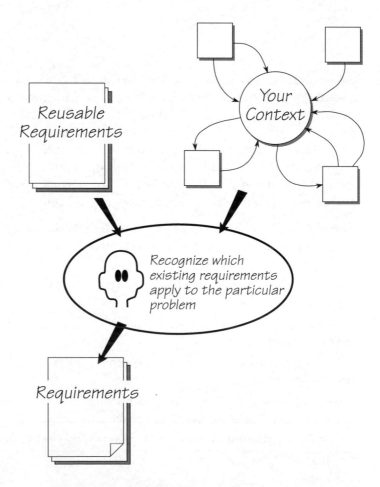

Reusable Requirements

Your Context

Recognize which existing requirements apply to the particular problem

Requirements

The stakeholders at the blastoff are wonderful sources of reusable components. Ask all the stakeholders about other documents that contain knowledge that is relevant to the work of the project. Consider whether someone else has already investigated subject matter domains that overlap with your project. Closely examine the blastoff deliverables. They provide a focus for identifying reusable knowledge that might not otherwise be found.

When you are trawling for requirements, continue to look for reusable requirements by asking the people you interview: 'Have you answered these questions, or questions like them before?' 'Do you know of documents that might already contain the answers to these questions?'

This fairly informal approach means that you will encounter potentially reusable requirements in many different forms. Some will be precisely stated and hence directly reusable, others will merely provide clues or pointers to sources of knowledge. One of the spin-offs of using a disciplined process for writing requirements specifications is that you naturally produce requirements that are more easily reused by future projects.

The blastoff deliverables provide a focus for identifying reusable knowledge that might not otherwise be found

One of the spin-offs of using a disciplined process for writing requirements specifications is that you naturally produce requirements that are more easily reused by future projects

Sources of Reusable Requirements

When you want to learn to cook the perfect fried egg, one of the best ways to get started is to ask to learn from someone whose fried eggs you admire. They tell you that the egg should be less than five days old, the butter – slightly salted is best – should be heated until it is golden but not brown. You break the egg and gently slide it into the bubbling butter and spoon the golden liquid over it until the white turns opaque. You serve it with a sprinkling of fresh coriander and offer the eater Tabasco sauce.

This is *informal experience-related reuse* of requirements; all of us do this when we ask questions of our colleagues. We want to learn from one person's experience so that we do not have to start our own endeavors from scratch. We might not always find out everything we want to know; we might make changes to what we are told, but we use it to build on other people's knowledge.

More *formal reusable requirements* for fried egg cookery come from cookery books. For example Jenny Baker, in her book *Simple French Cuisine*, instructs us to:

Heat sufficient oil ... fry the tomatoes with a garlic clove ... break the eggs on top and cook gently until set.

Italian Food by Elizabeth David advises us to:

Melt some butter ... put in a slice of mozzarella ... break two eggs into each dish ... cover the pan while the eggs are cooking.

Informal experience-related reuse of requirements: we do this when we ask questions of our colleagues. We want to learn from one person's experience so that we do not have to start our own endeavors from scratch

Once you know the context of your work, you can look for requirements specifications that deal with all or part of that context and use them as the source of potentially reusable requirements

READING

Three cookery writers who have made knowledge about cooking accessible and reusable are Elizabeth David, Jenny Baker and Delia Smith. Any of the books by these writers will help you improve your cooking skills and enjoyment of food. The three we have referenced are:

DAVID, ELIZABETH. *Italian Food*. Penguin Books, 1974.

BAKER, JENNY. *Simple French Cuisine*. Faber & Faber, 1992.

SMITH, DELIA. *How to Cook – Book One*. BBC Worldwide, 1998.

You can think of a cookery book as a requirements specification – it's just written for a different context of study than the one you are currently working on. Even though the above examples have differences, both have aspects that could be reused as a starting point for writing a new recipe for fried egg cookery. This means that once you know the context of your work, you can look for requirements specifications that deal with all or part of that context and use them as the source of potentially reusable requirements.

The above examples come from a domain of cooking fried eggs. Within that domain, each writer has written her specification from a specific viewpoint. Elizabeth David was writing about cooking eggs the Italian way, whereas Jenny Baker writes of eggs in France. The two writers give you specific instructions for producing the desired result in a particular situation. In other words, just like a normal requirements specification.

Now let's stand back a little and look at an abstraction. In her *How to Cook – Book One*, Delia Smith has investigated the *subject* of egg cooking with a view to learning as much as she can about the subject of eggs. She has made an abstraction of knowledge that is relevant regardless of whether you want to cook Italian, French or Trinidadian egg dishes. She writes about how to tell if an egg is fresh, how long to cook an egg, when to use oil, when to use butter, and so on. In terms of requirements engineering we could say that she has built a *domain model* on the subject of eggs.

A domain is a subject matter area. A domain model is a generic model of knowledge that applies to any product built for use in that domain. Consider the knowledge that Delia Smith passes on about eggs. It is usable for almost any recipe (specification) that involves eggs. We will see more about domain analysis later in this chapter.

You can reuse requirements or knowledge from any of the sources that we have discussed: colleagues' experiences, existing requirements specifications and domain models. The only thing needed is to be able to recognize the reusable potential of anything you come across. Recognition itself requires that you be able to abstract, so as to see past the technology and procedures that are part of existing requirements. Abstraction involves seeing past subject matters to find recyclable components. We will have more on abstraction later in this chapter. But first, let's look at making use of the idea of patterns.

Requirements Patterns

A pattern is a guide. It gives you a form to follow when you are trying to replicate, or make a close approximation of, some piece of work. For example, the stonecutters working on classical buildings used wooden patterns to help them to carve the column capitals to a uniform shape. The tailor uses patterns to cut the cloth so that each jacket is the same basic form, but minor adjustments are made to compensate for an individual client's body shape.

Now let's come to patterns in a requirements sense. Patterns imply a collection of requirements that make up some logical grouping of functions. For example, we can think of a requirements pattern for selling a book – determine the price; compute the tax, if any; collect the money; wrap the book; thank the customer. If this is a successful pattern, then it will pay you to use the pattern for any future bookselling activities, rather than reinvent how to sell a book.

Typically we use requirements patterns that capture the processing policy for a business event or use case. If we use the business event as a unit of work, then each pattern is bounded by its own input, output and stored data, and thus we can treat it as a stand-alone mini system.

Requirements patterns improve the accuracy and completeness of requirements specifications. You reduce the time to produce a specification because you reuse a functional grouping of requirements knowledge that has already been specified by other projects. You do this by looking for patterns that may have some application in your project. Keep in mind that the pattern is usually an abstraction and you may have to do a little work to adapt it to your own needs. However, the time saved in completing the specification, and the insights gained by using other people's patterns, are significant.

Refer to Chapter 4, Event-driven Use Cases, for more on the connection between business events and use cases

Christopher Alexander's Patterns

The most significant collection of patterns was published in *A Pattern Language*, written by a group of architects headed by Christopher Alexander. The book identifies and describes patterns that contribute to functionality and convenience for everyday human life within buildings, living spaces and communities. The book's intention is to present these patterns to architects and builders as guides for new building projects.

READING
ALEXANDER, CHRISTOPHER ET AL. *A Pattern Language*. Oxford University Press, 1977.

The Waist High Shelf illustrated in Figure 12.3 is the name of one of the patterns defined by Alexander and his colleagues. In this case they looked at many people, such as you and me, and observed what happens when we enter and leave our houses. Let's say that it is time to leave for work, you are in a hurry, and you need your keys, the shopping list for tonight's dinner and the library book that you have to return today. If these things are difficult to find you become irritated, probably forget something and have a bad start to the day. The Waist High Shelf pattern is based on the observation that we need somewhere to put our keys and whatever other bits and pieces we have when we arrive, so that we can easily find them when we leave.

The pattern specifies that there should be a horizontal surface at waist height (so that it is easy to reach), just inside the front door (so you do not have

Figure 12.3

Alexander defined the Waist High Shelf pattern because he observed 'In every house and workplace there is a daily "traffic" of the objects which are handled most. Unless such things are immediately at hand, the flow of life is awkward, full of mistakes: things are forgotten, misplaced.'

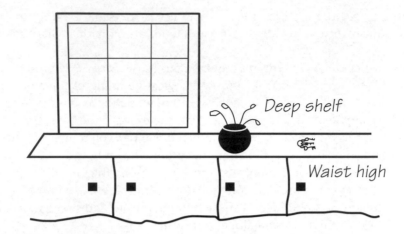

Deep shelf

Waist high

to carry objects any further than necessary), big enough for you to deposit items that are commonly transported in and out of the house. In the authors' house, the waist high shelf pattern implemented itself without us realizing it. We noticed that we naturally put our keys on one of the steps on the staircase that is on the right as you come through our front door. We also noticed that, without being told, our visitors also leave their keys on the 'waist high step'.

Note the role of the pattern. It is a guide, not a rigid set of instructions. It can be reused – there is no need to re-experiment and reinvent. It is a collection of knowledge or experience that can be adapted or used as is.

Now let us look at patterns as they apply to requirements.

A Business Event Pattern

PUTTING
THIS TO
WORK

Let's start by looking at an example of a requirements pattern, then we will discuss how the pattern was built and how it will be used by future projects. This pattern is based on the response to a business event:

> *Pattern Name: Customer Wants to Buy a Product*
> *Context: A pattern for receiving product orders from customers, supplying or back-ordering the product, and invoicing for the product.*
> *Forces: An organization has demands from its customers to supply goods or services. Failure to meet his demand might result in the customer seeking another supplier. Sometimes the product is unavailable at the time that the order is received.*
> *Solution: The following context model, event response model and class diagram define the pieces of the pattern. Each actor, process, data flow and data store, business object and association is defined in detail in attached text using the same names as are used in these models.*

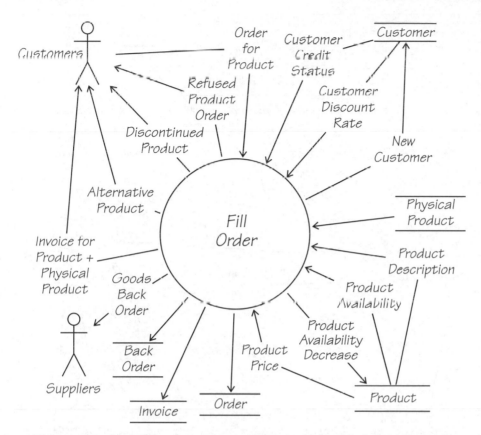

Figure 12.4

This context model
defines the boundaries
of the pattern Customer
Wants to Buy a Product.

The context model shown in Figure 12.4 is a summary of the subject matter covered by the pattern. You can look at the diagram to get an indication
of whether the details of the pattern might be relevant to the work that you
are doing. The flows around the boundary of the context indicate the kind
of work being done by this pattern. If these flows are compatible with the
inputs and outputs of your event, then the pattern is probably usable in your
project.

Once you know whether the pattern is suitable for your use, then it's time
to move on to the details. These can be expressed in a number of different
ways. The technique that you use depends on the volume and depth of your
knowledge about the pattern. For example:

● A step-by-step text description of what happens from the time a customer
  sends an Order for Product;

● A formal definition of all the individual requirements related to Fill Order;

● A detailed model that breaks the pattern into sub-patterns and their
  dependencies between each other before specifying the individual
  requirements.

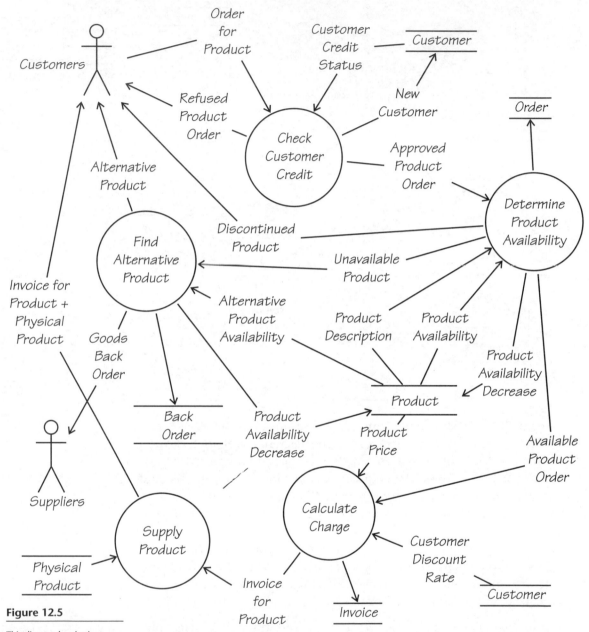

Figure 12.5

This diagram breaks the pattern, Customer Wants to Buy a Product, into five sub-patterns (groups of functionally related requirements) and shows the dependencies between them.

Figure 12.5 is an example of the last technique. It shows how a large pattern can be partitioned into a number of sub-patterns. From this we identify other potentially reusable clusters of requirements. For instance, the diagram has revealed a sub-pattern called Calculate Charge, and its interactions

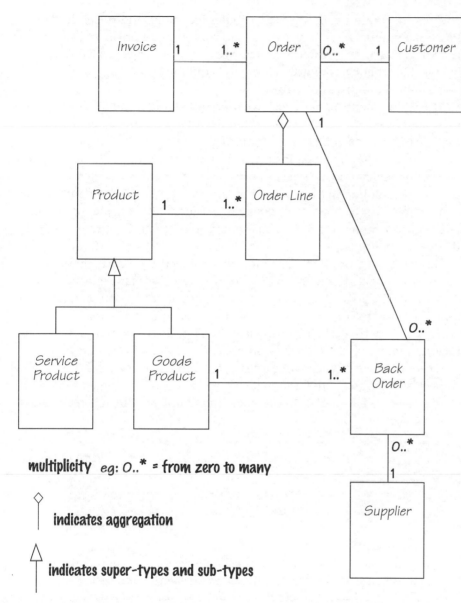

multiplicity *eg: 0..* = from zero to many*

⬦ indicates aggregation

△ indicates super-types and sub-types

Figure 12.6

This class diagram shows all the objects and associations between them that are part of the pattern Customer Wants to Buy a Product. Consider the business rules being communicated by this diagram. A customer may make zero or many orders, each one of which is invoiced. The order is for a collection of items. An item is a service or some goods. Only goods can be back-ordered. Now consider in how many situations these business rules, and the data and processes, can be reused.

with other sub-patterns. We can use this sub-pattern independently whenever we want to specify the requirements for calculating any type of charge. The interactions indicate which other patterns might also be relevant to us when we are interested in the pattern for calculating a charge.

The class diagram in Figure 12.6 shows us the objects that participate in the pattern Customer Wants to Buy a Product along with the associations between them. We can use the object-oriented paradigm to cluster the attributes and operations unique to each object. For instance the object

Product has a number of unique attributes like name and price; similarly it has some unique operations like calculate discounted price, and find stock level. If we have this cluster of knowledge about the object called Product it means that whenever we need to specify requirements for a product we can potentially reuse this knowledge.

The requirements pattern we have been discussing is the result of analyzing many business events – quite often from very different organizations – that deal with the subject of a customer wanting to buy a product. We derived the pattern by making an abstraction that captures all the common processing policy for this type of business event. Thus the pattern contains the business policy that applies when almost any customer wants to buy almost any kind of product. If your project includes a business event centered on a customer wanting to buy something, then this pattern is a realistic starting point.

Similarly, with other events, and other subject matters. Form your patterns by eliminating the idiosyncrasies that exist in many businesses and looking for the general case. Look past the specific to see the general. Look away from the technology that the organization currently uses, and see the business policy that is being processed. Think of the work, not in its current incarnation, but as a model for work that can be done in the future.

Of course there can be many patterns, covering many business events and subject matters. To file them so that they are accessible, we organize them in a consistent way according to the following template (which is really a pattern itself):

> *Pattern Name: A descriptive name to make it easy to communicate the pattern to other people*
> *Forces: The reasons for the pattern's existence.*
> *Context: The boundaries within which the pattern is relevant.*
> *Solution: A description of the pattern using a mixture of words, graphics and references to other documents.*
> *Related Patterns: Other patterns that might apply in conjunction with this one. Other patterns that might help to understand this one.*

Forming Patterns by Abstracting

Suppose that you are working on a system for a library. One of the business events within your context is almost certain to be 'Library User Wants to Extend Book Loan'. Figure 12.7 shows a model of the system's response to the event. When a Library User submits a Loan Extension Request the system responds with either Refused Loan or Loan Extension Approval.

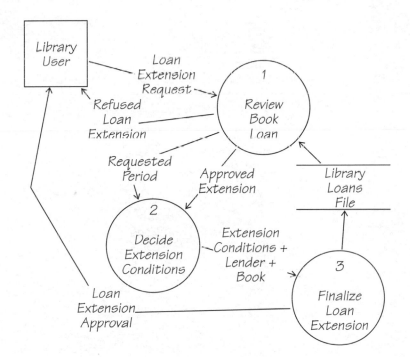

Figure 12.7

A summary of the Library system's response to the event Library User Wants to Extend Book Loan.

Your work on the project in the Library domain has led to the specification of detailed requirements for a particular product. A by-product of doing this work is that you have identified some useful requirements patterns, clusters of business event related requirements, that are potentially reusable on other projects in the Library domain.

When you specify the requirements using a consistent discipline you make them more accessible by other people and hence reusable. If you, or someone else, started another project for the library, a good starting point would be the specifications that you have already written. They are usually a prodigious source of recyclable requirements within this domain.

Now imagine that you are working on a system in a very different domain, that of satellite broadcasting. A business event within this context is 'Satellite Broadcaster Wants to Renew License'. When the satellite broadcaster submits a Broadcast License Request the system responds with either a Rejected License or New License. Figure 12.8 summarizes the system's response to the event.

When you work on the requirements for the Satellite Broadcasting project, you also discover requirements patterns that are potentially reusable on products within this domain.

Now let's look a little further afield. We have talked about the idea of identifying and reusing requirements patterns within a specific subject matter domain. Now let's consider how we can use patterns outside the originating domain.

READING

For some examples of reusable domain models refer to: HAY, DAVID. *Data Model Patterns: Conventions of Thought*. Dorset House, 1995.

Figure 12.8

A model of the Satellite Broadcasting system's response to the event Satellite Broadcaster Wants to Renew License.

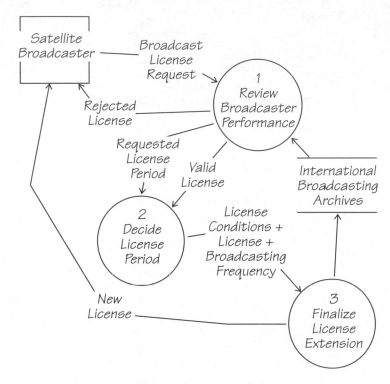

Making Abstractions

PUTTING THIS TO WORK

At first glance, the event responses to Library User Wants to Extend Loan and Satellite Broadcaster Wants to Renew License appear to be very different. And they are different in that they come from very different domains. However, let's look at the two event responses *and this time look for similarities*. If we find them we have a chance of deriving a more abstract pattern that could be applied to many other domains.

Both books and broadcasting licenses are Things to be Renewed. The business decides whether or not to agree to renew in response to requests from a Renewer. The business rules for renewing books or licenses have some similarities. For instance, the business checks whether the Renewer is eligible to renew the thing; it decides the conditions of renewal; it records the decision and informs the Renewer. By looking at several different responses we can make an abstraction: we can say we have some processing policy that is common to all renewable items. We also discover that some of the attributes of a Thing to be Renewed are the same regardless of whether we are talking about a book or a broadcasting license. Among others, each Thing to be Renewed has a unique identifier, a standard renewal period, and a renewal fee.

Figure 12.9 shows the result when we make an abstraction of the processing policy from the two business events. We are using abstraction to identify

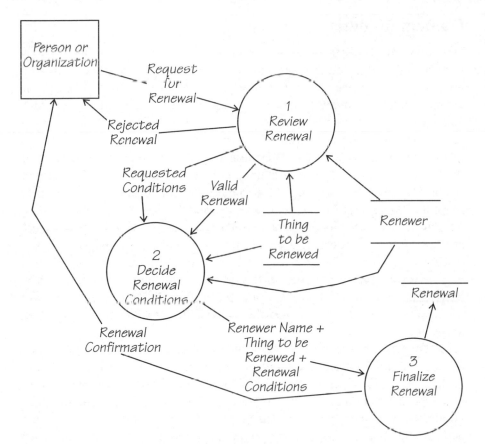

Figure 12.9

This event-response model is the result of finding the similarities between a business event response in the library domain and in the satellite broadcasting domain.

common characteristics. This means looking past what we see on the surface, and finding useful similarities or classifications. It means being able to ignore some characteristics to find common ones.

Ignore the physical artifacts and subject matters. For example, in Figure 12.9 we have ignored the artifacts of library books and broadcasting licenses. We have instead concentrated on the underlying actions that the two different systems are taking. We do this with a view to finding similarities that we may be able to use to our advantage. If, for example, we found that part of a route allocation system had functional similarities to a container storage system (one of the authors actually found these similarities) then work done for one system could be recycled for the other.

This comes down to seeing work at different levels of abstraction. To being able to categorize, or classify, in different ways. Being able to see that telescopes and glass spheres filled with water are both magnifying devices. Being able to spot similarities between apparently different things. Being able to disregard physical artifacts and see things in the abstract.

READING

GAMMA, ERICH ET AL. *Design Patterns: Elements of Reusable Object-Oriented Software.* Addison-Wesley, 1995. This is a leading book on object-oriented design patterns.

Domain Analysis

Domain analysis is the activity of investigating, capturing and specifying generic knowledge about a subject matter area. You could think of domain analysis as non-project systems analysis – the point of it is to learn about the business policy, data and functionality, not to build something. The knowledge gained about the domain is used, and hopefully reused, by any project that builds a product to be used within that domain.

Domain analysis works in the same way that regular systems analysis does. That is, you work with domain experts to extract their, hitherto unarticulated knowledge, and record it in a manner that allows other analysts to reuse it. This suggest that regular analysis models – event-response models, class diagrams, state models, data dictionary, and so on – are the most useful, as these kinds of models have the greatest currency in the analysis world.

Once the domain knowledge has been captured and recorded, then it becomes available to anyone who builds a product for that domain. The domain knowledge applies to any product for that domain. The point is not to rediscover knowledge that has always existed, but to reuse the models of knowledge.

Of course, there is always the problem of precisely what constitutes a domain. Simply saying 'banking' or 'insurance' or 'microsurgery' is not enough. The definition of a domain lies in its interfaces with other domains. It is what enters and leaves that defines the domain, not the domain name. Look back at the context model in Figure 12.4. It is the flows that enter and leave that define the scope of this domain, not its name of 'Customer Wants to Buy a Product'. However, once you have established the boundaries of the domain, it becomes far easier to identify useful business events, data and functions.

Domain analysis is a long-term project. That is, the knowledge gained is reusable, but this is of benefit only if you get the opportunity to reuse it. To invest in domain analysis is like any other investment – you must have a good idea that the investment will be paid back. In the case of domain analysis, the investment is rewarded if the domain knowledge is used by several projects in that domain. And keep in mind that there is no limit to the number of times that domain knowledge can be reused.

READING

Prieto-Díaz, Rubén and Guillermo Arango. *Domain Analysis and Software Systems Modelling.* IEEE Computer Society Press, 1991.

The point is not to rediscover knowledge, but to reuse models of knowledge

Trends in Reuse

When you build a model of some aspect of a system, you immediately make those aspects visible; as soon as you make them visible they are potentially reusable. Research and experience have provided many models for defining various aspects of requirements. For example, right at the project start you can make a system visible by drawing a context diagram to model the intended context of the work. You can partition the subject matter into business events, use cases and classes, each of which can be modeled. Which models you use is not important; what is important is that you and your colleagues all use the same models so that you have a communication medium for making your work visible and hence potentially reusable.

Reuse and Objects

Using the principles of object-orientation we partition and implement system knowledge so that everything relating to one class of subject matter is packaged together.

For instance in the IceBreaker system we have a class called Truck. This class contains all the attributes of truck like weight, registration number, model description. It also contains all the operations that are unique to a truck like Maintain Truck and Show Truck Capacity. The definition of the class called Truck is probably reusable in any system that deals with trucks or similar vehicles.

The increasing use of objects has encouraged more formality and consistency in the way people define and talk about system knowledge. This consistency has helped to raise consciousness about the possibilities of reuse. If we express our knowledge in a more consistent way, then it is more widely communicable and there is every chance that we can use it more than once. Another reason that object-orientation contributes to reuse is that it has led to convergence towards a common notation. The Unified Modeling Language (UML) is becoming a standard notation for building object-oriented models. If we have a standard form then we are less likely to spend our energy talking about notation and instead will focus on the content of our knowledge and how we can use it.

Reuse Is Now a Job?

Back in 1993, the Second International Workshop on Software Reusability was held in Lucca, Italy. Most of the papers presented at the conference focussed on the subjects of reusing code, design or architecture. In other words, the thinking was that only the hard artifacts – code, objects, and so on – could be reused. Very few papers at the conference looked at the idea of reuse earlier in the development cycle, namely the requirements themselves.

Things are changing. The practice of reuse is moving upstream and today we are seeing reuse of the more abstract artifacts. Requirements are commonly recycled, patterns are exchanged on the Internet. A working conference on patterns is held twice a year and results in the sharing of knowledge and publication of new patterns. This change in emphasis brings with it

READING

For a thorough discussion of the wide implications of reuse read: JACOBSON, IVAR, MARTIN GRISS AND PATRIK JONSSON. *Software Reuse: Architecture Process and Organization for Business Success.* Addison Wesley Longman, 1997.

READING

For an overview of the Unified Modeling Language refer to: FOWLER, MARTIN. *UML Distilled: Applying the Standard Object Modeling Language.* Addison-Wesley, 1997. See the bibliography for more UML titles.

Pattern Languages of Programs (PLoP). The annual conference for patterns writers and users. Browse http://www.cpl.uiuc.edu/~plop

READING

For more on thinking behind the reuse of analysis models refer to: ROBERTSON, SUZANNE AND KENNETH STRUNCH. *Reusing the Products of Analysis*. Second International Workshop on Software Reusability, Position Paper. Lucca, Italy, March 24–26, 1993.

Refer to the British Computer Society for information on the special interest group on reuse http://www.bcs.org.uk/ siggroup/siglist.htm

greater rewards. For instance, if a requirement has already been implemented, then it has a design and some code or objects associated with it. If you reuse the requirement, you probably get the design and the code/objects for free. By reusing earlier in the cycle, you get the advantage of the downstream products. But reusing late in the cycle does not bring the same advantages from the upstream products.

We have come a long way. In April 1998 we received the following email message:

We invite applications to investigate Software Reengineering Patterns as an approach to the problem of reengineering legacy systems. This project, funded under the EPSRC Managed Programme "Systems Engineering for Business Process Change", is jointly run by the Computer Science Department and the Management School of the University. Candidates should have excellent communication skills, and either a PhD in a related area or relevant industrial or commercial experience.

This advertisement and others like it indicate that we are starting to think of the discovery and management of reusable patterns as a real job. If we are prepared to invest in knowledge as a tangible asset then we can reap the benefits of requirements reuse.

Summary

We can and do informally reuse requirements knowledge by talking to our colleagues and reusing our own experience. Requirements modeling techniques produce visible deliverables like work context models, use case models, individual requirements specifications and many others, all of which serve to make requirements visible.

The visibility of requirements makes them potentially reusable to a much wider audience. Object-orientation is increasing sophistication in the use of modeling techniques. The interest in patterns and domain analysis is helping to make our industry more aware of the advantages and possibilities of reusing requirements.

Taking Stock of the Specification

13

in which we decide if our specification is
correct and complete, or if more work needs to
be done

By the time you are ready to take stock of your specification, you should feel that the specification is complete, or at least in a state where a progress review will be beneficial to you. This stocktake may be done several times in the development of the specification and it might coincide with particular development phases in your own project lifecycle. Keep in mind that this review is different from the Quality Gateway. The Gateway checks each requirement individually, whereas the stocktake considers all of the requirements and their effect on each other (Figure 13.1).

Chapter 10, Quality Gateway

The objective of the stocktake is to review the specification and find requirements that are:

- Missing
- Conflicting
- Ambiguous.

The review process is iterative until all problems have been resolved. We recommend that you keep a record of discarded requirements. This is to prevent their accidental reintroduction should they reappear, and to know what kinds of requirements are being rejected, with the aim of questioning their reappearance in future projects.

Once the bad requirements are weeded out, or rounded up and added in the case of the missing ones, the specification can be considered complete. But that is not the end of the review. There are several other things that are useful, indeed valuable, to do at this stage of development.

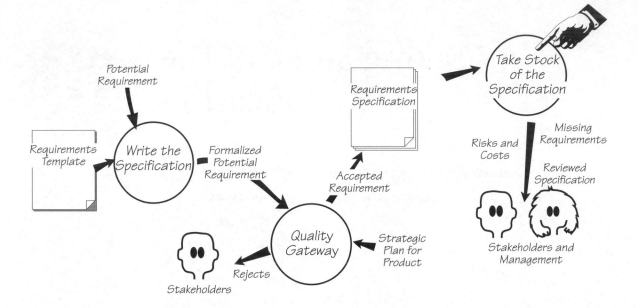

Figure 13.1

We have arrived at the point in the process where it is necessary to consider the specification as a whole. Individual requirements have been passed by the Quality Gateway, and now we assess them as a complete specification.

● Remeasure the effort required to build the product. This chapter contains a short tutorial on counting function points.

● Reanalyze the risks involved in completing the project. This does not mean avoiding risks, but getting an understanding of what they are. We talk about the major risks later in the chapter.

● Reassess the decision on whether to go ahead, or to abandon the project. See the section entitled Assess Your Product.

Find Missing Requirements

Firstly, all the requirements types that are appropriate to your product must be present in the specification. Use the template and its requirements types as a guide to determining that your specification contains all the appropriate types, and that there are not any others that should be included. The strategic plan for the product is usually an indicator of the types of requirements that may be missing. For example, if this is a financial product, and there are no security requirements, then something is definitely missing. Similarly, a safety critical product without safety requirements is certainly in trouble.

The functional requirements should be sufficient to complete the work of each use case. To check this, it is usually necessary to play through each of the use cases with the appropriate users, looking for missing actions. You are also looking for missing exceptions. Check that you have previously generated enough 'what if' scenarios to cover all eventualities, and that the functional requirements reflect this.

Check each use case against the non-functional requirement types. Does the use case have all the non-functional requirements that it needs and that are appropriate for this kind of use case? Use the requirements template as a checklist. Go through the non-functional requirements types, read their descriptions, and ensure that all possible non-functional requirements that can apply to the use case have been included.

Have All the Use Cases Been Discovered?

The strategy that we have described in this book shows you how to partition the work according to the business events that affect it. Then for each business event, determine the business response and how much of that response is to be carried out by the product. A use case is that part of the response done by the product. For each use case, you use trawling techniques to discover the requirements, and then they are written into the specification.

This strategy is effective, providing you have discovered *all* the business events. Missing events mean missing requirements. However, help is at hand.

We have devised a procedure for checking that all the events, and thus all the use cases, have been discovered. The procedure requires you to do some modeling using the regular systems analysis models – the ones that you build when you do systems analysis. This means that you may want to integrate the modeling effort with your requirements gathering or wait until the systems analysis is more complete to verify that you have gathered all the use cases.

The process is shown in Figure 13.2. We have used conventional data flow notation – an effective vehicle for describing an iterative process such as this. Follow along in the model as we describe each of the activities within it.

1 Define the Context

Determine the context of the work. Whichever model you choose, it must show the data that enters and leaves the work. Look at Figure 13.3.

The context is usually determined during the blastoff activity. It is necessary to have a clear scope for the work before beginning the requirements investigation. Thus this model is probably already to hand.

The context at this stage may be incomplete. The rest of this process will enhance and complete your context.

2 Identify the Business Events and 'Non-Events'

Determine the business events by studying the boundary data flows on the context diagram. Each incoming or outgoing flow is connected to a business

Chapter 4, Event-driven Use Cases, contains a complete coverage of how to determine business events from the context model

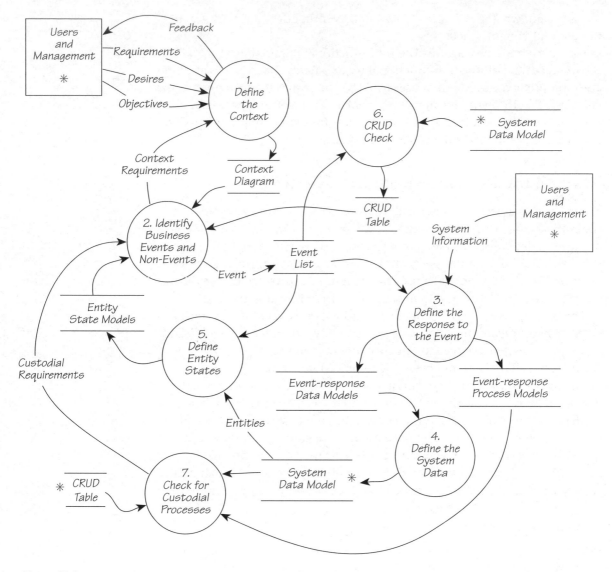

Figure 13.2

The procedure for determining that all the use cases have been found. The process is iterative, going through all the activities until the Identify Business Events and Non-Events activity fails to discover any new events.

event. Either it announces to the work that an external event has taken place, or it is the end product of the response to an event. Reponses to events take place inside the work. Some events will be connected to more than one flow.

Go around the perimeter of the work and, for each boundary data flow ask, 'What is the business event that causes this flow to be part of the context?' For each business event, add it to the list of events. The event list of the IceBreaker product is shown in Figure 13.4.

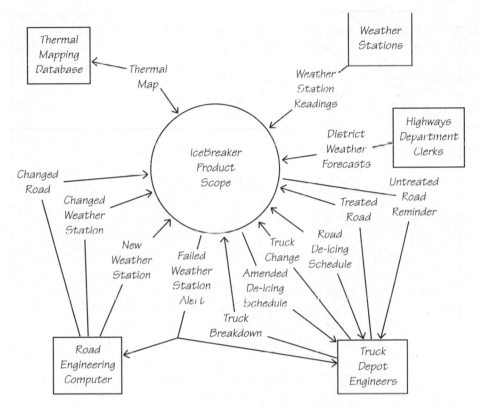

Figure 13.3

The context diagram of the work shows the data entering and leaving the scope of the system. These are referred to later as the boundary data flows.

The term 'non-events' is a play on words. Non-events are events that happen if the fundamental event does not happen. For example, if an event is Customer Pays for Services, the non-event is the customer does not pay. There is most likely some action to take under these circumstances – probably a temporal event such as Time to Send Reminder to Non-paying Customers. Not all events have non-events, but asking for each event, 'What happens if this event does not happen' will help you to discover some relevant missing events.

Look at the IceBreaker event list in Figure 13.4. The first event is 'Weather Station makes a reading'. This is a fundamental event. That is, it is part of the fundamental reason for the product's existence. Now, what happens if the weather station does *not* make a reading? If you talk to the users, they will tell you that if a weather station does not make any kind of transmission for four hours, it is deemed to be out of action, and the road engineering department must be notified.

Thus we have a new (non-)event Time to Notify Road Engineering of Failed Weather Station. You would add this event to the list, update the context model with the appropriate flows, and continue searching for more non-events. As an exercise, see if you can find the other non-events from the IceBreaker event list.

Figure 13. 4

The event list for the IceBreaker product. The list shows all the business events that cause the work to respond. The inputs and outputs are the boundary data flows connected to the event. When you have listed all of the boundary flows from the context model, you have determined all of the possible business events ... for the moment.

Event Name	Input Flows	Output Flows
1 Weather Station makes a reading	Weather Station Readings	
2 Weather Forecasting Bureau predicts weather	District Weather Forecasts	
3 Road Engineering makes a change to a road	Changed Road	
4 Road Engineering installs new weather station	New Weather Station	
5 Road Engineering makes change to weather station	Changed Weather Station	
6 Time to monitor weather station		Failed Weather Station Alert
7 Truck Depot makes a change to a truck	Truck Change	Amended De-icing Schedule
8 Time to schedule road de-icing		Road De-icing Schedule
9 Truck treats road	Treated Road	
10 Truck Depot reports problem with truck	Truck Breakdown	Amended De-icing Schedule
11 Time to monitor road de-icing		Untreated Road Reminder

3   Define the Response to the Business Event

Model the processing that takes place in response to the event, and the data needed to support the processing. You can use any kind of models for this, and they do not have to be complete and detailed, as long as they demonstrate the process and data involved in the response to each business event. Figure 13.5 provides an illustration.

READING

ROBERTSON, JAMES AND SUZANNE. *Complete Systems Analysis – the Workbook, the Textbook, the Answers.* Dorset House, 1994. This is a thorough treatment of event-response modeling.

We suggest that you either use a class diagram, collaboration diagram and sequence diagram, or an event-response data flow model and some kind of data model. Most model types will be satisfactory, provided they demonstrate the correct functioning of the process and the data necessary for the event response to do its work.

4   Define the System Data

Build a model of all the stored data needed by the system. This is usually easiest if you plug the event-response data models together by joining the entities that are the same on several models. Use an entity relationship

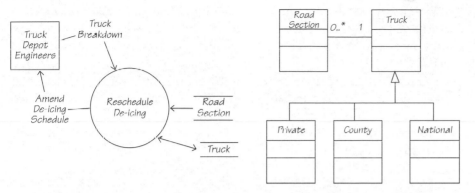

Figure 13.5

The process and the data used by the work to respond to the event 'Truck Depot reports problem with truck'. We have found it easier to model the data for a single event than for the entire system.

model, a class diagram, a relational model, or your preferred data model notation. As long as it shows entities, tables or classes, and the relationships between them, it will suffice. The system data model is progressively confirmed and added to by subsequent event-response data models.

Check that each entity on your model is well defined, that is, it qualifies according to the rules that apply to your choice of data model.

5   Define the States of the Entities

Build state models to show the states through which the entities pass. These models are often known as entity life history models.

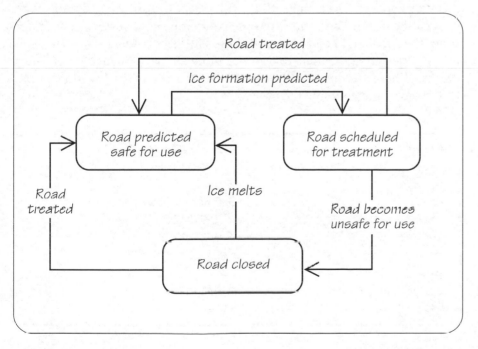

Figure 13.6

A state model showing the states of the entity called Road Section. Each state is a steady, continuous mode of behavior. An entity will remain in a state until an event occurs causing a transition to a new state.

READING

HAREL, DAVID. Statecharts: A Visual Formalism for Complex Systems. *Science of Computer Programming*, vol. 8, 1987.

Look at the model in Figure 13.6. To build such a model you need to determine the states that can apply to an entity. However, it is the transition between states that is of interest here – each transition is caused by an event.

You use the transitions – events – to reveal missing events. For example, in Figure 13.6, there is a transition out of the state Road Closed called Ice Melts. This is an event that was not previously considered, but obviously has an effect on the work. So this event is added to the event list and modeled like any other event.

6   CRUD Check

Each attribute on the data model must be Created and Referenced. Some are Updated and or Deleted. Build a table, such as the one shown in Figure 13.7 to determine if every entity has all the appropriate actions performed on it.

If an entity is referenced without firstly being created it means that the creating event has been missed. If it is created without being referenced then it indicates either a missing event or superfluous data. Some entities are updated and/or deleted, but for this to happen they must have been created.

Any holes in the CRUD table raise questions about the completeness of the work context. For example, the entities Depot, District and Sensor show no creating event. This means that the context is incomplete as it does not show the incoming flows to create these entities of stored data. This will result in revisiting the users to find out more about these missing business events. When they are found, record them on the event list, update the CRUD table, and continue the process.

Figure 13.7

The CRUD table. Each cell shows the number of the event that creates, references, updates or deletes the entity.

Entity	Create	Reference	Update	Delete
Depot		7		
District		2, 8, 10		
Reading	1	6, 8, 10		
Road	3	4, 8, 9, 103		
Road Section	3	4, 8, 10, 113, 9		
Sensor		1, 4		
Truck	7	8, 97, 10	7	
Weather Forecast	2	8, 10		
Weather Station	4	1, 6 5		

7 Check for Custodial Processes

Custodial processes are those that exist to maintain the stored data. It helps to think of processes as being either fundamental or custodial.

Fundamental processes are the ones that are connected to the reason for the system's existence. For example, analyzing the roads, recording the weather forecasts, scheduling the trucks to treat the roads.

Custodial processes maintain the stored data. They are necessary, because they maintain the data used by the fundamental processes. When the road engineers advise the IceBreaker system of a change to a road, a custodial process must be invoked to bring the data held about the road up to date.

Check that there are enough custodial processes to maintain all of the data shown on your system data model.

8 Repeat until Done

Stages 1 through 7 are iterative. That is, you must continue to go through the process – identifying events, modeling them, adding to system data, checking entity states, checking that the entities are created, referenced, updated, deleted – until stage 2 Identify Events and Non-events fails to reveal any new events. At that stage, you can be certain that there are no more events to capture.

Implementing the Checking

Completeness checking takes patience, but is not exactly rocket science. Once you understand the reasoning behind each one of the steps in the above completeness check, you can best implement it using some kind of automated CASE or requirements engineering tool. Consider the facilities provided by the tools at your disposal and map each stage of the checking process to the capabilities provided by the tools in your environment.

For a list of currently available requirements engineering tools, consult the Internet

Conflicting Requirements

Two requirements are conflicting if you cannot implement them both because their meanings are opposed. To implement one would mean not implementing the other. For example, if one look and feel requirement states that the product has to employ a large surface area to display information, and an operational requirement says that the product has to be used by someone while they move about on foot, then both cannot be implemented exactly as specified.

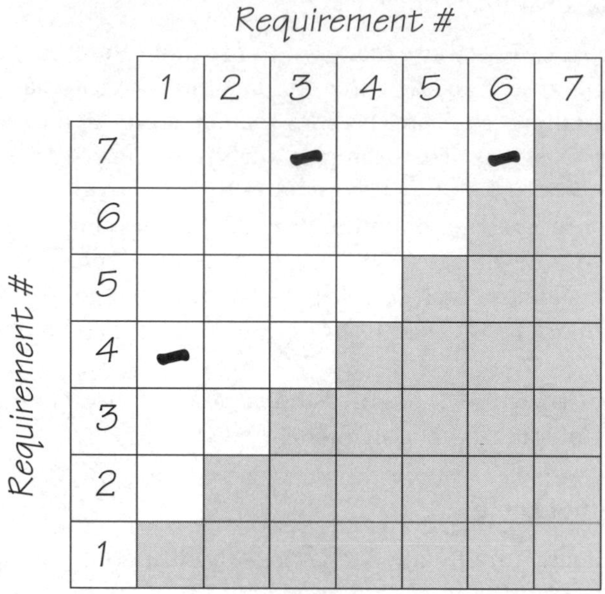

Figure 13.8

You can use a spreadsheet to compare requirements and identify conflicting requirements. For example, requirements 3 and 7 are in conflict with each other. If we implement a solution to requirement 3 it will have a negative effect on our ability to implement a solution to requirement 7 and vice versa.

As a first pass at finding conflicting requirements, sort the requirements into their types. Then examine all the entries that you have for each type, looking for pairs of requirements whose fit criteria are in conflict with each other. See Figure 13.8.

Of course it is possible for a requirement to be in conflict with any other requirement in the specification. To help you find conflicting requirements here are some clues to the situations where we most often find requirements in conflict:

● Requirements that use the same data (search by matching terms used);

● Requirements of the same type (search by matching requirement type);

● Requirements using the same scales of measurement (search by matching requirements whose fit criteria use the same scales of measurement).

A spreadsheet is a useful tool when you are doing this check. For non-functional requirements, consider the requirements that are of the same type. For example, a usability requirement should not, say, have a fit criterion specifying that users 'shall be able to carry out all the use cases without any training' if the users in question are research scientists dealing with masses of data. It should be as easy to use as is possible, but for such a product we would anticipate several months of training to use the product. Thus the fit criterion on the usability requirement is in conflict with the specification of the users.

Another technique that is helpful in identifying and assessing dependencies between requirements is Quality Function Deployment. (QFD) popularized in Japan in the 1960s. The intention is to make it easier for customers, marketing, development, production, design and managerial staff to work together from the time that a project is started. The heart of the technique is to communicate the *voice of the customer* (or the requirements) throughout the development of the product. QFD has a tool called the House of Quality (so called because it is in the shape of a house) which is a matrix for identifying functional and organizational interdependencies throughout the life of a product's development.

For functional requirements, look for conflicts in outcomes. For example, suppose that one requirement calls for the de-icing trucks to be routed by the *shortest* distance, and another specifies that the trucks must be given the *quickest* route. These two requirements do not necessarily mean the same thing, or may result in different outcomes.

Conflicts will arise because different users have asked for different requirements, or users have asked for requirements that are in conflict with the client's idea of the requirements. This is normal for most requirements gathering efforts. It indicates that you need to have some sort of conflict resolution mechanism in place.

You, the requirements analyst, have the most to gain by having conflicts resolved as rapidly as possible, and therefore we suggest that you play a lead part in resolving them. When you have isolated the conflicting requirements, approach each of the users separately (this is one reason why you record the source of each requirement). Go over the requirement with the user and ensure that both of you have the same understanding of the requirement. Reassess the satisfaction and dissatisfaction scales – if one user gives low marks to the requirement then he may not care if you drop it in favor of the other. Do this with both users and do not, for the moment, bring them together.

Talk to each user separately. Find out their reasoning – what is it that they really want as an outcome, and will it be compromised if the other requirement takes precedence? Most of the time we have been able to resolve conflicts this way. Note that we used the term 'conflict' and did not say 'dispute'. There was no dispute. There were no positions taken, no noses put out of joint by the other guy winning. They may not know who the other person is.

If you as a mediator are unable to reach a satisfactory resolution, then we suggest that you determine the cost of implementing the opposing requirements, assess their relative risks, and armed with numbers, call the participants together and see if you can reach some compromise. We have found that except in cases of extreme office politics, stakeholders are usually willing to compromise if they are in a position to do it gracefully without loss of face.

READING

For more on Quality Function Deployment refer to:

MACAULAY, LINDA. *Requirements Engineering.* Springer-Verlag

HAUSER, JOHN R. AND DON CLAUSING. The House of Quality. *Harvard Business Review*, 1988.

❝ *The foundation of the house of quality is the belief that products should be designed to reflect customers' desires and tastes – so marketing people, design engineers, and manufacturing staff must work closely together from the time a product is first conceived.* ❞

Source: John Hauser and Don Clausing

Fit Criteria

Each requirement carries a fit criterion. The fit criterion is a quantified goal that any implementation of the requirement must meet. Fit criteria are assigned either as the requirements are gathered, or during the Quality Gateway checks. While you take stock of the specification you are testing each fit criterion to see that it is a viable, valuable criterion for acceptance testing.

● Does the fit criterion meet the intention of the product objective? The objective for the product was determined by the blastoff. This objective is a guideline for all requirements. The fit criterion must be consistent with the product's objective, and should not attempt to enhance requirements to the point that they are outside the scope of the objective. Nor should the fit criterion in any way contradict the objective.

● Does it make an unnecessary demand when the objective can be met without this?

● Can it be readily tested? The testing people should advise you about the testability of the fit criterion. The requirements analyst will probably not be the person who tests the product. However, he must be sure that the fit criterion can be tested, and that the results of the tests will prove that the product unambiguously meets the requirement.

● Are the tests cost effective?

● Is the fit criterion subjective? If you have written that a transaction must be complete within 15 seconds, is there a reason for specifying 15 seconds? This number must be based on surveys, or empirical evidence that 15 seconds is the correct measure, and is needed by your client.

● Are the terms used in the fit criterion defined in the Naming Conventions and Definitions section of the specification?

● Is the terminology ambiguous? Note that numbers are rarely ambiguous, which is why we attach a quantification to the requirement instead of trying to define it using words.

Revise the fit criteria as appropriate. Keep in mind that the fit criterion is the real requirement. That is, in order to ensure that the product conforms to the requirement, the tester will test that the product meets the fit criterion. It is therefore important that the fit criterion is a precise statement of your client's wishes.

Ambiguous Specs

The specification should, as far as is practical, be free of ambiguity. You should not have used any pronouns and be wary of unqualified adjectives and adverbs – all of these introduce ambiguity. The word 'should' must not be used – it infers that the requirement is optional. But even if you follow these guidelines, some problems may remain.

The fit criteria are devices to quantify each of the requirements, and thus make them unambiguous. In Chapter 9 we have described fit criteria, and how they make each of the requirements measurable and testable. If you have correctly applied fit criteria, then the requirements in your specification will be unambiguous.

This leaves the descriptions of the requirements. Obviously the less ambiguity they contain the better, but a poor description cannot do much damage if the fit criterion is free of ambiguity. However, if you are concerned about it then we suggest that you select 50 requirements randomly. Ask a selection of stakeholders to give their interpretation of the requirement. If all the stakeholders agree as to the meaning of the requirement then set it aside. However, if the meaning of a requirement is disputed, then select five more. Repeat this until it becomes clear that the specification is acceptable, or the list of requirements to test is now so long that the problem is obvious to all.

If the problem is bad, then consider rewriting the specification using a qualified technical writer.

All the terms used in the specification are those that are defined in the Naming Conventions section of the specification. If every word has an agreed definition, and you have used the terms consistently, then the meanings through the specification must be consistent and unambiguous.

Risk Analysis

Risk analysis is not directly connected with requirements, rather it is a project issue. However, at this stage of the requirements process you have a complete specification of a product that you intend to build. You have invested a certain amount of time deriving a description of the product, and are about to invest even more time in building it. So now seems like a good time to pause for a moment and consider the risks involved in proceeding.

Risk analysis is about identifying the risks that the project faces along with the probability that a risk will manifest itself as a problem. There is quite a lot of help available for identifying risks. Several books have been published that can be used as checklists of risks. Capers Jones' book also gives the percentage of projects that have suffered from each risk, which can be used to help you assess the probability of the risk affecting your project.

Once you have assessed the risks that your project faces, and determined the probability that the risk could become a problem, then you determine your course of action. In some cases the impact if the risk becomes a problem

READING

JONES, CAPERS. *Assessment and Control of Software Risks.* Prentice-Hall, 1994.

is so severe, that it is worthwhile to take preventative action. In these cases you determine what it is you have to do to avoid that risk. In other cases – they have to be assessed on a project-by-project basis – it pays to have a contingency plan in the event of the risk turning into a problem. This applies to cases where the likelihood and the impact are slight enough that it is preferable to wait and see if the risk does in fact become a problem.

Many of the risks can be identified from the requirements specification. Look at the early part of the specification:

Product Constraints

1 The Purpose of the Product

2 Client, Customer and other Stakeholders

3 Users of the Product

4 Requirements Constraints

5 Naming Conventions and Definitions

6 Relevant Facts

7 Assumptions

Functional Requirements

8 The Scope of the Product

Is the purpose of the product reasonable? Is this something that your organization can achieve? Or are you setting out to do something that you have never done before, with only hysterical optimism telling you that you can successfully deliver the objective?

Is the client a willing collaborator? Or is he uninterested in the project? Is the customer represented accurately? While customer representative panels are useful, experience has shown that they are frequently wrong in their assessment of what the real customers want and need. Are all the stakeholders involved and enthusiastic about the project and the product? Hostile or unidentified stakeholders can have a very negative effect on your project. What are the chances that everybody will make the contribution that is needed? What risks are you running by not having the cooperation you need?

The users represent some serious risks. Are they properly represented? Are they able, and capable of telling you the correct requirements? Many project leaders often cite the quality of user contributions to requirements as their most serious and frequent risk.

Many system development efforts result in substantial changes to the users' work, and the way that they work. Have you considered the risk that the users will not be able to adapt to the new arrangements? Remember that humans do not like being changed, and your new product is bringing changes to your users' work. Are the users capable of operating the new product? Consider these risks carefully, as the risk of the users not being prepared to change may turn out to be a substantial problem.

Are the constraints reasonable, or do they indicate design solutions with which your organization has no experience? Is the budget reasonable for the effort needed to build the product? Unrealistic schedules and budgets is one of the most common risks cited by projects.

Are the assumptions reasonable, and should you be making contingency plans for the eventuality that one or more of the assumptions turns out not to be true?

Is the scope of the product correct? Have you taken it far enough to discover all the requirements? If the scope is not large enough, then the result will be a product that does not do enough for the user. This always results in early requests for modifications and enhancements to the product.

Also keep in mind that creeping user requirements, and incomplete requirements specifications, are very commonly cited risks. Look back over your requirements gathering effort and assure yourself that you gave the users and the client the appropriate opportunity to give you all their requirements, and that your gathering techniques allowed full participation from all the stakeholders.

Risk analysis does not make the risks go away, but it does mean that you and your management are aware of problems that might arise, and can make appropriate plans for monitoring and addressing them.

Measure Required Effort

Now that the requirements are all known, it is an ideal opportunity to measure the size of the product. It is common sense that you do not proceed past this point without knowing the size of the product to be built. Over the years our industry has established that for most size metrics, there is a standard amount of work to be done to implement one unit of the metric. For example, if you use function points to determine the size of the product, then there are industry-standard figures of the number of hours, or the number of dollars, it takes to implement one function point. Thus if you know the size of the product, then it is a relatively straightforward matter to translate size into effort required to build the product.

As an example of this, Capers Jones once gave a figure of US$1000 as the average cost of constructing one function point. (See Chapter 10, the section on Requirements Creep.) Let me hasten to add that Jones was in no way recommending that you use this number as if it would apply to you. Nor will it be accurate for all circumstances. Nevertheless it indicates that once you know your own cost per function point (or whatever size metric you use) estimating the effort needed to build a product can be done quite readily.

The keyword here is 'measure'

You can of course measure the size of your product any way that you and your organization think is appropriate. The key word here is 'measure'. If you are not already using a measuring method, then we suggest that you start with function point counting. While it is by no means the ultimate measuring method, it is widely used, and thus a lot is known about it, and a lot of information and statistics on function points is available.

Function points replace the earlier, and now thought to be dangerous, lines of code. Function points are not the only way to measure the size of a product. Some of the other methods available are Mark II Function points (these are a variation of standard function points), or Capers Jones' Feature Points (also a variation), or Tom DeMarco's Bang. There are various object-based counting methods. However, at the requirements stage of development, function points are convenient, and given what you know of the product at this stage, probably the most appropriate.

So if you do not already use another method, and would like to get started with function points, then please join us for this ...

Quick Primer on Counting Function Points

This is definitely not all there is to know about counting the size of a system using function points. However, it is sufficient to get started, and to make a quick sizing of your product.

Let's begin at the beginning.

Function points are a measure of software functionality. This means that you count the amount of work the automated product does. The amount of work is based on the data that is processed by the product, along with some processing characteristics. The idea being that the more data there is, and the more complex it is, the more functionality is needed. Function point counting can be applied to both procedural and object-oriented systems.

As the development proceeds, the models will become more accurate, and thus your measuring can become more accurate along with them. But we are still at the requirements stage, and so it is appropriate to:

● Count function points quickly. This is more important than being hyper-accurate. The intention is to get a quick and fairly accurate idea of what this product will cost.

● Count the function points for the product in its entirety, or for each of the event/use cases.

Let's start our counting with the context model.

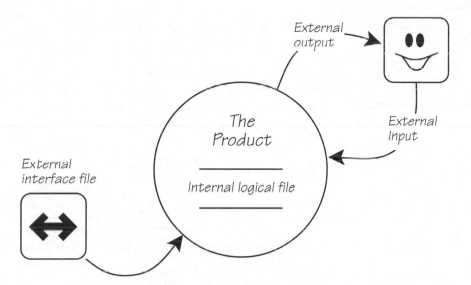

Figure 13.9

The components needed
to count function points.
The names used are
those in common usage
by the function point
counting community.

Note each of the labeled components on the context model in Figure 13.9. These are the components that will be used for the count. The External input is a flow of data that comes from an adjacent system. Similarly, an External output goes to an adjacent system. There is also an external query, however we feel it is appropriate to ignore it as it is a form of input and output and so will get counted here anyway. A data store that is controlled by the product is classed as an Internal logical file. There may be several of these. The function point counting authorities want to count disk files, or data base, so it does not matter if you show several files, or a single logical data store. The cooperative adjacent system is another system that supplies data to this event. This is measured as an External interface file – a file that is accessible to the product, but the product does not have responsibility to maintain it.

For each of these components in your own model:

**PUTTING
THIS TO
WORK**

- Count the Data Element Types. A data element type is a unique, user-recognizable, non-recursive field that is maintained on either an internal logical file, or an external interface file. You might know them as data elements or attributes. The count does not have to be highly accurate, as the method assigns low, medium and high according to ranges of elements, so an inspired guess as to the number may be good enough.

- Count the Record Element Types. Record elements are logical groupings of data elements, or just plain records if you prefer. Try and figure how many types of subject matter are covered in the data flows and data stores.

- Count the File Types Referenced. These are the data stores/files, internal or external, touched on by the processing.

Figure 13.10

For each component – either Internal Logical File, External Interface File, External Input or Output – translate the number of Data Element Types and Record Element Types/File Types Referenced into Unadjusted Function Point counts.

Internal Logical Files

	Data Element Types		
Record Element Types	1–19	20–50	51+
<2	7	7	10
2–5	7	10	15
>5	10	15	15

External Interface Files

	Data Element Types		
Record Element Types	1–19	20–50	51+
<2	5	5	7
2–5	5	7	10
>5	7	10	10

External Inputs

	Data Element Types		
File Types Referenced	1–4	5–15	16+
<2	3	3	4
2	3	4	6
>2	4	6	6

External Outputs

	Data Element Types		
File Types Referenced	1–5	6–19	20+
<2	4	4	5
2–3	4	5	7
>3	5	7	7

Next, the counts are translated into Unadjusted Function Point counts by referencing the table appropriate for the component. The tables are shown in Figure 13.10.

Look up the unadjusted function point count from the figure. Select the table that matches the component that you are measuring. The numbers in bold are the unadjusted function points assigned to the combination of data element types and record element types or file types referenced by that component. The basic idea is that the more data element types that have to be processed, and the more record or file types needed by the component, the higher the number of function points.

These are called 'unadjusted function points' as they have yet to be adjusted for the type of processing done by the product. This processing is assessed by the *general system characteristics* assigned to the product. Obviously some products are more complex, or harder to build than others and the characteristics make allowance for this.

For your product, assess each of the general system characteristics from the following list. These ratings change the unadjusted function points, rather like a degree of difficulty rating.

The general system characteristics are:

1   Data communications

2   Distributed data processing

3   Performance

4   Heavily-used configuration

5   Transaction rate

6   On-line data entry

7   End-user efficiency

8   On-line update

9   Complex processing

10   Reusability

11   Installation ease

12   Operational ease

13   Multiple sites

14   Facilitate change

Each of the characteristics is evaluated. This has to be done by someone who knows about the constraints of the product that you are building. At requirements time these may be assessments rather than measurements, but will be accurate enough provided they are done consistently.

READING

GARMUS, DAVID AND DAVID HERRON. *Measuring the Software Process*. Yourdon Press, 1996. This book has some commentary on general system characteristics.

Rate each characteristic by assigning a score of zero, meaning not applicable; through to 5, meaning that that characteristic has a strong influence throughout. To achieve consistency, have a single person give the ratings for all the factors.

Accumulate the scores for the 14 characteristics to give the total degree of influence. Multiply this by 0.01 then add 0.65. This gives a number in the range of 0.65 to 1.35, which is the factor that adjusts for the type of processing (or degree of difficulty).

Multiply the accumulation of the unadjusted function points by the adjustment factor to give the final adjusted function point count.

There. That's it. You have counted the function points.

That's not really it. At least, that is not all there is to function point counting, but it will get you started. It is also sufficient for the quick counts needed at requirements time.

Customer Value

Each requirement should carry a satisfaction and dissatisfaction rating. See Figure 13.11. The satisfaction rating is the measure of how happy your client will be if you successfully deliver the requirement, while the dissatisfaction rating measures how unhappy the client will be if you fail to deliver the requirement.

The satisfaction and dissatisfaction ratings measure the worth of the requirement to your client. They are normally appended to each requirement, however you may elect to have the ratings attached to each use case as a measure of the client's value for the successful delivery of that part of the work.

The client normally makes the satisfaction and dissatisfaction ratings. If the client is paying for the development of the product, then it stands to reason that he should be the one to put a value on the requirements. Some

Figure 13.11

The satisfaction and dissatisfaction scales measure your client's concern about whether requirements are delivered as part of the final product. A high score indicates that the client is happy that the requirement is successfully delivered, or very unhappy that it has not been included in the product.

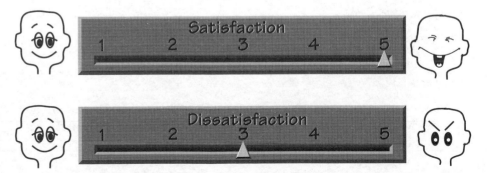

organizations prefer to have a small group of the principal stakeholders assign the ratings.

This is the best mechanism your client has to let you know which requirements are the most valuable. Use this idea to communicate with your client and to encourage him to tell you how he honestly feels about each requirement. If your client has trouble assigning ratings to the requirements, then you must do it yourself and check his reaction. Naturally, the value that you place on a requirement may be very different to that of your client. But he must bear the responsibility of the wrong requirements being implemented if he does not participate in this exercise.

Consider the value of a requirement after it has been rated. For example, if a requirement scores 5 for satisfaction, and 5 for dissatisfaction, then your client really wants that requirement. However, if a requirement scores 2 and 2, then the client doesn't care if this requirement does not make it to the final product. Requirements with low value should be either dropped from the specification, or delayed until the next release of the product.

This is the best mechanism your client has to let you know which requirements are the most valuable

READING

For more on customer value ratings refer to: PARDEE, WILLIAM J. *To Satisfy and Delight Your Customer.* Dorset House, 1996.

Assess Your Product

The purpose of the specification stocktake is to assess the correctness of the requirements specification, and the value, cost and risk attached to building the product.

Consider the model shown in Figure 13.12. It is a composite measure of the overall worth of the product. Suppose that you have devised a suitable scale for each of the axes. The low end of the scale is at the intersection of the axes, and the high end is at the extremities. Rank the risk, the size of product or effort to build, and the customer value along the corresponding scale. What does the profile look like? If you have high scores for effort and risk, and a low score for customer value, then you should consider abandoning the product – the benefit from having it is outweighed by the risk and effort to build it.

You can also use the same ranking model to compare the desirability of individual requirements, or clusters of requirements represented by product use cases. This is helpful when your requirements cannot be met within the constraints (usually time and budget) and you are trying to decide which ones should have priority.

The products that you would like to build are those that score highly for customer value and low on the other scales. You will not often see this nirvana-like state, but consider if the profile of your product indicates that it is one to build, or one to avoid.

Figure 13.12

Each of the axes represents one of the factors that determines if the product is worthwhile. The size axis can be assessed using function points, or some other size measurement, and represents the cost of construction. The customer value axis is assessed using the satisfaction and dissatisfaction ratings. The risk axis is a measure of the severity of risks determined by the risk analysis activity.

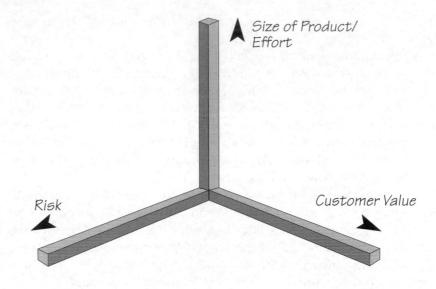

Summary

You take stock of the requirements specification for two reasons. One is to assess the state of completion, and the quality, of the specification. The other is to give you another chance to assess the overall value and desirability of the product, and whether it is worthwhile to continue developing this product.

Whither Requirements?

in which we consider some other issues for the *requirements*

Sometimes, the way we talk about the requirements process makes it sound as if it has a nice neat start and finish – once we specify the requirements for a product, then everything is taken care of. We would certainly like that to be the case. However, we know that requirements, like anything else, need to be managed. And not just while the specification is being written but for as long as the product exists.

We want to look at some of the management issues. This is not a complete treatise on managing a requirements effort, but there are some issues we feel are worthwhile exploring:

- Tools for recording and manipulating your requirements.
- Tailoring the requirements process to suit the project.
- Packaging the requirements for communicating to different people and organizations for different purposes.
- Tracing the requirements through the development of the product.
- Dealing with change.
- A post mortem to improve your process.

All of these issues have an impact on how you build the project management for your project.

What about Requirements Tools?

There are many products on the market that help with the requirements process. Tools can help with the requirements effort by applying automation to the clerical tasks of tracing requirements, linking test results to requirements, change management, semantic analysis, and so on. While these tools are undoubtedly useful, they should be treated as what they are – a tool. That is, an aid to your own efforts, and not a replacement for them. Despite the extravagant claims of some 258vendors, there is no requirements tool that can actually invent something, nor can any tool interview a user, nor can any tool know what it is that your client really wants.

We are not going to go over the features available on the various tools. By the time you read this the features would have changed, and some of the vendors would have gone out of business, and new ones appeared. If you want to know what is available, then we direct you to the Internet where you can find the most up-to-date information. We like the British Computer Society's site, and there are many others.

For information about currently available tools, the Internet is the best resource

Instead of looking at features, we want to look the other way. We want to take a look at the requirements for the tools.

Mapping Tools to Purpose

If there is an overriding message to come from this book it is: find the requirements before building the product. We can also say that this applies to buying a product. Before you, or your manager, succumb to the elaborate prose of the tool vendor salesman, consider what you want your tool to do. In other words your requirements for a requirements tool. If you requirement is to manage the requirements deliverables, then let's consider those deliverables.

Figure 14.1 is a class model of the key requirements deliverables, described in the template, along with the inter-deliverable associations that we need to keep track of in order to manage the requirements.

Let's look at this model. Each of the components is represented by a class. The classes are tagged with the section number from the Volere Specification Template. The associations between the classes show that there is a need to know the links between those classes. For example, the two classes Work Context and Business Event have an association, which indicates that there is a need to keep track of the links between the two. The 1 and the * indicate that for one Work Context there are potentially many Business Events. Consider this: if we have a work context, then we need to know how many business events affect it, as well as manage to link those business events back to the work context.

So this is a requirement. We would like a requirements tool to keep track of this association and alert us to any problems. We would also like the tool to record the details of the Work Context and each Business Event as defined in section 8 of the template. For example, the template tells us that, in order

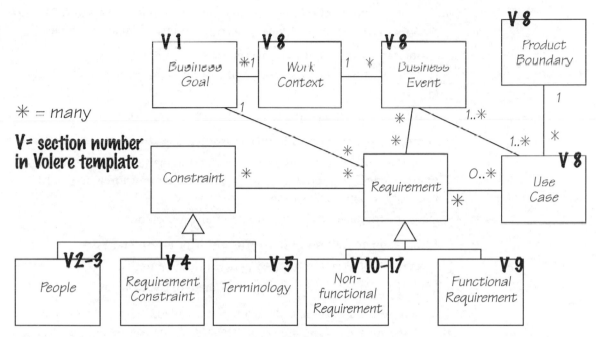

∗ = many

V= section number
in Volere template

to define Work Context we need to record things like the adjacent systems and the details of the interfaces between those adjacent systems and the work we are investigating.

Each of the classes and associations on the model identify some requirements-related knowledge that we have a need to record and manage. Look at the class called Requirement, see how it has an association with the class called Constraint. We see that each Requirement has an association with many Constraints and vice versa. To help us to think about the details, the model breaks both Requirements and Constraints into sub-classes. We see that there are three sub-classes – People, Requirement Constraint, Terminology – that share some characteristics common to any Constraint, while having their own unique characteristics.

When we look at the association between Requirement and Use Case we see that a Requirement has an association with zero to many (0..*) Use Cases. The reason for this is that we have some requirements that are associated with a Business Event, but when setting the product boundary we have decided that Requirement will not be part of the product hence it will not be associated with a use case. The requirements that we want to specify in the most detail are those that have an association with one or more use cases and hence will be part of the product.

The idea behind this is that you can use the class model as an overview of the requirements for a tool. Map the tool to the requirements using the following as a guide:

Figure 14.1

The class diagram shows the components of the requirements specification (the rectangles) and the necessary associations between them (the lines). The V indicates the section number of the Volere Specification Template that describes that component. The asterisks and numbers on the associations tell how many components can participate in the association.

● Use the requirements classes and associations in Figure 14.1 and the supporting details in the template and requirements shell as a checklist.

What can the tool help you to record?

● Has the tool got the facilities to record all the details for each class of knowledge?

● Can the tool record all the details for each association?

What can the tool do to identify problems and inconsistencies?

● Does the tool report on discrepancies and inconsistencies between classes of knowledge? (Refer to Chapter 10 Quality Gateway and Chapter 13 Taking Stock of the Specification.)

● Does the tool alert you to possible missing associations?

What can the tool do to help you monitor completeness?

● Does the tool alert you to missing definitions of terms?

● Does the tool analyze percentage complete of each class in Figure 14.1?

When you map your needs against the capabilities of a tool you will almost certainly discover some needs that are not completely met. This is not because there is anything inherently wrong with the tool, it is because requirements engineering is a relatively new field and the tools are being developed by many different people with different perspectives. Similarly, organizations are developing their own requirements processes because there is as yet no standard way of gathering requirements. So don't expect that any tool will do everything that you want.

This means designing your own requirements environment. Define how all parts, automated and manual, interface with each other. In other words you need your tools to support, as seamlessly as possible, all the activities that you carry out within your requirements process.

Tailoring the Process

The complete Volere Requirements Process model is in Appendix A

As we discussed early in the book, the Volere requirements process is a distillation of experience from many different projects, building different products, in different countries under different circumstances. The process provides a source from which you can select the parts that apply to your particular project. We have found that the most effective way to tailor the process is to focus on the deliverables. Tailoring is concerned with how much of each deliverable should you produce, what form should the deliverable take, who should produce them, how many review stages should each one go through.

Look at the process model to identify the generic deliverables produced by the process. Rather than getting lost in a sea of detail, get started by looking at the interfaces between the processes on Diagram 0 of the process model. For instance between the processes called Project Blastoff and Trawl for Knowledge there is an interface representing a deliverable called Work Context. When you tailor the process your aim is to decide how this (and all other deliverables) will be produced by your project. In some cases the deliverable will be produced by a number of people, possibly in a number of locations: in that case your process must define who will do what and how you will keep track of the pieces and eventually fit them together.

Your aim is to discover where and how you would most benefit from changes to your way of specifying requirements. If you have a current process for producing requirements specifications, then it will help you get your thoughts in order if you draw a rough Diagram 0 model of your current process. Review this diagram and mark any areas where you know you would like to make improvements.

To start with, concentrate on the deliverables on Diagram 0 of the generic process model; these deliverables are at a summary level and they will provide you with a way of talking about the big picture. When you are considering the overall requirements process you will identify parts of the process where you think it will benefit you to explore the deliverables described in the detailed lower levels of the model.

For each deliverable consider how each one would best be produced within your project environment using your resources. Ask:

- What is the deliverable called within your environment? Refer to the definitions of the terms used in the generic process model and identify the form of the equivalent deliverable in your organization.

- Does your current name for the deliverable help your communication or would changing it help you to remove misunderstandings? For example, we have found that a lot of projects have a catch-all description like project scope that means some combination of Work Context and Product Scope depending on who you are talking to. This loose terminology results in an enormous amount of wasted time.

- What is the deliverable used for within your environment? If the deliverable does not have an agreed purpose within your project then omit it from your process.

- Who produces the deliverable? Specify which parts of the deliverable are produced by whom. Also, when several people are involved you need to define the interfaces between their work.

If you have a current process for producing requirements specifications, then it will help you get your thoughts in order if you draw a rough Diagram 0 model of your current process. Review this diagram and mark any areas where you know you would like to make improvements

- When is the deliverable produced? Map your project phases to the generic process.

- Where is the deliverable produced? A generic deliverable is often the result of fragments that are produced in a number of geographical locations. Define the interfaces between the different locations and specify how they will work.

- Who needs to review the deliverable? Look for existing cultural checkpoints within your organization. Do you have recognized stages or phases in your projects when peers, users or managers review your specification?

- Now turn your attention to the generic processes that produce the deliverables and consider how they fit into your project. You might already have done a great deal of this thinking by examining the deliverables, this is simply a double check.

- Reflect the answers to the above questions by doing a rough sketch of a Diagram 0 process model and relevant lower levels for your project. Use this sketch to help you plan who will do what and how they will communicate with each other.

- If you discover that some deliverables are already effectively produced by your current process then you should retain those parts of your process and use the generic process to improve/replace the parts where you discover problems.

- You should also question any procedures that currently exist. Is there a good business reason for each activity that touches this deliverable?

An important issue when designing a process to fit your project is to consider your needs for the publication of the requirements specification. Some of this might occur to you when you are reviewing all the activities in your process. However, we find it is a good way to discover misunderstandings if we ask – when and why will we publish the requirements specification?

Publishing the Specification

PUTTING THIS TO WORK

When should you publish the specification? What should it contain? What form should it take? The requirements specification template provides a container for organizing this requirements knowledge and also provides one form for the arrangement of a published specification. However, there are many other ways to arrange the requirements knowledge and it will save enormous amounts of time if you choose the one that best suits the situation.

Harking back to our previous discussion, a well-designed requirements management tool makes it easier for you to publish the specification in different forms. But no matter what combination of tools you are using to maintain your specification the important thing is that you understand the benefit for each class of requirements knowledge and each association that you maintain. If you maintain these associations then you can publish the specification in whatever form is suitable for your purpose. Here are some typically useful publication versions for specific situations. We have annotated each part with the relevant sections of the requirements template.

Contractual Document

You have to publish a specification for a third party who will be responsible for building the product. This specification is the basis for your agreement with the third party.

- Product Constraints (sections 1–4).
- Definition of terms used in the specification (section 5).
- Relevant Facts (section 6).
- Assumptions (section 7).
- List of business events and work context diagram (section 8).
- Product boundary diagram (section 8).
- Class diagram or data model (section 8) conforming to the terms specified in section 5.
- Product use case list including fit criteria for each use case (section 8).
- Individual functional and non-functional requirements clustered by product use case (parts of sections 9–17).
- Estimate of size in function points.

See Chapter 13, Taking Stock of the Specification, for details of how to do a function point estimate of a requirements specification

Management Summary

Sometimes you need to publish a version of the specification that provides a management checkpoint. The amount of detail you include depends on the reason for the management checkpoint, but here is a list of the contents that are typically in such a document.

- Product Constraints (sections 1–4).
- Relevant Facts (section 6).
- Assumptions (section 7).
- Definition of terms used in the specification (section 5).
- Work context diagram (section 8).
- Business event list (section 8).
- Product boundary diagram (section 8).

- Product use case list including fit criteria for each use case (section 8).
- Estimate of size – a count of what you know, at this stage, about each of the classes of requirements. For instance, number of business events, number of use cases, number of functional requirements, number of non-functional requirements, number of terms. Depending on how far you have progressed you might be able to include the estimated number of function points (section 24).
- Percentage completed of each of the main classes of knowledge in the specification.

Marketing Summary

When your marketing department is working in parallel to make publicity plans then you need to publish a version of the specification that focusses on what the product will do for the customer.

- Product Constraints (sections 1–4).
- Definition of terms used in the specification (section 5).
- Work context diagram (section 8).
- Business event list (section 8).
- Product boundary diagram (section 8).
- Product use case list including fit criteria for each use case (section 8).
- If marketing is concentrating on a particular group of use cases, then include the detailed functional and non-functional requirements for those (parts of sections 9–17).

User Review

When you publish the specification for a user or group of users you want to focus on those parts of the specification that affect the work of those users. The most common purpose for publishing a version of the specification for the users is to verify that the specified product is the one that they are expecting. Another reason for publishing this version of a specification is to provide technical writers with the basis for the user manual.

- Work context diagram (section 8).
- Definition of terms used in the specification (section 5).
- Product boundary diagram (section 8).
- Product use case list including fit criteria for each use case (section 8).
- Individual functional and non-functional requirements clustered by product use case. Limit this to the use cases that are directly concerned with these users' work (parts of sections 9–17).

Taking Stock of the Specification

All sections of the specification. If you are reviewing individual use cases then arrange the requirements into use case related groups. If you are reviewing one particular type of requirement then arrange the requirements by type.

Requirements Traceability

A requirement is traceable if you can identify any part of the product that exists because of the requirement, and for any part of the product, you can identify the requirement that caused it. Requirements need to be traceable so that you can maintain consistency between the product and the world that is using the product.

If we want to change some aspect of the product we need to be able to identify which requirements are affected by the change. We need to be able to trace the effect of the change not just within the product but within the business affected by the product. Similarly, if there are new or changed requirements in the business we need to be able to trace which other business requirements and which parts of the implemented product are affected. So no matter what part of the world changes, we need to be able to trace the requirements both backwards and forwards.

During requirements specification we give each requirement a unique identifier, use consistent terminology to specify the requirement and identify which business events and which product use cases are associated with that requirement. So far, so good. When we design a solution to meet the requirements we need to keep track of which parts of each requirement are met by each piece of technology. The problem is that, when implemented, the requirements are translated into a different form – whatever form is appropriate for the technology – and are often fragmented because they are implemented using more than one piece of technology.

Let's use an example from the IceBreaker system to help us consider what we need to do to trace requirements.

Tracing a Business Event

We have talked about dealing with largeness and complexity by partitioning the context of the work into business events. Every time we make some kind of partitioning there is a need to consider traceability. In this case the traceability needed is to be able to connect the business event to the work context.

One of the business events in the IceBreaker system is:

> Business Event 10: Truck depot reports problem with truck
> Truck Breakdown (input flow from Truck Depot)
> Amended De-icing Schedule (output flow from Truck Depot)

The truck depot tells the engineers that one of the trucks has broken down. The engineers now need to reschedule the work of the broken-down truck. The engineers review the schedules of the trucks, find an available truck, reschedule the de-icing work and inform the truck depot

During the requirements process we study the work related to this event – the event response – so that we can determine how much of the work should be done by the product, and how much by the user. We looked at this back in Chapter 4 when we discussed event-driven use cases and how to determine the best product scope. The part of the event response that is done by the product is referred to as a product use case.

When we determined how much of the work should be done by the Ice-Breaker product, we came up with a product use case called:

Traceability need: to trace the use case(s) to the business event response(s) and vice versa. One way of doing this is by assigning a unique number to each business event and to each product use case and creating a connection between them.

> Use Case 10: Amend De-Icing Schedule whose user is the Truck Depot Engineer.

Here we have another traceability need because we have fragmented the event response by partitioning it into work that will be done by the product and work that will be done by the business. We need to be able to trace the use case to the business event response and vice versa. One way of doing this is by assigning a unique number to each business event and to each product use case and creating a connection between them. Bear in mind that we might have more than one use case related to a business event response. Also, the same use case might be related to more than one event response.

Traceability need: to trace all the use cases that are affected by a requirement and vice versa. One way of doing this is by giving each requirement an identification number and connecting it to the relevant use cases.

The detailed requirements specification for the product will contain detailed specifications (functional and non-functional) for all the requirements related to the use case like:

> Requirement number 81. The product shall record when a truck has gone out of service.

This requirement might turn out to be related to more than one use case which leads us to another traceability need. We must be able to trace all the use cases that are affected by a requirement. One way of doing this is by giving each requirement an identification number and connecting it to the relevant use cases.

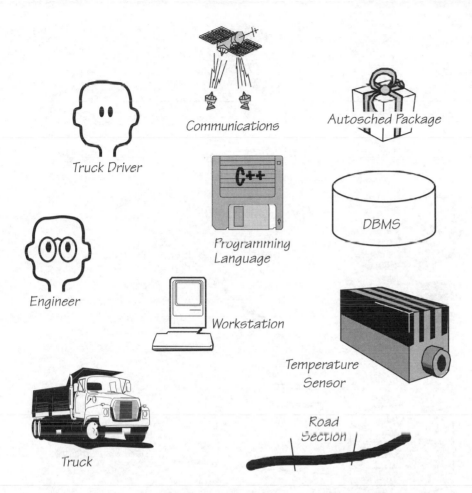

Figure 14.2

When we look at the technology that is available to us, including that which we can buy, we find these items are useful for implementing the business event.

When we do the detailed design we decide precisely which implementation technology will be used for each requirement. There might be several different types of technology used to implement the use cases within the product. There might also be several types of technology used to implement the parts of the event response that are outside the boundaries of the product.

Figure 14.2 identifies the technological raw material that we will use to implement the response to business event number 10 – Truck depot reports problem with truck. Some of this solution technology like the Temperature Sensor, Truck Driver, Engineer, Road Section and Truck might have been specified as a Requirements Constraint in section 4 of the specification – in other words whatever the solution, it must use this technology. Other parts of the technology like Autosched package, Workstation, C++, DBMS and Satellite technology have been selected by the designer taking into account the constraints such as budget.

When the designer decides which parts of the event response will be carried out by which pieces of technology, he is allocating all parts of the event

Figure 14.3

The event response for Truck depot reports problem with truck, is shown allocated to a variety of technology.

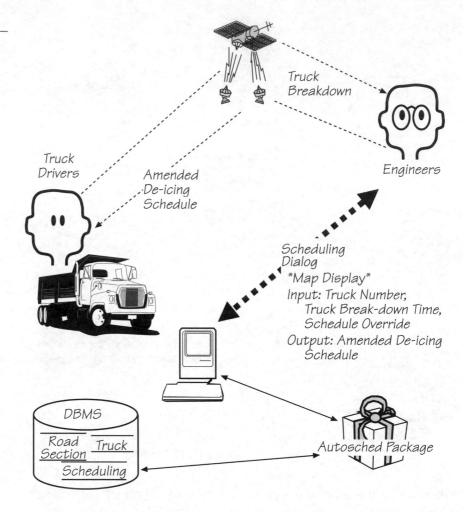

response to achieve the best fit implementation. The complete design defines how all the parts of the business event response will be implemented.

We see that the requirements for the response to the event – Truck depot reports problem with truck – are allocated to a variety of technologies (Figure 14.3). When a truck breaks down, the truck drivers communicate this to the engineers using the radio transmitter in their trucks. Then, to activate the product use case, the engineer uses a scheduling dialog on the PC to reschedule the work of the broken-down truck. We see that the requirements within the product use case are implemented using a mixture of C++ programs written for the PC, the Autosched package and the database management system. The engineer communicates the amended de-icing schedule to the appropriate truck using radio.

We need to keep track of which requirements – or parts of requirements – are implemented by which pieces of technology. We need this traceability so that we can ensure that the requirements specified are the ones that have been implemented.

Dealing with Change

When we put a product into the world and people start to use it to do work, experience shows us that there will be changes to the requirements. And these changes will continue throughout the life of the product.

Figure 14.4 illustrates the inevitability of change. You can build a product according to the defined requirements and make it available for use. As soon as people start to use a product it is likely that they will think of something that they would like to change that would make it easier for them to do their work.

The world changes – new technologies appear, new business opportunities open, new ways are found of doing things that we didn't do before. In fact, it is usually some change that kicks off a product development effort. Something has changed so much that the old product, whatever it was, cannot cope. And so a new product is built. Thereafter, the new product is changed and changed until it too becomes old, and then some large change causes the old product to be replaced by a yet newer one.

The product changes because our demands on it change. Consider the house in Figure 14.4. A house evolves over time. Do you live in exactly the same house that you first moved into? Houses change over time, because our needs change. We have babies, grannies, we can simply afford more, we want a new carpet, and so on. All these things are changes to requirements, and all cause changes to the product.

Like all things, there are good and bad changes. Good changes come when the product has been in use for a long time, and the user wants to extend its capabilities to accommodate some new requirements. *These requirements could not possibly have been foreseen by the original requirements analysts.* This is good because the life of the product is being extended, and the product itself is proving to be fundamentally sound. Bad change comes when the user asks for changes that either should have been foreseen, or the original scope of the requirements gathering was not nearly large enough.

By starting with a large enough scope – and we hasten to repeat our warnings about the scope being much more than the anticipated automated product – the product is far more likely to be suitable over the long term. It is more likely to be a closer match to the user's work, and it is more likely to fit seamlessly into the work environment.

Traceability need: to keep track of which requirements – or parts of requirements – are implemented by which pieces of technology. One way of doing this is to maintain up-to-date allocated business event-response models that are, as previously stated, cross-referenced to individual requirements and product use cases.

Figure 14.4

When a product is used it is likely to generate changes. Throughout the lifetime of the product the world will change which will in turn cause other changes to the product.

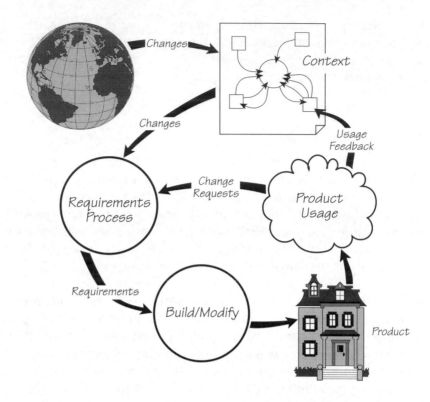

Changes in the World

However, there are many other changes that we cannot anticipate. These are new happenings in the world, things that we could not have anticipated when specifying the requirements for our product. For example, in our democracies governments change from time to time (no doubt we are all thankful for this) and the incoming administration brings new policies and new regulations. Some of these affect our products, and the way that we do work.

The world contains so many sources of requirements: people, technology, processes, politics, and so on. A requirements specification is based on a view of part of the world at a particular time. However, we know that the world is in a constant state of evolution. Interaction between all the requirements sources in the world is dynamic, continuous and unpredictable, and as the world changes so do the requirements.

The best products are the ones that are able to change as the world around them changes and the users become more sophisticated. Look at successful software products like Microsoft Word and Excel, Adobe Photoshop, UNIX, and so on. These products have increased their functionality many times over since their beginnings. The ability to change means that firstly we need some kind of feedback loop in our requirements process to enable us to recognize useful changes and secondly we need some way of controlling how, when and whether we implement them.

Requirements Feedback

Look at your requirements process and make sure that you are recognizing change by building in feedback loops. In other words, do you have mechanisms for users to give you their new thoughts regardless of the stage you have reached in the development of the product? We have seen some organizations where people are made to feel guilty if they change their minds about anything – especially if it has been written down. We are not advocating random and uncontrolled change, instead we are encouraging people to tell the truth so that you can make rational decisions about how to react to the change. If you do not allow for feedback, then your systems become obsolete – fast. Encourage feedback by asking people to review requirements and ask 'What could possibly happen to change this requirement and is there anything I can do to make that change less painful?'

Your mechanisms for encouraging requirements feedback must continue throughout the life of the product. The requirements change over time. We know this. So why not do what we do to all other products? Maintain them. Have a maintenance agreement with the product users (Figure 14.5). Visit the users for regular maintenance checks. Use trawling techniques like observation, interviewing and apprenticing with the user on a regular and ongoing basis. The same methods that got you the requirements in the first place can help you to find the new requirements and keep the product healthy.

Good feedback mechanisms help to recognize change but then we have to decide what to do about it. We need some kind of change control procedure so that we can define each change and monitor its status. In his survey on factors that contribute to successful requirements specification, Capers Jones reports that one of the major factors is use of requirements change control. As we mentioned in the discussion on traceability, without change control the real product and the product that we are managing are different things and the project gets out of control.

Requirements Post Mortem

When you finish your requirements specification you are usually under pressure to get on with the rest of the project. But before you leave your requirements process stop and give yourself a chance to learn from what you have

---

READING
The subject of how to recognize, model and examine feedback in systems is discussed in PETER SENGE'S *The Fifth Discipline*. Doubleday, 1990.

Factors that contribute to successful requirements specification:
- ● *Formal requirements gathering process*
- ● *Use of requirements change control*
- ● *Augmentation of written requirements with prototypes*
- ● *Use of requirements quality control*
- ● *Use of function points based on requirements*
- ● *Use of reusable requirements*

Source: *Jones, Capers.* **Survey on Requirements.** *Software Productivity Research, 1997.*

Figure 14.5

A requirements maintenance agreement involves regular maintenance checks with the product's users. Use trawling techniques to discover new and changing requirements as early as possible.

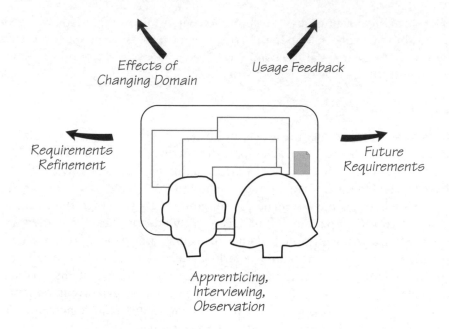

done. A post mortem is a tool for gathering the wealth of experience that will otherwise be lost – an expensive loss when a day or two's effort will retain it for all time. The result of the post mortem is a written summary of what you learned from your project and how you think other people might gain from your experience.

What to Look For

PUTTING THIS TO WORK

Focus on reviewing the effectiveness of the way that you gathered and specified your requirements. Look at each part of the process that you followed and identify the parts that worked well and the parts that did not.

Find the major mistakes, but don't allocate blame. The post mortem cannot be used as a witch hunt. If project members suspect that management will punish them for mistakes, then they will naturally cover up the mistakes. You can only really be effective in an organization that is free from fear.

Find the major successes, but don't reward. Don't reward as this will lead to people highlighting anything they did in the hope of being rewarded rather than looking at the project dispassionately. The post mortem process has to be kept completely separate from the personnel reward system.

The main question to ask in the post mortem is 'If you had to do it again, how would you do it and why?'

Post mortems work best in organizations that are free from fear

Running the Post Mortem

The way you run the post mortem depends on how many people are involved. Your aim is to get input from all the people who were involved in producing the requirements specification; there are a number of ways to do this. We illustrate a post mortem process in Figure 14.6.

The best advice that we can give is to tell you to appoint a facilitator. A facilitator is someone who has no vested interest in the project, and no self-interest in the outcome of the post mortem. His task is to gather the project experience.

The facilitator encourages each project member (manager, technical staff, client) to tell their own personal observations about the requirements. This

The Volere Process model in Appendix A contains a detailed procedure for running post mortems and writing reports. Refer to Do Requirements Post Mortem, Process 6

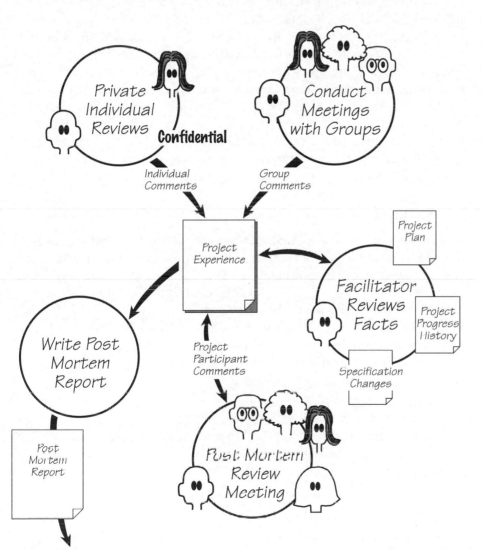

Figure 14.6

Your post mortem should have input from all the people who were involved in producing the specification.

gathering of individual comments is usually done by interviews, but can be done anonymously. Responses by individual project members are not publicized to encourage people to speak more freely.

Separate meetings are arranged by the post mortem facilitator, with homogenous groups of people involved in requirements – project management, project technical staff, and stakeholders. Each group considers the specification process from their own perspective and gives the facilitator additional issues to add to the list. The facilitator brings up points from private contact for clarification and concurrence. Each group is offered the chance to add or change the issues.

Now the facilitator, armed with some insights into the project and its participants, looks at the actual facts. For example, the facilitator might review the project plans and how the actual deliverables tracked to it, or count the changes to the specification after initial acceptance. The purpose of this research is to quantify the issues raised by the project members and to get more insights into why things happened the way they did.

The facilitator can hold a full project post mortem meeting for all personnel involved in earlier stages of the post mortem. At this time managers, technical staff, and clients come together to hear the findings described by the facilitator. All findings are presented, and each is up for discussion at this meeting.

Post Mortem Report

If no follow-on research is required from the full post mortem meeting, a final write-up of the post mortem report is written by the facilitator, often with the assistance of project members. The report is available for everyone in the organization to review, and includes contact names for further discussion on any issues. This report includes recommended procedures and tools, description of problems found and possible solutions to take, and any project disappointments or failures. The purpose of the report is to pass on experience, by making it as concise as possible. It also helps if it has an interesting table of contents, something like:

Requirements Post Mortem Report
Our requirements specification had successes and failures. This report shares our experiences so that you can profit from the successes and avoid the mistakes that caused the failures.

Contents

1 The most important things that we learnt

2 The history of the requirements (abridged, use diagrams to help)

3 The objectives – did we meet them?

4   The process we used – did it work?

5   Communication – within the team

6   Communication – with the world

7   Did we miss any stakeholders?

8   The tools we used and what we learnt

9   How we tested the requirements

10   Management – how did we do it?

11   Project Reviews – what we learnt

12   Design issues

13   Our greatest successes

14   Sources of embarrassment

16   Actions to take

READING

COLLIER, BONNIE, TOM DEMARCO AND PETER FEAREY. A Defined Process for Project Post Mortem Review. *IEEE Software*, 1996.

Your Notebook

Many years ago your authors developed the habit of having a personal note-book and using it to record observations, ideas, meeting notes, plans … anything that we feel like writing about or drawing a picture about. We use our notebooks for both personal and work-related subjects arranged in sequential order of writing. We have found that the habitual use of a personal note-book has some interesting effects.

You tend to write things down more often. It is purely for your own use so you are not inhibited by thinking – I haven't got time to write this really well. As long as you can read it that is all that matters.

The benefit of this is the amazing number of good ideas that you come across when you review your notebook – ideas that you do not remember thinking about are there for you to use. Your notebook becomes a tool for helping you to learn and to become more observant about the world. In other words, it becomes your own personal post mortem report.

The End

This brings us to the end of our book. We have taken you through a process for gathering requirements. But we hope that is not all we have done. Along the way we have tried to show you the little things about requirements – the small quality issues that make such a large difference to your work. Seemingly little things like searching for a measurement for 'an attractive product', or using apprenticing to understand what the guy on the factory floor is trying to achieve, or sketching a low fidelity prototype all make a difference. A difference that makes your work with requirements all the more enjoyable.

The authors are continuing their research on improving requirements. For more information on current projects, seminars and consulting services, please refer to our website www.atlsysguild.com

Please use this book as we intended. Not as a set of canonical rules that must be obeyed, but as a reliable companion to intelligent work. And as you work, take the time to observe (or better still measure) the difference that good requirements make to your development efforts and your products. It is a difference that is worth pursuing.

Appendix A

The Volere Requirements Process Model

a process for gathering and
testing requirements

This requirements process model is organized as a hierarchy of processes. To find more about the details of a process, look for the diagram or process notes with the same number. For example, in the Volere Process Model Summary (next page) there is a process (number 1) called Project Blastoff. Diagram 1 will show you more details about this process. On page 342 there is a dictionary that specifies the terms used in the model.

This is a model of the *generic processes* necessary to elicit, specify and review requirements. The model focusses on *content*. The *dependencies* between the processes are defined by the *interfaces*. This model does not imply any sequence; it is an *asynchronous* network. Any combination of processes can be active at any time.

The model is intended to provide you with a requirements process that you can tailor to your own environment. When you tailor the model you synchronize it to your own environment by repartitioning it to add checkpoints (reviews, milestones) that are suitable for your environment and identifying who will be responsible for carrying out each process. You also package the interfaces in the form that suits the way that you work.

An automated form of the model exists in the Process Continuum environment, which is available from Platinum Technologies at www.platinum.com.

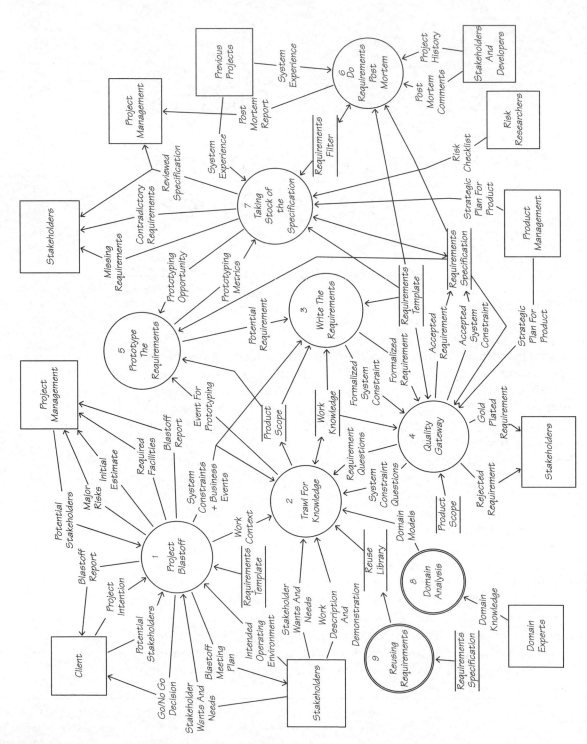

Diagram 0 Volere Process Model Summary

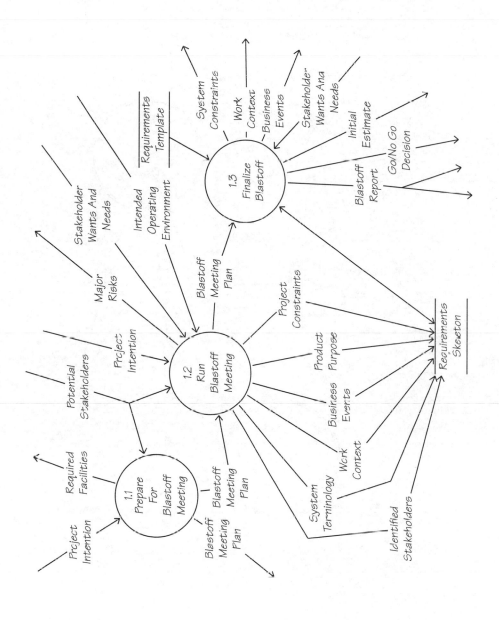

Diagram 1   Project Blastoff ● 279

Diagram 1   Project Blastoff

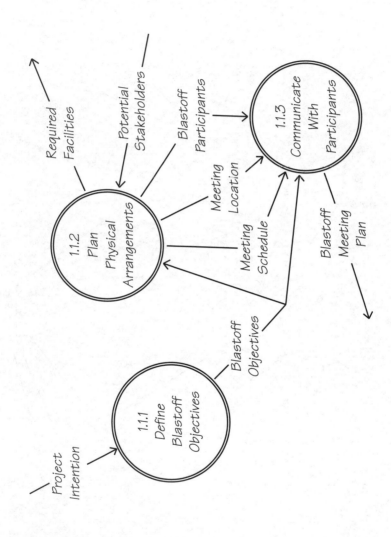

Diagram 1.1 Prepare For Blastoff Meeting

Define Blastoff Objectives (Process Notes 1.1.1)

Define the deliverables to be produced by the blastoff. Examine the Project Intention and decide whether the blastoff is to produce:

- System Objectives: this will always be produced.
- Work Context Model: there may be an existing model that will provide a starting point for this project, otherwise the blastoff must produce a new context model.
- Identified Stakeholders: always.
- Anticipated Developers: examine the kind of product wanted by the customer. Use previous project experience to determine the skills needed for this product. The anticipated developers is a list of the people/skills who are most likely to work on this project.
- System Events: these, at some level, will always be delivered by the blastoff.
- Event/Use Case Models: these are produced in a blastoff to prove the feasibility of the project. When the project is large, and there are no dominant transactions, then there is little use in producing use case models during the blastoff. However, when the project has a few critical transactions, preliminary use case/event models will be very helpful to determine if the product can be built.
- System Terminology: a preliminary terminology must be produced by the blastoff, unless there is a well-established standard terminology in use by the organization. For example, some industries have national or international standards for their terminology.
- Scenario Models: these fall into the same situation as events/use cases.

Plan Physical Arrangements (Process Notes 1.1.2)

The job of this process is to define the physical arrangements necessary to produce the Blastoff Objectives.

Determine the participants from the Potential Stakeholders in accordance with what is needed for the type of project. Include everybody that could possibly have a stake in the product. It is better to include possible stakeholders than exclude them. If they find they do not have a real interest in the product, they will certainly find that they have better things to do and leave your stakeholder group.

Plan the facilities and accommodation carefully. Keep in mind that you will have a number of people at the meeting. If you wish to keep them there, then make sure that you have adequate facilities to make their time well spent.

Make sure you have defined:

- The location of the blastoff meeting
- How to get there
- Name and contact details of the facilitator
- Dates and times
- Time needed for the blastoff. The number of days/hours
- List of participants.

Communicate With Participants (Process Notes 1.1.3)

Ensure that all the participants know the place and duration of the blastoff meeting. Send each participant an agenda and ensure that they understand what is expected of them before they arrive. It is important that you impress on participants the value to the product of them participating in the blast-off, why they are doing it, and the value of the product to your organization. Send a list of participants with each invitation. Each participant must respond and commit to being there, and you must be certain that they will come equipped to do the task.

Determine Product Purpose (Process Notes 1.2.1)

This task is to ask "What do we want this system for?" but not to say how we will achieve it. The System Purpose is a clear, unambiguous, measurable statement of precisely what product your client wants to get at the end of the project.

This should be a short statement, one or two sentences at most, or a few bulleted points.

The real intention of this task is to ask "Is this project feasible?" If you cannot state the objective so that all the stakeholders agree with it, then the project cannot achieve anything worthwhile. Similarly, you must be able to state the purpose such that you will know when you have achieved it. If your words demonstrate the criteria to be used to measure the purpose, then they will be strong and clear.

Failure to make a suitable statement of the Product Purpose means that you should seriously consider abandoning or deferring the project until your stakeholders can agree.

Each purpose statement should contain the following:

- A short description of the purpose (try to describe it in one sentence).
- The rationale behind the purpose – ask why the client has the purpose, what is the client's business advantage and how will he measure success?

Diagram 1.2   Run Blastoff Meeting ● 283

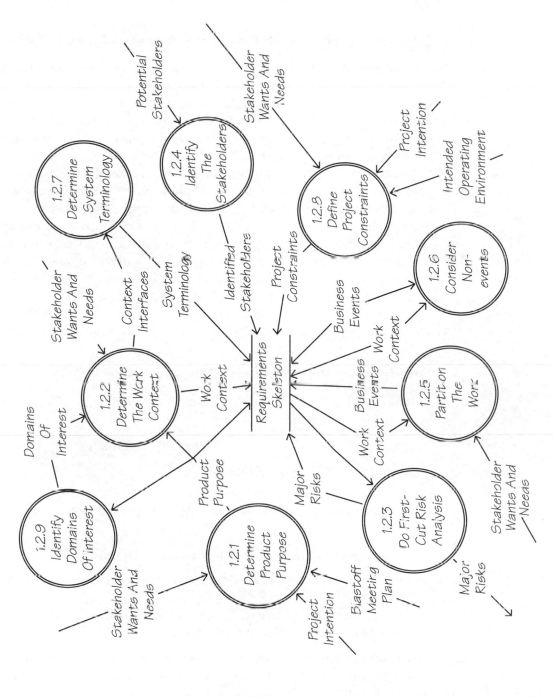

Diagram 1.2   Run Blastoff Meeting

● Fit criteria for the test(s) that you will apply to determine whether the purpose has been met.

Determine The Work Context (Process Notes 1.2.2)

The context is the starting point for requirements. The context diagram isolates the part of the world that you will study in order to satisfy the system objectives. The context diagram shows the interfaces between your project and other people, organizations and technology. It is the best place to reach the initial agreement on what part of the world is related to your project and what the system is expected to do.

The context is rarely as big as it should be – it should include all of the application domain. You must be careful not to have too small a context, or a context that represents only the intended computer system. Users often describe the system they want in terms of what they think is possible for a computer to do. Thus by accepting this description of a computer system as a context, you are missing other opportunities to automate or improve processes. Your context should include the business processes that are relevant to understanding the subject matter of your project. Some of the business processes carried out by your end-users (provided they help you to understand the application domain) will be within your detailed context of study.

Do First-Cut Risk Analysis (Process Notes 1.2.3)

An assessment of the major risks associated with building the desired product. It is necessary for the team to ask:

● "What are the main risks we face if we build this product?"
● "What will happen if that risk comes true?"

For example, suppose that the product is to be a new reservation system for a holiday tour operator. Major risks associated with this kind of system might be:

● "What happens if we are not ready for the holiday season?"
● "The system is to be used by travel agents. What if we build a system that takes too long to learn to use?"
● "The system must interface with airline systems. What happens if the airline systems change before our system is built?"

It is necessary to be brutally honest when stating risks. Some risks may seem like criticisms of people at the blastoff meeting; if necessary, make it possible to contribute risks anonymously.

Risks are the worst case scenarios that you can imagine. Suggested risks to examine are:

● Do we have an unrealistic schedule for delivering this product?

● What could happen if we don't have the product on time?

● Do we have unrealistic expectations for this product?

● Do we have the people skills we need to build this product?

● What new skills are needed?

● Have we built this kind of product before?

● What kind of things have gone wrong on other projects at our installation?

● What kind of things have gone wrong with this kind of system, at our installation or elsewhere?

● What have we done badly in the past?

● What external influences are there on the project? For example, are there proposed changes to laws affecting this product? Will the company be reorganized before the product is delivered?

● What new technology is needed for this product?

● Are we dependent on products being delivered by external forces?

● Are we making unrealistic assumptions about any other products that this project needs?

● Do we have the correct management structure for this project?

● Are we in danger of "gold plating" the product?

Remember that being honest about risks at this stage will considerably improve your chance of successfully building your product.

Identify The Stakeholders (Process Notes 1.2.4)

Identify all the people who have a vested interest in the product being built: these are the stakeholders. Stakeholders participate in the requirements gathering phase, as it is the stakeholders who determine the product they want built.

You are looking for people who will be affected by the product, or participate in its development. While the stakeholder list must not be so large as to include everyone in the building, neither must it exclude people who have a real interest in the product. To do so will result in later repercussions that may well scuttle your project.

Stakeholders must be individually named. Do not accept "someone from the accounting office".

A checklist of potential stakeholders is:

● Client – the person responsible for paying for the development

● Customer – the person(s) or group(s) who will buy the product

● User (potential at this stage) – the person(s) or group(s) who will use the product to do work

● Sponsor Name – the person responsible for arbitration and the well-being of the project

● Marketing Department

● Developer(s) – person(s) or group(s) responsible for developing the product

● Domain Expert(s) – sources of subject matter knowledge

● Technical Expert(s) – person(s) or group(s) who have expertise in the subjects relating to the product's non-functional requirements e.g. machines, legal, operational environment (see Volere Requirements Template for exhaustive list)

● Tester(s) – person(s) responsible for testing the quality of the requirements.

For each stakeholder identify:

● Stakeholder name

● Stakeholder specialization (e.g. accounting, pricing, manufacturing)

● Estimated amount of time the stakeholder will need to contribute to the project (it's difficult to know this at blastoff time because it depends on how much you know about the project. However it's worth considering whether you have an indication of the number of days/weeks and also the frequency of the involvement)

Partition The Work (Process Notes 1.2.5)

Partition the context into business events.

The term "events" is used here to mean the business events that have an effect on the work you are studying. These are the events that you will need to study in order to have enough knowledge to decide the best scope for the product.

Start by looking outside the system, and look for those happenings that result in a communication between an adjacent system and your work context. For example, when a customer places an order for some service from your system it is an event.

The system does not initiate the event, but has to respond to it. So when any signal arrives from outside your context, and your system must make some response, then this is an event.

Remember that these are business events, not the individual interface events that happen if the user clicks a button.

Consider Non-events (Process Notes 1.2.6)

Non-events are what happens if an event doesn't happen. For example, suppose that you have a fundamental event 'Customer pays for goods'. The non-event is what happens if the customer does not pay. Is there another event that happens, such as follow-up on bad payers?

Examine each business event and ask if there are one or more associated non-events. Add the new events to your list of business events.

Add the new data flows to your work context diagram.

Determine System Terminology (Process Notes 1.2.7)

Establish recognized names for the data items and other objects used by the developers and the users.

Begin with the context diagram. Write a description of the data flows around the context. The intention is to converge on common terms to be used for each of the data items used by the system.

The result of this task is a list of agreed terminology and definitions.

Define Project Constraints (Process Notes 1.2.8)

Define the mandated constraints on the way that the product must be produced.

Look for real constraints as distinct from opinions about how the problem should be solved:

● Solution constraints – technology that is mandated

● Deadlines – any known deadlines

● Financial Budget

● Current system constraints.

Each constraint should be testable. In other words, how will you know whether or not you have met the constraint?

For each project constraint ask "Why is it a constraint?" This will help you to distinguish between real project constraints and solutions posturing as constraints.

Refer to the Volere Requirements Template for more guidance in writing constraints.

Identify Domains Of Interest (Process Notes 1.2.9)

The product purpose is the basis for determining which subject matter domains we need to study.

For each product purpose statement we ask – "Does this objective mention or imply subject matter areas that we need to study in order to build this product?"

For example, suppose that one purpose is to provide rail transport for members of the general public. Then we can say that we need to study the domains of rail transport and the general public.

The next interesting question is how much of each of these domains is relevant to the product that we intend to build? We address that question when we set the context of the problem.

Write Blastoff Report (Process Notes 1.3.1)

Write a report describing what was accomplished by the blastoff meeting. The report should include:

- Work Context diagram with an explanation of the major decisions that determined the boundary of the work to be studied.

- Stakeholder list showing the stakeholders identified by the blastoff. Also include those people who were excluded as stakeholders, and say why.

- Developer list naming all people needed to work on this project.

- Preliminary event or use case list. Show those events/use cases identified so far. This list will not be complete, but serves as input to the first estimates of effort.

- System terminology as accepted at that point.

- Major risks. These are to be brought to management's attention.

- Initial estimate of effort needed to complete the project.

- Recommendation to proceed or not. In the case of the latter include reasons for not proceeding plus changes (if any) that would make it appropriate to proceed.

Remember that the Requirements Skeleton is the first step towards building a Requirements Specification. In other words, everything that you put in the Requirements Skeleton is used and built on by the processes involved in building the Requirements Specification.

Diagram 1.3   Finalize Blastoff ● 289

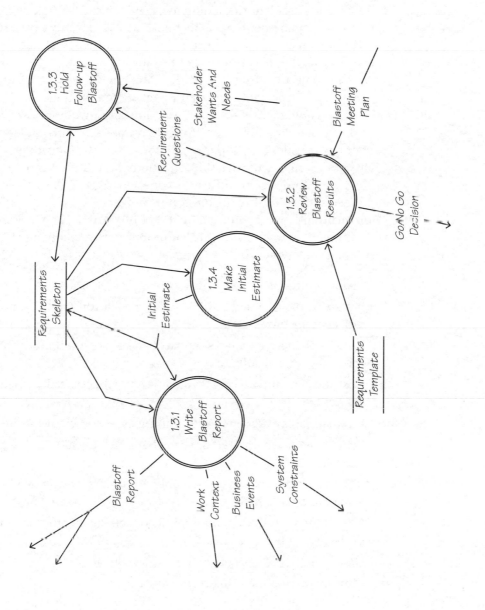

Diagram 1.3   Finalize Blastoff

Review Blastoff Results (Process Notes 1.3.2)

Look at the Requirements Skeleton and compare what has been collected with the requirements template. Determine if there is enough of a skeleton to reasonably complete the requirements specification. The template is a guide to the Requirements Specification that you have to write. The intention is not to have a complete specification at this stage, but to know if, given the time, the specification can be built.

Were the objectives from the Blastoff Meeting Plan met? In other words, are the blastoff deliverables enough to get started on the task of gathering the correct requirements? Are there any outstanding questions? Make a list of all the outstanding problems. If the deliverables are incomplete then the outstanding questions are input to a follow-up blastoff meeting.

This process makes the decision on whether the project is to go ahead.

The go/no go decision must be a conscious task. The question may be asked several times during the blastoff meeting.

Jim Highsmith and Lynne Nix in "Feasibility Analysis – Mission Impossible" *Software Development*, July 1996, produced the following checklist for identifying when you should NOT go ahead with a project:

1   Major political issues are unresolved by the blastoff.
2   Key stakeholders won't participate in the blastoff (and therefore probably the project).
3   Risks (probability of adverse consequences) are too high (technical, economic, organizational).
4   Cost and benefit ratio isn't favourable enough, especially when benefits are not measurable.
5   Internal staff's experience and training are insufficient for the project.
6   Requirements are unclear, or keep changing radically during the blastoff.
7   Risk and reward ratio is unfavorable. High risks usually need a high reward to be worthwhile.
8   Clients (in a multidisciplinary project) can't agree on exactly what the problems or objectives are.
9   No executive wants to be the project's sponsor.
10   Implementation planning seems superficial.

● There must be a measurable statement of the system objectives.
● The customers must be satisfied that the product is worthwhile.
● The developers must be satisfied that they are able to build the product.

- Both have to be satisfied with the estimates to build the product.
- The end-users have to be satisfied that the product will be beneficial to them.

If things do not look promising at this stage, it is far more economical to abandon the project now rather than in several years' time. Remember that the principal objective of the blastoff is to determine if the project is feasible.

Hold Follow-up Blastoff (Process Notes 1.3.3)

This is a mini blastoff meeting, run in the same way as the previous meeting, but run specifically to address the outstanding Requirements Questions. Unless these questions can be answered, the risk is too great to proceed with the project.

Keep in mind that you are trying to achieve the blastoff objectives, not to know everything about the system.

Make Initial Estimate (Process Notes 1.3.4)

Make your first estimate of the effort required to build the product.

The estimate at this stage does not have to be highly precise, but must be realistic. It can be based on such simple metrics as the number of events that the system has to respond to, or the number of use cases that will make up the system. The event/use case provides you with a manageable chunk that you can use as the basis for making an estimate. Estimate the average amount of effort for implementing one event and use this figure to estimate the effort for all the events within your context.

Depending on how much you know about the data, you may be able to make an initial function point count for the system. The type of count and the counting boundary (the context) have been defined, and an approximation of the data and transaction function types are also known. An estimate can also be made on simple metrics such as the complexity of the data. Roughly speaking, this is the number of data entities that the system will use. It is necessary to know the average cost of installing a data entity for this kind of estimate. While it is not the most accurate of possible estimates, it provides a starting point.

Keep in mind that previous history of effort required per function point (or whatever) will be tempered if this is the first time that you have used the proposed development technology. Allow generously for the learning curve.

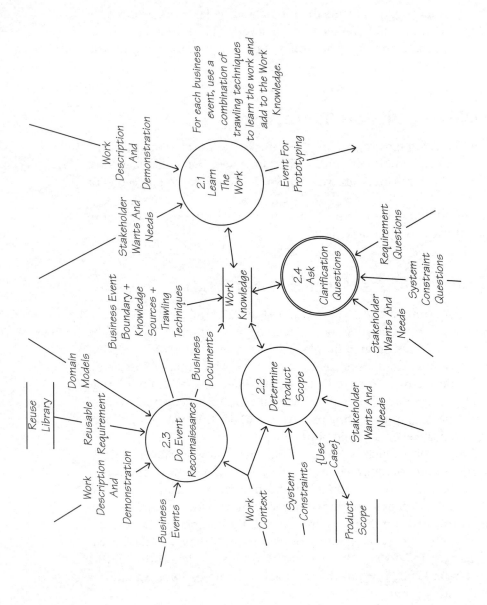

Diagram 2 Trawl For Knowledge

Diagram 2.1   Learn The Work ● 293

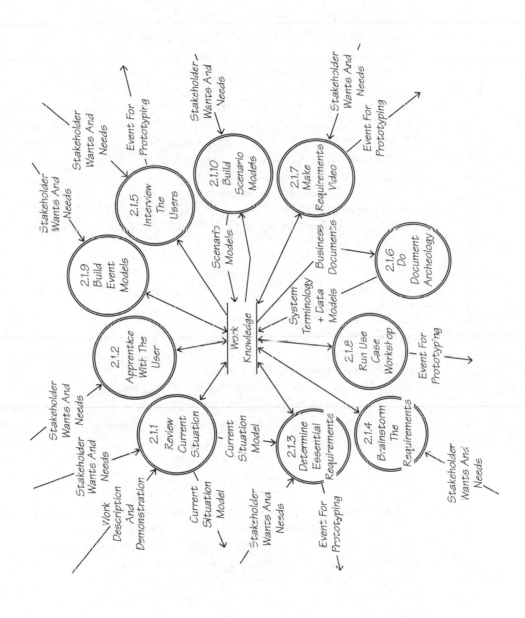

Diagram 2.1   Learn The Work

Review Current Situation (Process Notes 2.1.1)

When you review the current situation, keep in mind that you are not attempting to specify the system, but merely to establish the situation that the users currently face. It is highly likely that the users will describe their business in a way that includes the mechanisms they use to get the work done. These mechanisms are not requirements for the new system: you must look beyond them to see the underlying policy of the users' system.

Despite any bad reputation the current system may have, it is not totally worthless. It may have many functions that are making a positive contribution to the business. This means of course that there are some parts of the current system that must be included in any future system. You may implement them differently with new technology, but their underlying business policy will remain almost unchanged.

Thus the review of the current system is to ensure that you understand the situation before introducing any improvements.

The current situation model can be used as the input to business process reengineering.

Apprentice With The User (Process Notes 2.1.2)

This is based on the idea of masters and apprentices. The analyst becomes apprenticed to the user, and sits with the user to learn the job by observation and asking questions. It is unlikely that many users can explain what they do in enough detail for the analyst to capture all the requirements. Users cannot be expected to have the required presentation and teaching skills to present their work to others effectively. However, people are very good at explaining what they are doing while they are doing it. If the user is doing his job in his normal workplace, he can provide a running commentary and provide details that may otherwise be lost. It is probably only while working that the user is able to describe his task precisely, tell you why he is doing things, and what exceptions can occur.

Apprenticeship removes the need to talk in generalizations. If we are away from our work, we tend to describe it in abstract terms, and describe generalized cases. The abstraction is useful in one sense, but it does not hold enough detail for it to work every time. (You can see this effect when a user shows you his work-around for special cases.) By sitting alongside the user, the apprentice receives a running commentary and gets to see all the cases, and the actions the user takes for each.

Finally, the apprentice learns the task, and demonstrates this by actually doing the job under the user's eyes.

Use this approach:

- When the user is not good at abstraction
- When the user does not have time to talk to you.

Determine Essential Requirements (Process Notes 2.1.3)

The objective is to find the underlying essence of the system, and not accidentally reintroduce an existing technology or a requirement that exists because of an existing technology.

The developer is also looking for the skills that people use, and how they see themselves when they do the work. What conceptualizations and metaphors do they use?

Abstract by seeing the application without its technology. For example, a bank in London had 20 different products. Each product was (on the surface) a different way of guaranteeing that exporters got paid for their goods in foreign countries. The products ranged over letters of credit, guaranteed foreign bank loans, guaranteed funds, and so on. The way the users handled each of these products looked at first to be different. However, a common essence emerged as the developers studied the real work and looked past the current technology. The end result was that we were able to make a single core implementation, and then dress it differently for each of the products. In some cases, this different window dressing was little more than changing a few titles on screens.

Brainstorm The Requirements (Process Notes 2.1.4)

Brainstorming is a method for generating ideas. The intention here is to produce as many requirements for the new product as possible. Do not be concerned whether or not the ideas from the brainstorm session are all usable. The intention is firstly to create as many ideas as possible. Subsequently, you will eliminate any that are too expensive, impractical, impossible, and so on.

There are some simple rules for brainstorming:

- Participants in the brainstorming process should come from as wide a range of disciplines with as broad a range of experience as possible. This brings many more creative ideas to the session.
- Suspend, at least defer, judgment, evaluation and criticism. Simply record requirements as they are generated. The practice of not judging, evaluating or criticizing is the fastest way to develop a creative and energized atmosphere for the brainstorm group.

- Produce LOTS of ideas. Come up with as many ideas as possible. Quantity will in time produce quality.

- Try to come up with as many ideas as you can that are unconventional, unique, crazy, wild. The wilder the idea, the more creative it probably is, and the more likely to turn into a really useful requirement.

- Piggyback a new idea on an old one. That is, build one idea on top of another.

- Write every idea down, without censoring. "Ideas disappear faster than water evaporates unless written down." (Alex Osborne, the founder of brainstorming)

- If you get stuck, 'seed' the session with a word pulled randomly from a dictionary. This word acts as a starting point in the process of generating ideas.

After the brainstorming session, the results can be evaluated, and the best requirements can be explored by more conventional methods.

Interview The Users (Process Notes 2.1.5)

Interviewing the users is the traditional approach to requirements gathering. However, used on its own it may not be the most effective. We strongly suggest that interviews are not the sole method of gathering, but that interviews are used in conjunction with other techniques when they will be more effective.

The requirements engineer can draw up questionnaires in advance. While this gives some structure to the following interview, we have found that users have to be highly motivated to actually fill them in prior to meeting the engineer. We suggest that you send the user, or whoever you are interviewing, an agenda of the topics that you wish to cover. This at least gives the user a chance to have material to hand, or ask subject matter experts to be present.

The user should not be completely passive during the interview. We strongly urge you to build models – event response, use case, scenario, and so on – while you are talking with the user during the interview. This gives you and your user immediate feedback, and allows you to test the accuracy of what you are being told. We prefer that the user participate in your modeling efforts. You must make allowances for their notational idiosyncrasies: you can correct them later.

You can also interview the user while watching the work being done. This has the advantage of you being able to direct your questions to the task at hand, and gives the user a better chance to describe the task. People are not good at describing their jobs, but are usually good at telling you what they are doing while they are doing it.

When people describe things to you, especially such conceptual and difficult things such as requirements, they usually have difficulty in being precise. They will also describe things in abstract terms, and have difficulty defining precisely what they mean. You can use laddering to help get over this problem. The idea of laddering is that you can conceptually go up or down from what they are saying, depending on what you need to know. Going down the ladder means that you decompose what you are told to find the layer of fact below the statement, and then decompose again to find the next lowest layer. You might also need to ladder up. That is, move the conversation to a higher level of abstraction.

For example, you may be asked for a system that responds quickly to customers' needs. To go down the ladder means that you have to ask for a meaning, or measurement for "quickly". "While the customer is on the telephone" is a measurement, and the next lowest level will give you "You have to find the customer's record in one second." By going down the ladder of abstraction, you arrive at a deterministic answer.

Going up the ladder is also useful. It leads to outcomes and criteria, for example, "The system has to respond quickly so customers do not become impatient."

Think about the level of the interview, and always try other levels. They are often very revealing.

Do Document Archeology (Process Notes 2.1.6)

Document archeology is determining the underlying processes that are requirements from inspecting the documents and files that the organization uses. It should not be used on its own as a requirements gathering technique, but as the prelude to more intensive interviews and as the basis of modeling efforts.

Document archeology starts with you collecting samples of all documents, reports, forms, files, in fact anything that is used to record or send information. Regular telephone calls should not be excluded.

Inspect the document (for simplicity's sake, the term "document" will mean all of the above) looking for nouns, or "things". These can be column headings, named boxes on forms, or simply the name of a piece of data on the document.

For each noun, ask:

● What is the purpose of this thing?
● Who uses it, why and what for?

- What are all the uses the system makes of this thing?
- If I have thing A, must I also have thing B, and must I not have thing C?
- Can this thing have a value? For example, is it a number or a code or quantity?
- If so, to what collection of things does it belong? (Data modeling enthusiasts will immediately recognize the need to find the entity that owns the attribute.)
- What is that thing used for?
- Does the document contain a repeating group of things?
- If so, what is the collection of things called?
- Can I find a link between things?
- What process makes the connection between them?
- What are the rules attached to each thing? In other words, what piece of business policy covers the thing?
- What processes ensure that these rules are obeyed?
- Which documents give the users the most problems?

These questions will not in themselves reveal all the requirements for the system. They will, however, give you plenty of material and direction for further investigation. We also suggest that you use document archeology as part of your data modeling approach. The questions raised by data modeling are always very revealing.

Make Requirements Video (Process Notes 2.1.7)

Video can be used to co-develop software. The users and developers participate in workshops and brainstorms, and the proceedings are videotaped. Interviews and on-site observations are also taped. The tapes are used firstly to record, and then confirm, the proceedings. Additionally videotapes can be shown to developers who do not get the opportunity to meet face to face with the users.

Video can be used as an adjunct to interviewing and observing the users in their own workplace. Users have their own way of accomplishing tasks. They have their ways to categorize the information that they use, and ways to solve problems that they have found worked well for them in their own situation. Thus by using video to capture the users at work, you are capturing their ways of doing their jobs and their concerns, and not imposing your own expectations and preferences.

Video can also be used in a more structured way, one use case or event at a time. Select the use case and ask the users to work through typical scenarios that they encounter with that activity. As they work, the users describe the special circumstances, the additional information they use, the exceptions, and so on. The shrugs, grimaces and gestures that are normally lost when taking notes are faithfully recorded for later playback and dissection.

Run Use Case Workshop (Process Notes 2.1.8)

The workshop is conducted between the appropriate customer/user and the requirements team. The first part of the workshop is to generate the scenarios. This needs input from the users/customers. The idea is to talk through a use case/event and to extract from the user the essential things that have to happen when this event takes place. You are trying to define a series of user-recognizable steps that complete the work of this event. You ask the user to verify/improve/change the steps that you have written down. The resulting use case scenario is a very rough sketch of the requirements for the use case.

After the use case workshop, the requirements engineers go back to their office and derive and specify the individual requirements from the knowledge in the use case scenarios.

Build Event Models (Process Notes 2.1.9)

You are looking at the functional part of the system. Break the whole system into its constituent business events. We will use the term event to signify this partitioning as a convenient way to look at each of the system's functions.

The objective of partitioning the system into events is to provide a way of breaking up the system in a consistent and communicable way. Event partitioning is nothing more than a special knife for carving a system into logical, minimally related, pieces. However, despite its simplicity, it gives you several advantages:

● The events are minimally connected, thus you can study isolated pieces without getting involved in all the details of the system.

● Events can be readily measured using function points, or other measuring methods. Thus it is easier to make estimates that are based on real measurements.

● Management can use event partitioning to monitor progress.

● The main benefit to the requirements process is that events allow you to separate the actions of the system, and deal with the system's functionality in a way that is familiar to your users.

Finding Events:

● The work context is the best place to identify events. All of the data flows that connect the system to the outside world are somehow part of an event. Start by looking for the adjacent systems that communicate with the work context. Each discrete business data flow connected to them is a potential event. Some of these will be simple data flows that have to be stored by the system. Others will be complex interactions with the adjacent system that persist until the piece of business has been completed.

● Some of the data that flows from the system does so as a result of a temporal event. Use this to identify more of the events. Ultimately, you must be able to account for all of the data flows that bound the system. The flows will either trigger an event, or they are the result of one. Some events have both input and output flows.

Once you have listed all the events, consider the functionality of each. It may be necessary to model some of the events in order to see the requirements more clearly, however, at this stage you should try not to get bogged down in detailed modeling. It is suggested that scenario models may be the tool that gives you enough of a description of each function to write its functional requirements.

Build Scenario Models (Process Notes 2.1.10)

Scenarios are specific stories built to illustrate the way that a user might operate an intended system. The scenario is built to illustrate the user's viewpoint of a specific event and is used to clarify the implications of a requirement.

Scenarios can be built using a variety of media. The simplest scenario might be straight text, but is more likely to be pictures or diagrams. In fact, you should use any format and medium that feels comfortable to the user.

Study The Adjacent Systems (Process Notes 2.2.1)

For each Business Event:

● If you have built an event-response model as part of the process of learning the work then use that model to help you study the adjacent system and the event processing

otherwise

● Depending on your knowledge of the event and the complexity of the event, it might help you to sketch an event-response model.

Look for Business Opportunities for how the product can help to achieve the Product Purpose within the Project Constraints

Diagram 2.2   Determine Product Scope ● 301

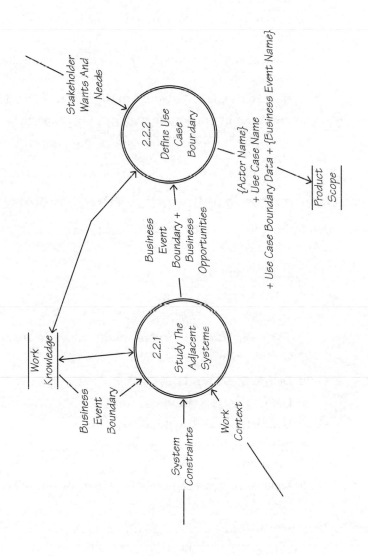

Diagram 2.2   Determine Product Scope

For each Input Dataflow and Output Dataflow between an adjacent system and a process consider the System Constraints and the Work Context and ask:

● What work does the adjacent system do in order to produce or use the interface?

● Are we studying enough of the adjacent system to be able to identify business opportunities?

● Is there any work done by the adjacent system that could be done by the product?

● Could all/some of the work done by the process be done by the product?

● Are there any opportunities for helping people to be better at their jobs?

● What are the aspirations, desires and concerns of the adjacent systems?

Define Use Case Boundary (Process Notes 2.2.2)

Determine the Use Case(s) for Business Events
   For each Business Event:

● Consider the Business Opportunities
● Review the Work Knowledge

      Decide the boundary between the Product and the Actor
      For each Use Case (there might be more than one per business event):

● Define the Actor Names
● Define the Use Case Name
● Define the Use Case Boundary Data
● Record the Product Context by adding the Use Case to a Use Case Diagram
● Make sure you keep track of which Business Event Name(s) is/are related to this use case.

   If there are more than 15–20 use cases then a Use Case Diagram will be too complex and you will need to draw a leveled Use Case Diagram

Gather Business Event Knowledge (Process Notes 2.3.1)

This activity is concerned with taking stock of all the Work Knowledge that exists for each business event. Use the event boundaries as a guide for gath-

Diagram 2.3   Do Event Reconnaissance ● 303

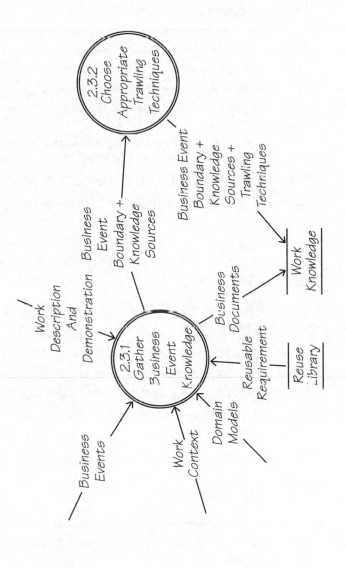

Diagram 2.3   Do Event Reconnaissance

ering together all the work knowledge and the sources of that knowledge. The results of this activity are the starting point for learning the detailed work.

For each Business Event:

● Look for any business documents that might contain knowledge about the work related to the event.

● Look for reports, forms, specifications, user manuals, organization charts, feasibility studies, product documentation, marketing blurb – any document that might contain requirements buried in its depths.

● List the names of sources of the work knowledge:
  – People within the boundaries of the work context
  – Adjacent systems
  – People outside the boundaries of the work context
  – The name of a group of people that might have knowledge of this event.

● Are there any domain models that contain knowledge about this event?

● Are there any reusable requirements that contain knowledge about this event?

Choose Appropriate Trawling Techniques (Process Notes 2.3.2)

To choose the most appropriate trawling techniques for a business event you need to consider:

● What are the potential sources of knowledge?

● What type of requirement are you searching for: policy architecture, stored data, person/machine interface, essential activity?

● Will you be able to speak directly to people?

● Is the knowledge conscious, unconscious or undreamt of?

Here are some guidelines on the strengths of a number of trawling techniques:

Review Current Situation:

● Good for uncovering unconscious requirements.

● Helps when adding new requirements or doing maintenance changes to an existing system.

● Use as the basis of business process reengineering.

Apprentice With The User:

● Helps to uncover unconscious and conscious requirements.

● Useful when users are "too busy" to talk.

  Determine Essential Requirements:

● Helps to separate requirements from solutions.

● A good way to understand the real purpose of the system.

● Helps in uncovering unconscious requirements and provides insights that trigger undreamt of requirements.

  Interview the Users:

● A good technique for discovering conscious requirements.

  Brainstorming:

● Helps uncover undreamt of requirements. Very useful when inventing new products with unknown/potential users.

  Use Case Workshops:

● Involves the users in explaining vague/complex/difficult events.

● Good for uncovering conscious and unconscious requirements.

  Document Archeology:

● Used when your source of information is documents.

  Build Event Models:

● If the business event boundaries are vague then investigate them by doing some detailed systems analysis modeling.

  Make Requirements Video:

● Useful when users' time is limited. Can be studied, analyzed and used by a group after the video is made.

● Helps when the context is vague.

Ask Clarification Questions (Process Notes 2.4)

Review Requirement Questions and System Constraint Questions. Use the Requirements Template to help you.

  Can you determine the Requirement Type?

  Are there any Measurement Examples for this type of requirement?

  Which of the Stakeholders is most likely to be able to provide the answers to these questions?

  What is the best medium/way to ask the question?

  Your question should include everything that is already known about the requirement.

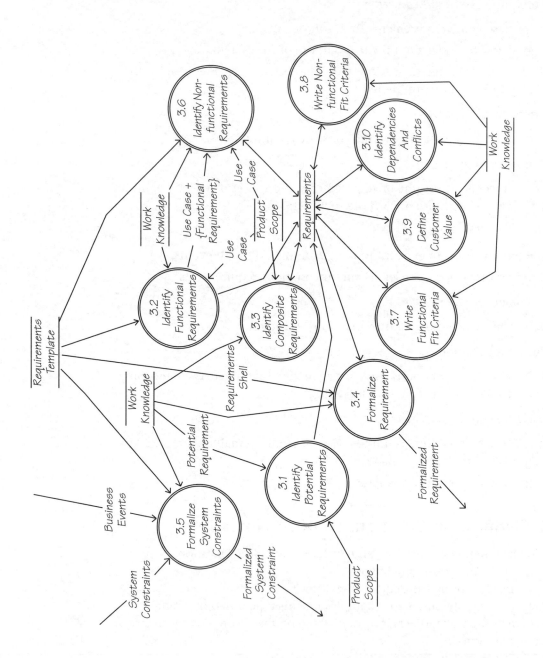

Diagram 3 Write The Requirements

Identify Potential Requirements (Process Notes 3.1)

Not all requirements are discovered as a result of setting a context and working towards a logical and connected partitioning. Instead many individual requirements are discovered during Trawling for Knowledge.

This process analyzes the Potential Requirements discovered as a result of trawling.

For each Potential Requirement:

- Write a description using the form: The product shall ... followed by the action that the product must take.
- Give the requirement a unique number.
- Review the Product Context and see if you can identify which use case(s) this requirement is connected to.
- Record the source (preferably names of people) of the requirement.
- Record the requirement rationale. Ask why is this requirement important to the business?

Identify Functional Requirements (Process Notes 3.2)

For each Use Case in the Product Context:

   When the Use Case is large and/or complex and/or unfamiliar it is difficult to make the leap directly from the Use Case to the requirements. In this case Use Case steps provide a stepping stone to the functional requirements.

   From the point of view of the actor(s), make a list of all the steps that the product must go through in order to do the work of the Use Case.

   For each Use Case Step:

      Find the functional requirements by breaking the use case step into testable one-sentence statements. Ask what the product has to do to complete the work of this step. Questions that help are:

- What data must be received by the product?
- What data must be produced by the product?
- What data must be recorded by the product?
- What checks must be made by the product?
- What decisions must be made by the product?
- What calculations must be made by the product?

      Each of the above questions might produce a number of functional requirements.

For each requirement:

● Write a description using the form: The product shall ... followed by the action that the product must take.

● Give the requirement a unique number.

● Attach the use case number to the requirement.

● Record the source (preferably names of people) of the requirement.

● Record the requirement rationale. Ask why is this requirement important to the business?

Identify Composite Requirements (Process Notes 3.3)

A Composite Requirement is a requirement that does not have its own testable fit criteria. Instead it is a "summary" of a number of other individually testable requirements.

Composite Requirements are useful as a way of talking about the combined effect of a number of individually testable requirements. Sometimes a Composite Requirement is a sign of vagueness or uncertainty.

Composite Requirements are often also known as "High Level Requirements".

It is useful to have a Composite Requirement for each Use Case. Then you can summarize the requirements at the Use Case level but you still have connections to each of the testable requirements that compose that Use Case.

When you define a Composite Requirement be sure that you have a reason for doing so and that you are not simply taking refuge in generality.

Formalize Requirement (Process Notes 3.4)

Refer to the Requirements Shell that is packaged with the Requirements Template.

For each Requirement use the shell as a guide and define each of the components defined on the shell.

For detailed advice and examples of each type of requirement refer to the Requirements Template.

Formalize System Constraints (Process Notes 3.5)

Refer to the Requirements Shell that is packaged with the Requirements Template.

For the Product Purpose and the Project Constraints use the shell as a guide and define each of the components defined on the shell.

For other types of system constraints (Client, Customer, User ...) refer to the Requirements Template.

For detailed advice and examples of each type of system constraint refer to the Requirements Template.

Identify Non-functional Requirements (Process Notes 3.6)

You can use the Functional Requirements as a trigger to help you find the Non-f unctional Requirements by adopting the following approach:

For each Use Case:

For each Functional Requirement:

For each Type of Non-functional Requirement listed in the Requirements Template:

Should there be one or more of these Non-functional Requirements to support this Functional Requirement?

You can also use a higher level approach and look for Non-functional Requirements by comparing the Use Case with each of the Types of Non-functional Requirements.

Write Functional Fit Criteria (Process Notes 3.7)

The objective of this process is to take a Requirement and use the Work Knowledge to produce a Requirement Fit Criterion for a Functional Requirement.

This process is looking for unambiguous criteria that make it possible to classify any solution to the requirement as either "fits the requirement" or "does not fit the requirement".

The template contains many examples of how to determine requirement measurements.

For each requirement:

Fit Criteria for a functional requirement specify how you will know that the product has successfully completed the required action.

Provided that you have defined the terms (refer to section 5 of the Requirements Template) that you have used in the description and purpose/rationale of the requirement, then your fit criteria will take the form of:

- The specified retrieved data will agree with the specified data that was input ...

- The specified checked data will agree with the specified checking rules ...

- The result of the calculation will agree with the specified algorithm ...
- The specified recorded data will agree with the specified retrieved data ...

In other words, if your terminology is unambiguously defined it is part of the definition of Fit Criteria for functional requirements.

Write Non-functional Fit Criteria (Process Notes 3.8)

The objective of this process is to take a Requirement and use the Work Knowledge to produce a Requirement Fit Criterion for a Non-functional Requirement.

This process is looking for unambiguous criteria that make it possible to classify any solution to the requirement as either "fits the requirement" or "does not fit the requirement".

The template contains many examples of how to determine requirement measurements.

- Decide what type of requirement you are dealing with – the template will help with this.

- Is it really a requirement? Requirements are often mistakenly stated as solutions. If this is the case then you need to ask the Stakeholder(s) what the real requirement is independent from how you might solve it.

- If the requirement is concerned with something that you can touch, see, smell, hear or taste then it is easier to find an objective measurement.

- If a noun is not concerned with something that you can touch, see, smell, hear or taste then you have a nominalization. A nominalization is created when a verb describing an ongoing process has been turned into a noun. For example, we could say that maintenance is a nominalization.

- Suppose that you come across a requirement: Maintenance must be reliable. Maintenance is a nominalization. You can clarify a nominalization by trying to bound the meaning. Turn the nominalization back into a verb and ask the question who is nominalizing about what and how are they doing it. In this example ask: who is maintaining what and how are they doing it. This technique will help you to identify the real meaning of the requirement and from there you will be able to define an appropriate fit criterion.

- Some requirements are vague nominalizations because nobody really knows what they mean or want.

Define Customer Value (Process Notes 3.9)

Define the Customer Value by asking the customer to look at the requirement from two points of view:

- Customer Satisfaction: "How happy will you be (on a scale from 1 to 5) if
  I give you a solution that satisfies the fit criteria for the requirement?"

- Customer Dissatisfaction: "How unhappy will you be (on a scale from 1 to 5)
  if I do not give you a solution that satisfies the fit criteria for the requirement?"

Your aim is to understand the Customer's real priorities and to guide the
Customer in communicating his greatest importances. The aim is to have
some rational basis for making choices about which/when/whether to
implement requirements.

The same procedure is used when you have several different groups of
customers each with different priorities. Your aim is to discover and record
the different priorities so that you can make reasoned choices and tradeoffs.

Identify Dependencies And Conflicts (Process Notes 3.10)

Whenever you find a requirement that is in conflict with another require-
ment(s) then you should record the conflict.

A conflict is an indication that you have a situation that requires some
kind of negotiation.

The first step to resolving conflict is to recognize that it exists and start to
think about it independently from the people whose opposing views might
be thought to "cause" the conflict.

You might not discover all the conflicts at this stage. Later, when you review
the requirements specification, you will do a more formal search for conflicts.

Review Requirement Fit Criteria (Process Notes 4.1)

The purpose of the Requirement Fit Criteria is to set communicable limits
that the people involved in the project can understand well enough to test
each solution.

Ask your testers to help with this process.

Does the Formalized Requirement or Formalized System Constraint have
a Requirement Fit Criterion such that:

- The Requirement Fit Criterion provides an unambiguous way of testing
  any eventual solutions such that any solution either conforms with the
  Requirement Fit Criterion or it does not?

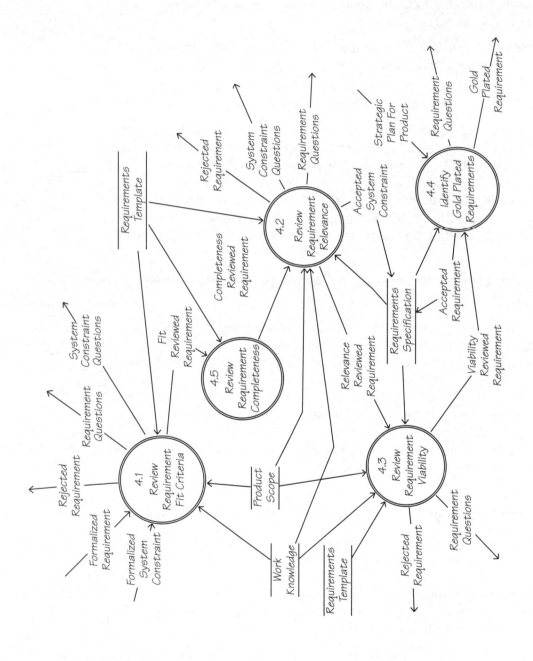

Diagram 4 Quality Gateway

Some requirements are easier to quantify than others. Functional requirements are the easiest of all because they are bounded by a tight context and we have had much more experience in quantifying them.

For instance, suppose we say that there is a Requirement for a Customer to send us Orders. We can specify exactly what data describes a Customer, how many customers we have and the projected growth/attrition rate. So we could say that the Requirement Fit Criterion for Customer is that any solution must record all of the defined data values for the defined number of customers and must be able to cope with the defined projected growth.

If, on the other hand, we say that when a Customer sends us an Order we must respond fast then we have a performance requirement that does not have an unambiguous Requirement Fit Criterion. It would be impossible to test a solution such that we can say whether or not it conforms to this requirement, because everyone can interpret "fast" however they want to. So we need to quantify how fast. This forces many questions out into the open. Does "fast" have a different value in different circumstances? Does "fast" have the same value for all customers or all types of orders?... The idea is to arrive at a value, range of values or statement that can be used to test the fit of eventual solutions to that requirement.

The more abstract the concept, the more difficult it is to come up with a specific value for a Requirement Fit Criterion, however, provided you really have a requirement relevant to the context, it is always possible to come up with a Quality Measurement that conforms to our definition.

Suppose you have a requirement that says that the system's automated interfaces must be "easy to use". Now we need a Requirement Fit Criterion for "easy to use". Remember we are looking for criteria for testing whether a solution satisfies the requirement. In this case it's impossible to find a number, but we can still ask the question "How will we know whether a given solution fits this requirement?"

In this case perhaps we can agree that:

● A test panel of novice users must be able to get an answer to a query of grade 3 complexity within five minutes of first encountering the product.

Raise a question for any requirement or system constraint that does not have a testable fit criteria.

Review Requirement Relevance (Process Notes 4.2)

Is the Requirement within the Product Context?
   If not then raise a question because it might be an irrelevant requirement.
   Is the Requirement really a requirement or is it a solution?

Solutions masquerading as requirements are most common in the case of non-functional requirements or system constraints.

Look at the context of study and ask whether this requirement is a constraint that is imposed by the context. If the answer is yes then you have a real requirement. If the answer is no, then you have a constraint that has been imposed by somebody because of their implementation bias, or because they have an incomplete understanding of the context.

Review Requirement Viability (Process Notes 4.3)

Given the Current Situation and the Context of the project, is this requirement viable?

Is the organization mature enough to cope with a system that satisfies this requirement?

Do we have the technological skills to satisfy this requirement?

Would it be more realistic to scrub the requirement?

You are trying to raise questions early about requirements that are not viable within the conditions of this project.

Identify Gold Plated Requirements (Process Notes 4.4)

Review each requirement to determine whether it is a real requirement or whether it is "gold plating".

The key question is: does the requirement contribute to the Strategic Plan For the Product? Go back to the purpose of the project (requirement types 1) and compare this requirement against the measurable purpose.

Sometimes, even though a requirement is gold plated, you might choose to include it because it helps to overcome a personality or political problem. The important issue is to know that the requirement is gold plated and to have a stated reason for including it.

Review Requirement Completeness (Process Notes 4.5)

Review the requirement against the Requirements Shell in the Volere Requirements Specification Template.

If any of the components listed on the requirements shell are missing then:

● Highlight the missing components.
● Record the reason for the absence of the component.
● Question whether the requirement needs more trawling for knowledge.

Diagram 5   Prototype The Requirements ● 315

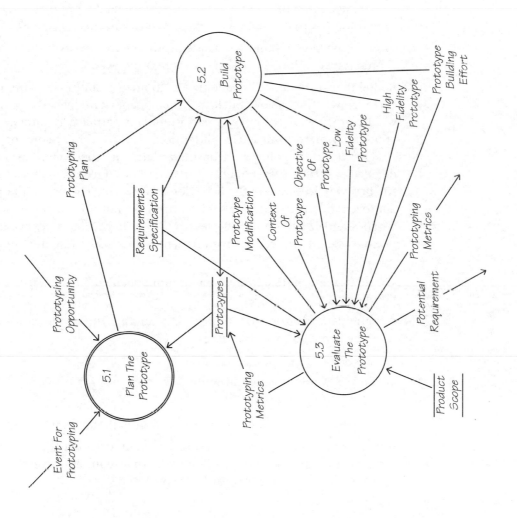

Diagram 5   Prototype The Requirements

Plan The Prototype (Process Notes 5.1)

This task decides what sort of prototype is best for a given Prototyping Opportunity.

Make a prototyping plan to satisfy this objective by considering the following:

- Do you need to build a new prototype from scratch? Are there any existing prototypes that could be used/adapted to suit this objective?
- Would it be best to build a separate prototype for this event/use case, or should it be combined with one or more other events?
- Rather than automatically building a high fidelity (automated) prototype, consider whether a low fidelity (pencil, paper and person) prototype would satisfy your objective. A paper model is particularly suitable when you are trying to focus a user's attention on the essential content of the system (business policy and business data). In these circumstances a detailed event/use case model and an experienced requirements analyst is the best way to simulate the behavior of a system. The paper and pencil approach diverts the user's attention from the automated system characteristics and highlights the system purpose. If you have an event with non-measurable functional requirements, then use a low fidelity prototype.
- Would it help you to consider one or more detailed business scenarios by building a scenario model?
- A high fidelity (automated) prototype is suitable when you want to illustrate the behavior of an interface

  or

  When you cannot define the context of an event

  or

  When you have > 50% unmeasurable non-functional requirements.
- If you decide on a high fidelity prototype, then consider the prototyping tools available to you and choose the one that requires the least effort to satisfy the objective for this particular prototype.

Build Low Fidelity Prototype (Process Notes 5.2.1)

Task to build a low fidelity prototype.

A low fidelity prototype is a simulation model which is built using pencil, paper and an experienced person. The aim of the model is to bring alive those aspects of the system that are related to the objective of the prototype.

Diagram 5.2   Build Prototype ● 317

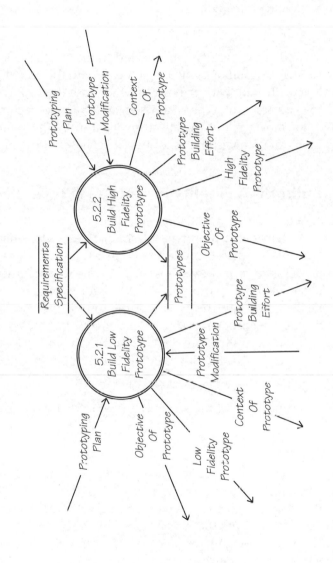

Diagram 5.2   Build Prototype

Types of models that might be suitable are:

- A detailed event/use case model
- A scenario model for the event/use case
- An entity/state model
- A context diagram
- A sketch of a screen layout.

Modify the prototype to respond to the Usage Feedback. The Usage Feedback is the result of using the prototype with the user(s). Ideally the prototype is actually built with the user in which case this task is done in parallel with the task Test Prototype With Users, and the usage feedback is immediate.

Keeping track of the effort involved in building the prototype provides input for doing estimates for the later phases of the project.

Build High Fidelity Prototype (Process Notes 5.2.2)

Task to build a high fidelity prototype.

A high fidelity prototype is a simulation model which is built using some kind of automated product and an experienced person. The aim of the model is to bring alive those aspects of the system that are related to the objective of the prototype. The best prototyping products are those which help to highlight the aspects of the system that are relevant to the user. A prototyping product is counter-productive if it makes it necessary for a user to know things that are only relevant to the internal system design.

Types of high fidelity prototypes that might be suitable are:

- A simulation of a user interface
- A simulation of the system's behavior for a given event/use case
- A simulation of the system's behavior for a combination of events/use cases.

When building a high fidelity prototype you are in an awkward position. You want to build a prototype that makes the system look as real as possible so that the user will give you relevant feedback. On the other hand, you want the user to remember that this is not really the real system and you can't deliver all the functionality just like that. You can reflect the unreality by the names you use. For instance, if a user sees the customer name is Alice in Wonderland, it's a continual reminder that there's a lot to do before this is a real system.

Modify the prototype to satisfy the usage feedback. The Usage Feedback is the result of using the prototype with the user(s). Ideally the prototype is actually built with the user in which case the usage feedback is immediate.

If the prototyping product has an interface that is understandable to the user then the prototype can be built with the user; in this case this task is done in parallel with the task Test Prototype With Users. Otherwise it is better for the analyst to build the prototype and then test it with the user.

Keeping track of the effort involved in building the prototype provides input for doing estimates for the later phases of the project.

Test High Fidelity Prototype With Users (Process Notes 5.3.1)

This task tests the prototype with the user(s). Ideally this task is done in parallel with the task of building the prototype. However if, due to the prototyping product, the process of building the prototype involves procedures that are irrelevant to the user, then it is better to build the prototype before showing it to the user.

The trouble with high fidelity prototypes is that they are often so convincing that the user is sure that they are real, and that you can build the whole system in half an hour. Remind the user(s) that this is a prototype. It's like a stage set – it appears to be real until you look behind the facade and discover thin air.

Demonstrate the prototype to the user(s) and ask questions like:

● Does this behave as you expected?

● Can you imagine yourself using a product that works like this to do useful work?

● Is there anything about the prototype that irritates you?

Review the Objective Of the Prototype and ask whether the prototype is leading you toward satisfying the objective.

Depending on the Objective Of the Prototype you might decide to leave the prototype with the users for a period of time so that they can experiment with it and give you feedback at a later date.

Identify any Prototype Modifications that are necessary to bring the prototype closer to satisfying the Objective Of the Prototype.

If you have satisfied the Objective Of the Prototype then the Usage Feedback is user comments, new requirements, requirements changes as a result of using the prototype.

Test Low Fidelity Prototype With Users (Process Notes 5.3.2)

This task tests the prototype with the user(s). Ideally this task is done in parallel with the task of building the prototype because the process of building

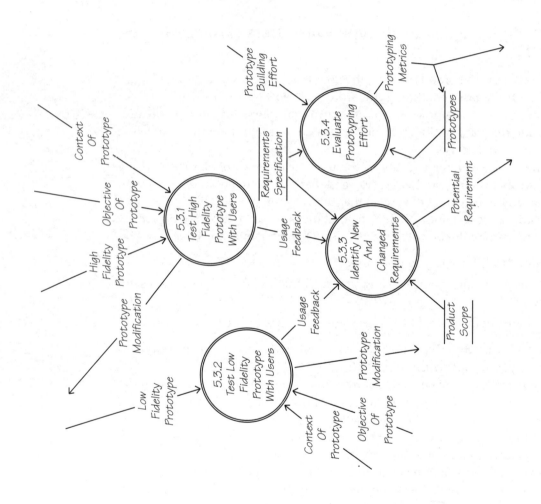

Diagram 5.3 Evaluate The Prototype

a low fidelity prototype makes the business problem clear to the user. Review the Objective Of the Prototype and ask whether the prototype is leading you towards satisfying the objective.

Ask questions like:

- Is there any information missing from the prototype?
- Are the business rules correct?
- Does the prototype cover the intended Context Of the Prototype?

Identify any Prototype Modifications that are necessary to bring the prototype closer to satisfying the Objective Of the Prototype. If you have satisfied the Objective Of the Prototype then the Usage Feedback is user comments, new requirements, requirements changes as a result of using the prototype.

Identify New And Changed Requirements (Process Notes 5.3.3)

This task reviews the Usage Feedback that is generated as a result of using the prototype. The aim is to discover new potential requirements by comparing the usage feedback with the requirements in the requirements specification and the Strategic Plan For the Product.

- Does the specification already contain a requirement that satisfies this Usage Feedback?
- Can this Usage Feedback be expressed as a Measurable Requirement?
- Does this Usage Feedback contribute to the Strategic Plan For the Product?

If the Usage Feedback passes these preliminary tests then treat it as a Potential Requirement. Before it can be added to the Requirements Specification, it will have to pass through the Quality Gateway like all other Potential Requirements.

Evaluate Prototyping Effort (Process Notes 5.3.4)

This task evaluates the Prototype Building Effort and defines some Prototyping Metrics. These metrics are input to the task of estimating how long it will take to analyze and design similar sized components in the real system.

- Calculate the number of function points contained in this prototype.
- What problems did you experience when building this prototype?
- What lessons did you learn?

The metrics will be used to help identify future Prototyping Opportunities and to help make estimates for future stages of the project.

Conduct Private Individual Reviews (Process Notes 6.1.1)

The facilitator has private contact with each project member (developer, stakeholder, manager). The contact is often by questionnaire. These individual responses by project members are never publicized and often the questionnaire is unsigned. Another way of gathering input from individuals is by asking them to talk into a tape recorder. The purpose of this initial private contact is to provide the facilitator with a realistic guide to the issues of the project.

Sample questions:

- If you had to do it again, what would you do differently?
- What would you do the same way?
- What was your best experience?
- What was your worst experience?
- Which tools were most helpful?
- Which tools impeded progress?
- How do you rate the traceability of your requirements?
- Would you work with the same team again? Why?
- What single change would result in most improvement to product quality?
- How do you rate management support?
- What did you learn by doing this project?

Conduct Separate Meetings With Groups (Process Notes 6.1.2)

This is a series of meetings between the post mortem facilitator, or a team of facilitators if the project had many personnel, and project management, developers, users and clients in homogenous groups. The purpose is to understand that particular group's experience of the project.

During these sessions the facilitator might bring up points for clarification that have arisen as a result of his private reviews. Each group is asked for its input to add to or change the issues.

Diagram 6   Do Requirements Post Mortem ● 323

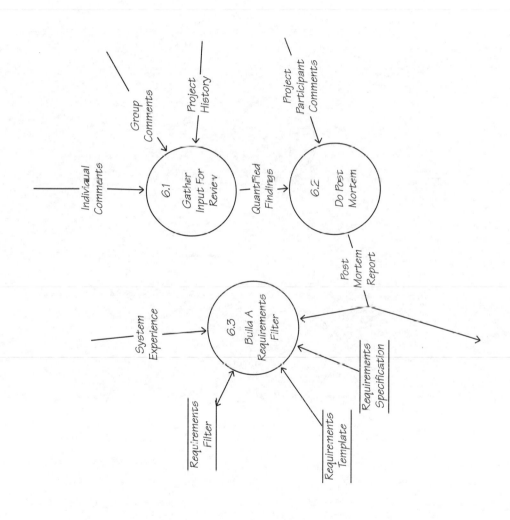

Diagram 6   Do Requirements Post Mortem

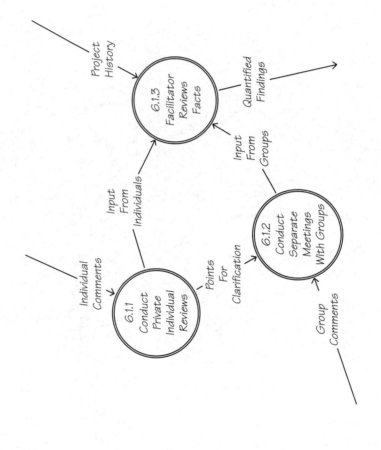

Diagram 6.1   Gather Input For Review

Facilitator Reviews Facts (Process Notes 6.1.3)

The facilitator, or team of facilitators, takes time to review the facts gathered from individual and group input and reviews the actual history of the project. The aim is to quantify the findings.

● Compare the plan for producing the requirements specification with the actual progress. What are the differences?

● How many changes were made during the requirements specification process?

● Is the project suffering from requirements creep?

● The facilitator also compares the project plans with the actual progress and reviews the changes to the specification.

Hold Post Mortem Review Meeting (Process Notes 6.2.1)

The Post Mortem review meeting is for all the people who have been involved in any of the earlier stages of the post mortem (individual reviews or group reviews). Managers, clients, technical staff and all stakeholders meet to hear the findings described by the facilitator(s). The conduct of the review is:

● Remind participants of the objective of the post mortem: to learn from experience by capturing and packaging the noteworthy experiences of the project so that other people can benefit from the knowledge.

● The facilitator presents each finding.

● The participants discuss the finding and any new comments are noted by the facilitator.

● If there is disagreement on any points then the facilitator notes both opinions.

Produce Post Mortem Report (Process Notes 6.2.2)

Your aim is to have as many people as possible read the post mortem report with interest. You need to design the report so that it captures people's attention and is easy to find one's way around.

● Write the report in clear straightforward language.

● Avoid words whose only purpose is to provide bulk.

● Be honest.

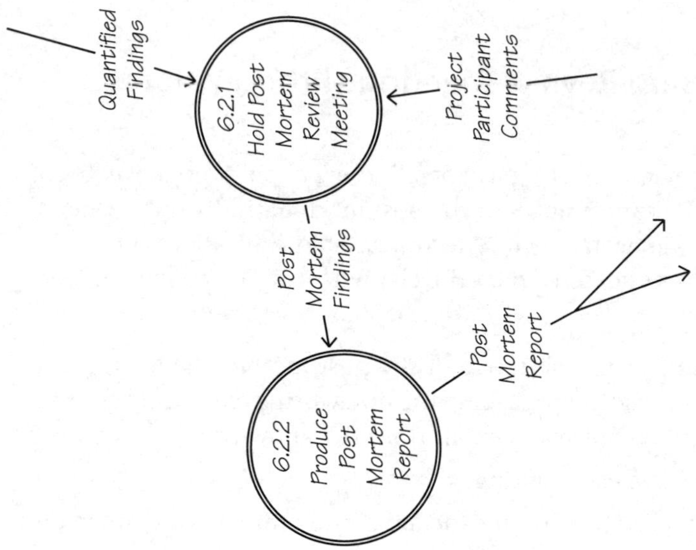

Quantified
Findings

6.2.1
Hold Post
Mortem
Review
Meeting

Project
Participant
Comments

Post
Mortem
Findings

6.2.2
Produce
Post
Mortem
Report

Post
Mortem
Report

Diagram 6.2 Do Post Mortem

● Use pictures to help with explanations

● Include quotes from project participants

● Maintain anonymity unless individuals have requested otherwise.

Here is a sample table of contents for a Post Mortem Report:

Post Mortem Report on Requirements Specification

Our project had successes and failures. This report shares our experiences so that you can profit from the successes and avoid the mistakes that caused the failures.

Contents

1   The most important things that we learned

2   The history of the project (abridged)

3   The project objectives – did we meet them?

4   The process we used – did it work?

5   Communication – within the team

6   Communication – with the world

7   The tools we used and what we learned

8   How we tested our requirements

9   Management issues

10 Project reviews

11 Requirements issues

12 Design issues

13 Some things we really did right

14 Why our faces are red

15 Actions to take

Identify Filtration Criteria (Process Notes 6.3.1)

The purpose of a requirements filter is to provide an objective measurement of the quality/degree of uncertainty/degree of completion (the content) of a requirements specification irrespective of the form in which it is produced. The filter provides a way of applying a fixed measurement to variable artifacts.

The filter is relevant when requirements specifications are:

● Produced by another organization

● Produced in diverse forms

● Produced by a variety of people who work in different ways.

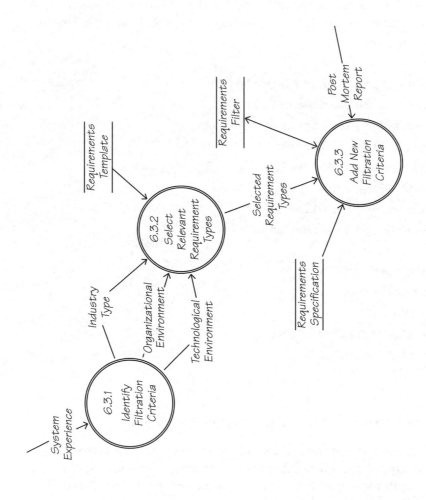

System Experience

6.3.1
Identify
Filtration
Criteria

Industry
Type

Organizational
Environment

Technological
Environment

Requirements
Template

6.3.2
Select
Relevant
Requirement
Types

Selected
Requirement
Types

Requirements
Filter

6.3.3
Add New
Filtration
Criteria

Post
Mortem
Report

Requirements
Specification

Diagram 6.3 Build A Requirements Filter

The filter is used as a tool for trapping missing requirements, irrelevant requirements and inconsistent requirements.

The first step in building a filter is to identify the Industry Type for which it will be used. For example, a banking system would have different filtration criteria from an air defense system, simply because requirements that are very important in one industry might be totally irrelevant in another.

Next define the organizational environment in terms of the roles of people involved in producing your requirements specifications.

Describe the typical technology that applies to your projects for this industry type.

Select Relevant Requirement Types (Process Notes 6.3.2)

For each requirement described in the Requirements Template ask the question:

● Does this requirement apply to the Industry Type or Organizational Environment or Technological Environment for which I am building a Requirements Filter?

If the answer is yes then add the requirement to the Requirements Filter.

Thinking about a requirement will often trigger off ideas about other requirements that are not mentioned in the Requirements Template. If you think of any other requirements that are relevant to the Requirements Filter that you are building, then add them to the Requirements Filter.

Add New Filtration Criteria (Process Notes 6.3.3)

This task is concerned with making your Requirements Filter more useful by adding new knowledge to it.

Every time you produce a Requirements Specification for this Industry Type/Organizational Environment/Technological Environment, review the spec to see if it includes any types of requirements that are not included in the filter. Add the new types of requirements to the Requirements Filter and they become additional criteria for reviewing future requirements specifications.

Identify Missing Requirements (Process Notes 7.1.1)

If you have built a Requirements Filter, then use it to drive this task. Otherwise use the Requirements Template.

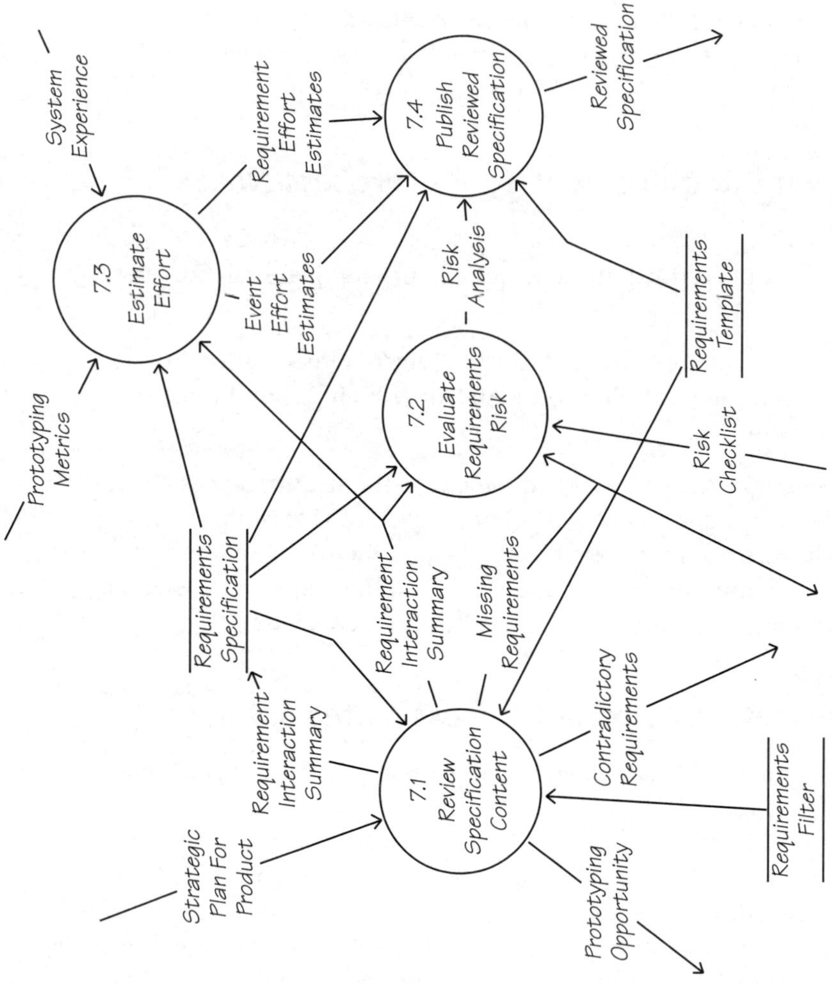
7.1
Review
Specification
Content
7.2
Evaluate
Requirements
Risk
7.3
Estimate
Effort
7.4
Publish
Reviewed
Specification
System
Experience
Prototyping
Metrics
Requirement
Effort
Estimates
Event
Effort
Estimates
Risk
Analysis
Reviewed
Specification
Requirements
Template
Risk
Checklist
Requirements
Specification
Requirement
Interaction
Summary
Missing
Requirements
Requirement
Interaction
Summary
Strategic
Plan For
Product
Contradictory
Requirements
Requirements
Filter
Prototyping
Opportunity

Diagram 7 Taking Stock of the Specification

Diagram 7.1   Review Specification Content ● 331

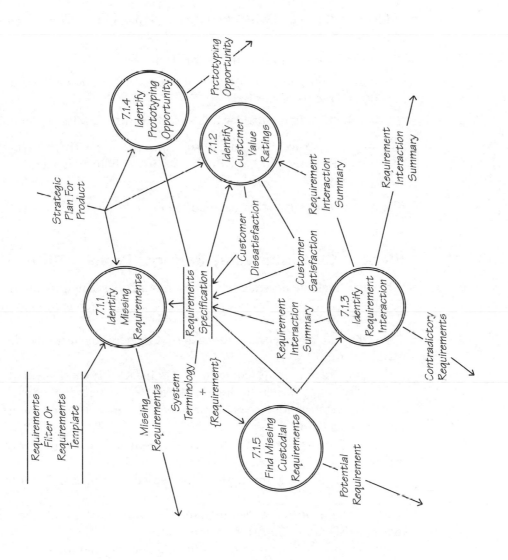

Diagram 7.1   Review Specification Content

Remember that each Requirement should already have been individually reviewed. Your concern here is to cross-check the requirements to discover any missing ones.

For each Requirement Type in your Filter/Template ask these questions to discover Requirements that have been missed:

- Identify all Requirements of this Type defined in the Requirements Specification.

- If there are no Requirements of this Type:
  - If the Strategic Plan For the Product indicates that there should be Requirements of this type
  - Tell the Requirements Trawling step that this is a Missing Requirement.

Compare each event/use case in your specification with each type of Non-functional Requirement. Ask this question to help you identify Missing Requirements:

- Is this type of non-functional requirement relevant to this use case/event?

Identify Customer Value Ratings (Process Notes 7.1.2)

It helps to evaluate design alternatives if you know which requirements are absolutely vital and which ones are there because someone thought it would be "nice".

Ask your stakeholders to grade each requirement for customer satisfaction on a scale from 1 to 5.

1 = quite happy if this requirement is satisfactorily implemented

5 = very happy if this requirement is satisfactorily implemented

Ask your stakeholders to grade each requirement for customer dissatisfaction on a scale from 1 to 5.

1 = slightly perturbed if this requirement is not satisfactorily implemented

5 = extremely grumpy if this requirement is not satisfactorily implemented

The dependencies between requirements will help you to assign the customer satisfaction and dissatisfaction ratings. For example, if you have a requirement with a satisfaction rating of 5 and that requirement is dependent on three other requirements, then it is likely that the dependent requirements will also have a satisfaction rating of 5.

The point of having a satisfaction and a dissatisfaction rating is that it guides the stakeholders to think of the requirements from two different perspectives, and helps you to uncover what they care about most deeply.

You can add the satisfaction and dissatisfaction rating of a requirement to give you an overall indication of the value that the customer places on that requirement.

Identify Requirement Interaction (Process Notes 7.1.3)

Two requirements interact if a design solution to one of them makes it more difficult or easier to do anything about the other. Identifying requirement interaction at the specification stage provides input to evaluating requirements risk and estimating effort.

Requirement interactions exist when:

- Two functions use some of the same policy
- Two functions use some of the same data
- Two functions have contradictory measurements
- The solution to one requirement has an effect (either negative or positive) on the solution to another requirement.

Identify Prototyping Opportunity (Process Notes 7.1.4)

Task to identify which parts of the requirements would benefit most from the building of a prototype.

For each Event or Use Case in the Requirements Specification ask the following questions:

- Does the Event/Use Case have high customer reward or penalty, or is it composed of a set of requirements that have high customer reward or penalty?
- Is the Event/Use Case central to the Strategic Plan For the Product?
- Is the Event/Use Case composed of more than 50% unmeasurable requirements?
- Can we specify the benefit of building a prototype for this Event/Use Case?

For one Event/Use Case, if the answers to these questions is yes, then you have identified a Prototyping Opportunity.

The point of building prototypes during requirements specification is to try to find requirements that have been forgotten or to clarify requirements that are not clear. Steve McMenamin refers to prototypes as "requirements bait".

Find Missing Custodial Requirements (Process Notes 7.1.5)

Custodial processing relates to the maintenance of the system's stored data. Most systems store data that must be able to be changed. For example, the addresses of customers change from time to time. The processing necessary to keep the addresses up to date is nothing to do with the fundamental activities of the system.

For each item of stored data, determine if it has any maintenance requirements. Should the user be able to change, or perhaps delete it? Can the custodial activity be part of a fundamental process, or does it require you to establish a new event/use case?

Also, examine the context model for data flows from the outside that indicate data to be changed. Look for flows that directly change stored data, such as "Customer Address Change". As some of these may be missing from the context, look for flows that bring data into the system that may need to be changed. For example, there may be a flow that establishes a new customer. The data stored by this activity would at some stage in the future have to be changed. If it is missing, add the changing data flow to the context, and make it a requirement to change the stored data.

Consider all of the external entities for the system. Where one of these is a service provider, for example it manufactures goods handled by the system, or transports goods, then there may be a need to create, change and delete the information held about this external entity.

Similarly, inspect all of the data items stored by the system and determine if it needs to be maintained in any way.

Finally, determine if the maintenance is to be a separate requirement, or can it be included in the same events/use cases as other, fundamental requirements.

Look For Likely Risks (Process Notes 7.2.1)

This task looks for all the risks that are likely in your project. The completeness of the requirements specification is a powerful indicator of likely risks. There is nothing wrong with having risks provided you look for them, define them and monitor them. The problems are caused when people push the risks under the carpet and then get a nasty surprise when an unrecognized risk turns into a problem.

Many risk checklists have been produced by researchers and some of these are suggested in the Bibliography. Use one of these checklists as your starting point and add new risks as you encounter them.

For each risk on the checklist:

Diagram 7.2   Evaluate Requirements Risk ● 335

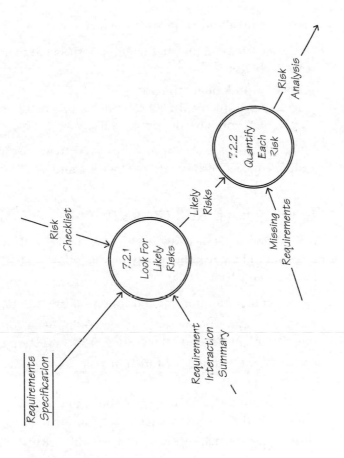

Diagram 7.2   Evaluate Requirements Risk

● Review your Requirements Specification to see whether there is any indication of this risk. For instance, one of the risks on your checklist is Inadequate Customer Involvement. Does anything in your Requirements Specification indicate that you have this risk? Suppose that in the section on User Participation Requirements you see that specific User Names and Roles have not been specified. This indicates a likely risk. If they can't specify who will be involved then it's likely that nobody will be available when they are needed for the project.

For each requirement in your specification:

● If the requirement measurement is not specified then that is an indication of a likely risk.

● Can you think of anything that might go wrong with analyzing, designing and/or implementing a solution to this requirement? If your answer is yes, then you have discovered a likely risk.

If you discover a risk for a requirement then it is likely that dependent requirements will also be affected by the same risk.

Quantify Each Risk (Process Notes 7.2.2)

This task does a detailed assessment of each of the likely risks. Quantify each one of your likely risks by specifying the following risk elements defined by Tim Lister and Tom DeMarco:

● Risk Number: (to monitor and communicate the state of the risk).

● Risk Description: (one sentence describing what problem might occur), e.g. We might need to involve users from an external organization.

● Risk Weight: number of function points involved in this risk, e.g. 200 function points.

● Risk Probability: percentage probability of this risk materializing, e.g. 30% based on what we know after specifying the requirements.

● Risk Cost: estimated cost associated with this risk materializing, e.g. $100,000.

● Risk Schedule Impact: estimated effect on the schedule, e.g. +3 months; +6 months.

● First Indication: e.g. none of the stakeholders within our organization is prepared to define the requirements for value based investment.

Look at each Missing Requirement and ask the question:

● Is this type of requirement relevant within the system; would I expect to have this requirement specified?

For instance, in a safety critical system you would expect to have detailed specification of requirements that relate to damage to people and property, whereas in an inventory control system it would be reasonable for this type of requirement to be absent.

If you determine that a relevant requirement is missing then quantify it as a risk and add it to the Risk Analysis.

The resulting Risk Analysis contains an assessment of all the risks that you have identified as a result of reviewing your Requirement Specification.

Identify Estimation Input (Process Notes 7.3.1)

Each of your requirements that has passed through the Quality Gateway will contain a measurement. You can use your measurable requirements as input to estimating the effort needed to do the project.

If your Requirements Specification includes events or use cases, then you have manageable chunks that you can use as the input to your effort estimation.

For each event/use case you should have:

- Event Name.
- All the Functional Requirements that are connected by this event.
- All the Non-functional Requirements that are connected by this event. If you have not identified the non-functional requirements then you can still do an estimate based on events, however you will have to use an estimated weighting for the impact of the non-functional requirements.
- A definition of all the data that is input to or output from the event. This might come from the world outside the system or it might be stored data.
- If you have an event description or specification it will make the estimate more accurate.

If your Requirements Specification does not include events or use cases, then you can use the individual requirements as input to your effort estimation.

Use the functional requirements to estimate the effort based on the essential functions and data within your context of study. The non-functional requirements provide input to help you weight the estimates depending on the number and difficulty of the non-functional requirements that relate to each functional requirement.

Estimate Effort For Events (Process Notes 7.3.2)

If you have all of the required inputs to the necessary level of detail, then for each event estimate the effort using Albrecht function points.

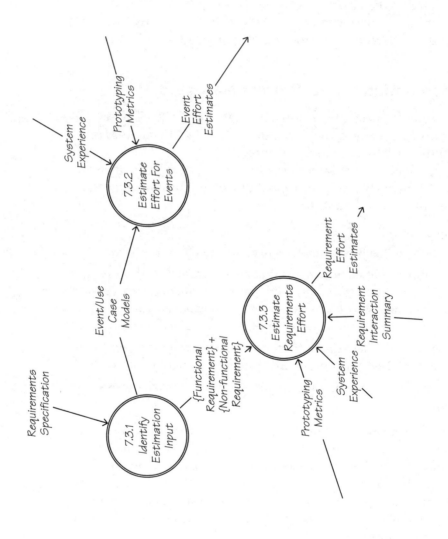

Diagram 7.3 Estimate Effort

Think of the events/use cases as mini systems that combine a number of related requirements. Throughout the project, you can use the events as a project management and communication tool.

System Experience from other projects run under similar conditions provides input for how long it took to develop a similar event under similar conditions. This input, if you have it, helps you to weight the estimates more accurately. System Experiences that you should look for are:

● Developer experience

● Management experience

● Stakeholder experience

● Experience with the intended technology.

If you have built any prototypes then you can use the prototyping metrics as input to estimating the effort necessary for similar events within the system.

Event Effort Estimates = {Event Name + Estimated Function Points}
+ Total Estimated Function Points For All Events
+ Estimate of What Effort a Function Point means in this environment

The US industry standard according to Capers Jones is: $1000 per implemented function point.

Estimate Requirements Effort (Process Notes 7.3.3)

You would use this approach if you have not identified event-related clusters of requirements. Estimate the effort using Albrecht function points.

System Experience from other projects run under similar conditions provides input for how long it took to develop a similar event under similar conditions. This input, if you have it, helps you to weight the estimates more accurately. Project conditions that you should look for are:

● Developer experience

● Management experience

● Stakeholder experience

● Experience with the intended technology.

If you have built any prototypes then you can use the prototyping metrics as input to estimating the effort necessary for similar events within the system.

Requirement Effort Estimates = {Requirement Id + Estimated Function Points}
+ Total Estimated Function Points For All Requirements

+ Estimate of What Effort a Function Point means in this environment

The US industry standard according to Capers Jones is: $1000 per implemented function point.

Design Form Of Specification (Process Notes 7.4.1)

This task designs the media that you will use to communicate the contents of the requirements specification. The most common form is to print the specification on paper. However today's technology provides some other alternatives.

- CD-ROM
- A web page
- A Lotus Notes document.

The way that you design the form of the specification (typeface, color(s), graphics, indexing) makes a great deal of difference to whether anyone will be able/want to read it. Consider the idea of using a graphic designer to advise you on the form of your specification.

Assemble The Specification (Process Notes 7.4.2)

When you assemble the specification make sure that you make it easy for the reader to find his or her way around.

Use the requirements template as a guide for organizing the specification. Add an index.

Diagram 7.4   Publish Reviewed Specification ● 341

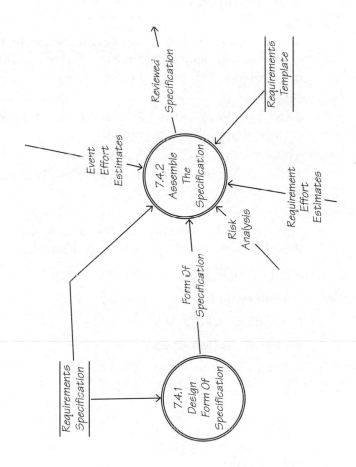

Diagram 7.4 Publish Reviewed Specification

Dictionary of Terms Used in the Requirements Process Model

Accepted Requirement
> [Functional Requirement | Non-functional Requirement | Project Constraint]
> A requirement that has passed through the Quality Gateway and will be included in the requirements specification

Actor Name
> An actor is a human being (usually), a job, another computer system, another organization – anything that interacts with the product. Every use case has at least one actor

Assumptions
> Refer to section 7 of the Volere Requirements Specification Template for more details about assumptions

Blastoff Meeting Plan
> Advice to the stakeholders on the schedule, location and objectives for the Project Blastoff Meeting

Blastoff Objectives
> Deliverables to be produced by the blastoff are some combination of the following depending on the Project Intention:
>
> - System Objectives
> - Context Model
> - Identified Stakeholders
> - Anticipated Developers
> - System Events
> - Event/Use Case Models
> - System Terminology
> - Scenario Models

Blastoff Participants
> Name and contact details for each of the people who are invited to attend the Project Blastoff

Blastoff Report
> Report describing what was accomplished by the Blastoff Meeting

Business Documents
> Reports, forms, specifications, user manuals – any document that might contain requirements buried in its depths

Business Event
> Business Event Name
> + (Event Input + Adjacent System Name)
> + {Event Output + Adjacent System Name}
> The work context boundaries of a business event

Business Event Boundary
> Event Name
> + {Input Dataflow + Adjacent System Name}
> + {Output Dataflow + Adjacent System Name}
> The boundary for studying a business event

Business Events
> {Business Event}
> A list of the business events within the work context. This first-cut functional partitioning is the basis for future detailed analysis and design work. Refer to section 8 of the Volere Requirements Specification Template for more detailed information about Business Events

Business Opportunities
> Ideas for how the product can help to achieve the Product Purpose within the Project Constraints

Client Name
> The name of the person or organization who will pay for the development of the product

Context Interfaces
> Named interfaces between your system and the world outside your scope of study

Contradictory Requirements
> Contradictions between requirements, discovered during requirements review

Current Organization And Systems
> Description of the people who work for the organization, their roles, their responsibilities, their interaction and the technology that they use to do their work

Current Situation Model
> A model that describes aspects of an existing system. The model usually focusses on the current partitioning of the problem and the interfaces between the pieces

Customer Name
> The name of the person(s) or organization(s) who will or are expected, to buy the product

Customer Value Ratings

>   Customer satisfaction on a scale from 1 to 5.
>   1: quite happy if this requirement is satisfactorily implemented
>   5: very happy if this requirement is satisfactorily implemented
>   Customer dissatisfaction on a scale from 1 to 5.
>   1: slightly perturbed if this requirement is not satisfactorily implemented
>   5: extremely grumpy if this requirement is not satisfactorily implemented

Domain Models

>   Models that capture the essence of a particular area of subject matter

Event Effort Estimates

>   Estimated effort in implementing a solution to a use case/event

Event For Prototyping

>   Produced when we suspect that building a prototype might lead to a better understanding of the requirements for this event or the discovery of other requirements

Event/Use Case Model

>   Event Name + {Functional Requirement}
>   + {Non Functional Requirement}
>   + Event Input
>   + Event Output
>   + (Event Description + Product Boundary +{Actor Name})
>   A model that isolates the effect of one event/use case on the processes and data within the context of a system and identifies the product boundary and actors

Event/Use Case Models

>   {Event/Use Case Model}

Existing Documents

>   Reports, forms, specifications, user manuals – any document that might contain requirements buried in its depths

Fit Reviewed Requirement

>   Description of Requirement
>   + Purpose of Requirement
>   + Requirement Source
>   + Requirement Type
>   + Unique Identifier for a Requirement
>   + Requirement Fit Criteria
>   + Customer Satisfaction
>   + Customer Dissatisfaction
>   + Requirement Dependencies
>   + Requirement History

Formalized Requirement
> [Functional Requirement | Non-functional Requirement]
> A potential requirement that has been formally written according to the guidelines in the Volere Requirements Specification Template

Formalized System Constraint
> System Constraints
> A system constraint that has been formally written according to the guidelines in the Volere Requirements Specification Template

Functional Requirement
> Requirement
> Refer to section 9 of the Volere Requirements Specification Template for more details of the Functional Requirement

Go/No Go Decision
> Recommendation based on blastoff results on whether or not to proceed with the project plus reason for recommendation

Gold Plated Requirement
> A requirement that is not essential to solving the stated business objectives

Group Comments
> Post mortem comments made by the group

High Fidelity Prototype
> An automated prototype

Identified Stakeholders
> Client Name
> + {Customer Name}
> + Sponsor Name
> + {User Group}
> + {Developer}
> + {Domain Expert}
> + {Technical Expert}
> People who have been identified to have an interest in the product and whose input is required during requirements gathering. Refer to sections 2 and 3 of the Volere Requirements Specification Template for more detailed information on Stakeholders

Individual Comments
> Post mortem comments made by an individual. Might be a need to keep these confidential

Initial Estimate
> First-cut estimate of the effort required to build the system

Input From Groups
> Input from groups collected by the facilitator

Input From Individuals
> Input from individuals collected by the facilitator

Intended Operating Environment
> Details of the environment in which the product will be installed

Intended Operating Environment Description
> A detailed description of the hardware, software, people and environmental factors under which the product must operate

Knowledge Sources
> Any person, place, organization or document that contains or might contain knowledge about the work within the work context

Low Fidelity Prototype
> A non-automated prototype usually built using some combination of graphic models, screen layouts and written examples

Major Risks
> A blitzed list of the major risks associated with building this product

Meeting Location
> Address of the place at which the Blastoff Meeting will be held

Meeting Schedule
> Time(s) and Date(s) for which the Blastoff Meeting is scheduled

Missing Requirements
> Requirements types that should be included

Non-functional Requirement
> Requirement
> Refer to sections 10–17 of the Volere Requirements Specification Template for more details about non-functional requirements

Objective Of Prototype
> Why we are building the prototype. What we expect to gain. What are the questions to which we require answers

Points For Clarification
> Meetings with individuals sometimes raise questions for the facilitator to clarify when meeting with groups

Post Mortem Comments
> Individual Comments
> + Project Participant Comments
> + Group Comments

Post Mortem Report
> A report whose purpose is to communicate noteworthy experiences of the project in a form that is usable by other people

Potential Requirement
> This has been discovered as a result of learning the work. It might turn out to be a requirement but we will not be sure until it has been formalized and has passed through the Quality Gateway

Potential Stakeholders
> A list of people considered to have an interest in the project

Product Purpose
> Business problem(s) that this product is intended to solve plus criteria for determining whether the objective(s) have been met. Refer to section 1 of the Volere Requirements Specification Template for more details about product purpose

Product Scope
> Use Case
> + {Business Event Name}

Project Constraints
> Constraints on the way that the product must be produced:
> - technology to be used/not used
> - budget
> - time
> - operating environment
>
> Refer to section 6 of the Volere Requirements Specification Template for more details about Project Constraints

Project History
> Project Plans + Project Progress History + Specification Changes

Project Intention
> Guideline from the customer on the:
> - product desired from the project
> - anticipated budget
> - technological constraints
> - problem the product is intended to solve
> - anticipated scope
> - reasons for doing the project

Project Participant Comments
> Comments made by participants at the post mortem meeting

Prototype Building Effort
> Time To Build Prototype
> + Context Of Prototype
> + Form Of Prototype

Prototypes
{[Low Fidelity Prototype | High Fidelity Prototype]
+ Prototyping Metrics}

Prototyping Metrics
Context Of Prototype
+ Number Of Function Points
+ Form Of Prototype
+ Time To Build Prototype
+ Problems Experienced
+ Lessons Learned
Measurements of how long it took to build a particular prototype within a particular environment

Prototyping Opportunity
Context Of Prototype
+ Objective Of Prototype
+ Interested Stakeholders
+ {Requirement}

Prototyping Plan
Context Of Prototype
+ Objective Of Prototype
+ Interested Stakeholders
+ [Low Fidelity | High Fidelity]
+ Existing Prototypes
+ Prototyping Tool

Quantified Findings
The result of the facilitator reviewing all comments from individuals and from groups

Rejected Requirement
A requirement or constraint that has failed to pass through the Quality Gateway

Relevance Reviewed Requirement
A requirement that has passed the Quality Gateway's relevance test

Relevant Facts
Refer to section 6 of the Volere Requirements Specification Template for more details about relevant facts

Required Facilities
All the physical arrangements necessary to satisfy the Blastoff Objectives including:

● Accommodation

● Stationery

- Catering
- Equipment

Requirement

Requirement Number
+ Requirement Type
+ {Use Case Number}
+ Requirement Description
+ Requirement Rationale
+ Requirement Source
+ Fit Criteria
+ Customer Satisfaction
+ Customer Dissatisfaction
+ {Requirement Dependency}
+ {Requirement Conflict}
+ Supporting Materials
+ Requirement History

This identifies all the components of a complete functional or non-functional requirement. The components are gradually added during the process of trawling for knowledge and writing the requirements

Requirement Interaction Summary

Lists interactions between requirements. Two requirements interact if a design solution to one of them makes it more difficult or easier to do anything about the other. Identifying requirement interaction at the specification stage provides input to evaluating requirements risk and estimating effort

Requirement Measurement

Description of Requirement
+ Purpose of Requirement
+ Requirement Type
+ Unique Identifier for a Requirement
+ Requirement Fit Criteria
+ Customer Satisfaction
+ Customer Dissatisfaction

Requirement Questions

Outstanding questions that prevent a project blastoff from being considered complete or prevent a requirement or constraint from passing through the Quality Gateway. Contains everything that is currently known about the requirement or constraint

Requirement Type
[Functional | Non Functional]

Requirements
{Requirement}

Requirements Filter
A tool for assessing the completeness of a requirements specification

Requirements Skeleton
Product Purpose
+ Work Context
+ Identified Stakeholders
+ Business Events
+ System Terminology
+ Initial Estimate
+ Major Risks
+ Project Constraints
+ Intended Operating Environment Description
The Requirements Skeleton is used to keep track of the knowledge discovered during the blastoff

Requirements Specification
Product Purpose
+ Product Context
+ Identified Stakeholders
+ {Use Case}
+ System Terminology
+ {Functional Requirement}
+ {Non-functional Requirement}
+ {Project Constraint}
+ Assumptions
+ Relevant Facts
+ Project Issues
+ Requirement Interaction Summary

Requirements Template
Template for a Requirements Specification. See sample Volere Requirements Specification Template

Reusable Requirement
A requirement that has been put into the Reuse Library because it is considered to be a candidate for reuse

Reuse Library
{Reusable Requirement}
A collection of potentially Reusable Requirements

Reviewed Specification
Requirements Specification

+ Risk Analysis
+ Effort Estimates

Risk Analysis
Detailed assessment of all the risks identified by doing a risk analysis of the Requirements Specification

Risk Checklist
Risk checklists produced by researchers like Capers Jones and Barry Boehm

Stakeholder Wants And Needs
Functional requirements, non-functional requirements and constraints that the stakeholders want the system to have

Strategic Plan For Product
Product Management's input on the constraints to apply to the product. External influences might cause this to change during the course of the requirements specification

System Constraints
Product Purpose
+ Identified Stakeholders
+ Business Events
+ System Terminology
+ Project Constraints
+ Relevant Facts
+ Assumptions

System Experience
Relevant experience of the stakeholders in building similar products, using similar technology, dealing with similar problems, working in a similar environment

System Terminology
Definition of the terms that people use within the context of this project. Refer to section 5 of the Volere Requirements Specification Template for more details about System Terminology

Trawling Techniques
A variety of techniques used by requirements engineers and business analysts for discovering requirements

Usage Feedback
User comments, new requirements, requirements changes as a result of using a prototype

Use Case
Use Case Name
+ {Actor Name}
+ Use Case Boundary Data

User Group
    User Group Name
    + User Group Skills

Work Context
    A summary of the parts of the world that we intend to study in order to satisfy the system objectives. The model shows the adjacent systems (square boxes), our specific interest in each adjacent system (interfaces) and the intersections of those adjacent systems (context process). Refer to section 8 of the Volere Requirements Specification Template for more detailed information about Work Context

Work Description And Demonstration
    Current Organization And Systems
    + Business Documents
    + Stakeholder Experience

Work Knowledge
    Work Context
    + Business Documents
    + Market Surveys
    + Job Descriptions
    + Company Reports
    + Current Organization And Systems
    + Stakeholder Experience
    + {Business Event Boundary + Knowledge Sources + Trawling Techniques}
    + {Potential Requirement}
    + Event Models
    + System Terminology
    + Data Models
    + Scenario Models
    Any artifact that contains knowledge about the subjects within the context of the work

Appendix B

Volere Requirements Specification Template

a guide for writing a rigorous
requirements specification

Table of Contents

Preamble

Volere

Volere is the result of many years of practice, consulting and research in requirements engineering. We have collected the most effective ideas for successful requirements and packaged them into a process for gathering correct requirements, and a template for writing rigorous requirements specifications.

This template is a guide. It is complementary to the techniques that we have discussed in this book, and we assume that you are making use of the book's contents when using this template. If you need explanations for any parts of the template, then you will find them in the body of the book.

We suggest that you write requirements using the shell. The shell is shown in Figure B.1. This is a mechanism for ensuring that you collect all the necessary components for your requirements.

This template is updated from time to time and updates are posted on the Atlantic Systems Guild web site at www.atlsysguild.com.

The template itself is copyright. However, you may make use of it. You can use it as it stands, modify it or copy it for internal use, provided you acknowledge the copyright. You may use it as a basis for your own requirements specifications, whether you are writing for in-house consumption, or you are working as a contractor, or you plan on selling your specification. However, you may not sell this template, or use it for commercial gain without prior written permission.

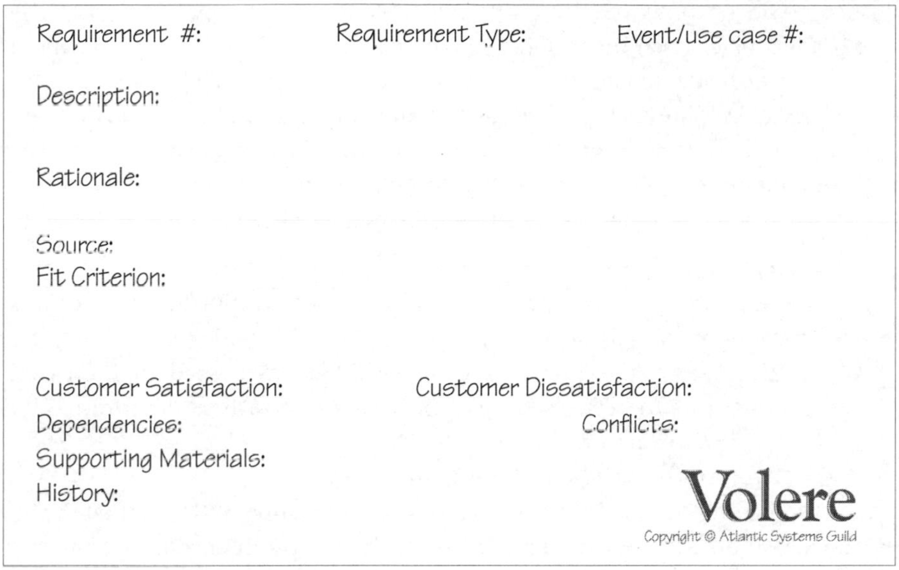

Requirement #:	Requirement Type:	Event/use case #:

Description:

Rationale:

Source:
Fit Criterion:

Customer Satisfaction:	Customer Dissatisfaction:
Dependencies:	Conflicts:
Supporting Materials:	
History:	

Volere
Copyright © Atlantic Systems Guild

Figure B.1

The Volere shell is a convenient way of ensuring that you have all the components necessary for complete requirements.

1 The Purpose of the Product

1a The user problem or background to the project effort

Content
A description of the work and the situation that triggered the development effort. It should also describe the work that the user *wants to do* with the delivered product.

Motivation
This statement justifies the project.

Considerations
You should consider whether or not the user problem is serious, and whether and why it needs to be solved.

1b Goals of the product

Content
This boils down to one, or at most a few sentences that say 'What do we want this product for?' In other words, the real reason that the product is being developed.

Motivation
Projects without a clearly stated, and readily understandable, goal are in danger of wandering in the desert of product development.

The purpose has to give some business advantage. Typically the advantage is that the product will increase the organization's value in the market place, reduce the cost of operations, or provide better customer service. Whatever the advantage, it must be measurable. The advantage, or benefit, from developing the product must have some objective measurement that allows you firstly to determine if the product is worthwhile, and secondly to determine if the delivered product meets the goal.

Examples

'We want to give an immediate and complete response to customers ordering our goods over the telephone.'

The measurement of this goal would be expressed in increased turnover due to better response, or increase in ratings determined by customer satisfaction surveys.

'We want to be able to forecast the weather.'

The measurement of this goal is increased value in the market. If the customers for this product (golf clubs) have a product that can forecast weather accurately, then they can save money by watering golf courses more efficiently. The measurement must be expressed in money terms. That is, how much value will the product represent in the market.

Considerations

There is a real danger of this purpose getting lost along the way. As the development effort heats up, and the customer and developers discover more and more what is possible, it may well be that the product as it is being constructed wanders away from the original goals. This is a bad thing unless there is some deliberate act by the client to change the goals. It may be necessary to appoint a person to be 'custodian of the goals', but it is probably sufficient to make the goals public, and periodically remind the developers of them. It should be mandatory to acknowledge the goals at every review session.

2   Client, Customer and other Stakeholders

2a   The client is the person(s) paying for the development, and will become owner of the delivered product

Content

This item must give the name of the client. It is permissible to have several names, but more than three negates the point.

Motivation

The client has the final acceptance of the product, and thus must be satisfied with the product as delivered. Where the product is being developed for in-house consumption, the roles of the client and the customer may be filled by the same person. If you cannot find a name for your client, then perhaps you should not be building the product.

Considerations

Sometimes, when building a package or a product for external users, the client is the marketing department. In this case, a person from the marketing department must be named as the client.

2b The customer is the person(s) who will buy the product

Content

For in-house development, the customer is the person who will have the final say on whether the product is acceptable. This is usually the management of the department that is to deploy the product. Name this person. Note that it may be the same as the client.

For mass-market products, the customer is the person who will buy the product off the shelf. In this case define the characteristics of the target customers in sufficient detail that the requirements analysts can imagine the customer and shape the requirements accordingly.

Note that for some mass-market development efforts, the marketing department may be a surrogate customer. In this case, ensure that the marketers give you as complete a description as possible of their target customer.

Note that international customers may have different characteristics from domestic ones.

Motivation

The role of the customer is to decide whether or not to buy the product, or to deploy it. The product must be built to satisfy the aims of the customer whilst conforming to the constraints of the client. Even if your customers are people who work for another part of the client's organization, they might still have the authority to decide whether or not to use the new product.

2c Other stakeholders

Content

The names of other people and organizations who are affected by the product or whose input is needed in order to build the product.

Examples of stakeholders include:

● Management, or the project sponsor

- Business subject matter experts
- Technology people
- System developers
- Marketing people
- Product managers
- Testers and quality assurance people
- Inspectors such as safety inspectors or auditors
- Lawyers
- Usability experts
- Professional bodies for your industry.

Also check each of the adjacent systems from the context diagram. They may need representation in your requirements gathering activities.

Motivation
Stakeholders have demands on products. Failure to find all the stakeholders will result in missed requirements.

3   Users of the Product

3a   The users of the product

Content
A list of the potential end-users or operators of the product. For each category of user, provide the following information:

- Category of user – such as schoolchildren, road engineers, project managers.
- User work tasks – summarizes the users' responsibilities.
- Subject matter experience – the users' knowledge of the business. Rate as novice, journeyman or master.
- Technological experience – this describes the users' experience with relevant technology. Rate as novice, journeyman or master.
- Other user characteristics – describe any other characteristics of the users that may have an effect on the requirements and eventual design of the product. Describe things like:
  - Physical abilities/disabilities
  - Intellectual abilities/disabilities
  - Attitude to job

– Attitude to technology

– Education

– Linguistic skills

– Age group

– Gender.

Motivation

Users are human beings who interface with the product to do their work. The more you know about the user the more likely you will deliver a product that fits in with the user's way of working, and conforms to the user's metaphors and preferences.

The description of the user is taken into account when you define the usability requirements for the product (section 11 in this template).

Examples

Users can come from wide, and sometimes unexpected, sources. Consider the possibility of your users being clerical staff, shop workers, managers, highly-trained operators, general public, casual users, passers-by, illiterate people, tradesmen, students, test engineers, foreigners, children, lawyers, remote users, people using the product over the telephone or Internet, emergency workers. Almost anybody might be a user.

3b   The priorities assigned to users

Content

Attach to each category of user a priority rating. This gives the importance and precedence of the user. Prioritize the users into:

● Key users. These are critical to the continued success of the product. Give greater importance to requirements generated by this category of user.

● Secondary users. They will use the product, but their opinion of it has no effect on its long-term success. Where there is a conflict between secondary users' requirements and those of key users the key users take precedence.

● Unimportant users. This category of user is given the lowest priority. It includes infrequent, unauthorized and unskilled users, and people who misuse the product.

Percentage of this type of user – this is intended to assess the amount of consideration given to this category of user.

Motivation

If some users are considered to be more important to the product, or the organization, then this should be stated because it should affect the way that you design the product. For instance, you need to know if there is a large customer who has specifically asked for the product, and if they do not get what they want then the results could be a significant loss of business.

Some users may be listed as having no impact on the product. This means that the users will make use of the product, but have no vested interest in it. In other words, these users will not complain, nor will they contribute. Any special requirements from these users will have a lower design priority.

4 Requirements Constraints

This section describes constraints that have an effect on the requirements and the eventual design of the product.

4a Solution constraints

Content

This specifies constraints on the way that the problem must be solved. You can think of these as mandated solutions. Carefully describe the solution, and a measurement of how you will test compliance. If possible, you should also explain the reason for using the solution.

Motivation

To identify constraints that must be part of the final product. Your client, customer or user may, for any number of reasons, have design preferences. If these are not met then your solution is not acceptable.

Examples

'The product must use the current two-way radio system to communicate with the drivers in their trucks.'
'The product must use the Windows NT operating system.'
'The product must be a hand-held device.'

Considerations

We want to define the boundaries within which we can solve the problem. Be careful because anyone who has experience/exposure to a piece of technology tends to see requirements in terms of that technology. This tendency leads people to impose solution constraints for the wrong reason and it's very easy for false constraints to creep into a specification. If you impose false constraints the danger is that you do not have the creative freedom to come up with the best solution to the problem. The solution constraints should only be those that are absolutely non-negotiable.

4b   Implementation environment

Content
This describes the technological and physical environment in which the product will be installed. This includes automated, mechanical, organizational and other devices. These include the non-human adjacent systems.

Motivation
To describe the technological environment into which the product must fit. The environment places design constraints on the product. This part of the specification provides enough information about the environment for the designers to make the product successfully inter act with its surrounding technology.

The operational requirements (section 13) are derived from this description.

Considerations
All the component parts of the current system, regardless of their type, should be included in the description of the implementation environment.

If the product is to affect, or be important to the current organization, include an organization chart.

4c   Partner applications

Content
This describes applications that are not part of the product but with which the product will collaborate. These can be external applications, commercial packages or pre-existing in-house applications.

Motivation
To provide information about design constraints that are caused by using partner applications. By describing or modeling these partner applications, you discover and highlight potential problems of integration.

Considerations
Examine the work context model (section 8) to determine if any of the adjacent systems should be treated as partner applications. It

might also be necessary to examine some of the details of the work to discover relevant partner applications.

4d Commercial off-the-shelf software

Content
This describes COTS that must be used to implement some of the requirements for the product.

Motivation
The characteristics, behavior and interfaces of the commercial software are design constraints, and may have an effect on the requirements.

Considerations
The use of a specific package has been mandated before the full extent of the requirements was known. When gathering requirements you may discover requirements that are in serious conflict with the behavior and characteristics of the package. In light of your discoveries you must consider whether the package is a viable choice, or if the conflicting requirements will have to be discarded.

4e Anticipated workplace environment

Content
This describes the workplace in which the users will work and use the product. This should describe any features of the workplace that could have an effect on the design of the product.

Motivation
To identify characteristics of the physical workplace that may have an effect on the requirements for the product. That is, the product may have to compensate for any difficulties in the workplace, or may be able to take advantage of workplace features.

Examples
'The printer is a considerable distance from the user's desk.' This constraint suggests that printed output should be de-emphasized.

'The workplace is noisy.' The implication is that audible signals might not work.

'The workplace is outside.' To allow for this, the product must be waterproof, have displays that are visible in sunlight and allow for the effect of wind on any paper output.

'The user will be standing up or working in positions where he must hold the product.' This suggests a hand-held product.

Considerations

The physical work environment constrains the way that work is done. The product should overcome whatever difficulties exist, however you might consider a redesign of the workplace as an alternative to having the product compensate for it.

4f How long do the developers have to build the product?

Content

Any known deadlines, or windows of opportunity, should be stated here.

Motivation

To identify critical times and dates that have an effect on product requirements. If the deadline is short, then the requirements must be kept to whatever can be built within the time allowed.

Considerations

State deadline limitations that exist by stating the date and describing why it is critical. Also identify prior dates where parts of your product need to be available for testing. The reasons for having to meet deadlines might be:

- To meet scheduled software releases.
- There may be other parts of the business or other software products that are dependent on this product.
- Windows of marketing opportunity.
- Scheduled changes to the business that will use your product. For example the organization may be starting up a new factory and your product is needed before production can commence.

You should also ask questions about the impact of not meeting the deadline like:

- 'What happens if we don't build the product by ...?'
- 'What is the financial impact of not having the product by ...?'

4g What is the financial budget for the product?

Content

The budget for the product, expressed in money or available resources.

Motivation

The requirements must not exceed the budget. This may constrain the number of requirements that can be included in the product.

The intention of knowing the budget is to determine if the product is really wanted.

5   Naming Conventions and Definitions

Definitions of all terms, including acronyms, used in the project

Content
A dictionary containing the meaning of all the names used within the requirements specification.

This dictionary should build on the standard names that your organization, or industry, uses. The names should also reflect the terminology in current use within the work area.

The dictionary contains all the important names that are used by the project. Select names carefully to avoid giving a different, unintended meaning. For each name write a succinct definition. This definition must be agreed by the appropriate stakeholders.

Motivation
Names are very important. They invoke meanings that, if carefully defined, can save hours of explanations. Attention to names at this stage of the project helps to highlight misunderstandings.

The dictionary produced during requirements is used and added to throughout the project.

Examples
De-icing Truck – a vehicle used for spreading de-icing substances on roads in winter.

Considerations
Make use of existing dictionaries and glossaries. Obviously it is best to avoid renaming existing items unless they are so ambiguous that they cause confusion.

From the start of the project emphasize the need to avoid homonyms and synonyms, and explain how they increase the cost of the project.

Later on, as the analysis progresses, this description will be expanded to define the term using its elementary data items. In other words, this glossary evolves into a data dictionary.

6   Relevant Facts

External factors that have an effect on the product, but are not mandated requirements constraints

Content

Statements describing other forces, systems, activities in the world that may have an effect on this product. Relevant facts do not always translate directly to requirements, but they might.

Include in this section any facts that you feel have a bearing on the requirements, and do not seem appropriate for other sections of the specification.

Motivation

To alert the requirements analysts and developers of conditions or facts that might contribute to, or have a bearing on, the requirements. These facts will also have an effect on the eventual design of the product.

Examples

'One ton of de-icing material will treat three miles of single lane roadway.'

'The existing application is 10,000 lines of C code.'

7   Assumptions

Content

A list of the assumptions that the developers are making. These can be about anything that has an effect on the product.

Motivation

Assumptions are, in a sense, the opposite of facts. They are not true, but they might well be in the future. This section exists for two reasons: to make people declare the assumptions that they are making, and to make everyone on the project aware of assumptions that have been made.

Examples

Assumptions about what your developers expect to be ready in time for them to use. For example, other parts of your products, the completion of other projects, software tools, software components, and so on.

Assumptions about the technological environment in which the product will operate. These assumptions should highlight areas of expected compatibility.

Assumptions about the capabilities of the users

The software components that will be available to the developers.

Other products being developed at the same time as this one.

Availability and capability of bought-in components.

Dependencies on computer systems or people external to this project.

Assumptions about new laws or political decisions.

Considerations

It is necessary to talk to the developers to discover any unconscious assumptions that they have made. Treat the developers like users of technology and ask them questions like:

- 'What software tools are you expecting to be available?'
- 'Will there be any new software products?'
- 'Are you expecting to use a current product in a new way?'

8 The Scope of the Product

8a The context of the work

Content

The context diagram identifies the work that you need to investigate in order to build the product. Note that this includes more than the intended product. Unless we understand the work that the product will support, there is little chance of building a product that will fit seamlessly into its environment.

The adjacent systems on the example context diagram (see Figure B.2), for example Weather Forecasting Bureau, indicate other subject

Figure B.2

The work context defines the scope of the work by defining the flows of information that enter or leave the work. In other words, the responsibility of the work begins when an incoming flow arrives, and ends when the outgoing flow leaves. The external entities are *adjacent systems*. These are the other products or people that surround, and interact with, the work.

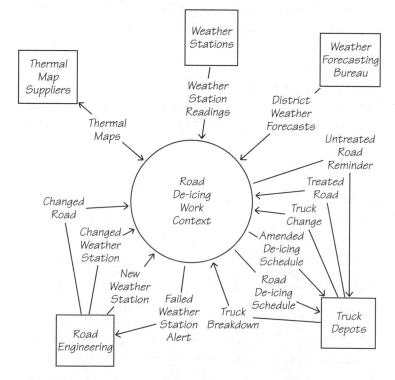

matter domains (systems, people and organizations) that need to be understood. The interfaces between the adjacent systems and the work context indicate why we are interested in the adjacent system. For the District Weather Forecasts, we are interested in the transmission medium, frequency, location of the Weather Forecasting Bureau, the contact person, and the reason for the transmission.

Motivation

To clearly define the boundaries for the work study and requirements effort.

Example

An example of a context diagram is shown in Figure B.2.

The work context diagram shows the work as a single activity and its connections to the outside world, represented here by the adjacent systems. The flows of information between the work and the adjacent systems precisely define the responsibilities of the work, and those of the adjacent systems.

8b   Work partitioning

Content

An event list, identifying all the business events to which the work responds. The business events are user-recognizable actions that happen to the work. The response to each event represents a portion of work that contributes to the total functionality of the work.

The event list includes:

- Event Name
- Inputs and outputs. These are the flows that trigger the response to the event, or flows that are the result of a response. These flows are shown on the context diagram.

Motivation

To identify logical chunks of the work that can be used as the basis for discovering detailed requirements. These business events also provide the sub-systems that can be used as the basis for managing detailed analysis and design.

Example

An example of an event list is shown in Figure B.3.

Figure B.3

An event list showing the business events that affect the system, with their triggering incoming data flows and their resulting outgoing flows.

Event List

Event Name	Input and Output Flows
1 Weather Station transmits reading	Weather Station Readings (in)
2 Weather Bureau forecasts weather	District Weather Forecasts (in)
3 Road engineers advise changed roads	Changed Road (in)
4 Road Engineering installs new weather station	New Weather Station (in)
5 Road Engineering changes weather station	Changed Weather Station (in)
6 Time to test Weather Stations	Failed Weather Station Alert (out)
7 Truck Depot changes a truck	Truck Change (in) Amended De-icing Schedule (out)
8 Time to detect icy roads	Road De-icing Schedule (out)
9 Truck treats a road	Treated Road (in)
10 Truck Depot reports problem with truck	Truck Breakdown (in) Amended De-icing Schedule (out)
11 Time to monitor road de-icing	Untreated Road Reminder (out)

8c   Product Boundary

Content

A use case diagram identifies boundaries between the users and the product. A sample use case diagram is shown in Figure B.4.

You derive the use cases by deciding where the product boundary should be for each of the business events. These decisions are based on your knowledge of the work and the requirements constraints. Refer to Chapter 4 for details of deriving the use cases from business events.

The use case diagram is an effective way of summarizing all the use cases relevant to the product. If you have a large number of use cases – we find 15–20 is around the limit, then it is better to list the use cases and model each one individually. For each use case on the list you should have: use case number, use case description and use case fit criterion.

9   Functional and Data Requirements

9a   Functional Requirements

Content

A description of an action that the product must take.

Example

'The product shall issue an alert if a weather station fails to transmit readings.'

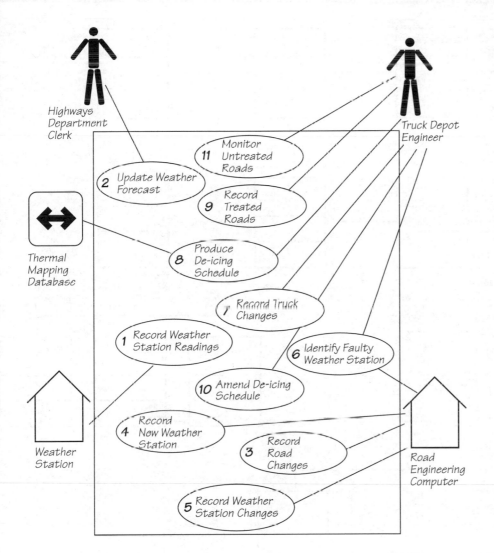

Figure B.4

The use case diagram shows the use cases that make up the functionality of the product. The actors that surround the product are shown diagrammatically as autonomous, cooperative or active. (See Chapter 4, Event-driven Use Cases, for an explanation of these terms.) Use cases are convenient groupings of requirements.

'The product shall produce an amended de-icing schedule when a change to a truck means that previously scheduled work cannot be carried out as planned.'

Fit Criterion

Each functional requirement must have a fit criterion. The fit criterion is a target that makes it possible to test whether the requirement was in fact implemented as specified in the delivered product.

For functional requirements, the fit criterion depends on the action being required. For example, if the function is to record some data, then the fit criterion would say that the data must be able to be

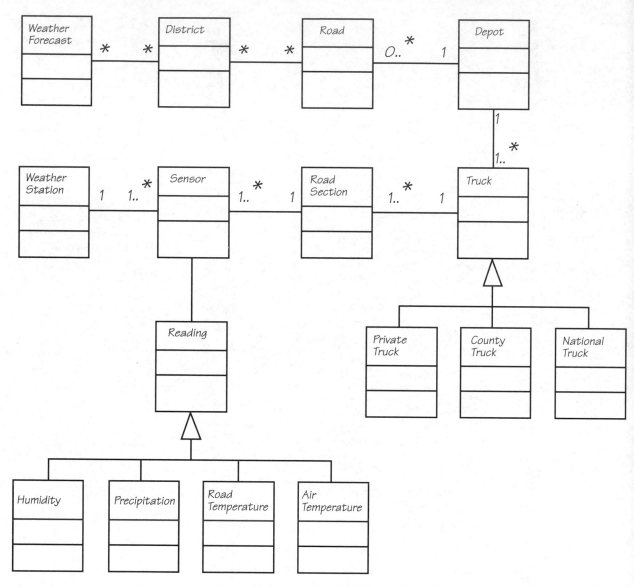

Figure B.5

A class diagram shows the essential subject matter for the product. This model may later be used as the basis for object design, but for the moment it is used to identify the data that is important to the product.

retrieved and must match certain standards. For calculations, the resulting data must conform to predicted results.

9b Data requirements

Content

A specification of the essential subject matter/business objects/entities/classes that are germane to the product. This might take the form of a first-cut data model, an object model or a domain model. Alternatively you may feel that it is adequately dealt with by defining the terms in the dictionary described in section 5.

Motivation

To clarify the product's subject matter and thereby trigger requirements that have not yet been thought of.

Example

An example class diagram is shown in Figure B.5.

Considerations

There may be other class or data models that are suitable as a starting point for your project. It is quite usual to find that there are overlapping class diagrams from other products.

10   Look and Feel Requirements

The spirit of the product's appearance

Content

The requirements for features of the product that are related to the way a potential customer will see the product. For example, if your client wants the product to appeal to the business executive, then a look and feel requirement is that the product has a conservative and professional appearance. Similarly if the product is for sale to children, then the look and feel requirement is that it be colorful and look like it's intended for children.

Keep in mind that this is not the design for the product. Its purpose is to communicate the requirements for the appearance.

Motivation

Given the state of today's market and people's expectations, we cannot afford to build products that have an inadequate appearance. Once the functional requirements are satisfied, it is often the appearance of products that determines whether they are successful or not. Your task in this section is to determine precisely how the product shall appear to its intended consumer.

Examples

'The product shall have the same layout as the district maps that the engineering department uses now.'

'The product shall use the company colors.'

'The product shall be colorful and attractive to a teenage audience.'

'The product shall appear authoritative.'

Considerations

The look and feel requirements specify your client's vision of the product's appearance. The requirements may at first seem to be rather vague – 'conservative and professional appearance' – but these will be quantified by their fit criterion. The fit criterion in this case gives you the opportunity to extract from your client precisely what is meant, and gives the designer precise instructions on what is to be accomplished.

Product or interface design may overlap the requirements gathering process. This is particularly true if you are using prototyping as part of your requirements process. As prototypes develop it is important to capture the requirements that relate to the look and feel. In other words, be sure that you understand your client's intentions instead of merely having a prototype to which the client has nodded his approval.

11   Usability Requirements

11a   Ease of use

Content

This section describes your client's aspirations for how easy it will be for the intended users of the product to operate it. The product's usability is derived from the abilities of the expected users of the product and the complexity of its functionality.

Motivation

To guide the product's designers into building a product that will meet the expectations of its eventual users.

Examples

'The product shall be easy for 11-year-old children to use.'
'The product shall help the user to avoid making mistakes.'
'The product shall make the users want to use it.'
'People with no training, and possibly no understanding of English, shall use the product.'

Fit Criterion

These requirement examples may seem simplistic, but they do express the intention of the client. To completely specify what is meant by the requirement it is necessary to add a measurement of acceptance. We call this a fit criterion. The fit criteria for the above examples would be:

[An agreed percentage, say 90%] of a test panel of 11 year olds shall be able to successfully complete [list of tasks] within [specified time].

One month's use of the product shall result in a total error rate of less than [an agreed percentage, say 2%].

An anonymous survey shall show that [an agreed percentage, say 75%] of the users are regularly using the product after [an agreed time] familiarization period.

Considerations

Refer back to section 3, Users of the Product, to ensure that you have considered the usability requirements from the perspective of all the different types of users.

It may be necessary to have special consulting sessions with your users and your client to determine whether there are any special usability considerations that must be built into the product.

You could also consider consulting a usability laboratory that has experience with testing the usability of products that have constraints (sections 1–7 of this template) similar to yours.

11b Ease of learning

Content

A statement of how easy it should be to learn to use the product. This will range from zero time for products intended for placement in the public domain (for example, a parking meter) to a considerable time for complex, highly technical products. (We know of one product where it was necessary for graduate engineers to spend 18 months in training before being qualified to use the product.)

Motivation

To quantify the amount of time that your client feels is allowable before a user can successfully use the product. This requirement will guide designers in how users will learn the product. For example, the designers may build elaborate interactive help facilities into the product, or the product may be packaged with a tutorial. Alternatively, the product may have to be constructed so that all of its functionality is apparent upon first encountering it.

Examples

'The product shall be easy for an engineer to learn.'

'A clerk shall be able to be productive within a short time.'

'The product shall be able to be used by members of the public who will receive no training before using it. They may have seen the advertising campaign.'

'The product shall be used by engineers who will attend five weeks of training before using the product.'

Fit Criterion

Fit criteria for the above example requirements are:

An engineer shall produce a [specified result] within [specified time] of beginning to use the product, without needing to use the manual.

After receiving [number of hours] training a clerk shall be able to produce [quantity of specified outputs] per [unit of time].

[Agreed percentage] of a test panel shall successfully complete [specified task] within [specified time limit].

The engineers shall achieve [agreed percentage] pass rate from the final examination of the training.

Considerations

Refer back to section 3, Users of the Product, to ensure that you have considered the ease of learning requirements from the perspective of all the different types of users.

12   Performance Requirements

12a   Speed requirements

Content

Specifies the amount of time available to complete specified tasks. These often refer to response times. They can also refer to the product's ability to fit into the intended environment.

Motivation

Some products, usually real-time products, must be able to perform some of their functionality within a given time period. Failure to do so may mean catastrophic failure (for example, a ground-sensing radar in an aeroplane fails to detect a mountain ahead) or the product will not cope with the required volume of use (a server for an ATM network).

Examples

'Any interface between a user and the automated product must have a maximum response time of two seconds.'

'The response must be fast enough to avoid interrupting the user's flow of thought.'

'The product must poll the sensor every ten seconds.'

'The product must download the new status parameters within five minutes of a change.'

'Complete summaries of the day's trading shall be available one minute after the close of trading.'

Fit Criterion

For speed requirements the fit criteria have to be testable measurements of performance. They would enhance the above requirements by fully stating the conditions under which the product must meet the target times.

Considerations

There is a wide variation in the importance of different types of speed requirements. If you are working on a missile guidance system then speed is extremely important. On the other hand, an inventory control report that is run once every six months has very little need for speed.

12b Safety critical requirements

Content

Quantification of perceived risk of possible damage to people, property and environment.

Motivation

To understand and highlight the potential damage that could occur when using the product within the expected operational environment.

Examples

'The product shall not emit noxious gases.'

'The heat exchanger must be shielded from human contact.'

Fit Criterion

The product shall be certified to comply with the Health Department's standard E110-98. This is to be certified by qualified testing engineers.

No member of a test panel of [specified size] shall be able to touch the heat exchanger. The heat exchanger must also comply with safety standard [specify which one].

Considerations

If you are building safety critical products then you will probably have safety experts on your staff. These safety experts are the best source of the relevant safety critical requirements for your type of product. The safety experts will almost certainly have copious information that you can use.

Consult your legal department. They will be aware of the kinds of lawsuits that have resulted from product safety failure. This is probably the best starting place for generating relevant safety requirements.

12c   Precision requirements

Content
Quantification of the desired accuracy of the results produced by the product.

Motivation
To set the client and user expectations for the precision of the product.

Examples
'All monetary amounts must be accurate to two decimal places.'

'Accuracy of road temperature readings will be within plus or minus two degrees Celsius.'

12d   Reliability and availability requirements

Content
This section quantifies the necessary reliability of the product. This is usually expressed as the allowable time between failures, or the total allowable failure rate. Alternatively, you could express it as the expected availability of the product.

Motivation
It is critical for some products not to fail too often. This section allows you to explore the possibility of failure and to specify realistic levels of service. It also gives you the opportunity to set client and user expectations about the amount of time that the product will be available for use.

Examples
'The product shall be available for use 24 hours per day, 365 days per year.'

'The product shall be available for use between the hours of 8:00 a.m. and 5:30 p.m.'

'The product shall achieve 100 hours MTBF (mean time between failure).'

'The product shall achieve 99% up time.'

Considerations
Consider carefully whether the real requirement for your product is that it is available for use, or that it does not fail at any time.

Consider also the cost of reliability and availability, and whether it is justified for your product.

12e Capacity requirements

Content
This section specifies the throughput of processing and the volume of data to be stored by the product.

Motivation
To ensure that the product is capable of processing the expected volumes. To set expectations and force revelation of the expected capacities.

Examples
'The product must be able to cater for 300 simultaneous users within the period from 9:00 a.m. to 11:00 a.m. Maximum loading at other periods will be 150.'

'During a launch period the product must cater for up to 20 people in the inner chamber.'

13 Operational Requirements

13a Expected physical environment

Content
This section specifies the physical environment in which the product will operate, and any special requirements that exist because of this environment.

Motivation
To highlight conditions that might need special requirements, preparation or training. These requirements ensure that the product is fit to be used in its intended environment.

Examples
'The product is to be used by a worker, standing up, outside in cold, rainy conditions.'

'The product will be used in noisy conditions with a lot of dust.'
'The product must be able to fit in a pocket or purse.'
'The product will be used in dim light.'

Considerations
The operational requirements are largely derived from the description of the workplace in section 4, Requirements Constraints. This section of the specification should be written in conjunction with the usability requirements in section 11.

13b Expected technological environment

Content

Specification of the hardware and other devices that make up the operating environment for the new product.

Motivation

To identify all the components that interact with, or are part of, the new product. This allows effective management of the acquisition, installation and testing of the integrated products.

Considerations

Special considerations should also be given if the product is to be embedded in another device.

13c Partner applications

Content

Description of other applications that the product must interface with.

Motivation

Requirements for interfacing to other applications often remain undiscovered until implementation time. The intention is to avoid rework by discovering these requirements early.

Examples

'We must be able to interface with any HTML (HyperText Markup Language) browser.'

'The new version of the spreadsheet must be able to access data from the previous two versions.'

'Our product must interface with the applications that run on the remote weather stations.'

Fit Criterion

For each inter-application interface describe the information that you will use to determine if the implemented product works successfully with the partner application.

14 Maintainability and Portability Requirements

14a How easy must it be to maintain this product?

Content

A quantification of the time necessary to make specified changes to the product.

Motivation

To make everyone aware of the maintenance needs of the product.

Examples

'New MIS (Management Information System) reports must be available within one working week of the date the requirements are agreed.'

'A new weather station must be able to be added to the product overnight.'

Considerations

There may be special requirements for maintainability, such as this product must be able to be maintained by its end-users, or developers who are not the original developers. This has an effect on the way that the product is developed, and there may be additional requirements for documentation or training.

14b   Are there special conditions that apply to the maintenance of this product?

Content

Specification of the intended release cycle for the product and the form that the release will take.

Motivation

To make everyone aware of how often it is intended to produce new releases of the product.

Examples

'The maintenance releases will be offered to end-users once a year.'

Considerations

Do you have any existing contractual commitments or maintenance agreements that might be affected by the new product?

14c   Portability requirements

Content

A description of other platforms or environments into which the product must be installed.

Motivation

To quantify client and user expectations about the platforms on which the product will be able to run.

Examples

'The product is expected to run under Windows 95 and UNIX.'

'The product might eventually be sold to the Japanese market.'

'The product is designed to run in offices, but we intend to have a version which will run in restaurant kitchens.'

Considerations

Ask questions from your marketing department to discover unstated assumptions that have been made about the portability of the product.

15   Security Requirements

15a   Is the product confidential?

Content

Specification of who has authorized access to the product, and under what circumstances that access is granted.

Motivation

To understand and highlight the expectations for confidentiality aspects of the product.

Examples

'Only direct managers can see the personnel records of their staff.'

'Only holders of current security clearance can enter the building.'

Considerations

Is there any data that is sensitive to the management? Is there any data that low level users do not want management to have access to? Are there any processes that might cause damage or might be used for personal gain? Are there any people who should not have access to the product?

Avoid solving how you will design a solution to the security requirements. For instance, don't design a password system. Your aim here is to identify what the security requirement is. The design will come from this description.

Consider asking for help. Computer security is a highly specialized field, and one where improperly qualified people have no business being. If your product has need of more than average security, we advise that you make use of a security consultant. They are not cheap, but the results of inadequate security can be even more expensive.

15b File integrity requirements

Content

Specification of the required integrity of databases and other files.

Motivation

To understand the expectations for the integrity of the product's data.

Considerations

How will the information be used? What is the impact on the customer's business if the information is out of date? Will there be a ripple effect if two different users have different versions of the product?

15c Audit requirements

Content

Specification of the required audit checks.

Motivation

To build a product that complies with the appropriate audit rules.

Considerations

This section may have legal implications. You are advised to seek the approval of your organization's auditors for what you write here.

16 Cultural and Political Requirements

Are there any special factors about the product that would make it unacceptable for some political reason?

Content

This section contains requirements that are specific to the sociological and political factors that affect the acceptability of the product. If you are developing a product for foreign markets then these requirements are particularly relevant.

Motivation

To bring out in the open requirements that are difficult to discover because they are outside the cultural experience of the developers.

In the case of political requirements the requirements sometimes appear irrational.

Examples

'The product shall not use icons that could be considered offensive in any of our market countries.'

'Our company policy says that we shall buy our hardware from Dell.'

'The chief auditor shall verify all the user interfaces.' (This last one is a pure political requirement. There can be no other reason for its existence.)

Considerations

Question whether the product is intended for a culture other than the one with which you are familiar. Ask whether people in other countries or in other types of organizations will use the product. Do these people have different habits, holidays, superstitions, or cultural norms that do not apply to your own culture?

Did you intend to develop the product for a Macintosh, when the office manager has laid down an edict that only Windows machines are permitted?

Is a director also on the board of a company that manufactures products similar to the one that you intend to build?

Whether you agree with these political requirements has little bearing on the outcome. The reality is that the product has to comply with political requirements even if you can find a better/more efficient/more economical solution. A few probing questions here may save some heartache later.

17 Legal Requirements

17a Does the product fall under the jurisdiction of any law?

Content

A statement specifying the legal requirements for this product.

Motivation

To comply with the law so as to avoid later delays, lawsuits and legal fees.

Examples

'Personal information must be implemented so as to comply with the Data Protection Act.'

'The product must conform with the disabled access laws.'

Fit Criterion

Lawyers' opinion that the product does not break any laws.

Considerations

Consider asking the company lawyers to help you identify the legal requirements. At the very least, be aware of the laws that apply to the type of product that you are developing.

Are there any copyrights that must be protected? Alternatively, do any competitors have copyrights that you might be in danger of infringing?

Is it a requirement that developers have not seen competitors' code or even have worked for competitors?

Is there any pending legislation that might affect the development of this product?

17b Are there any standards with which we must comply?

Content
A statement specifying applicable standards and referencing detailed standards descriptions.

Motivation
To comply with standards so as to avoid later delays.

Example
'The product must comply with the appropriate MilSpec (Military Specification) standards.'

'The product must be developed according to SSADM standard development steps.'

Fit Criterion
A measurement that allows you to be able to certify that the standard has been adhered to.

Considerations
It is not always apparent that there are applicable standards because their existence is often taken for granted. Consider the following:

- Are there any industry bodies that have applicable standards?
- Has the industry a code of practice, watchdog or ombudsman?
- Are there any special development steps for this type of product?

18 Open Issues

Issues that have been raised and do not yet have a conclusion

Content
A statement of factors that are uncertain and might make a significant difference to the product.

Motivation
To bring uncertainty out in the open and provide objective input to risk analysis.

Examples

'Our investigation into whether or not the new version of the processor will be suitable for our application is not yet complete.'

'The government are planning to change the rules about who is responsible for de-icing the motorways, but we do not know what the changes might be.'

Considerations

Are there any issues that have come up from the requirements gathering that have not yet been resolved? Have you heard of any changes that might occur in the other organizations/systems on your context diagram? Are there any legislative changes that might affect your product? Any rumors about your hardware/software suppliers that might have an impact?

19 Off-the-Shelf Solutions

19a Is there a ready-made product that could be bought?

Content

List of existing products that should be investigated as potential solutions. Refer to any surveys that have been done on these products.

Motivation

To give consideration to whether or not a solution can be bought.

Considerations

Is it possible to buy something that already exists or is about to become available? It may not be possible at this stage to say with a lot of confidence, but any likely products should be listed here.

Also consider whether there are ready-made products that must *not* be used.

19b Can ready-made components be used for this product?

Content

Description of the candidate components, either bought-in or built by your company, that could be used by this project. List libraries that could be a source of components.

Motivation

Reuse rather than reinvention.

19c Is there something that we could copy?

Content

List of other similar products.

Motivation
Reuse rather than reinvention.

Examples
'Another electricity company has built a customer service system. Their hardware is different from ours but we could buy their specification and cut our analysis effort by approximately 60%.'

Considerations
While a ready-made solution may not exist, there may well be something that, in its essence, is similar enough that you could copy and possibly modify to better effect than starting from scratch.

20   New Problems

20a   What problems could the new product cause in the current environment?

Content
A description of how the new product will affect the current implementation environment. This section should also cover things that the new product should *not* do.

Motivation
The intention is to discover early any potential conflicts that might otherwise not be realized until implementation time.

Examples
'Any change to the scheduling system will affect the work of the engineers in the divisions and the truck drivers.'

Considerations
Is it possible that the new product will damage some already existing product? Can people be displaced, or affected by the new product?

This requires a study of the current environment. A model highlighting the effects of the change is a good way to make this information widely understandable.

20b   Will the new development affect any of the installed systems?

Content
A description of how the new product is expected to work with any existing systems.

Motivation

Very rarely is a new development intended to stand completely alone. Usually there is some existing system that the new one must co-exist with. This question forces you to look carefully at the existing system and examine it for potential conflicts with the new development.

20c Will any of our existing users be adversely affected by the new development?

Content

Details of any adverse reaction that might be suffered by existing users.

Motivation

Sometimes existing users are using a product in such a way that they will suffer ill effects from the new product/feature. Identify any likely adverse user reaction, determine whether we care and what precautions we will take.

20d What limitations exist in the anticipated implementation environment that may inhibit the new product?

Content

Statement of any potential problems with the new automated technology or new ways of structuring the organization.

Motivation

The intention is to make an early discovery of any potential conflicts that might otherwise not be realized until implementation time.

Examples

'The planned new server is not powerful enough to cope with our projected growth pattern.'

Considerations

This requires a study of the intended implementation environment.

20e Will the new product create other problems?

Content

Identification of situations that we might not be able to cope with.

Motivation

To guard against situations where the product might fail.

Considerations

Will we create a demand for our product that we are not able to service? Will the new product cause us to fall foul of laws that do not currently apply? Will the existing hardware cope?

There are potentially hundreds of unwanted effects. It pays to answer this question very carefully. Also refer to section 23, Risks.

21 Tasks

21a What steps have to be taken to deliver the product?

Content

Details of the lifecycle and approach that will be used to deliver the product. A high-level process diagram showing the tasks and interfaces between them is probably the most effective way to communicate this information.

Motivation

To specify the approach that will be taken to deliver the product so that everyone has the same expectations.

Considerations

Depending on the level of maturity of your process, the new product will be developed using your standard approach. However, there are some circumstances that are special to a particular product and will necessitate changes to your lifecycle. While these are not a product requirement, they are needed if the product is to be successfully developed.

If possible, attach an estimate of the time and resources needed for each task based on the requirements that you have specified. Tag your estimates to the events/use cases/functions that you specified in sections 8 and 9.

Do not forget data conversion, user training and cutover. We have listed these because they are usually ignored when projects set implementation dates.

21b Development phases

Content

Specification of each phase of development and the components in the operating environment.

Motivation

To identify the phases necessary to implement the operating environment for the new product so that the implementation can be managed.

Considerations
Identify which hardware and other devices are necessary for each phase of the new product. This may not be known at the time of the requirements process, as these devices may be decided at design time.

22   Cutover

22a   What special requirements do we have to get the existing data, and procedures to work for the new product?

Content
A list of the cutover activities. A timetable for implementation.

Motivation
To identify cutover tasks as input to the project planning process.

Considerations
Will you be using phased implementation to install the new product? If so, describe the requirements that will be implemented by each of the major phases.

What data conversion has to be done? Are there special programs to be written to transport data from an existing product to the new one? If so, the requirements for this program(s) are to be described here.

What manual backup is needed while the new product is installed?

When are each of the major components to be put in place; when are phases of the implementation to be released?

This section is the timetable for implementation of the new product.

22b   What data has to be modified/translated for the new product?

Content
List of data translation tasks, and identification of the data to be translated for the new product.

Motivation
To discover missing tasks that will affect the size and boundaries of the project.

Considerations
Every time you make an addition to your dictionary (section 5) ask the question 'What are the places where this data is held and will the new product affect those implementations?'

23   Risks

23a   What risks do you face when you develop this product?

All projects involve risk. By this we mean the risk that something will go wrong. Risk is not necessarily a bad thing, as no progress is made without taking some risk. However, there is a difference between unmanaged risk – say shooting dice at a craps table – and managed risk where the probabilities are well understood, and contingencies made. Risk is only a bad thing if the risks are ignored and they become problems. Risk management is assessing which risks are most likely to apply to the project, deciding a course of action if they become problems, and monitoring projects to give early warnings of risks becoming problems.

This section of your specification should contain a list of the most likely and the most serious risks for your project. Against each risk include the probability of that risk becoming a problem. Capers Jones' book *Assessment and Control of Software Risks* (1994) gives comprehensive lists of risks and their probabilities; you can use these as a starting point.

It is also useful input to project management if you include the impact on the schedule, or the cost, if the risk does become a problem.

23b   What contingency plans are you making?

Some of the above risks are serious. That is, if they become a problem, the consequences are such that your product may not function correctly, or be seriously impaired. If it is not possible to avoid or prevent the risk from becoming a problem, then are there contingency actions that you can take if the risk manifests itself?

Probably the best known example of *not* having a contingency plan is the baggage-handling system at Denver International Airport. The new, automated baggage system did not work as planned when it was implemented. However, there was no contingency plan in place should it not work. That is, there was no way that the bags could be manually transported to and from the planes. Thus the entire airport was not able to open for many months after it was ready (except for the baggage system).

Most product development efforts will face some risks becoming problems. So most specifications should contain contingency plans.

24 Costs

The other cost of requirements is the amount of money or effort that you have to spend building them into a product. Once the requirements specification is complete, you can use one of the estimating methods to assess the cost, and express this in a monetary amount or time to build.

There is no best method to use when estimating. However, your estimates should be based on some tangible, countable, artifact. If you are using this template then, as a result of doing the work of requirements specification, you are producing many measurable deliverables. For example:

● Number of input and output flows on the work context

● Number of business events

● Number of use cases

● Number of functional requirements

● Number of non-functional requirements

● Number of requirements constraints

● Number of function points.

The more detailed work you do on your requirements the more accurate will be your deliverables. Your cost estimate is the amount of resources you estimate each type of deliverable will take to produce within your environment. You can do some very early cost estimates based on the work context. At that stage, your knowledge of the work will be general and you should reflect this by making the cost estimate a range rather than one figure.

As you get more knowledge about the requirements we suggest you try using function point counting – not because it is an inherently superior method – but because it is so commonly accepted. So much is known about it, that it is possible to make easy comparisons with other products, and other installations' productivity.

It is important that your client knows at this stage what the product is likely to cost. You usually express this as a total cost to complete the product, but you may also find it advantageous to be able to point out the cost of individual requirements.

Whatever you do, do not leave the costs in the lap of hysterical optimism. Make sure that this section includes meaningful numbers based on tangible deliverables.

25   User Documentation

25a   The plan for building the user documentation

Content
List of the user documentation that will be supplied as part of the product.

Motivation
To set expectations for the documentation and to identify who will be responsible for creating it.

Considerations
What level of documentation is expected? Will the users be involved in the production of the documentation? Who will be responsible for keeping the documentation up to date? What form will the documentation take?

26   Waiting Room

Requirements that will not be part of the agreed product. These requirements might be included in future versions of the product

Content
Any type of requirement.

Motivation
To allow requirements to be gathered, even though they cannot be part of the current development. To ensure that good ideas are not lost.

Considerations
The requirements gathering process often throws up requirements that are beyond the sophistication of, or time allowed for, the current release of the product. This section is a hold-all for requirements in waiting. The intention is to avoid stifling your users and clients by having a repository for future requirements. You are also managing expectations by making it clear that you take these requirements seriously but they will not be part of the agreed product.

Glossary

Adjacent system   A system (person, organization, computer system) that provides information to, or receives information from, the work that we are studying. We need to study the adjacent system to understand why and how it communicates, as well as understanding the reason that it communicates with our work.

Business event   Something that happens to the business, or the work, that makes it respond. Business events are such things as 'Customer pays an invoice', 'Truck reports all roads have been treated', 'Time to read electricity meters'.

Client   The person who pays for the development of the product. See also *customer*.

Constraint   A global requirement that restricts the way that you produce the product. For example, the budget for development is a constraint as it restricts the number and sophistication of the requirements.

Context   The subject matter, people and organizations that might have an impact on the requirements for the product. The context of study, or the work context, identifies the work that is to be studied, and the adjacent systems that interact with this work. The product context identifies the scope of the product and its interactions with users and other systems.

Customer   A person who buys the product. See also *client*.

Data flow   Data that moves from one process to another. Usually represented by a named arrow.

Design   The act of crafting a technological solution to fit the requirements, within the constraints.

Developer   Someone who contributes to the development of the product. For example, a systems analyst, designer, tester or programmer.

Event-driven use case   The work done by the product in response to a business event. Once the desired response to a business event is established, the requirements analyst and designer determine how much of that response is to be done by the automated product. The use case is a convenient way of identifying a user and a group of requirements that carry out a specific task for that user.

Fit criterion   A quantification or measurement of the requirement such that you are able to determine if the delivered product satisfies, or fits, the requirement.

Function point   A measure of the functionality of software products. Function points were first proposed by Allan Albrecht and today the method for counting function points is specified by the International Function Point User Group.

Functional requirement   Something that the product must do. Functional requirements are part of the fundamental processes of the product.

Non-functional requirement   A property, or quality, that the product must have, such as an appearance, or a speed or accuracy property.

Product   That which you are about to build, and for which the requirements are written. In this book, product usually means a software product, but the requirements can be for any kind of product.

Prototype   A simulation of the product using either software prototyping tools, or low fidelity whiteboard or paper mock-ups. The purpose of the prototype is to prompt the users for more requirements.

Requirement   Something that the product must do, or a property that the product must have.

Requirements Analyst   The person who has responsibility for producing the requirements specification. The analyst does not necessarily do all of the requirements elicitation, but does have responsibility for coordinating the requirements effort.

Requirements Specification   A document that contains the requirements. The specification defines the product, and may be used as a contract to build the product.

Scenario   A simulation that explores a specific instance of a use case. One use case can have many scenarios. Used for the purpose of discovering requirements.

Stakeholder   A person with an interest in the product. For example, the client for the development, a user, or somebody who builds the product. Some stakeholders are remote, for example an auditor, a safety inspector, the company lawyer.

System   In the context of this book, system means a business system. It never means the computer, or the software system.

Systems Analysis   The craft of modeling the system's functions and data. Systems analysis can be done using data flow modeling as defined by DeMarco, event response modeling as per McMenamin and Palmer, or any of the many object-oriented methods. Jacobson's approach is probably the best known of these. See the Bibliography for references.

Use case   An amount of work as seen from the viewpoint of the user of the product. See *event-driven use case*.

User   The person, or system, that manipulates the product. Also known as end user.

Work   A business area of the organization that we have to understand. It is also used to mean the work that the user is intended to do. The product is to become a part of this work.

Bibliography

Alexander, Christopher. (1964). *Notes on the Synthesis of Form*. Cambridge MA: Harvard University Press

Alexander, Christopher et al. (1977). *A Pattern Language*. New York: Oxford University Press

Baker, Jenny. (1992). *Simple French Cuisine*. London: Faber & Faber

Beyer, Hugh and Karen Holtzblatt. (1998). *Contextual Design. Defining Customer-Centered Systems*. San Francisco: Morgan Kauffmann

Boehm, Barry. (1989). *Software Risk Management*. Los Alamitos, CA: IEEE Computer Society Press

Bolton, Robert. (1979). *People Skills. How to Assert Yourself, Listen to Others and Resolve Conflicts*. New York: Simon & Schuster

Booch, Grady, James Rumbaugh and Ivar Jacobson. (1998). *Unified Modeling Language User Guide*. Reading, MA: Addison Wesley Longman

Brun-Cottan, Françoise and Patricia Wall. Using Video to Re-present the User. *Comm. ACM*, May 1995, vol. 38, no. 5

Burgess, Anthony. (1975). *Language Mad'e Plain*. London: Fontana

Buzan, Tony with Barry Buzan. (1995). *The Mind Map Book*. London: BBC Books

Carroll, John. (1995). *Scenario-Based Design*. New York: John Wiley

Charette, Robert. (1989). *Software Engineering Risk Analysis and Management*. New York: McGraw-Hill

Checkland, Peter. (1981). *Systems Thinking, Systems Practice*. Chichester: John Wiley

Checkland, Peter and J. Scholes. (1991). *Soft Systems Methodology in Action*. Chichester: John Wiley

Collier, Bonnie, Tom DeMarco and Peter Fearey. A Defined Process for Project Post Mortem Review. *IEEE Software*, July 1996

Cook, Steve and John Daniels. (1994). *Designing Object-Oriented Systems*. Hemel Hempstead: Prentice-Hall

David, Elizabeth. (1974). *Italian Food*. Harmondsworth: Penguin Books

Davis, Alan. (1993). *Software Requirements – Objects, Functions and States*. Englewood Cliffs, NJ: Prentice-Hall

DeGrace, Peter and Leslie Hulet Stahl. (1990). *Wicked Problems, Righteous Solutions.* New Jersey: Yourdon Press

DeMarco, Tom. (1997). *The Deadline.* New York: Dorset House

DeMarco, Tom and Tim Lister. (1987). *Peopleware. Productive Projects and Teams.* New York: Dorset House

Ellinor, Linda and Glenna Gerard. (1998). *Dialogue: Rediscovering the Transforming Power of Conversation.* New York: John Wiley

Fenton, Norman and Shari Lawrence Pfleeger. (1997). *Software Metrics: A Rigorous and Practical Approach.* London: International Thomson Computer Press

Fisher, Roger and William Ury. (1991). *Getting to Yes.* New York: Penguin

Fowler, Martin. (1997). *UML Distilled: Applying the Standard Object Modeling Language.* Reading, MA: Addison Wesley Longman

Function Point Counting Practices Manual. Westerville OH: International Function Point Users Group

Gamma, Erich and Richard Helm, Ralph Johnson, John Vlissides. (1995). *Design Patterns: Elements of Reusable Object-Oriented Software.* Reading, MA: Addison-Wesley

Garmus, David and David Herron. (1996). *Measuring the Software Process.* New Jersey: Yourdon Press

Gause, Donald and Gerald Weinberg. (1989). *Exploring Requirements: Quality Before Design.* New York: Dorset House

——————————. (1990). *Are Your Lights On? How to Figure Out What the Problem Really Is.* New York: Dorset House

Gilb, Tom with Susannah Finzi. (1988). *Principles of Software Engineering Management.* Wokingham: Addison-Wesley

Harel, David. Statecharts: A Visual Formalism for Complex Systems. *Science of Computer Programming,* vol. 8, 1987

Hauser, John and Don Claussing. The House of Quality. *Harvard Business Review,* May–June 1988, pp. 63–73

Hay, David. (1995). *Data Model Patterns: Conventions of Thought.* New York: Dorset House

Hayakawa, S.I. (1970). *Language in Thought and Action.* London: George Allen & Unwin

Highsmith, Jim and Lynne Nix. Feasibility Analysis – Mission Impossible. *Software Development,* July 1996

Jackson, Michael. (1996). *Software Requirements and Specifications: A Lexicon of Practice, Principles and Prejudices.* Harlow: Addison Wesley Longman

Jacobson, Ivar, Martin Griss and Patrik Jonsson. (1997). *Software Reuse: Architecture Process and Organization for Business Success.* Harlow: Addison Wesley Longman

Jacobson, Ivar, Grady Booch and James Rumbaugh. (1998). *The Objectory Software Development Process*. Reading, MA: Addison Wesley Longman

Jacobson, Ivar, Magnus Christerson, Patrik Jonsson and Gunnar Övergaard. (1992). *Object-Oriented Software Engineering – A Use Case Driven Approach*. Harlow: Addison-Wesley

Jones, Capers. (1991). *Applied Software Measurement*. New York: McGraw-Hill

Jones, Capers. (1994). *Assessment and Control of Software Risks*. Englewood Cliffs NJ: Prentice-Hall

Jones, Capers. (1997a). *Software Quality – Analysis and Guidelines for Success*. Boston MA: International Thomson

Jones, Capers. (1997b). *Survey on Requirements*. Burlington: MA: Software Productivity Research

Kovitz, Benjamin. (1999). *Practical Software Requirements – A Manual of Content and Style*. Greenwich CT: Manning

Latour, Bruno. (1996). *ARAMIS or The Love of Technology*. Boston MA: Harvard University Press

Loucopoulos, Pericles and Vassilios Karakostas. (1995). *System Requirements Engineering*. London: McGraw-Hill

Macaulay, Linda. (1994). *Requirements Engineering*. London: Springer-Verlag

Maguire, Steve. (1994). *Debugging the Development Process*. Redmond, Washington: Microsoft Press

Maiden N.A.M, C. Ncube and A. Moore. (1998). *Acquiring Requirements for Commercial Off-The-Shelf Package Selection: Some Lessons Learned*. City University

McConnell, Steve. (1993). *Code Complete*. Redmond, Washington: Microsoft Press

McMenamin, Steve and John Palmer. (1984). *Essential Systems Analysis*. New York: Yourdon Press

Norman, Donald. (1990). *The Design of Everyday Things*. New York: Doubleday

Pardee, William. (1996). *To Satisfy and Delight Your Customer*. New York: Dorset House

Peters, Tom. (1997). *The Circle of Innovation*. New York: Alfred A. Knopf

Petrowski, Henry. (1993). *The Evolution of Useful Things*. London: Pavilion

Pfleeger, Charles. (1997). *Security in Computing*. Englewood Cliffs NJ: Prentice-Hall

Pfleeger, Shari Lawrence. (1998). *Software Engineering – Theory and Practice*. Englewood Cliffs NJ: Prentice-Hall

_____. A Framework for Security Requirements. *Computers and Security*, 1991, vol. 10, no. 6, pp. 515–23

Prieto-Diaz, Rubén and Guillermo Arango. (1991). *Domain Analysis and Software Systems Modeling*. Los Alamitos CA: IEEE Computer Society Press

Robertson, James and Suzanne Robertson. (1994). *Complete Systems Analysis: the Workbook, the Textbook, the Answers*. New York: Dorset House

Robertson, Suzanne and Kenneth Strunch. (1993). *Reusing the Products of Analysis*. 2nd Int. Workshop on Software Reusability, Position Paper. Lucca, Italy, March 24–6

Rumbaugh, James, Ivar Jacobson and Grady Booch. (1998). *Unified Modeling Language Reference Manual*. Reading, MA: Addison Wesley Longman

Russell, Peter. (1979). *The Brain Book*. London: Routlege & Kegan Paul

Schank, Roger. (1990). *Tell Me a Story – Narrative and Intelligence*. Evanston IL: North western University Press

Schelling, Thomas. (1980). *The Strategy of Conflict*. Boston MA: Harvard University Press

Senge, Peter. (1990). *The Fifth Discipline*. New York: Doubleday

Shlaer, Sally and Steve Mellor. (1988). *Object-Oriented Systems Analysis*. Englewood Cliffs NJ: Yourdon Press

_____. (1992). *Object Lifecycles – Modeling the World in States*. Englewood Cliffs NJ: Yourdon Press

Smith, Delia. (1998). *How to Cook – Book One*. London: BBC Worldwide

Sobel, Dava. (1995). *Longitude: The true story of a genius who solved the greatest scientific problem of his time*. London: Penguin

Somerville, Ian and Pete Sawyer. (1998). *Requirements Engineering – A Good Practice Guide*. Chichester: John Wiley

Thomsett, Rob. (1993). *Third Wave Project Management: A Handbook for Managing the Complex Information Management Systems of the 1990's*. New York: Prentice-Hall/Yourdon Press

Tufte, Edward. (1997). *Visual Explanations*. Cheshire, CT: Graphics Press

United States Marine Corps. (1994). *Warfighting*. New York: Currency Doubleday

Wiegers, Karl. (1996). *Creating a Software Engineering Culture*. New York: Dorset House

_____. Listening to the Customer's Voice. *Software Development*, March 1997

Weinberg, Jerry. (1992–97). *Quality Software Management: Volume 1 Systems Thinking; Volume 2 First-Order Measurement; Volume 3 Congruent Action; Volume 4 Anticipating Change*. New York: Dorset House

_____. (1998). *The Psychology of Computer Programming – Silver Anniversary Edition*. New York: Dorset House

Winograd, Terry, John Bennett, Laura de Young and Bradley Hartfield. (1996). *Bringing Design to Software*. New York: ACM Press

Index